FORGING A CONSENSUS

VICTOR L. RUSSELL, editor

Forging a Consensus

HISTORICAL ESSAYS ON TORONTO

Published for the Toronto Sesquicentennial Board by
UNIVERSITY OF TORONTO PRESS
Toronto Buffalo London

© City of Toronto Sesquicentennial Board 1984
Printed in Canada

ISBN 0-8020-3409-8 (cloth)
ISBN 0-8020-3410-1 (paper)

Design: William Rueter RCA

Canadian Cataloguing in Publication Data

Main entry under title:
Forging a consensus

Includes bibliographical references and index.
ISBN 0-8020-3409-8 (bound). – ISBN 0-8020-3410-1 (pbk.)

1. Toronto (Ont.) – History – Addresses, essays,
lectures. I. Russell, Victor L. (Victor Loring),
1948–   II. Toronto (Ont.)

FC3097.4.F67 1984   971.3′541   C84-099338-2
F1059.5.T6857F67 1984

42,093

Contents

Contributors

VICTOR L. RUSSELL is manager of the City of Toronto Archives. Formerly a manuscript editor at the Dictionary of Canadian Biography, he has written several articles and a book on historical Toronto.

PAUL ROMNEY is a free-lance historian currently completing a book on the office of the attorney-general in nineteenth-century Ontario. He has written several articles on the history of Toronto and Ontario.

GREGORY S. KEALEY is a member of the Department of History at Memorial University of Newfoundland. He is editor of the journal *Labour/Le Travailleur* and author of several books and articles on the history of the working class in Canada. He was awarded the Macdonald Prize in 1980 and the Corey Prize in 1984.

BARRIE DYSTER is a lecturer in the Department of Economic History at the University of New South Wales, Australia. He completed a doctoral thesis at the University of Toronto on mid-nineteenth-century Toronto. He is currently preparing a history of the working class in Australia.

NICHOLAS ROGERS is a member of the Department of History at York University, Toronto, and a specialist in the social history of eighteenth-century England.

vii Contributors

J.M.S. CARELESS is a University Professor at the University of Toronto. Twice winner of the Governor-General's award, he is the author of many books and articles on Canadian history. He has just completed a history of Toronto to 1918.

ROGER RIENDEAU teaches at Innis College, University of Toronto. He is currently completing a history of Mississauga.

PATRICIA PETERSEN is a lecturer at the University of Toronto, currently completing her doctoral thesis on city government structures in Toronto and New York state. Active in Scarborough politics, she served as chairman of the Scarborough Planning Board.

CHRISTOPHER ARMSTRONG and H.V. NELLES are members of the Department of History at York University, Toronto, and have collaborated on several articles on the history of public utilities in Canada and a book on the Sunday streetcar controversy in Toronto in the late nineteenth century.

FRANCES FRISKEN is a member of the Division of Social Science at York University. She has written on both urban transportation and metropolitan politics and is currently studying the evolution of selected government services in the Metropolitan Toronto region since 1950.

GUNTER GAD is a member of the Department of Geography at the University of Toronto. He has advised the City of Toronto Planning Board and other government agencies on office development.

DERYCK HOLDSWORTH is an editor with the Historical Atlas of Canada project and is a specialist in the historical geography of the industrial city.

JAMES LEMON is a member of the Department of Geography at the University of Toronto. After receiving his doctorate at the University of Wisconsin, he taught at UCLA before coming to Toronto in 1967. In 1972 he won the Albert J. Beveridge Award from the American Historical Association for the best book on American history for that year. Aside from numerous articles on colonial America, he has just completed a history of Toronto since 1918.

Acknowledgments

I NATURALLY begin my acknowledgments with thanks to the contributors, all of whom made my duties as editor a pleasure. At the same time, their professionalism has assured a very high standard of scholarship throughout the volume. I wish to extend my thanks to the Sesquicentennial Publications Committee for the opportunity to be involved in the project, and especially to R. Scott James, the committee's chairman, for his support. I would like also to acknowledge the expert advice of the committee's consultant, Paul Irwin. My friend and colleague Paul Romney receives my sincere thanks for his relentless encouragement and useful suggestions. Two institutions deserve special mention: the City of Toronto Archives, which endured my periodic absences and from time to time my preoccupied presence; and York University Archives, where, thanks to Hartwell Bowsfield, I had a quiet place to hide and work. Karen Lunn spent many hours at the keyboard without complaint entering revisions into the computer, and Glenda Williams retyped many sections. John Parry copy-edited the manuscript; William Rueter designed the book; and Wendy Cameron prepared the index. On a personal note, I wish to acknowledge the support of Donna Russell.

FORGING A CONSENSUS

VICTOR L. RUSSELL

Preface

THIS NEW VOLUME joins a grow-
ing family of works on the history of Toronto, sponsored by the Corporation
of the City of Toronto in honour of its successive jubilees. The first was the
Memorial Volume by the Reverend H. Scadding and J.C. Dent. Commissioned to celebrate the city's semi-centennial in 1884, the volume comprises
laudatory, though sometimes nostalgic 'memoirs' or essays by two noteworthy nineteenth-century scholars. The authors proudly trace the history of the
city from its founding in 1793, through its incorporation as a city, to a view of
what was, for them, modern Toronto. Fifty years later, the publications
committee of the city's centennial celebration commissioned author and
journalist J.E. Middleton to write *Toronto's 100 Years*. Though different in
style and form from its Victorian relation, Middleton's work was essentially
the same in argument: it was a chronicle of the city's rise from nineteenth-
century colonial outpost to twentieth-century metropolis.

That civic boosterism and a sense of pride should be the predominant tone
of these jubilee volumes is understandable. Although both books, and indeed
both celebrations, were launched during difficult economic times, civic
officials and civic-minded Torontonians seldom missed an opportunity to
applaud their city's growth. In his inaugural speech in 1884, Mayor A.R.
Boswell boasted of Toronto that 'given the many cities I have visited in my
time in England, on the continents of Europe and America, I can say with
truth there is no place better.' In 1934 Mayor W.J. Stewart declared: 'We have
much to be thankful for as we approach the One Hundredth Anniversary of
our corporate existence, notwithstanding the troublous and difficult times ...

Toronto has made amazing strides since it first aspired to city status ... and we have cause to be hopeful and jubilant as we enter our centennial year.'

The circumstances of today's jubilee are similar in certain respects to those of 1884 and 1934. That the city finds itself in a period of 'economic distress' was a major theme of Mayor Art Eggleton's inaugural speech in December 1982. As in the past, however, civic pride in the Corporation's achievement in making Toronto 'The City That Works' dominates the mood of the celebrations. As Mayor Eggleton remarked: 'Yes, Toronto is a great city. But it didn't become one by accident.'

It was also no accident that the organizers of Toronto 150, very early in their deliberations, pondered how to add to the family of jubilee publications. The resulting publication program has not only sustained the tradition established by previous celebrations but, I believe, also greatly enhanced it. The program had three aspects: grants in support of books about Toronto to be published privately in 1984, a system of endorsements whereby other relevant publications would receive approval of the sesquicentennial board, and (the centrepiece of the program) the production of two official publications. The first was Edith Firth's award-winning *Toronto in Art* (Fitzhenry & Whiteside, 1983). In the tradition of Scadding, Dent, and Middleton, this beautifully produced and well-written volume was intended for a wide and popular readership. The second is this book.

The decision to publish a volume of scholarly essays on the history of Toronto is evidence of a growing sophistication in the Corporation's approach to its past. As editor of the proposed volume, I knew I could draw readily on the new but already well-established area of historical urban studies, encompassing history, geography, and political science. And, although once again preoccupied with explaining and understanding the 'Rise of Toronto,' the resulting book is not a work of expansive civic pride, like those of 1884 and 1934, but a judicious evaluation of Toronto's past. Though critical, however, it is far from negative. Indeed, these essays provide evidence of the apparent success of the municipality in its handling of the problems of urban development as the city grew from a colonial capital of 9,000 inhabitants to Canada's largest metropolis.

Toronto's growth has been far from extraordinary among North American cities, and its success as a major urban centre has not been wholly due to the mere accretion of size or wealth. Rather, it was based on the development of a distinctive civic culture that allowed Toronto to become, at least by reputation, 'The City That Works.' This is, I would suggest, a central theme of the city's history. In the broadest terms, the underlying theme of this volume is the gradual synthesis, in a British community on North American soil, of a civic culture that was not British, yet was distinctly un-American. It is the development of this distinctive civic culture, based on stability and consensus, that made Toronto unique among cities in North America.

The city of Toronto was incorporated with a single, clearly defined mandate: to solve the problems of a small, but rapidly growing colonial town. The execution of that mandate was complicated by the existence, in the 1830s and 1840s, of deep social fissures that were primarily ethnic and religious, but also, to a lesser extent, those of class. Part I of the book opens by delineating the dimensions of the social and political fragmentation that existed in Toronto in the first two decades after incorporation. Paul Romney's description of Toronto in 1834 introduces the players and sets the stage, concluding that Toronto's first year was 'a term marked by strife within both the council chamber and the political community at large.' Gregory Kealey follows with an investigation of that prominent agent of 'sectarian wrangling,' the Orange Order, which he suggests was an expression not only of ethnic and religious, but also of proletarian consciousness. Barrie Dyster pursues this theme with an analysis of an Orange leader, 'Captain' Bob Moodie.

As the city grew through the railway boom of the 1850s, the fierceness of the struggle was gradually diffused by the emergence of a social and political consensus, or perhaps in Kealey's words 'a new bourgeois hegemony.' The values of efficiency, order, and stability, catchwords of a pervasive 'ethos of development,' cut across class and ethnic lines and produced a civic culture based on consensus that was to become one of Toronto's distinctive features. As Romney notes: 'The politics of ethnic and ideological fragmentation would give way to those of pluralistic consensus: a limited tolerance of diversity founded on unquestioned participation in a British and Protestant empire and a new dominant ideology of commercial and industrial advance.' The new Toronto was, to be sure, a society of dramatic inequalities. But those inequalities were mitigated by a substantial rise in material well-being, which convinced even many of the poorer citizens that they had a vested interest in supporting the new order.

The Corporation contributed to the forging of this consensus in three principal ways. It fostered the city's economic growth directly by investing heavily in railway development and indirectly by providing municipal services such as water, gas, sewers, and paved roads. Its fire and police departments served to ensure the safety of persons and property. And, finally, it acted as a kind of civic cheerleader.

Nicholas Roger's paper on the police force is presented as a case study of this phenomenon and a demonstration of the strategies adopted by the Corporation in changing the police from agents of sectarian violence to agents of the requisite social order. Part I ends with J.M.S. Careless's appraisal of the semi-centennial activities of 1884 which saw the whole community demonstrate and celebrate 'pride in city, country, and empire.' Toronto had forged a distinctive civic culture which it celebrated; it was, in Careless's words, the city's 'First Hurrah.'

Part II, 'The Triumph of Consensus,' focuses mainly on the corporation's role in assuring the material well-being on which Toronto's distinctive civic culture was based. Roger Riendeau begins the section with an investigation of the dramatic increase in municipal services during the first three decades of the twentieth century. Patricia Petersen provides an account of the only structural change in civic government made necessary by the Corporation's interventionist strategy: the creation of the board of control. Christopher Armstrong and H.V. Nelles explore the city's move to municipal ownership of utilities. Frances Frisken analyses the achievements of the city-owned transportation system. Geographers Gunter Gad and Deryck Holdsworth survey the changing physical environment with a study of office building development as Toronto grew to the major metropolitan centre in Canada and touch on the Corporation's changing role in this sphere.

Several of these papers highlight the emergence of a new theme: the increasing tendency of the Corporation to go beyond merely fostering the creation of wealth to directing its application in the public interest. Riendeau, in particular, documents the 'formidable contributions of municipal government in promoting a positive social and economic role for the state.' Municipal government in Toronto had, he concludes, 'raised the standards for the level of public service that a modern urban society could expect.'

As is traditional in jubilee publishing, the volume concludes with a discussion of Toronto today: 'Toronto among North American Cities: A Historical Perspective on the Present,' by James Lemon. But Lemon's critical analysis is far from the civic boosterism of traditional jubilee volumes. In a free-wheeling but historically rooted piece that incorporates many of the issues raised in preceding papers, he tries to define exactly how and why Toronto differs from other North American, especially American, cities.

Yet Lemon, even though ambivalent, ultimately agrees that Toronto is in fact 'worldy, wealthy, personable, and relatively problem free' and has enjoyed (and continues to enjoy) a degree of material well-being and 'civilization' unknown to many North American cities. But he concludes, 'If Toronto is to remain the "city that works ... a model of the alternative future," then its citizens will need to keep their wits about them.' As civic leaders in Toronto have always recognized, and as Mayor Eggleton reminds us, cities do not become, or remain, great by accident.

PART ONE

Forging the consensus

PAUL ROMNEY

A struggle for authority

Toronto society and politics in 1834

THE PLACE was changing. On the northern outskirts, workingmen's cottages were springing up on the park lots between Yonge Street and the square brick pile of Osgoode Hall to the west: Macaulaytown was being born. Long columns of residential development straggled westwards along Lot, Hospital, Newgate, and King streets. Leaving Ketchum's tannery, Sheldon and Dutcher's foundry, and Armstrong's axe factory in their rear, they bypassed the waterfront mansions of the elect and closed in on the garrison from the opposite direction to that taken by the invading American soldiery in 1813.[1]

While frame construction flourished on the outskirts, red brick was ousting it from the centre. Merchant shops three and four storeys high began to supplant the wooden structures of the first decades and plug the gaps left by haphazard early growth. Behind the residential vanguard, commerce also marched westward along King Street, throwing up an outpost as far afield as York Street, where James Chewett had erected 'a splendid block of lofty brick houses ... to comprise eight or ten tenements for stores or dwelling houses, with an extensive hotel at the corner.'[2]

Beyond the town, with its fringe of wooded park lots, market gardens, orchards, and the occasional dairy farm, woodland was vanishing before the pioneer's axe. On Yonge and Dundas streets, the ruts had deepened and the undergrowth finally failed as these erstwhile slashes in the forest at last became highways of settlement and commerce. Urban eyes began to view the back country as a profitable railway route and a source of pure water to refresh the town.[3]

Disrupted by industrialization, overpopulation, and agrarian crisis, Britain spilled out its huddled masses, yearning to breathe free: free from hunger or the constraints that an old, stratified society clamped on enterprise. Irish, English, Scots; farming folk, artisans, labourers, and a thick sprinkling of higher station and education but small or ruined fortune; they flocked to the unpeopled continent, and some few of them found their way to the inland domain called Upper Canada. Many of these headed for vacant soil north and west of the contemptible, shanty town capital, so assumingly called York; others planted themselves in the townlet's own abundant mud. In 1827, Little, Muddy York was the abode of only 1,817 counted inhabitants. By 1830 it was home to nearly 3,000, and three years afterwards to more than 6,000 people. In 1834, its bounds spread to embrace the new sprawling purlieus, it would boast more than 9,000. Even this calculation omitted a host of transients who thronged the waterfront and the meaner interior streets, exhausted by arduous journeying or pausing to take new bearings before pressing on in search of a permanent home. Eleven and twelve thousand were numbers boasted in the press as the year passed.[4]

The townsfolk of the capital had always been used to strangers in the streets: a stream of commercial travellers, of soldiers, of farmers come to market or to transact business at the land offices; the annual influx of politicians for the parliamentary session; the periodic advent of theatrical troupes from south of the border. Litigants clustered constantly, drawn by the incessant round of court sittings at the headquarters of judicial administration: the court of requests, the quarter sessions, the district court, the twice-yearly assizes, the four terms of the court of King's Bench. Aspirant healers arrived to undergo examination by the provincial medical board or to present the British credentials that would earn them a certificate without that formality. And always there were immigrants in search of a place where they might prosper. But the number of these passengers was small; some of them were frequent visitors, and they fitted into the pattern of daily life. York's sudden flood of new denizens, and their co-migrants who came to cultivate the back country, broke that pattern. They made York a new place. In 1834, the capital must have been almost as much a sea of strange faces to the old inhabitants as it was to the newest comer.

Always disproportionately British, it became still more so.[5] A 'Yankee' accent, heard in a tavern or within the crowded quadrangle enclosed by the new red-brick market building, was as likely to betoken a farmer as a townsman. The more cultivated American tones of the Loyalist élite – prominent, but never predominant among the capital's patriciate – would soon begin to fade in the councils of the town, if not yet of the government: the British lawyers, doctors, and other professional men who flooded into the capital were at least their equals in capacity and education and would not long be denied the place their talents deserved.

The proportion of Scottish residents was declining, but in such an active and vociferous part of the community this may not have been noticeable. They were especially prominent among the merchants who flocked to exploit the new bonanza. Disposing of more capital than most of the established merchants, they imposed new patterns of trading: wholesale specialization, commodity specialization, direct importing from Britain. The days of the general storekeeper, who bought from Montreal wholesalers, were numbered. To an official élite anxious to establish its city's commercial pre-eminence by means of a railway and other institutions requiring large amounts of capital, the influx of new money was most welcome. In 1833, several leading merchants were elevated to the town magistracy: a necessary accession of strength to that overburdened amateur body, but also a symbolic admission of them and their co-equals in commerce to junior membership of the élite.[6]

The advent of the Irish was certainly noticeable. The Irish carter (usually Anglican) and the Irish labourer (often Catholic) became prominent features of the new metropolis. So too, as Irish residential clusters proliferated on the outskirts of the town (Catholics mainly to the east, Protestants to the north and west), did the Irish storekeeper and the Irish tavern-keeper. All these were sometimes the same man: a carter was a labourer with a horse and wheels, a storekeeper a labourer with a few provisions and a barrel of beer on the premises, a tavern-keeper a storekeeper who – often without troubling to obtain a licence – allowed patrons to consume the liquor he sold them on the spot and stay for more. As this Irish lower class began to multiply in the meaner streets and lanes, some of its more prominent members would assume a new shape: the Irish constable.

If the Scots dominated business, and the Irish were mostly unskilled and semi-skilled labourers, the English supplied a disproportionately large share of the administrators and professional men. Doctors, architects, civil engineers, teachers, and government clerks were more likely to hail from south of Hadrian's Wall than elsewhere in the kingdom. The one exception was the lawyers. The provincial élite, anxious to preserve this most lucrative of professions for its sons, had secured its monopoly by a law barring anyone from legal practice who had not served five years under articles in Upper Canada.[7] Unlike British medical credentials, British legal qualifications counted for nothing.

English, Irish, and Scots all contributed their share of artisans and manufacturers: the carpenters, bricklayers, shoemakers, tailors, blacksmiths, tinsmiths, butchers and bakers, the brewers and soap-makers. York's relatively high cash incomes – from government office, from commerce, from professional (especially legal) practice, from land speculation – also sustained a variety of less essential trades: jewellers, watchmakers, confectioners, carvers and gilders, portrait painters. A wheelwright and wagon-maker could specialize as a coach-builder, a blacksmith as a coach-spring maker.[8]

The way a family prayed was related to its source of income. York was the seat of an oligarchy committed to the ascendancy of the Church of England in the colony. Naturally, the families of most government employees at every level were Anglican. So, too, were those of most professional men and leading merchants, the other components of the town's élite. The Church of Scotland also claimed several leading merchants, but these were mainly the more recent arrivals. The Reverend William Rintoul's congregation had been formed only in 1830, and the most prominent of the established Scots merchants – Alexander Wood, William Allan, William Proudfoot, and George Monro – had gravitated to the Church of England (long the only organized congregation in the town), where they were ministered to by a fellow countryman and Presbyterian apostate, the Very Reverend Archdeacon of York, Dr John Strachan. They were readily embraced by a church that aspired to universality in the province, and the economic interests they shared with the patriciate kept them in the fold even after other communions had been formed. The men who met each other in the boardroom of the Bank of Upper Canada tended to worship together at the Church of St James.[9]

At the other end of the social scale – the mainly Irish semi- and unskilled labouring element – the Church of England split the field with that of Rome. By far the largest denomination in the capital, it also claimed a good share of the artisans and manufacturers, especially the immigrants of recent vintage, among whom the practitioners of luxury trades were strongly represented. The non-luxury artisans and manufacturers, though, formed the backbone of the dissenting congregations: Secessionist Presbyterian, Methodist, Congregationalist, and Baptist. These, together with the Church of Scotland, were less autonomous congregations than overlapping connections.

Rintoul's congregation of St Andrew's Church included communicants of Baptist orientation and voluntarist Scottish Presbyterians who preferred the Scottish form of worship to that offered by the Irishman James Harris at Knox Church to his mingled Irish, Scots, and North American–born congregation. It also contained an obstreperous fifth column of Congregationalists, who would secede in 1834 to set up their own communion. Harris's heterogeneous gathering was itself hardly the abode of harmony. Harmony was very much the issue to Scots such as William Lyon Mackenzie and his brother-in-law, master mariner John McIntosh, son-in-law of the Baptist minister, Alexander Stewart, for they did not like his unfamiliar hymn tunes. Ethnic similitude brought Harris a compensating clutch of Irish Presbyterians who were politically out of sympathy with his Scots and North American communicants; while Methodists were to be found at his altar (much to the disgust of a newly arrived Scottish minister) even before Egerton Ryerson arrived back from England to try to patch together a union between his own Episcopal Methodists and the insurgent British Wesleyans in 1833.[10]

Despite the impulse toward unity of the few politicians among them, the Methodists fissured with true sectarian zeal. The Primitive Methodists set up on their own in 1830, only to cast off the following year a splinter calling itself the Canadian Protestant Wesleyans. Ryerson's attempted union with the British Wesleyans would lead to schism within the year as a militant residue – small in York, larger in the countryside – refused to give up their separate existence as Episcopals.[11]

The brittleness of York's Protestant sects – the Baptists, too, were not immune – reflected the nature of the community, if indeed it could be called a community. The mix of British nationalities was one that could be met with nowhere in Britain itself. It created a society in which perhaps everyone – not just the overwhelmed North Americans – was conscious of belonging to a minority. The resulting sense of insecurity fostered a zealous adherence to one's spiritual and cultural lights. Ethnic consciousness may even have grown as the town itself became more securely rooted, less of an outpost in the wilderness, and the feeling of inhabiting a huddle of huts on the edge of nowhere was lost. Not in the Protestant sects alone, with their strongly individualistic ethos, but even in the spiritually authoritarian Church of Rome, an organizational rupture resulted from the antipathy between the lower-class Irish, who formed the bulk of the congregation, led by their priest, Father William O'Grady, and the few leading laymen (some North American–born, some Irish), who sided with the province's Scottish bishop, Alexander Macdonell.[12]

The Church of England avoided rupture partly because it was the spiritual fastness of an embattled élite. Its privileges were entrenched in the same authoritarian constitution that sustained the oligarchy's own dominance over the provincial administration. The oligarchy, with their connections and dependants, formed a phalanx in defence of both. The hierarchical organization of the church meant that the few upper-class dissidents in Archdeacon Strachan's congregation could not secede without abandoning their church altogether; but no other denominational allegiance was quite *comme il faut*.

For these reasons, Anglicans conducted their political and personal quarrels outside the church.

Political quarrels were one of York's distinctive entertainments. To Joseph Gould, a young farmer from the town's eastern hinterland, himself later a prominent reformer and entrepreneur, it seemed on his first visit to the capital in 1830 that 'the people of York were all politicians ... and excitement ran so high that quarrels between neighbours were of frequent occurrence.'[13] Indeed, how could York not be the political cockpit it was? It was the capital of a newly but intensely politicized colony; a place where those Scottish zealots, Archdeacon Strachan and William Lyon Mackenzie, might glower at each other daily in the street; a permanent exhibit of the whole social hierarchy in all its polyethnic, multistratified diversity: high officials and oligarchs in their mansions and spreading parks, merchants in their opulent red-brick emporia, artisans and labourers in their frame shanties, back-country farmers driving their wagons to and from the market: farmers like young Gould, to whom the city's inhabitants seemed to dress well and live sumptuously, without visible means of support.[14] Where else could a political quarrel be got going, if not here?

The reform movement had congealed, as a communion of intellectual critics of the status quo with substantial, if unreliable, mass support, in the mid- and late 1820s. The discontent generated by a variety of sectional grievances had resulted in the return of an oppositionist majority to the house of assembly in 1824. A series of public campaigns had followed: first against specific grievances, such as the administration's seeming intent to disfranchise as aliens most of the colony's North American–born electors and its attempt to enhance the privileges of the Church of England, and later a movement aimed at superseding the colony's authoritarian constitution by one that would make the administration responsible to the people as represented in the house of assembly.[15]

York was not as susceptible to these issues as many county constituencies. Its population was more British and more Anglican than the province's as a whole. The administration's influence over the electorate was strong at the seat of government, especially under an electoral system that ordained open, not secret voting. In 1828, when Upper Canada as a whole elected the most radical house of assembly in its history, York returned the attorney-general, John Beverley Robinson, as it had in the two previous contests.[16]

But the capital had witnessed at close quarters several of the outrages that a harassed administration, or the oligarchy that dominated it, had inflicted on its critics in the years 1826–8. It had seen William Lyon Mackenzie's printing-shop wrecked by young members and friends of the patrician families; the judicial persecution of another journalist, Francis Collins; the dismissal of a newly installed judge, John Walpole Willis, for disparaging the administration of justice in the province. Robinson's opponent in 1828 had been a Methodist of Canadian birth, Dr Thomas David Morrison. In 1829, when the new lieutenant-governor, Sir John Colborne, removed Robinson from the forefront of politics by appointing him chief justice, the Reformers chose as their candidate an Anglican of good family, also Canadian-born but with an audibly Irish father. Robert Baldwin won the by-election easily.[17]

He did not last long. In 1830, the death of King George IV required a new general election. In November the province, influenced perhaps by the more conciliatory style of Lieutenant-Governor Colborne, elected a conservative majority to the house of assembly. It was not that the voters had become reconciled to the men and policies they had rejected in 1824 and 1828, but many of them were willing to refrain for a while from strident opposition and see what the new imperial political order had to offer by way of reform. Even the previous February the district sheriff, William Botsford Jarvis, had come within nine votes of Baldwin at a second by-election occasioned by informalities in the first. In November he was the town's contribution to the new conservative majority.[18]

At the beginning of 1834, then, the town of York was represented in the legislature by the leading local officer of the provincial administration; but another election was pending and the Tories had lost a good deal of whatever popularity they had enjoyed in 1830. This was partly their own fault, partly William Lyon Mackenzie's, and partly that of the Whig government in Britain.

Mackenzie had embroiled the conservative majority of the house of assembly in a row as beneficial to his reputation as it was damaging to theirs. They had been provoked by his insults into expelling him from the house, only to see him overwhelmingly returned by his constituents in the county surrounding the little capital. They ejected him again; he was elected again; and so it went for the next two years. While all this was happening, the spiky Scottish journalist sailed off to Britain to present the grievances of an oppressed people to the new Whig administration. When the house persisted in spurning his company, in effect unconstitutionally disfranchising the electors of the county of York, the colonial secretary, Lord Goderich, dismissed both the attorney-general and the solicitor-general of the colony, Henry John Boulton and Christopher Hagerman, for their part in the affair.[19]

A new colonial secretary soon partly retracted Goderich's action, reinstating Hagerman and sending Boulton off to be chief justice of Newfoundland;

but the new attorney-general was sent out from Britain. Robert Jameson's appointment was obviously a comment on either the political unacceptability or the professional incapacity of the conservative Upper Canadian lawyers who might have expected to be considered for this, the most lucrative post in the province; either way, it was a slap in the face for the provincial élite. The political damage to the Tory cause was increased by the assembly's stubborn refusal to let Mackenzie take his seat, even after Sir John Colborne had publicly repudiated their conduct by ordering him sworn in as an MPP.[20] The Tories' posture as defenders of the British tie against a traitorous opposition had also been discredited by the rash words of the leading Tory journalist in the capital. George Gurnett had reacted to Goderich's dismissal of Boulton and Hagerman by hinting that the colony's loyal inhabitants, their minds 'unhinged' by the insult, were themselves beginning to grasp the merits of political independence from Great Britain. This entire train of events made it seem as if the Tory politicians had been discountenanced by, and had in their turn repudiated, the imperial authority whose proper representative they claimed to be.[21]

Newspapers like Gurnett's *Courier of Upper Canada* were an unrivalled means of political propaganda and tended – at least in a highly politicized place such as York – to be strongly biased in their presentation of news. Nowadays the printed word still carries authority to the unsophisticated reader; yet the sheer volume of often trivial and mutually contradictory writing that inundates us has devalued it, just as that other product of the printing press, the banknote, has devalued money. To most Upper Canadians, print meant three things: first, the Bible; second, official proclamations; third, the newspaper; and the last of these enjoyed much of the authority belonging to the first two. Most people saw only one paper and believed it implicitly. If they saw two of opposing views, they accepted one as scripture and rejected the other as the teachings of the Antichrist. In 1838, John Beverley Robinson would blame newspaper propaganda for the rebellion that had menaced the capital the previous December: how else could discord have entered the Garden of Eden that was Upper Canada?[22]

In January 1834, Gurnett's was only one of five intensely partisan papers that were busy fuelling and fanning York's political furnace. Three of them had been founded elsewhere in the colony, but their proprietors had been lured to York like rowdies to a street brawl. William Lyon Mackenzie had started the *Colonial Advocate* at Queenston in 1824, but had forsaken that small border town for the barely larger capital before the end of the year, intent on preaching against the oligarchy in its den. The Englishman Gurnett, then editor of the *Gore Gazette* in Ancaster, had been invited to the capital by the official oligarchy (probably with the explicit sanction of Sir John Colborne) in the black year of 1829, when the newly arrived governor had decided that the official *Upper Canada Gazette* should henceforth abstain from partisan propaganda. Gurnett's links with the oligarchy were known almost at once, and the *Courier* was frequently cited by Reformers as 'demi-official': hence the furore surrounding his outburst of May 1833. Thomas Dalton had moved his *Patriot and Farmer's Monitor* from Kingston to York in 1832. A Reformer turned Tory, he now vilified his old comrades with the same insatiable malignity he had once vented on the government and its Kingston allies.[23]

York's other two papers were published by Irish Catholics. Francis Collins had founded his *Canadian Freeman* in 1825. His zeal in opposing the oligarchy and the administration had made him Reform's foremost martyr in 1828, when his conviction for a libel against Attorney-General Robinson earned him a year in prison and a draconian fine. By 1834, repelled by Mackenzie's occasional anti-Catholic tirades and his attacks on the conservative Bishop Macdonell, he was more inclined to oppose Mackenzie than the government. The capital's newest paper, the *Canadian Correspondent*, had been set up only in 1833 to counteract Collins's and Macdonell's influence on the Catholic community. Its chief proprietor was a lawyer, James King, but its principal voice was that of William O'Grady, recently ousted by Macdonell as priest and pastor of York's Roman Catholics. O'Grady, who soon bought King out, proclaimed his Irishness by hymning the glory of Daniel O'Connell, the 'Great Liberator' of Britain's Catholics, at every opportunity. He disparaged the provincial establishment with a characteristic velvet-tongued sententiousness that provoked Dalton of the *Patriot*, the most satirical-sarcastic of Upper Canadian journalists, to nickname him PERSE-CUTED VIRTUE (Dalton often resorted to capitals to emphasize a gibe).[24]

The newspaper format lent itself to satire. So did the new city's new name: an anonymous broadside disguised as a newspaper boasted the dateline *Tory-on-toe*. Yet *The Porcupine!* itself developed no political point of view, even though nearly all its butts were Tories: it was a literary charivari, which pilloried offenders against popular morality.[25] Alexander Wood, magistrate and retired merchant, and Robert G. Anderson, chief teller of the Bank of Upper Canada (both old friends of Archdeacon Strachan) were denounced by innuendo as homosexuals; Dr Christopher Widmer, magistrate and chairman of the provincial medical board, as an adulterer; Simon Washburn, the district magistrates' clerk of the peace, as a philanderer with a barren wife. Some government lawyers were assailed for quite slight offences: Attorney-General

Jameson for stupidity, Solicitor-General Hagerman for his monstrous nose, and John Godfrey Spragge, a commissioner of the court of requests who would one day be vice-chancellor of Upper Canada, for ignorance of the law. Perhaps to be a lawyer was offence enough: two others of the fraternity, the Irishman James King and the Englishman William Henry Draper, were branded hag-ridden and bastard respectively.[26]

Reformers did not escape scot-free. Martin O'Beirne, a Roman Catholic merchant tailor who was, like King, a leading partisan of William O'Grady, was accused of having interfered with his girl pupils when a school teacher in Ireland. O'Grady himself was indirectly poked at by *The Porcupine!*'s repeated claim to emanate from 'No. 44 Lot Street (sign of Daniel O'Connell).' Daniel Bancroft, the leader of the Toronto printers' union, who in 1834 was fronting for William Lyon Mackenzie as a publisher of the *Advocate* (Mackenzie had dropped the '*Colonial*' in December 1833), was characterized in obscure but vivid language as one who walked 'as if he had a red hot poker stuck in his A – – e.' If the publisher of *The Porcupine!* had any friends, he did them the favour of keeping quiet about it.[27]

Squibs like *The Porcupine!* are in-group affairs: they say (or affect to say) what everyone knows about people everyone knows. But Toronto in 1834 was rapidly ceasing to be that sort of place. Each year it acquired several hundred new inhabitants who had no idea who Archdeacon Strachan and William Lyon Mackenzie were, let alone Alexander Wood and Simon Washburn. For the Reformers this represented a setback, for the Tories an opportunity. The newcomers had not witnessed the wrecking of Mackenzie's printing-shop, the judicial persecution of Francis Collins, the dismissal of Judge Willis. They knew nothing of the Alien Question, which had first fired the Reform movement and (though settled in 1828) still stoked the hostility of many North American–born colonists to the administration; in fact, they might have applauded such an attack on ethnically alien people whom they often met in adversary economic relations. The large part of them who were Anglicans were unlikely to share in the great unsettled grievance of the 1820s, the Church of England's claim to pre-eminence in the colony. If Mackenzie, as his growing republicanism made likely, were to do or say something that offended patriotic Britons in general and not just the oligarchy and its connections; if the latter could manage to stop blacking their own eyes with ill-judged swings at him; if these things happened, the Tories might again be able to command the votes – if not the affections – of the majority, as they had until 1824 and again in 1830.

The storm centre of Toronto politics in 1834 was the municipal council chamber. This was so simply because Mackenzie was chosen as the city's first mayor. His election on 3 April inaugurated the most astounding train of events in Toronto's municipal history. The cholera epidemic that struck the sweating city in mid-summer was a perfect metaphor for the evil humours oozing from the body politic.

At the beginning of the year, the town was still governed by the district magistrates, an unpaid body of prominent citizens appointed by the provincial government. Their main duty was to protect life and property by enforcing the criminal law and by promulgating and enforcing fire and sanitary regulations. To this end they commanded an unpaid constabulary (whose members, appointed annually, were obliged to serve on pain of a fine) and met as necessary, either as a police court to administer summary justice or in special session to handle administrative tasks. More serious matters were referred to the court of quarter sessions, which the magistrates formed four times a year to try cases with the aid of a jury. Until 1833, when special comissionerships had been set up, they had also been responsible for forming a court of requests to hear suits for small debts. In performing all these duties they were assisted by two principal paid officials. Their chief clerical officer was the clerk of the peace. Their chief executive officer was the high constable, who since 1826 had also been inspector of police for the town of York, charged with enforcing fire and sanitary regulations in the capital.[28]

This system was inadequate for a growing town. The sheer volume of work was too great for an amateur board of government to undertake willingly or an unpaid, part-time constabulary to discharge efficiently. Many of the leading citizens had just banded together in a fire insurance company, and the volunteer fire brigade needed beefing up (the new city's first by-law would be a package of fire regulations).[29] But the increased taxes necessary to provide a full-time, paid magistracy and constabulary, to improve the fire brigade, and to furnish essential amenities such as sewers, sidewalks, and paved streets could legitimately be levied only by an elected authority. Only such an authority, too, could acceptably trench on the citizens' liberty in certain other necessary ways, such as banning the building of wooden shanties in crowded areas. Upper Canada's élite rejected the idea of 'responsible government,' but the exigencies of local government required that its own capital be put in charge of the governed.

By 1833, several efforts had been made to do so, but all had foundered on the prevailing political polarization. The Tory-controlled provincial government grappled with the problem of creating an electoral system liberal enough to legitimize the municipal government while minimizing the chance that it would lead to the election of Reformers. How high a property qualification should be imposed on voters? How high a qualification should determine eligibility to office? Should the mayor be elected by the voters at large or by the municipal council? This riddle of political engineering evoked a variety of solutions, the most elaborate being one that envisaged a bicameral legislature with a six-man upper house and a sixteen-man lower house: a miniature houses of parliament for a town of less than ten thousand![30]

The act of incorporation of 1834 originated in a bill drafted by four moderate, upper-class Reformers: Robert Baldwin, the ex-MPP; John Rolph, the pre-eminent surgeon and lawyer; George Ridout, a district court judge; and James E. Small, a vice-president of the Upper Canada Bible and Tract Society.[31] The four had been deputed by a committee elected by a meeting of the citizens; only such men could command a degree of confidence – even grudging, partial confidence – in every sector of a polarized public. Even so, their bill was too liberal for the Tory-controlled legislature and underwent amendment in both houses. It proposed two different property qualifications for voting, a higher one for electing both aldermen and common councilmen and a lower one for electing councilmen only. The mayor was to be chosen by the voters qualified to vote for aldermen, and voting was to be by secret ballot – one of the main planks of the Reform platform. The final statute ordained open voting and had the mayor chosen by the city council as a whole from among the aldermen.[32]

But how could the city's political structure be given a conservative bias without exposing the government to charges of oppressive legislation? The tories found an ingenious answer. Having come under fire for proposing to stiffen the subcommittee's proposed voting qualifications, they turned about and created a broader electorate than the original bill had envisaged, balancing this concession by imposing a high qualification for election to office. The Reformers' strength in Toronto was to be found mainly in the middle ranks of society – the politically intelligent and independent-minded small masters and skilled journeymen of the manufacturing sector. The Tories extended the electorate to include many of the semi- and unskilled labouring element, consisting mainly of newly arrived Anglican or Roman Catholic Irishmen, which was economically more dependent, less sensitive to the Reformers' political and sectarian grievances, and maybe more susceptible to the persuasive influence of a glass of whisky or a dollar tip.[33] Much of the clamour over municipal politics in the press in 1834 was a struggle for the Irish vote.

Clever as these provisions were, in 1834 they did not do as the Tories hoped. During the early months of the year, the biggest political story in the capital was that of Mackenzie's latest vain efforts to claim his seat in the house of assembly as MPP for the county of York – a place to which even the lieutenant-governor and the colonial secretary said he was entitled. Mackenzie's inclusion among the Reform candidates for council turned the city's first elections into a referendum on the Tories' sins. True, not all the electors voted a straight party ticket. An individual had four votes in each ward in which he was enfranchised (two for alderman, two for common councilman), yet only one of the five wards returned four representatives of the same political colour (see Table 1). Still, politics undeniably played a part in the voting, and the Reformers had the discipline to exploit their political appeal to the full by putting up only one candidate for each seat. Representatives of the city's social élite did especially badly: four of the six magistrate candidates lost, including all three appointed prior to 1833. 'The Irish of this City have nobly done their duty,' reported O'Grady. 'They cheerfully ranked in the cause of reform.'[34] When all the votes had been tallied, twelve Reformers and only eight Tories glowered at each other round the council table.

Or rather, eleven Reformers: one was doing his glowering in private. John Rolph had been featured on both the Reform and the conservative ticket for St Patrick's Ward. He was an acceptable choice for mayor to the Tories, at least after they found themselves in a minority and deprived of their most prominent candidates, and he may even have stood for council in the expectation of becoming mayor. After the election he apparently learned to his chagrin that his Reform colleagues were bent on choosing Mackenzie, and he resigned his seat even before the new council was sworn in (see Table 2). Rolph was the only certified gentleman among the elected councillors and had played a large part in drafting the city's act of incorporation. Since he was also a founding leader of the Upper Canadian Reform movement, he may have felt it beneath his dignity to sit below Mackenzie at the council board. He had stayed aloof from party politics since moving to York in 1830 and may also not have relished the year of toe-to-toe partisan infighting that might be feared with Mackenzie as mayor.[35]

Any such fears on Rolph's part were well founded. The events of the past two years had crystallized Mackenzie's status as the personification of opposition to the provincial establishment. His elevation to the chief magistracy of the capital was a crowning challenge to the powerful interests whose headquarters it was. How likely were those interests to respond peaceably? The last sixteen years had shown them ready to abuse their official powers, and even to employ sheer illegal violence, to assert their position. On the one hand, there was the legal persecution of Robert Gourlay and Francis Collins, and Mackenzie's repeated expulsion from the house of assembly; on the other, the wrecking of Mackenzie's printing-shop in 1826 and his battering at Hamilton in March 1832 by thugs led by a magistrate, William Kerr.[36]

TABLE 1
General election, March 1834

Candidates for alderman		Candidates for common councilman	
St Andrew			
Dr Thomas D. Morrison (R)	95	John Armstrong (merchant) (T)	97
John Harper (R)	89	John Doel (R)	96
Dr Grant Powell (T)	85	Alexander Armstrong (R)	81
Robert Stanton (T)	82	J. Johnston (T)	74
St David			
William Lyon Mackenzie (R)	148	Franklin Jackes (R)	150
James Lesslie (R)	129	Colin Drummond (R)	136
Dr Christopher Widmer (T)	95	Thomas Bright (T)	119
Peter Paterson (T)	95	Charles Stotesbury (T)	119
James King*	52		
William Bergin*	38		
St George			
Thomas Carfrae, Jr (T)	40	John Craig (T)	32
John Elmsley (T)	32	George Gurnett†	31
Dr John Tims (R)	28	Edward Perry (R)	31
George Ridout‡	2	James Hunter (R)	29
		John Roddy (T)	15
St Lawrence			
George Monro (T)	100	William Arthurs (R)	161
George Duggan, Sr (T)§	99	Lardner Bostwick (R)	90
Peter McDougall (R)	97	Alexander Dixon (T)	80
Joseph Cawthra (R)	97	William C. Ross (T)	51
Thomas Helliwell (T)	22	John Ernest (T)	16
St Patrick			
Dr John Rolph (RT)	128	James Trotter (T)	81
George Taylor Denison, Sr (T)	103	Joseph Turton (R)	81
Thomas Elliott (R)	44	John McIntosh (R)	60
		James Newbiggin (T)	30

*Probably Roman Catholic sectional candidates
†Returned by the returning officer's casting vote; *Courier of Upper Canada* 27 March 1834, in Metropolitan Toronto Library, Carfrae Scrapbook
‡Nominated, in preference to Tims, by a mainly conservative electors' meeting, though he was a moderate Reformer; unidentified newspaper clipping, Carfrae Scrapbook
§Probably an Orange sectional candidate, was unseated at the subsequent election scrutiny in favour of Cawthra; Council Journal, 1 May 1834. Monro and Helliwell were the official Tory candidates; *Courier of Upper Canada*, reprinted in *Brockville Recorder* 4 April 1834.
SOURCE: *Canadian Correspondent* 29 March 1834

TABLE 2
By-elections 1834

Ward, office, month	Outgoing member	Winner	Loser
St Patrick alderman (April)	Dr John Rolph (R, T)	Dr John Tims (R)	Robert Blevins (T)
St Lawrence common councilman (September)	Lardner Bostwick (R)	Joshua G. Beard (T) 72	Charles Baker (R) 35

SOURCES: *Canadian Correspondent* 26 April 1834; *Advocate* 11 September 1834

Rolph's own brother had been a victim of politically motivated violence. George Rolph, whose reform ties offended the Gore District's tory leadership, had been tarred and feathered at his home in Dundas by nocturnal assailants. They escaped virtually unpunished, but George Rolph had been hounded from his office as district clerk of the peace. One of those accused of the outrage now belonged to Toronto's city council: George Gurnett of the *Courier*, whose invitation to York had followed hard on his unsuccessful application to the government for the newly vacant clerkship.[37] Gurnett's unsleeping assiduity in the Tory cause had been evinced at York only a few days after his friend William Kerr had seen action at Hamilton, when he was prominent among the disrupters of a public meeting organized by Mackenzie and his supporters.[38] It was perhaps the first time a political rally in the Home District had been broken up by thuggery, but such action against Reformers would become common as the decade advanced. Considering the political climate of Upper Canada in 1834, and of Toronto in particular, John Rolph did not need clairvoyance to predict trouble ahead at Toronto city hall.

Circumstances certainly provided ample room for troublemaking. The new corporation's financial situation was precarious. A major purpose of the legislature in incorporating the capital had been to create a local authority that could legitimately levy higher taxes than the appointed district magistracy; but the act of incorporation left the taxes to be imposed according to the general provincial assessment law. This was highly inequitable as applied to a sizeable urban area. Dwelling houses were assessed fixed rates that bore little relation to their value. Corner stores were taxed as merchant shops if they stocked any imported goods at all, even a few oranges.[39] The magistrates had been entitled to raise only a penny in the pound (1/240 of assessed value), plus a special town rate of £100 a year. The city was obliged by its charter to pay the magistrates a penny in the pound merely for the use of the district jail and court house – a provision that would engender strife between the council and the magistrates, partly because of the city's financial plight and partly because of the jail's deplorable state.[40] Obviously, the new council would have to increase taxes substantially if it were to fulfil its expected functions. The Tory minority would cynically oppose the threepenny rate the Reformers imposed and exploit it to discredit them with the poorer ratepayers.[41]

Another potential embarrassment for Mackenzie in particular was the mayor's judicial functions. One of his main responsibilities (it was for this that he, alone of the council, received a salary under the city charter) was to hold a daily police court. He also presided at the city quarter sessions, or mayor's court.[42] These duties entailed fining or imprisoning people for acts that were habitual, or else important to their livelihood, such as drunk and disorderly conduct, beating their wives and children, Sabbath-breaking, creating nuisances to the public health, and selling liquor without a licence.[43] This put Mackenzie, as a politician dependent on public favour, in a bind. The standards of conduct he had to enforce were strongly upheld by the heavily nonconformist middle ranks of Toronto society who were the backbone of Reform in the capital: an element dedicated to hard work, self-improvement, and temperance – in a word, respectability. They were quite antipathetic, however, to many of the lower-class Irish voters, whose support was also essential to the Reformers' success. Mackenzie's enemies would exploit this dilemma, too, with equal unscrupulousness.[44]

Three cases Mackenzie heard in his magistral capacity in June gave them a field day. In March, participants in a St Patrick's Day dinner had been involved in a fracas that led to the indictment of three of them – a district magistrate and two government clerks – for assault and battery before Mackenzie at the mayor's court. The magistrate was acquitted, the clerks convicted. It is probable from the evidence that the jury's verdict was just, but what really incensed the Tory press was the sentences Mackenzie imposed: a £5 fine and a week in jail. Their outrage was sharpened by another case, in which the brother of a Reform councilman was also convicted of assault and battery, but with a strong recommendation to mercy by the jury. Mackenzie fined him only five shillings.[45] A fortnight later, the mayor evoked new extremes of fury by sentencing a habitually drunken woman to the stocks after she had insulted him in court.[46]

The mayor's court cases lent themselves to Tory propaganda partly because of their fortuitous conjunction. Thomas Turton's light fine was not unreasonable, in view of the jury's recommendation; it might not even have been noticed, but for the contrast with the clerks' unhappy fate. Here was class conflict: a Tory district magistrate and two salaried officials arraigned before the people's tribune (or an unprincipled demagogue, depending on one's point of view). The *Patriot* trumpeted that Mackenzie had chided the convicts for thinking themselves better than their victim merely because their salaries let them wear better coats. Mackenzie's paper remarked, though, that a fine meant nothing to men who were well paid out of the public treasury: a week in jail was more likely to make them think twice about throwing their weight around. Their acquitted co-defendant did not escape censure: 'The behaviour of Dr King while conducting his own case during the trial, was the most insolent and impudent we ever witnessed in any Court of Justice. As a bad sample from the magistracy of the Home District, we readily consign him to the sober judgement of our fellow citizens.'[47]

But while the Tory papers might have made a meal of all three cases under any circumstances, ethnic politics gave them a special savour. The two clerks were Irish, and Dr John King (lawyer King's brother) was not merely Irish but a Roman Catholic. Mackenzie was alleged to have told the convicts, 'It will teach you not to go to St Patrick's dinner again.'[48] Thomas Turton's victim was a Catholic Irishman, and the occasion of their quarrel a dispute over religion. Of the Woman in the Stocks, otherwise known as the MOTHER OF A FAMILY IN THE STOCKS, the *Patriot* shrilled: 'We understand the poor woman thus exposed, is an Irish Roman Catholic, did this consideration weigh upon the generous mind of his Lordship? We know he hates them.'[49]

Even more yards of print were devoted to another subject, which had nothing to do with Mackenzie's conduct as mayor. This was his newspaper's publication of a letter sent him by the Scottish radical MP, Joseph Hume. Hume had taken a special interest in Upper Canadian political questions, and he remarked of Mackenzie's unconstitutional expulsion from the house of assembly in December 1833 that it 'must hasten that crisis which will terminate in independence and freedom from the baneful domination of the Mother Country and the tyrannical conduct of a small and despicable fraction in the Colony.'[50]

In the minds of the provincial oligarchy, Upper Canada's authoritarian constitution and its status as a British colony were intimately linked. The constitution was the institutional basis of the oligarchy's political predominance; the oligarchy and its apologists defended that predominance by arguing that reform would endanger the British connection. Hume's words were just as ambiguous as Gurnett's outburst a year earlier, but by implying that oligarchy and the imperial tie would fail together they stressed the link between the two. Mackenzie's publication of a letter that spoke of both in opprobrious language seemed to offer his enemies a twofold opportunity:

first, to identify opposition to the status quo with treason, and second – by identifying Mackenzie, the personification of such opposition, with treason – to check the long run of favourable publicity the last few years had brought him.

They exploited it for all it was worth. Tory activists hit the streets to gather signatures on a loyal address to the crown. Councilman Gurnett himself brought the subject into the municipal arena by a motion of censure on the mayor; his and Alderman Morrison's speeches pro and con were declaimed to an overflowing council chamber.[51] At the beginning of July, leading Tories moved to revive the British Constitutional Society, first set up early in 1832 to combat Mackenzie's agitation over his expulsion from the house of assembly. William Henry Draper was elected president; the vice-presidents included all three Tory aldermen (Carfrae, Monro, and Denison), as well as the ousted George Duggan and Dr John King. Gurnett pulled the strings as secretary. In order to exploit any embarrassment moderate Reformers might feel at being linked with treason, the society was declared open to 'every Adult Male Inhabitant of this City, of respectable character, without distinction of political party,' who would pledge himself to support the British connection.[52]

Gurnett's first major act as secretary was to get in touch with his old Tory friends in the Gore District to arrange a display of political theatre. On a warm, sunny day in mid-July, two steamers sailed into Toronto harbour, bearing a deputation said to be more than 900 strong. One of the vessels fired a salute of several guns, which was answered by a cannon stationed for the occasion on a wharf. A committee of the society went on board to greet the visitors, who then disembarked to march in procession with the society to the government house at the west end of the city. There they presented a loyal address to Lieutenant-Governor Colborne. When the procession returned to the docks, the Toronto contingent marched past the visiting deputation to display its own strength. An ox was roasted whole. Early in the proceedings, Mayor Mackenzie was reported to have visited the waterfront, hoping to find some illegality that would allow him to exert his 'little brief authority'; but he had not dared to act. He had also been seen later, skulking with his crony Alderman James Lesslie among the chimney-pots atop Lesslie's store in order to spy on the returning procession.[53]

With a provincial general election expected daily, this was a demonstration that had to be answered. Mackenzie called a meeting at the market on 29 July to discuss matters connected with the public welfare, in particular the unfair tax laws. Operating this Tory law was making the Reformers unpopular, and Mackenzie was determined that the blame should rest where it belonged: on

Sheriff Jarvis, who had not done all he should, as the city's MPP, to correct the situation. Since Jarvis was expected to defend his seat at the coming poll, it was doubly useful to the Reformers to flush him out of his cool Rosedale garden and make him answer to the people amid the heat and dust of the market-place.

The meeting was rowdy. Mackenzie had called it for the evening, so that working people could attend it, and he spoke for so long that it was getting dark when Jarvis began to reply. The meeting was adjourned until the next day, but Mackenzie did not wait to stage his own little act of political theatre. The *Patriot* reported that he 'was followed to his house, by all the street laborers in the employ of the Corporation, for the special benefit of whose blessed presence the late hour of meeting had been appointed by his Lordship.'[54] He was not even present the next afternoon when the tragedy occurred. As Jarvis was proceeding with his speech, the packed gallery collapsed, shooting its occupants into the butchers' stalls beneath. Four people were killed – some of them fatally gored by butcher's hooks as they fell – and dozens injured.

Mackenzie's absence did not prevent the Tory press from blaming him for the disaster. He was condemned for calling the original meeting, for setting it in the evening, for delaying it until more of his supporters had time to arrive, for speaking too long, for giving a speech designed to create antagonism between rich and poor. It was held up as a monstrous thing to set a meeting for a time when working folk could attend it and to criticize laws that threw an unfair tax burden on the poor. The second day's tragedy was said to have been provoked by the rowdiness of a group of Reformers that included Mackenzie's brother-in-law and one of his printers. A group of the mayor's men were said to have cheered as the gallery collapsed. His colleague on council, Dr Morrison, was alleged to have looked on the carnage with smiles of satisfaction and pronounced it a judgment on its Tory victims.[55]

A worse calamity was in progress even before the collapse of the market gallery. Cholera again stalked the streets. The first case had been identified on 26 July, and it soon became clear that it was even more virulent than the first epidemic of 1832. It put an end to electioneering for a while, but not to political discord.

The emergency turned the corporation's financial difficulties into a severe handicap. The special fund of £250 voted by council was exhausted within a fortnight. Lieutenant-Governor Colborne had turned down the board of health's appeals for help, and he reconsidered only after the superintendent of the cholera hospital complained that he was not getting the supplies he needed. By that time, the board of health had to be reorganized because the chairman, Dr Morrison, and the two Tory members, Gurnett and Carfrae, refused to serve any longer.[56]

Colborne seems at this time to have told Alderman John Tims, the other medical man on the board, that he would help the city if the hospital were placed under a medical committee consisting of Tims himself, Morrison, Dr Christopher Widmer, and Dr John Rolph. Accordingly, the board's new chairman, Alderman James Lesslie, wrote to ask for £500 in aid and announce that the board had appointed Colborne's nominees 'to take under their direction in conjunction with the resident Surgeon all matters that may appertain to the medical Treatment, Diet or Regimen of the Patients during the continuance of the disease.'[57] Colborne replied by offering to assume all the expense of the hospital provided it were placed 'under the Entire Charge' of the four physicians.[58]

This might seem too good an offer to refuse, but tempers were frayed by the heat and the crisis and the new board received it as a deep affront. Even in his first letter, Lesslie had blamed the board's difficulties on the iniquitous tax laws and the Tory councillors who, though now condemning the board as inefficient, had voted against higher taxes in May. Now he told Colborne tartly that the city charter made it the duty of the board – and of no one else – to safeguard the public health. Colborne had earlier claimed to be unable to help the board; now it appeared that he could, but he seemed intent on humiliating it by withholding his aid unless it were to be administered by a committee of his own choosing. Though the hospital had been placed under his nominees' medical supervision, financial control must rest with the city. If Colborne chose not to co-operate, the board would 'continue nevertheless to fulfill to the best of its ability the Important trust imposed in it by the Citizens, leaving the Public to judge how far His Excellency has shown a reasonable desire to co-operate with the municipal authorities for the general good in a time of great public calamity.' Colborne responded with an unconditional offer of £250.[59]

The newspapers devoted a lot of print to the board's internal quarrels and its row with the lieutenant-governor. Gurnett blamed the breakup on the interference of Mackenzie (who was himself a member) with its decisions. He crowed that Dr Morrison and the mayor were no longer on speaking terms. The *Advocate* ascribed Morrison's resignation to disagreement with the board of health's decision to apply again to the government for help; but this leaves it unclear whether he objected to Colborne's terms for granting aid or the board's for accepting it.[50] The squabble between the city and the government was discreditable to both sides, but such quarrels were common throughout the Canadas in both 1832 and 1834 as doctors and officials grappled with the invisible enemy in their midst.[61] The prevailing political tone of Toronto in 1834 made them doubly likely.

Even before the epidemic had ended, leaving perhaps 500 dead in the city, politics returned to the forefront of the public mind. An election was a public spectacle. There was only one polling place in each riding, no matter how large. There the public would gather at the appointed time for the nomination of candidates. After speeches from the nominator and seconder of each, and then from the candidates themselves, the polling began. Voting was a public act. Each aspiring elector would approach the returning officer to claim his privilege and announce his choice, which would be recorded next to his name in the poll book. The poll lasted for six days: a necessary provision where voting depended on a property qualification and one man might be enfranchised in several widely dispersed constituencies. It was a system that placed a premium on getting your supporters to the hustings early, in order to build up a lead that might influence the floating voters.

It also helped if you could establish a physical presence at the hustings that might deter hostile voters from trying to exercise their franchise. To do this, it helped to have the Irish on your side. Wherever they settled in large numbers, they added a new sound to the clamour of partisan rhetoric: the crack of clubs on skulls. A large, mainly disfranchised lower class, they energetically embraced the one means available to them to project themselves into the political processes that affected their lives.[62] Most of them, as Anglicans partaking of a strongly loyalist political culture, were more likely to act on the government side; but in Toronto in the 1830s there was also a robust minority of Catholics who were willing to brawl for Reform. Their chief was a blacksmith, Daniel Sullivan, head of a family of fearsome reputation. 'Not a row of any consequence takes place but the name of Sullivan is connected with it,' declared a new Orange newspaper. 'This name carries terror along with it, to every peaceable and well-minded citizen.'[63]

Sullivan had last been in court in September, when he was fined for beating up an Orangeman who had dared to parade with a few comrades on 12 July, wearing the sash of his order. The very first day of the election found the brawny hero brawling near the hustings. Wroth waxed he and wrought woe; dole dealt he there to faith-foes. Further violence the next day reached a climax in the evening, when a gang of Orangemen rioted outside Sullivan's house at the foot of Yonge Street, smashing all the windows. On the third evening it was the turn of Sullivan and his friends to go on the rampage. Their roistering ended in tragedy. As they charged and chanted their way along King Street toward the market, they clashed with a band of constables led by the high bailiff, William Higgins. One of Sullivan's companions fell to the ground, his life ebbing from the great wound carved in his side. Soldiers stood guard into the small hours to keep the peace.[64]

The actual polling furnished its own kind of excitement. Sheriff Jarvis's first rumoured opponent at the hustings had been Alderman Lesslie; but experience taught that the Reformers were more likely to win with an Anglican gentleman of moderate politics than a nonconformist radical, and Mackenzie's friend gave way to James Small.[65] Small had been Robert Baldwin's rival in the town of York by-election of 1829 and had twice opposed Mackenzie unsuccessfully in county elections. This time he jumped ahead to lead 64–46 at the end of the first day, but Jarvis all but made up the deficit on the second and the rivals ran neck and neck to the finishing post. Eventually Small squeaked home by 258 votes to 250. The loser grumbled that he had a majority of eight but had been beaten by ineligible Reform voters. 'Notwithstanding all their villainy, I was within two or three of beating them, when they thrust upon [sic] some perjured rascals and those two or three in attendance being luke-warm, thinking all was over refused to vote.'[66]

The house of assembly was once more controlled by a Reform majority (including Mackenzie and Dr Morrison, who had both been elected in York county). The Reformers began to prepare for January's municipal elections. Their political organization, the Constitutional Reform Society (or Canadian Alliance Society, as it was about to rename itself to emphasize its sympathy with the Lower Canadian Reformers led by Papineau), set up ward committees late in November to marshal the Reform vote. Daniel Sullivan was named to the St George's Ward committee, along with Judge Ridout, among others.[67] Small's victory in October was encouraging, but hardly a certain augury. Would the Reformers receive credit for the by-laws they had passed, the miles of sidewalks and pedestrian crossings they had laid down in the mud, their refusal to use the borrowing powers granted to the council by the act of incorporation to plunge the city into debt? Would the Tories benefit from Hume's 'baneful domination' letter, the widespread discontent at increased municipal taxation, the sheer volume of opprobrious clamour they had kicked up about Mackenzie's performance as mayor?[68] Mackenzie himself was renominated for St David's Ward against his will: he had closed down his newspaper in November to prepare to resume his duties as an MPP, and he was also anxious to give up the burdens of a conscientious municipal councillor.[69] It was at this juncture that two bombshells blew up in his face.

On 20 November, Mackenzie and Alderman Lesslie had sentenced two prostitutes to two weeks in prison, directing that they be kept in a part of the jail to which male prisoners had no access.[70] Later that day, the mayor visited the jail to see how these orders were being observed and apparently found the women at large among the imprisoned debtors. The jailer, Charles Barnhart, was employed by Sheriff Jarvis, not the city. He and Mackenzie were old enemies (he had relatives at Streetsville, in Mackenzie's riding, and before the general election had campaigned there against the mayor). Outraged at the neglect of his and Lesslie's orders, Mackenzie complained to Lieutenant-Governor Colborne.

Barnhart told a different story. He claimed that the women had been committed with orders to deny them access to fire, but the day had got so cold that the under-jailer had let them warm themselves at the stove in his private room, where no male prisoners were. One of the debtors backed Barnhart up, adding that when the mayor had found the women out of their cell he had stormed off in a rage, ordering them to be shut up without fire or light. For his part, Sheriff Jarvis noted that the women had been sentenced to hard labour, which could only mean breaking stones – hardly a fit punishment for women, he suggested.

Mackenzie's first reaction was simply to set the record straight. He and Lesslie had meant only to ensure that the prostitutes should be locked up in the separate ward where women had normally been placed. They had been sentenced to 'labour' (not hard labour), which meant cleaning cells and washing the prisoners' linen. The debtor's story was a fabrication by someone he did not know. As an afterthought, the mayor sent the deputy city clerk to the jail to check the warrant of commitment. Appended to the direction to segregate the women, John Elliott found the words '& to keep from fire.' They were obliterated by a thick pen-stroke but quite legible.

Confronted by an apparent forgery of a court document, Mackenzie at once placed the matter before the grand jury of the mayor's court. The jury presented that the document had been altered 'by some person or persons unknown' after being delivered to the jailer, but named no culprit. Shortly afterwards, two successive numbers of the *Toronto Recorder*, a new Orange paper, published Barnhart's story together with the compromising allegations of Barnhart himself, Sheriff Jarvis, and the debtor. Mackenzie published his own version in O'Grady's paper, also with supporting documents. He pursued Barnhart with complaints to Colborne and Attorney-General Jameson but found them reluctant to act on his grievance. Barnhart for his part drummed up a bundle of affidavits to support his story, but with one exception they were all by people who were under his control or possessed an obvious grudge against the mayor and need not be taken seriously.[71]

The exception certainly deserves notice. George Gurnett and his fellow councilman James Trotter swore that they had heard the prostitutes sentenced in the police court 'to be kept at hard labour in the jail without fire and candle.' Authoritative testimony against the mayor, it might seem. Yet the disputed words in the warrant of commitment said nothing about depriving the women of light, but mentioned fire alone. Since the evidence also favours Mackenzie's claim to have sentenced the women to labour, not hard labour, it is difficult not to conclude that the two Tory councilmen conspired to perjure themselves in order to discredit him.

While Mackenzie was struggling in these toils, the election killing returned to haunt him. Neither the coroner's jury nor the grand jury of the district assizes had been able to detect Patrick Burns's killer, but shortly before Christmas a group of the dead man's friends came to the mayor with testimony incriminating his own chief of police, William Higgins. These men were Reform supporters, but not unconditionally, and they represented the part of the community most likely to be alienated by the jail scandal (at least one of the prostitutes was Irish). With the municipal elections barely three weeks away, there was no chance of sweeping this business under the rug even temporarily. Mackenzie held a public hearing in the police court and committed Higgins to stand trial at the spring assizes on a charge of murder.

Higgins was a respected local official. For years he had been high constable of the Home District, and he had continued to hold that post after becoming high bailiff of the city. His committal sparked off a furore in the papers along predictable partisan lines. O'Grady's paper, called the *Correspondent and Advocate* since Mackenzie had closed his, characterized the dead man as 'an old, kind-hearted and confiding Irishman,' struck down 'while he, under influence of the prevailing excitement was cheering his favourite candidate.' Other evidence portrayed him as a drunkard out for blood.

When Higgins's case came before the assize grand jury in April, the accused man was exonerated and presentments returned for riot against other parties, including Daniel Sullivan and his brother-in-law. The jury maintained that Burns had been felled by an axe aimed at Higgins, not by Higgins with a sword. The Tory newspapers seized the occasion to stress Mackenzie's apparent intimacy with Sullivan and the possible political motive behind his committal of Higgins.[72]

If the high bailiff's committal was politically motivated, it was a futile ploy. The election of January 1835 was a disaster for the Reformers. They swept St Andrew's Ward this time, but the Tories scooped the rest (see Table 3). On this occasion there was no excess of candidates to split the Tory vote, but the main difference from 1834 was the collapse of Reform support. James Lesslie ascribed this in his diary to the Reformers' over-confidence and consequent laziness, but it looks as though some of their own candidates were not too eager for re-election. Mackenzie's reluctance is well attested, and he shared it

TABLE 3
General election, January 1835

Candidates for alderman		Candidates for common councilman	
*St Andrew**			
John Harper (R)	65	John Doel (R)	64
Dr Thomas D. Morrison (R)	63	John Armstrong (axemaker) (R)	60
Robert Stanton (T)	59	Robert Marchant (T)	56
John Ewart (T)	53	John Armstrong (merchant) (T)	52
St David			
Robert Baldwin Sullivan (T)	126	Charles Stotesbury (T)	126
George Duggan, Sr (T)	123	George Henderson (T)	119
James Lesslie (R)	74	Franklin Jackes (R)	74
William Lyon Mackenzie (R)	69	Malcolm McLellan (R)	74
St George			
Thomas Carfrae, Jr (T)	46	John Craig (T)	43
Edward Wright (R)†	43	Alexander Rennie (T)	42
George Gurnett (T)	42	Edward Perry (R)	40
James E. Small, MPP (R)	33	James Hunter (R)	34
St Lawrence			
George Munro (T)	122	Joshua G. Beard (T)	118
Dr John King (T)	117	Alexander Dixon (T)	116
Charles Baker (R)	41	William Arthurs (R)	37
Joseph Cawthra (R)	37	William Musson (R)	32
St Patrick			
Richard Hull Thornhill (T)	84	George Nichol (T)	86
George Taylor Denison, Sr (T)	83	James Trotter (T)	86
Dr John Tims (R)	36	John Anderson (R)	34
Joseph Turton (R)	33	Thomas Eliott (R)	32

*The return for this ward was invalidated and a new election held, but the four Reformers won by increased majorities; Council Journal, 13 February 1835; *Patriot* 20 February 1835.
†At the subsequent election scrutiny, Wright was unseated in favour of Gurnett.
SOURCE: *Patriot* 16 January 1835

with Lesslie, for one.[73] Neither man would stand in 1836, when the Reformers won again.

So ended the first term of Toronto's municipal history, a term marked by strife within both the council chamber and the political community at large. Even catastrophe had sharpened dissension rather than muting it. The collapse of the market gallery had been exploited by Tory journalists to stimulate hatred of their opponents; the cholera epidemic had promoted quarrels that, if not essentially political, certainly had political overtones. Such extremes of antipathy were the mark of a badly fissured, a disintegrated society.

The focus of this discord was the mayor. Mackenzie was perhaps a brusque, quarrelsome sort of man – not merely one whose business was political controversy, but one likely to provoke it by tactlessness even when he did not intend it. Still, no one achieves political importance under representative institutions unless he embodies widely held views and aspirations, and Mackenzie's very prominence gives the lie to Chief Justice Robinson's idea of Upper Canada as a Garden of Eden. Moreover, in 1834 as so often before and afterwards, Mackenzie's Tory adversaries met him more than half-way. Alderman George Monro, a district magistrate, had led the way early in April by refusing to quit the council chamber at council's bidding while it was investigating the validity of his election for St Lawrence Ward. In vindicating council's authority by having Monro ejected by the high bailiff, Mackenzie had given his enemies their first chance to trumpet his tyrannical temper to the world; but the fault had been Monro's.[74]

The struggle for authority that this episode epitomized was one of the underlying themes of Toronto municipal politics in 1834. It is hard for us to conceive how sorely it grated on the provincial establishment and its minions to see Mackenzie elected to the mayoralty, the first popular tribune in recent memory to occupy a prominent post of executive authority in the province. To the oligarchy he was a threat, to its creatures a reproach by his refusal to compromise with power for the sake of personal gain. In small matters as well as large he challenged its ideas of what was fitting: by his refusal to adopt a fancy regalia, his insistence that his salary should be the minimum dictated by the act of incorporation, his refusal to accept even that until the inequitable assessment law was amended.[75]

Yet the position of Mackenzie and his Reform colleagues was not easy. They had won power, but they had still to establish their legitimacy. Several of the most controversial episodes of that first term reflected the need they felt to enforce their authority over an overweening élite and its familiars: not only Monro's eviction and the exemplary chastisement of the government clerks, but also the board of health's quarrel with Lieutenant-Governor Colborne and the mayor's insistence on having his say in the running of the district jail. If some of their conduct seems unduly petty or contentious, consider what they faced. Consider the provincial establishment's record of pursuing its enemies by foul means. Consider Barnhart's unpunished forgery of a legal instrument, his master the sheriff's libellous declaration that the prostitutes had been sentenced to hard labour, the supporting perjuries of councilmen

Gurnett and Trotter. These events of December 1834 were not a sport: they were part of a pattern of legal and illegal intimidation and chicanery in defence of the status quo that stretched back to the persecution of Robert Gourlay.

The full story of these overt and covert abuses of executive power, abuses that deprived the existing political order of its claim to legitimacy and so contributed to the outbreak of rebellion in 1837, has yet to be told. Only when imperial intervention and a further surge of British immigration had combined to change the terms of Upper Canadian politics, abolishing the old polarities of oligarchic authoritarianism and Yankee egalitarianism, would legal persecution, 'dirty tricks,' and (above all) Orange violence cease to be important political factors. The union of Upper and Lower Canada in 1841 would destroy the oligarchy's institutional power base; the concession of responsible government in 1848 would finally shatter its vision of a pastoral domain ruled by a colonial gentry; but the decisively British character of the population by that time would still its fears that Upper Canada might become a brawling Yankee chaos. While these changes unfolded, Toronto's patricians would cling to an ever more illusory social ascendancy, with the connivance of both a thriving but prudent merchant class and an unruly Orange militia, the latter composed mainly of plebeian immigrants who drew social fulfilment from acting as shock troops in what they were willing to see as a struggle between Empire loyalism and Yankee insurrectionism.

In the new era inaugurated by the advent of responsible government, the politics of ethnic and ideological fragmentation would give way to those of pluralistic consensus: a limited tolerance of diversity founded on unquestioned participation in a British and Protestant empire and a new dominant ideology of commercial and industrial advance. Even then, when the term *Tory* no longer denoted devotees of oligarchy but the most pragmatic champions of the new materialism, Toronto would still normally be, to reformers of a new era, what it had been to a wag in 1835: 'Tory-on-Toe.'

NOTES

1 The most succinct account of Toronto's physical aspect in 1834 is Frederick H. Armstrong 'Toronto in 1834' *Canadian Geographer* x (1966). See also Armstrong 'Toronto in Transition: The Emergence of a City, 1828–1838' PhD thesis, University of Toronto, 1966.
2 *Canadian Courant* (Montreal) 12 October 1833, quoted in Edith G. Firth ed *The Town of York, 1815–1834: A Further Collection of Documents of Early Toronto* (Toronto 1966) 82
3 F.H. Armstrong 'Toronto's First Railway Venture' *Ontario History* LVIII

(1966); Firth *Town of York* xxxii, 74–5, 236, 287; City of Toronto Archives (hereafter CTA), RG1A, Journal of the Common Council (hereafter Council Journal), 21 November 1834, 24 January 1835

4 Firth *Town of York* lxxxii; *Advocate* (Toronto) 2 October 1834; *Correspondent and Advocate* (Toronto) 15 January 1835

5 The observations in the following paragraphs are partly impressions gleaned from my current research on Toronto, using the nominal census of 1842: Public Archives of Canada (hereafter PAC), RG31, Statistics Canada, census records. It should be noted that the PAC microfilm of this document is incorrectly targeted.

6 Firth *Town of York* 288–9; Paul Romney, 'Voters under the Microscope: A Quantitative Meditation on the Toronto Parliamentary Poll Book of 1836' paper presented to the Canadian Historical Association, June 1983, 19–21 (copy at CTA)

7 Paul Romney 'A Conservative Reformer in Upper Canada: Charles Fothergill, Responsible Government and the "British Party," 1824–1840' paper presented to the Canadian Historial Association, June 1984 (copy at CTA)

8 Romney 'Voters under the Microscope' 30

9 Firth *Town of York* lvii–lviii, 36 n1; G.M. Craig 'Strachan, John' in *Dictionary of Canadian Biography* (DCB) IX (Toronto 1976); Barrie Dyster 'Proudfoot, William' DCB IX; R.I.K. Davidson, 'Monro, George' in DCB X (Toronto 1972); M.L. Magill 'William Allan: A Pioneer Business Executive' in F.H. Armstrong et al *Aspects of Nineteenth-Century Ontario: Essays Presented to James J. Talman* (Toronto 1974)

10 Firth *Town of York* lvii–lviii, lx, 98 n, 133 n, 196; Lawson Memorial Library, University of Western Ontario, Diary of the Reverend William Proudfoot, excerpted in ibid 211–17; Ronald John Stagg 'The Yonge Street Rebellion of 1837: An Examination of the Background and a Re-assessment of the Events,' PhD thesis, University of Toronto, 1976, 214–15, 228–9, 300

11 Firth *Town of York* liv–lvii; Goldwin French *Parsons and Politics: The Role of the Wesleyan Methodists in Upper Canada and the Maritimes from 1780 to 1855* (Toronto 1962) 136–53

12 Firth *Town of York* lviii–lx; J.E. Rea *Bishop Alexander Macdonnel and the Politics of Upper Canada* (Toronto 1974) 99–116

13 W.H. Higgins *The Life and Times of Joseph Gould* (Toronto 1887) 58

14 Ibid 54

15 This account of York and Upper Canadian politics is based on G.M. Craig *Upper Canada: The Formative Years, 1784–1841* (Toronto 1963) 188–209 and Firth *Town of York* xxxvi–xlv, 90–138

16 Robert E. Saunders 'Robinson, Sir John Beverley' in DCB IX

17 Alan Wilson 'Colborne, John, 1st Baron Seaton' in ibid; J.M.S. Careless 'Robert Baldwin' in Careless ed *The Pre-Confederation Premiers: Ontario Government Leaders, 1841–1867* (Toronto 1980); R.M. Baldwin and J. Baldwin *The Baldwins and the Great Experiment* (Toronto 1969); Victor Loring Russell *Mayors of Toronto 1 1834–99* (Erin, Ont, 1982) 20–3; William Canniff *The Medical Profession in Upper Canada, 1793–1850* (Toronto 1894) 522–4

18 Robert J. Burns 'Jarvis, William Botsford' in DCB IX

19 Craig *Upper Canada* 210–15; Frederick H. Armstrong and Ronald J. Stagg 'Mackenzie, William Lyon' in DCB IX; Hereward Senior and Elinor Senior 'Boulton, Henry John' in DCB IX; S.F. Wise 'The Rise of Christopher Hagerman' *Historic Kingston* XIV (1965); S.F. Wise 'Tory Factionalism: Kingston Elections and Upper Canadian Politics, 1820–1836' *Ontario History* LVII (1965)

20 David B. Read *The Lives of the Judges of Upper Canada and Ontario* (Toronto 1888) 188–200; Charles Lindsey *The Life and Times of Wm. Lyon Mackenzie* 2 vols (Toronto 1862), 1 293–8

21 *Courier of Upper Canada* (Toronto) 1 May 1833, cited in Craig *Upper Canada* 215

22 Paul Rutherford *The Making of the Canadian Media* (Toronto 1978) 1. See also Joseph Gould's account of his 'first lesson in politics,' gleaned from the *Colonial Advocate*; Higgins *Joseph Gould* 55–6, also ibid 91.

23 Edith G. Firth ed *Early Toronto Newspapers, 1793–1867* (Toronto 1961). For Gurnett, see Frederick H. Armstrong 'Gurnett, George' in DCB IX and Romney 'Conservative Reformer in Upper Canada.'

24 John Charles Dent *The Story of the Upper Canadian Rebellion* 2 vols. (Toronto 1885) 1 171–4, 195–212; Rea *Bishop Alexander Macdonnel* 99–116

25 The *Porcupine!* was published in September 1835, not 1834, but it is too much fun to ignore. There is a copy in the Baldwin Room of the Metropolitan Toronto Library (MTL).

26 Firth *Town of York* 62 n, 103 n; George Metcalf 'William Henry Draper' in Careless ed *Pre-Confederation Premiers*; Brian H. Morrison 'Spragge, John Godfrey' in DCB XI (Toronto 1982). Widmer's philandering is noted in Paul Romney 'Widmer, Christopher' in DCB VIII (forthcoming). Wood's homosexuality is documented in MTL, William Dummer Powell Papers. I am indebted for this reference to Mr James Fraser, recently of the City of Toronto Archives.

27 Sally F. Zerker *The Rise and Fall of the Toronto Typographical Union* (Toronto 1982) 22, 25, 30; Elizabeth Hulse *A Dictionary of Toronto Printers, Publishers, Booksellers and the Allied Trades* (Toronto 1982) 11, 15, 275

28 James Hermeston Aitchison 'The Development of Local Government in Upper Canada, 1783–1850' PhD thesis, University of Toronto, 1953, especially parts 1 and 5; Aitchison 'The Courts of Requests in Upper Canada' *Ontario History*

XLI (1949); Armstrong 'Toronto in Transition' 57–67; Paul Romney 'The Ordeal of William Higgins' *Ontario History* LXVII (1975) 69–70

29 *Statutes of the Province of Upper Canada*, 1833, 3 William IV cap 18, 'An Act to Incorporate a Company under the Style and Title of the British America Fire and Life Assurance Company'; Firth *Town of York* xxxi, lxxii, 290

30 Firth *Town of York* lxxii–lxxiii, 279–81

31 G.M. Craig 'Rolph, John' in DCB IX; Frederick H. Armstrong 'Small, James Edward' in DCB IX; Thomas H.B. Symons 'Ridout, George' in DCB X

32 Firth *Town of York* lxxiv–lxxviii, 290–6; 4 William IV cap 23 (1834) sec 15, 27

33 Firth *Town of York* lxxv–lxxvi, 294–6; Romney 'Voters under the Microscope'

34 *Canadian Correspondent* (Toronto) 29 March 1834

35 F.H. Armstrong 'William Lyon Mackenzie, First Mayor of Toronto: A Study of a Critic in Power' *Canadian Historical Review* XLVIII (1967) 314–16. The old magistrates were Robert Stanton, Dr Grant Powell, and Dr Christopher Widmer; the new creations were George Monro, George Taylor Denison, and Peter Paterson.

36 Lindsey *Life and Times of Wm. Lyon Mackenzie* I 246–9

37 Josephine Phelan 'The Tar and Feather Case, Gore Assizes, August 1827' *Ontario History* LXVIII (1976); PAC RG5 A1, Civil and Provincial Secretaries' Offices, Canada West, Upper Canada Sundries, vol 93, pp 51997–2000 (G. Gurnett to Z. Mudge, 17 April 1829), vol 94, pp 52171–3 (John Carey to Sir J. Colborne, 8 May 1829)

38 Firth *Town of York* xliii, 132–7; F.H. Armstrong 'The York Riots of March 23, 1832' *Ontario History* LV (1963)

39 *York Commercial Directory, Street Guide and Register ... 1833–4* (York 1833) 143; Council Journal, 3 July 1834, 8 January 1835; *Advocate* 3 July, 18 September, 2 October 1834; *Patriot and Farmer's Monitor* (Toronto) 7 July, 29 July 1834

40 CTA RG1B, City Council Papers, W. Rowan to William Lyon Mackenzie, 9 May 1834; same to same, 30 July 1834, and attachments; PAC RG5 A1, vol 142, pp 77497–500 (Mackenzie to Rowan, 9 June 1834); Council Journal, 21 April, 22 April 1834; *Advocate*, 5 June, 11 September 1834; Paul Romney 'William Lyon Mackenzie and His Enemies' unpublished paper (copy at CTA). The magistrates were empowered to levy a tax of up to 4 pence in the pound by a statute of 1833 (3 William IV cap 28).

41 Council Journal, 19 May, 27 May 1834

42 Ibid 12 November 1834

43 One of the first things Mackenzie did after his election was to tour the slums with the high bailiff (chief of police). They found 'the obscure parts of the city' thronged with 'persons unlicensed selling beer, whiskey and other

strong liquors, and affording place and room for gambling and vice in its blackest shapes'; PAC RG5 A1, vol 141, pp 76923–6 (Mackenzie to W. Rowan, 7 May 1834); see also vol 142, pp 77497–500 (same to same, 9 May 1834).

44 In *Correspondent and Advocate*, 24 December 1835, William O'Grady noted: 'The most vicious part of the present system appears to be, the Aldermen being obliged to sit as police magistrates in judgement upon that class of persons upon whom they are in a great measure dependant for their seats, and no one can be insensible to the effect this is likely to have on their decisions.' Cf *Advocate* 20 March 1834, reprinted in Firth *Town of York* 300.

45 CTA RG7E, Proceedings of the Mayor's Court, 2 June, 3 June 1834; *Advocate* 5 June, 12 June, 10 July 1834; *Canadian Correspondent* 12 July 1834; *Patriot* June and July 1834 passim; Paul Romney 'William Lyon Mackenzie as Mayor of Toronto' *Canadian Historical Review* LVI (1975) 423

46 *Patriot* 20 June, 24 June, 27 June 1834. Ellen Halfpenny was appearing in the police court for the third time in four weeks: *Advocate* 22 May, 12 June, 26 June 1834. Section 74 of the act of incorporation authorized the magistrates to commit drunk and disorderly persons to the stocks.

47 *Advocate* 5 June 1834; ibid 12 June 1834; *Patriot* 13 June 1834; Canniff *Medical Profession* 459–62

48 *Patriot* 6 June 1834

49 Ibid 20 June 1834; ibid 10 June 1834

50 *Advocate* 22 May 1834; Craig *Upper Canada* 219–20; *Dictionary of National Biography* 'Hume, Joseph (1777–1855)'

51 *Patriot* 23 May–24 June 1834, passim; *Canadian Correspondent* 14 June, 21 June, 5 July, 12 July 1834; *Cobourg Star* 25 June, 2 July 1834

52 *British Constitutional Society of Upper Canada* 19 July 1834 (broadside, copy at MTL)

53 *Patriot* 18 July 1834

54 *Advocate* 31 July 1834; *Patriot* 1 August 1834

55 *Patriot* 1 August 1834

56 Council Journal, 31 July, 8 August 1834; PAC RG7 G16C, Upper Canada, Civil Secretary's Letterbooks, vol 31, pp 200, 205–6 (W. Rowan to Alderman Morrison, Chairman Board of Health, 7 August 1834; Rowan to James Lesslie Esq., Chairman Board of Health, 9 August 1834)

57 PAC RG5 A1, vol 143, p 78269, vol 144, pp 78596–8 (Lesslie to Rowan, 9 August 1834, and attachment numbered out of sequence); J.M.S. Careless 'Lesslie, James' in DCB XI; Canniff *Medical Profession* 651

58 PAC RG7 G16C, vol 31, p 204 (Rowan to Lesslie, 9 August 1834). The medical committee was appointed on 9 August at Colborne's behest, not on 24 July at the board of health's, as suggested in Geoffrey Bilson *A Darkened House:*

Cholera in Nineteenth-Century Canada (Toronto 1980) 85: see PAC RG5 A1, vol 143, p 78269 (extract from minutes of board of health)

59 PAC RG5 A1, vol 144, pp 78570–3 (Lesslie to Rowan, 9 August 1834); RG7 G16C, vol 31, p 208 (Rowan to Lesslie, 12 August 1834)

60 *Patriot* 9 August, 12 August, 15 August 1834; *Advocate* 14 August 1834; *Canadian Correspondent* 16 August 1834; *Kingston Chronicle and Gazette* 16 August 1834

61 Bilson *Darkened House* Chapters 1–4

62 For discussion of the Irish impact on Upper Canadian politics during the 1820s and 1830s, see Hereward Senior 'Ogle Gowan, Orangeism, and the Immigrant Question, 1830–1833' *Ontario History* LXVI (1974); Graeme H. Patterson 'Studies in elections and Public Opinion in Upper Canada' PhD thesis, University of Toronto, 1969, chapter 4.

63 *Toronto Recorder* 15 July 1835; ibid 18 July 1835; Paul Romney 'Sullivan, Daniel' in DCB XI

64 Proceedings of the Mayor's Court, September 1834; *Patriot* 14 October 1834; Romney 'Ordeal of William Higgins'

65 *Advocate* 13 March 1834; *Canadian Correspondent* 6, 13 September 1834

66 Alden G. Meredith ed *Mary's Rosedale and Gossip of 'Little York'* (Ottawa 1928) 94–5; *The Correspondent* 11, 18 October 1834; Armstrong 'Small, James'

67 *Correspondent and Advocate* 27 November 1834; Eric Jackson 'The Organization of Upper Canadian Reformers, 1818–1867' *Ontario History* LIII (1961), reprinted in J.K. Johnson ed *Historical Essays on Upper Canada* (Toronto 1975)

68 Armstrong 'William Lyon Mackenzie'; Romney 'William Lyon Mackenzie as Mayor of Toronto'

69 *Correspondent and Advocate* 18 December 1834; ibid 22 January, 18 February 1835. See also PAC RG5 A1, vol 148, pp 80668–75 (Mackenzie to W. Rowan, 2 December 1834): 'I shall gladly look forward to the day which ending my term will free me from the responsibilities of an office I do not like.'

70 For context see Romney 'William Lyon Mackenzie and His Enemies.'

71 PAC RG5 A1, vol 148, pp 80981–1001 (W.B. Jarvis to W. Rowan, 23 December 1834, and attachments)

72 *Patriot* 28 April 1835; *Toronto Recorder* 10 January 1835; Romney 'Ordeal of William Higgins'

73 Dundas, Ontario, Museum, Diary of James Lesslie, 1 January, 18 January 1835

74 Armstrong 'William Lyon Mackenzie' 317; Romney 'William Lyon Mackenzie as Mayor of Toronto' 425–6

75 *Patriot* 25 March, 28 March 1834; ibid 6 March 1835; Romney 'William Lyon Mackenzie as Mayor of Toronto' 432–3

GREGORY S. KEALEY

Orangemen and the Corporation

The politics of class during the Union of the Canadas

L ABOUR AND POLITICS in early Victorian Canada have received rather different treatments at the hands of historians. The former remained virtually ignored until the last decade, while the latter represented the major focus of historical writing. The rise of social history in Canada has commenced the process of investigating the lives of the common people, but has tended to ignore their role in politics. Fortunately, the view that discussions of politics and the state, and hence of power, somehow belonged to an 'old' history no longer prevails. A major task for historians has become the analysis of politics and political systems from a resolutely social perspective.[1] This analysis, especially a close scrutiny of the social basis of political cleavage, will make a contribution to our consideration of the interaction of class and politics.

In Victorian Toronto a major component of the political system was, of course, the Orange Order. An organization largely composed of plebeians and, later in the cities, proletarians, the order was a secret society with deep roots in the Irish struggle. Its proud trinity of crown, empire, and Protestantism provided its members with an ideological tradition, but one that had to be constantly reformulated in the Canadian context. While giving guidance in matters political, it promised no certainties as the bitter internal Orange conflicts of the period amply demonstrate.[2] Often viewed simply as a reactionary dogma, static and unchanging, the order has more often than not played the villain in liberal views of nineteenth-century Canadian history.

Attempts to study the Orange Order have proven controversial, and, more important, all have dismissed the utility of class analysis. In Barrie Dyster's thoughtful and sensitive study of pre-Confederation politics in Toronto,[3] it was proposed that there was a 'relative absence of overt class associations or class politics in Toronto during the two decades between 1840 and 1860.'[4] This thesis, combined with his argument that ethnic and religious identities substituted for those of class, fails to recognize the ways class was imbricated in these struggles. Indeed, it assumes that class is pre-eminently an economic category. Dyster, then, in his search for a recognizable 'modern' version of class politics, fails to recognize what Przeworski did, that 'classes are not given uniquely by any objective positions because they constitute effects of struggles, and these struggles are not determined uniquely by the relations of production ... Class struggles are structured by the totality of economic, political, and ideological relations; and they have an autonomous effect on the process of class formation.'

Simply, ethnicity and religion do not stand outside class. In this period of rapid class formation, class, even more than usual, cannot be found through the search for it as a determined sociological structure. Instead, class is to be discovered as a relationship, an effect of struggles, that is in constant motion as the process of class organization, disorganization, and reorganization continues. The search for the working class as a continuous, recognizable, historical subject in such a period is bound to fail, and yet class struggle was certainly not absent from Toronto or Canadian politics in this period.[5] As Dyster partially recognized, an older hegemonic system based on the gentry paternalism of the Family Compact was giving way to new forms of bourgeois hegemony. The class struggle involved battles between old and new segments of the Canadian élite, as well as the necessity of reintegrating the masses on some new basis as the older gentry/crowd relation dissolved.

The years of the Union of the Canadas were eventful ones, the story of responsible government and the genesis of Confederation being all too familiar. Yet when viewed from the perspectives of politically conscious Toronto Orangemen, these and the similar 'great' political events of the period begin to take on an unfamiliar appearance. The order, though founded for many purposes, was a political machine that in Toronto was involved in some 29 riots over the thirty years from Durham to Confederation. No fewer than 16 of these had direct political inspiration. These 16 riots included 4 election poll battles, 4 altercations at public meetings, and 8 politically inspired effigy burnings and street demonstrations (see Table 1).

Toronto had gained incorporation as a city in 1834 with a population of around 9,000. By 1848 the city had grown to 23,000, and Irish famine immigrants swelled that to over 30,000 by the time of the 1850 census. The city had reached almost 45,000 by 1861. At the time of the first religious census of the city in 1841 the city was approximately 17 per cent Roman Catholic. The Catholic proportion of the population had grown to 25 per cent by 1848, and this held constant with minor 1 per cent increases in the two subsequent decennial censuses.[6] The city's steady growth and shifting demographic composition were more than matched by its economic transformation as industrialization marched forward. The coming of the railways, protective tariffs, and the impetus provided by the American Civil War all provided Toronto's nascent industrialists with significant opportunities of which they were quick to take advantage.[7]

With industrial transformation came a growing wage-earning class and significant growth in trade union activity. The 1850s saw perhaps the first and certainly the most sustained period of widespread labour militancy in Canada to that point.[8] In Toronto, there were at least fourteen strikes in the years 1852–4, a level of strike activity not to be matched again until the labour upsurge surrounding the shorter-hours movement of 1872.[9] When combined with the massive unrest on Canadian public works in the 1840s and 1850s, it becomes only too clear that these decades witnessed the emergence of overt class conflict on a scale previously unknown in Canada.[10] Trade unionism was, however, only one of the effective and growing working-class institutions of this period. Workers were active in others. While primarily organized on ethno-religious lines, these organizations nevertheless performed services of great import for their primarily working-class members. In the Irish Roman Catholic community, there was the Hibernian Benevolent Society, in the Protestant and British community, the Orange Order.

The Orange Order was active in Toronto at least from the early 1820s, and some accounts put its arrival in the late 1810s. As early as 1823, Toronto Reformer William Warren Baldwin tried to introduce legislation to ban the order. The formal history of Orangeism in Canada, however, commences with Ogle Robert Gowan's creation of a Canadian grand lodge in 1830.[11] Subsequently, 12 lodges were founded in Toronto in the 1830s, 17 in the 1840s, and 15 in the 1850s,[12] the lodge structure in Toronto remaining stable in the 1860s with some 20 functioning lodges. The membership in these lodges fluctuated, but for the late 1850s and early 1860s there were approximately 1,100–1,200 full members of the order in Toronto.[13] In an adult male non-Catholic population of around 8,000, this 15 per cent obviously played a significant role. Indeed, when we remember that many of the non-members probably had passed through lodges at some point in their lives, one is struck by the pervasiveness of the institution.

In Toronto there were two main theatres of organized politics after 1834. The first was the Corporation. Although ostensibly non-partisan throughout

TABLE 1
Toronto riots 1839–66

Date*	Occasion	Participants	Outcome
15 October	1839 Durham meeting	Orange, Corporation vs Reformers	Petition to Legislative Assembly
April	1840 Celebration of the queen's marriage	Attack *Examiner* Orange, Corporation	
	1841 Election riot	Orange vs Reform: Election victory procession	Legislative Assembly investigation
	1841 Election riot (Streetsville)	Orange vs Reform	Controverted election
8 November	1843 Effigies of Baldwin and Hincks burned	Orange vs Party Processions Act	–
12 July	1844 Twelfth	Orange vs city magistrates	Trial
March	1849 Effigies of Mackenzie et al	Orange vs Prominent Reform over Rebellion Losses	–
May	1849 Effigy of Elgin	As above	–
October	1849 Riot vs Elgin	As above	Trial
	1851 Attack Anti–Clergy Reserves meeting	Orange, Corporation vs Grits	–
	1851 As above	Orange, Corporation vs Grits	–
4 July	1853 Fight with Hibernians	Orange vs Green	–
27 July	1853 As above	Orange vs Green	–
3–4 January	1855 Municipal election poll riot	Orange	Trial and controverted election
29 June	1855 Fire riot	Police vs firemen	Trial
July	1855 Circus riot	Orange crowd vs circus	Trial
January	1857 Municipal election poll riot	–	–
12 July	1857 Attack on policemen	Orange vs Green	Trial
12 July	1857 Attack on Catholic cathedral	?	–
August	1857 Omnibus riot	Carters	
17 March	1858 St Patrick's Day procession	Orange vs Green	Trial
12 July	1858 Twelfth	Orange vs Green	Trial
August	1859 Agnes Street parkland	?	–

TABLE 1 (*Continued*)
Toronto riots 1839–66

Date*	Occasion	Participants	Outcome
September	1860 Visit of Prince of Wales	Orange	–
October	1860 Melinda Street riot	Firemen vs rolling mill workers	
	1861 Fire department demonstration	Firemen vs police	–
	1863 Separate schools	Orange	
May	1864 Corpus Christi procession	Orange	
November	1864 Guy Fawkes Day	Hibernian	

*This list is not necessarily comprehensive. It is based on the Toronto press and on Orange sources. It certainly does not include every incidence of assault or rowdyism at election time.

the period, there was never any doubt about the Corporation's politics. Following the delegitimation of Reform after the Rebellions were suppressed, the Corporation developed into an impenetrable bastion of Orange-Tory strength. Toronto mayors throughout this period, while drawn from various elements of both the dying patrician order and the emerging bourgeois community, often shared titular membership in the Orange Order and always found themselves in an uneasy relationship to the order's plebeian demands. This tense reciprocity held equally true for aldermen and councillors, two of whom were elected from each of Toronto's wards (five until 1847, when a sixth ward was added, and then a seventh in 1853). Until 1859 the elected members of council then chose the mayor. In 1859 popular election of the mayor was instituted, but it survived only until 1866, when the choice was returned to the elected council. Although the Tory hold on the mayor's chair was broken briefly in 1859–60 with the election of Adam Wilson, Toronto voters quickly returned to tried and true Tory politicians for the remainder of the period of popular election (see Table 2). John George 'The 10,000 pound job' Bowes and Francis Henry 'Old Squaretoes' Medcalf restored the Tory ascendancy by holding the mayor's office from 1861 to 1866.

Toronto's second political theatre was provincial. The city elected two members to the legislative assembly of the Canadas. They were elected at large for the entire city until 1861 when the city was split into Toronto West and Toronto East, with one member for each constituency. The city remained predominantly Conservative throughout the period, returning Reformers

TABLE 2
Mayors of Toronto 1840–66

Year	Mayor	Occupation	Political affiliation	Birthplace
1840	John Powell	Lawyer	Compact	Canada
1841	George Munro	Merchant	Tory	Scotland
1842–4	Henry Sherwood	Lawyer	Compact	Canada
1845–7	William Henry Boulton	Lawyer	Compact	Canada
1848–50	George Gurnett	Journalist	Conservative	England
1851–3	John George Bowes	Merchant	Conservative	Ireland
1854	Joshua George Beard	Merchant	Conservative	England
1855	George William Allan	Lawyer	Compact	Canada
1856	John Beverley Robinson, Jr	Lawyer	Compact	Canada
1857	John Hutchison	Merchant	Conservative	Scotland
1858*	William Henry Boulton	(see 1845)		
1859–60†	Sir Adam Wilson	Lawyer	Reformer	Scotland
1861–3	John George Bowes	(see 1851)		
1864–6	Francis Henry Medcalf	Foundry owner	Orange	Ireland

*Boulton resigned on 8 November 1858 and was succeeded for the two remaining months of his term by David Breakenridge Read, a lawyer.
†From 1859 to 1866 mayors were directly elected.
SOURCE: Victor L. Russell *Mayors of Toronto 1 1834–1899* (Erin, Ontario, 1982)

only in 1841, with the extraordinary efforts of Lord Sydenham, in 1857 and 1858 when George Brown managed to win a seat, and in 1863 when the separate school issue led to the return of two Toronto Reformers. Thus of the nineteen provincial campaigns fought in Toronto in the Union period, Reformers won only six times (see Table 3).

What was the Corporation and what was its political hold on the loyalties of the Toronto Orangemen, who were universally recognized to have constituted its core and were continuously condemned as its enforcers? The elected council stood at the centre of the Corporation, but the Corporation's appointed officials also provided strength. In the 1840s and 1850s the number of positions under council patronage was limited, but they included the city clerk, the city treasurer, the city inspector, the deputy inspector of licences, the police force (initially consisting of the high bailiff and four constables), two assessors, and five tax collectors. (Chief constables and chief engineers 1840–66 are listed in Table 4.) Added to these offices, however, were the equally important patronage powers of licensing the city's inns and taverns

TABLE 3
Legislative Assembly elections in Toronto 1841–66

Year	Type of election	Winning candidates	Losing candidates
1841	General	J.H. Dunn*	H. Sherwood
		Isaac Buchanan*	George Munro
1843	By-election	H. Sherwood	Captain J.S. Macaulay
1844	General	H. Sherwood	J.H. Dunn*
		W.H. Boulton	
1847	General	H. Sherwood	J. Beaty*
		W.H. Boulton	
1851	General	G.P. Ridout	H. Sherwood
		W.H. Boulton	T. O'Neill*
			F.C. Capreol
1853	By-election	H. Sherwood	O.R. Gowan
1854	General	J.H. Cameron	H. Sherwood
		J.G. Bowes	W.H. Boulton
			G.P. Ridout
1857	General	G. Brown*	W.H. Boulton
		J.B. Robinson, Jr	J.G. Bowes
1858	By-election	G. Brown*	J.H. Cameron
1861	General	J. Crawford	G. Brown*
		J.B. Robinson, Jr	A. Wilson*
1863	General	A.M. Smith*	J. Crawford
		J. MacDonald*	J.B. Robinson, Jr

*Reform candidates
SOURCE: Toronto press 1840–63

and carters and cabmen, of hiring labourers for corporation work, and of appointing special constables in unusual circumstances such as for the supervision of elections. This combination of positions and favours endowed the council with an extraordinary network that touched plebeian life in numerous places.

Control of the publicans, for example, provided the Corporation with crucial support. The inroads of the temperance movement were still relatively weak, and the tavern was central to working-class life. As one critic of the system noted: 'The power of licensing or rather deciding upon the qualifications of applicants for licenses ... will and must inevitably be abused if entrusted to the caprice of an elected magistracy. It will be prostituted to seduce the wavering, to reward the compliant, to punish the refractory. The influence exercised by tavernkeepers at public elections is notorious, and we feel that the means which the existing corporation have employed for securing or coercing this influence are sufficient to justify the preceding observation.'

TABLE 4

Chief constables and chief engineers of
Toronto 1840–66

Chief constables 1840–66

1837–46	George Kingsmill
1847–52	George L. Allen
1852–8	Samuel Sherwood
1859–73	Captain William S. Prince

Chief engineers 1840–66

1838–41	Thomas D. Harris
1842–6	Robert Beard
1847	James Armstrong
1851–77	James Ashfield

SOURCE: J.E. Middleton *The Municipality
of Toronto* (Toronto 1923) 788–9

Our best description of the intricacies of this process comes from the report of the commissioners appointed to investigate the 1841 Toronto election riot.[14] No fewer than five tavern keepers or former tavern keepers testified that they had lost or now expected to lose their licences for having opposed the Corporation's candidates in the first legislative assembly elections of the United Canadas. Irish publican Peter Harkin, for example, explained that upon his arrival in Toronto in 1840 he was instructed to apply to an alderman for a tavern licence. In return for a small bribe (£2) he received a licence, and the same alderman later helped defend him against an earlier charge of unlicensed selling and had his fine remitted. Shortly thereafter, however, Harkin refused to support the Tory candidates in the coming election. He was then offered £30 or £5 a day to keep open house for the Tory candidates. He again refused and later cast his vote for the Sydenham candidates. Following those events his old fine was executed and he was subsequently charged and fined for refusing to help fight a fire.[15]

This pattern of rewarding friends and punishing enemies was also described by John Lindsay, former city constable, Irish publican, and Orangeman. After a short stint as a city constable, Lindsay had become the proprietor of the North of Ireland Tavern. He attributed his successes in both positions to his prominence in the Orange Order. In 1839, however, he decided to attend the Durham meeting held on Yonge Street, north of Toronto. Before this meeting he was asked by City Inspector William Davis, acting on the behest of Clarke Gamble and the Corporation, to attend the Durham meeting to oppose the Reformers. His noncommittal response, and his later refusal to don a purple ribbon offered by Alderman Alexander Dixon who was riding in a wagon with Alderman John Armstrong and four city constables, began his problems. Lindsay's indignation at the constables' subsequent attack on the Reformers, which was led by Sheriff William B. Jarvis, with obvious aldermanic approval, caused him to support the Reformers when the meeting divided. This was duly noted by the sheriff who indicated that he would pay later. And so Lindsay did. He was refused his licence renewal and then prosecuted when he continued to sell. During the 1841 election campaign both Tory candidates offered him a licence in return for his support, and later City Inspector Davis also indicated that money and an open house designation were his in return for abstaining, or at least splitting his vote. He again refused and after the election was again charged with selling without a licence. His frequent petitions for a licence also failed.[16]

The importance of taverns in plebeian life cannot be overestimated. At its incorporation in 1834, Toronto had approximately 78 taverns, or one for every 120 individuals.[17] According to testimony before the 1841 Riot Commission, the Reform council of Dr Thomas David Morrison had reduced this to 36 by 1836–7. The return of a Tory council to power had led to a massive growth in taverns (119) and the additional ubiquitous beer licences (21).[18] This total of 140 licensed drinking places provided a legal bar for approximately every 100 Torontonians, the largest numbers of the period. In addition, there were reputed to be many unlicensed houses. A quick perusal of the licences issued for 1841 turns up Corporation stalwarts such as John 'Tory' Earls, City Inspector Davis, Deputy Inspector of Licences James Bell, and Constable Thomas Earls.[19]

The Tories in this period appear to have been manipulating their licensing control to allow the tavern to expand. This growth in licences would eventually work against them when respectable Torontonians, increasingly influenced by evangelical reform, began to demand stringent enforcement. Nevertheless customary plebeian culture, supported and extended by the Corporation in return for electoral aid, would later prove extremely resistant to attempts at regulation. The small riots and frequent attacks on licence inspectors that commenced in the 1850s became a familiar component of cultural struggle in late Victorian Toronto, despite the city's later familiar 'dry' reputation.

One example of the Corporation's use of drinking places was Allen's Coleraine Tavern, which provided a home for a number of Orange lodges, an open house for the unsuccessful Monro-Sherwood party in the 1841 election campaign, and a launching pad for the subsequent riot. Further, Allen was identified by a number of witnesses as the man who had recruited the Orangemen from the outlying area who were the aggressors in the day's violence. There was also persuasive testimony that Sherwood's brother, Samuel, later Toronto's police chief, had put Allen up to this. The ostensible rationale for the riot was the rumour that the victorious Reform procession would carry two coffins labelled 'The Corporation' and 'The Family Compact.' Clearly, as the riot demonstrated, the Corporation was far from dead, no matter what the election result.[20]

Tavern licences were but one part of the Corporation's elaborate system. Cartage and cab licences were used in a similar fashion. Perhaps more important, however, was the control that the Corporation enjoyed over the police force. The appointment of the high bailiff and the constables provided far more than jobs for loyal Orangemen. A monopoly of legal violence, and the power to choose when to enforce the law, were significant weapons. Again the 1841 commissioners noted:

A force thus constituted must be liable, in times of political excitement, to be employed as political instruments in behalf of those to whom the corporation may be friendly. The authority legally invested in these men, their habitual intercourse with the lower classes, the impression that they possess the ear of their employers, the favouritism they may be enabled to suggest, the petty and indirect tyranny they may be permitted to exercise, all combine to degrade a force of this nature into formidable engines of oppression; and when we find, as in the late election, that the Corporation has cast itself into the political arena as a hot partizan of one of its own party – the Mayor of the City – in a bitter and unsuccessful contest, we can hardly be surprised that a stringent and unscrupulous use has been made of the machinery at their disposal.[21]

The commissioners' call for a 'well-regulated and efficient police force ... appointed, directed, and governed by authorities remote from, superior to, and independent of local bias or interference' found little initial support, although, as we shall see, by the late 1850s this view would become dominant. In the mean time Orange membership was the major credential for a position on the Toronto police, a force which, like other urban police forces, expanded rapidly in the 1840s and 1850s. Francis Hincks, for example, recounted on numerous occasions the story of the promotion of Constable Wallace to a permanent position on the Toronto police, after his attack on Hincks during the Yonge Street riot of 1839.[22]

At the centre of the informal Corporation world was City Inspector Davis.

With responsibility for public works and therefore a labour force, he stood at the centre of the city's patronage network. Naturally, it was he who orchestrated the more vociferous support of the Corporation when it was needed. Davis has been termed the 'marshall of the mob'[23] by one historian, and the *Globe* called him the man 'who has bullied the inhabitants of the city for many years, who has ruled the corporation with a rod of iron, who knows all the corporation rascalities from the beginning to the end, who controls the town elections as he thinks proper, the bosom friend and pitcher of Mr. Henry Sherwood.'[24] Not too surprisingly, when Davis finally was removed from office by Mayor William Henry Boulton in 1845, the *Globe* greeted the news with considerable enthusiasm. Other members of the Corporation remained less convinced, and the mayor faced a serious challenge to his prerogative to fire without consulting the council. The central issue raised by the firing of Davis was control of the police. Boulton had removed Constable George Earls from the force for drunkenness. Earls, the brother of infamous Orange innkeeper and carter John 'Tory' Earls, found an avid supporter in Davis, who apparently spread the rumour that Boulton himself had been drinking on the evening in question.[25] This proved too much for Boulton who, while an alderman in 1841, had failed in an early attempt to get Davis fired. Davis meanwhile re-emerged shortly thereafter as an elected councillor and continued to play an important Corporation role.[26]

When William Coffin and Nicholas Fullam, the Toronto riot commissioners, summarized their 1841 investigation into the workings of the Corporation, they concluded with a full assault on Orangeism. 'Spread extensively through the City of Toronto,' the order's 'evil influence' was 'direct, obvious and tangible.' Moreover, the order's 'portentous influence aggravated the evils of political acrimony and revived feuds and feelings, religious prejudices and party animosities, which had almost ceased to exist.' The commissioners concluded: 'The existence of Orangeism in this Province is a great and growing evil, which should be discountenanced, denounced, and repressed by the exercise of every authority and influence at the disposal of the Government.'[27]

The proposal was quickly acted on. In 1842 the ministry of Robert Baldwin successfully introduced electoral reforms that were primarily aimed at Orangeism. The new law, which proved ineffective and was seldom enforced, outlawed the exhibiting of party flags and colours, treating at public places, the carrying of firearms, assault and battery, and bribery during elections. It also introduced multiple polling stations to diffuse the potential for violence, separated the nomination process from the polling for the same reason, and limited the polling to two days.[28]

Equally ineffectual, as it turned out, but far more bitterly contested were two further Baldwin reforms, the Party Processions Act and the Secret Societies Act of 1843. Although Parliament passed both, only the first was enacted, because Governor-General Lord Metcalfe reserved the latter for British consideration and it was subsequently disallowed.

In Parliament the opposition to these measures was led by Toronto Orange spokesmen Henry Sherwood and George Duggan. Sherwood, scion of the Brockville élite, had transferred his political career to the metropolis, where he found himself dependent on Orange support. Duggan, in contrast, owed his very presence in politics to his prominence in the order. The debate itself was initially focused on the pseudo-issue of the right to appeal under the Party Processions Act, but the discussion heated up considerably when the true anti-Orange motives of the act were alluded to in Francis Hincks's attack on Duggan for his role in the 1839 Yonge Street riot and for Orange violence at the poll in his election victory in York county, which was later successfully challenged by the loser. Duggan responded by accusing the government of trying to outlaw its opposition; if the violent acts described by Hincks were so reprehensible, why had there been no indictments? And again invoking the straw man of the right of appeal, he closed: 'They will not put down these evils by any moderate means; no it must be by the iron heel of power, and the victim must be imprisoned whether guilty or not.'[29]

The debate on the outlawing of all secret societies except the Masons, which in effect meant only the Orange Order, was even more heated and ended in the expulsion of Tory leader Allan MacNab from the assembly by the Speaker. Here again Sherwood and Duggan were prominent, with the former wisely warning that such proscription would fuel the growth of the order and the latter defending Orangemen's loyalty. This bill was also opposed by some moderates who felt it went too far. Toronto Orangemen certainly thought so, and after the bills were passed they gathered in front of Baldwin's residence to burn him and Francis Hincks in effigy. The aim of Baldwin's bill was clear enough. Under its terms members of a secret society would be barred from jury service and holding office under the crown and any innkeeper or tavern keeper who allowed secret societies to meet on his premises would have his licence revoked. Duggan's argument that such a bill was aimed at breaking the back of the political opposition to Reform highlights the crucial Orange basis of Tory support.[30]

The Orange response too should be noted. Orangemen took to the streets, for, like other plebeian groups, they assumed that the streets were theirs for political purposes. Gathering between 11 p.m. and midnight, a large body of Orangemen paraded with a cart, on which was mounted a gallows bearing effigies of Baldwin and Hincks. The effigies wore the label 'traitors,' and the cart was decorated with Orange slogans including 'No Surrender.' With the accompaniment of 'the most indecent ribaldry,' the effigies were burned at the house of Dr W.W. Baldwin.[31] This resort to effigy burning, which would be common in Toronto for the next decade, was an established form of plebeian political protest. Needless to say, the attempt to deny them the streets for their marches only further entrenched the crucial importance of the 12 July processions. Those, like John Neilson, who predicted that such prohibitive legislation would increase the strength of the order proved correct.

Tory opposition mounted quickly. 'Never will these societies, and the Orangemen of Canada in particular, forget the debt of hatred they owe to the party who have cast shame and obloquy upon them.'[32] Moreover, the various 1843 pieces of Reform legislation and the breakdown of Sydenham's carefully constructed alliance certainly did not help John Henry Dunn, who was trounced by Henry Sherwood and W.H. Boulton in the 1844 parliamentary election in Toronto. Reformers unsuccessfully protested the result, alleging bribery, corruption, illegal oaths, and the 'gross partiality of the Returning officer.' Reform opinion rationalized the defeat by blaming 'the corporation which has always been a political body supporting the Family Compact tyranny.' The methods of the Corporation involved 'spending immense sums of money every week in various buildings and improvements in the city, by which means they are able to secure the votes of hundreds and to intimidate many more. They have the control of licensing taverns, carters, and cabmen, and it is well known that these bodies are nearly in every individual case Orangemen.'[33]

The attempt at banning the order proved ineffectual, not only because of Orange intransigence but also because Governor-General Metcalfe soon found himself fighting his Reform ministry and thus of necessity turning to the Tories and their Orange allies.[34] Ironically, Gowan, the Orange grand master, enjoyed perhaps his greatest political influence in the middle years of the decade as a trusted adviser to the new Tory ministry. These were relatively quiet years, partially, no doubt, because of the order's political prominence. Orange leaders initially tried to prevent any too overt testing of the Party Processions Act, although many of their followers refused to heed their advice. In Toronto, for example, the first 12 July after the ban saw the Orange leadership lead its members on an excursion to Niagara Falls. This intentional ploy to prevent a direct challenge to the act almost backfired when some 1,500–2,000 Irish Catholic navvies employed on the Welland Canal turned out to prevent any procession. The timely intervention of Niagara magistrates prevented a riot, when they managed to convince the outnumbered Toronto Orangemen that discretion was the better part of valour and that disarming and avoiding party tunes would maintain the peace. Meanwhile, in Toronto itself, Orangemen from outside the city refused to obey the injunction against demonstrations and instead marched into the city. On this occasion, undoubtedly because this contravened the Orange design as well as the law, the Toronto magistrates intervened. Led by important Orange aldermen George Gurnett and Alexander Dixon, a saddler, the Toronto constables met the procession and ordered it to disband. The response was a donnybrook in which Gurnett was assaulted. Following the reading of the Riot Act, a number of arrests were made. Not surprisingly, at least one of those arrested had been involved in the 1841 election riot.[35]

The return to power of a Conservative ministry in late 1844 ended such difficulties, and Toronto Orangemen proceeded to march on the 12th with regularity for the rest of the decade, blatantly repudiating the law. These processions were relatively quiet, and, although they were formally illegal, no action was taken against them, despite the frequent complaints of the Reform papers.[36]

In this brief interlude of relative quiet the fights in Toronto occurred within the Conservative forces and focused on the growing tension between the rising plebeian elements of the party and the older, declining patricians – the Compact Tories. Constantly acting as mediators in these struggles were the 'Corporation Beauties,' as the *Globe* termed the aldermanic corps. Prominent in this role were figures such as George Gurnett and the Beard brothers, who acted as a 'sturdy bridge between the compact gentry and the mass of horny-handed townsmen within that predominant caste of post-Rebellion Torontonians who professed strident loyalism.'[37] This tension was manifest in the fight to remove City Inspector Davis; but the conflict was also apparent before provincial elections, when it was necessary to nominate Tory candidates for the city. In 1844, for example, an initial attempt to place G.P. Ridout on the ballot was resisted by Orangemen who felt Ridout was insufficiently loyal.[38] The Corporation's choice was former Mavor George Munro, but the nomination instead went to William Henry Boulton, who was acceptable to both patricians and aspiring bourgeoisie. Boulton, although a descendant of the Compact, appears as an example of the transitional political figures who, despite their patrician roots, were not too proud to play the emerging democratic game. Returned in 1844 to the legislature, he was to enjoy the faithful support of Toronto voters until his financial difficulties of the late 1840s and early 1850s publicly embarrassed him.[39] His patrician tendencies, however, remained evident in his remarkable propensity to resign public office when he failed to get his own way.

Other Irish and Orange political figures continued to encounter resistance.

Ogle Gowan, for example, used these relatively quiet years to pursue his goal of Irish political unity and the conversion of the Tory party into a moderate political force prefiguring the Liberal Conservative party of Sir John A. Macdonald. He paid dearly, however, for his Orange connections and his battles with the Compact Tories. This combination of disabilities kept him out of the cabinet. Ironically, he also lost the leadership of the order in 1846 to Belleville's George Benjamin, who appears to have been a better administrator than Gowan and also a more traditional Tory in his attitudes, especially toward the Anglican church.[40] Other Irish politicians with close ties to the Orange Order also suffered from Gowan's disability. Former Orange District Master George Duggan, for example, made a determined try for the Toronto mayor's chair on numerous occasions and failed. He came closest in 1847 by opposing incumbent Boulton on avowedly national grounds. His narrow 12-to-11 defeat pitted Compact Tories and a few Reformers against his Orange supporters, although the alliances were also coloured by the ongoing war between the Denisons and the Boultons, the great families of St Patrick's Ward. With the exception of the patrician lawyer Robert Baldwin Sullivan in 1835, the only Irish-born, council-selected mayor in this period was successful merchant John George Bowes, 1851–3. When popular election arrived briefly in the late 1850s and early 1860s Toronto voters chose two Irishmen of the three mayors elected – Bowes again, 1861–3, and (more significantly) Orange leader, former machinist, and foundry-owner Francis Henry Metcalf, 1864–6, the first Toronto mayor who was not a lawyer, merchant, or journalist[41] (see Table 3). The 1847 provincial election disaster for the Tories was not reflected in Toronto, where Boulton and Sherwood easily won re-election. The sole Reform candidate, James Beaty, tried to make much of his mechanic background but to no avail. The *Globe* complained in the aftermath of the election that 'Toronto was not ripe for freedom' and blamed 'the retainers and toadies of the Corporation' for the defeat.[42]

The return to power of a new Reform ministry in 1848 and the crisis that ensued brought the few years of harmony to a rapid and violent close. Yet before analysing the series of savage conflicts surrounding the Rebellion Losses Bill and the Annexation Manifesto, it is worth noting the democratic reforms undertaken by this Reform ministry. Baldwin's Municipal Corporations Act of 1849 completed the work commenced by Sydenham in 1841 of bringing elective government to the local level. Until 1842 the appointed justices of the peace meeting in the court of quarter sessions had held all responsibility in the area of local government. In the pre-rebellion period the Reformers and William Lyon Mackenzie had backed the popular election of the magistrates, but this reform had not been accomplished. The 1840 Sydenham legislation had provided the districts with their first elected councils, though limiting the franchise and office-holding to the successful and retaining a central government veto. Baldwin had tried to extend these actions with his 1843 Municipal Act, but though it passed the assembly it was not implemented after the Baldwin ministry resigned. The succeeding Tory government failed to act in the field with the exception of a moderate democratic extension in 1846, when the elected councils were allowed to choose their own warden from among the elected councillors and to appoint their own officials.

Every commentator on these acts has recognized them as an attack on the old Tory magistracy. The extension of democracy to the local level, while still limited, nevertheless incorporated a broader populace into the electoral process. Baldwin asserted this as a major rationale of the act, arguing that local institutions would have 'the effect of creating a school of practical statesmen.' The 1849 act also finally regularized the legislative framework for urban areas which until then had evolved through specific pieces of legislation for each newly incorporated town or city.[43]

But what of the crisis of 1849? How did Toronto Orangemen deal with the most significant challenge of this period to their ideology? Not too surprisingly, they reacted in the streets. In March, May, and again in October, Toronto Orangemen expressed their discontent in riotous gatherings. In March they greeted the news of the Rebellion Losses Bill and the return to Toronto of William Lyon Mackenzie with a procession with effigies that visited the homes of prominent Toronto Reformers. In front of Robert Baldwin's house the effigies of Baldwin and Francis Hincks were burned, along with numerous tar barrels. The crowd then visited the house of John McIntosh, where Mackenzie had been staying, and threatened to wreck it. Instead they only broke windows and doors and then marched to the houses of Dr John Rolph and of George Brown, where similar actions ensued.

Predictably, Reform opinion was infuriated, especially when no charges were laid. A number of Torontonians petitioned Lord Elgin for an investigation, arguing that they were 'at the mercy of a drunken, reckless mob, which may at any moment issue forth from the low taverns and brothels of the city and make the political opinions of their victims a pretext for violence and proceed to attack the dwellings and threaten the lives of those who may happen to have incurred their displeasure.'[44] Moreover, as the Globe pointed out, apparently the only Torontonians who remained unaware of the crowd's plans before the attack were Mayor Gurnett and High Bailiff Allen. Two other members of the Corporation, Aldermen Dempsey and

Denison, played prominent roles in leading the crowd. Thus, when Gurnett responded to press criticism by trying to set up an investigation, his council flatly refused. Alderman Denison argued that the government was at fault since it had first refused to hang Mackenzie and now allowed him to return to Toronto. He asserted: 'If it were not for the law I would not scruple a minute to take his life.' Alderman Duggan then attacked the mayor for calling out the troops on the following evening to prevent a recurrence of the rioting. Finally, rather than support the mayor's call for an investigation of the riot, the council instead endorsed the crowd's opposition to the Rebellion Losses Act.[45]

Approximately one month later, and following a week of riots in Montreal which included the burning of the Parliament buldings, the Toronto crowd also rallied to demonstrate its opposition to Elgin's signing of the Rebellion Losses Bill. Some 100–150 Orangemen met in a Queen Street tavern and then marched to city hall. This procession had been formally announced early in the week, so on this occasion the mayor had called out the military. When the crowd carrying the effigy of Elgin reached city hall, it was met by the mayor, the council, and the troops. The soldiers were present, however, only to guarantee the safety of the citizenry's property, and they did not interfere with the effigy burning. Alderman Beard, the city's deputy sheriff, was accused by the *Globe* of having led the procession. His subsequent denial claimed that he had only appeared to be leading the crowd because in his official capacity he had convinced the crowd not to attack the homes of John McIntosh, John Rolph, and John Montgomery.[46]

There was, of course, considerable fear by officials of what 12 July would bring in 1849. Yet Elgin's and Russell's cool and confident predictions that 'nothing of consequence' would occur proved accurate and Toronto remained relatively quiet.[47] In Hamilton Orangemen marched with arms[48] and in the St Catharines area there was a fatal encounter between Roman Catholic navvies and Orangemen celebrating the Battle of the Boyne in a tavern.[49] The relative quiet in Toronto led one local Reformer and secret Elgin informant to write dismissively of the 'constant meetings and caballings of the Orange associations,' which he was certain signified little. He assured Elgin that 'the late attempt at a riot here, the effigy burning, and all the demonstrations of the same character, were the work of a few Tory aldermen' and that the 'masses took no interest.' Moreover, the 12 July procession had involved only 400 Orangemen, which suggested to him that 'respectable Orangemen were ashamed of Annexation.'[50]

There can be no question that the ranks were now indeed split. The extensive involvement of Ontario Orange leaders such as Gowan in the British

American League eventually provided the institutional wherewithal to break openly with annexation, but it took them a considerable length of time to clarify their position. Meanwhile, anonymous broadside writers had a field-day as they tried to rally the forces of loyal Protestant Britons to the cause. In August, for example, Toronto citizens awakened to find emblazoned on their city's walls:

PROCLAMATION

'TO YOUR TENTS, O, ISRAEL'

BRITONS OF THE CITY OF TORONTO — BRITONS OF THE HOME DISTRICT

Shall the rank rebels be permitted to tell us that they will drive the bloody Tories out of the country? Up to your duty and let us no more slumber! The Political Judas Iscariot [Elgin] ... is expected to arrive in Toronto ... Shall Elgin ... be permitted to be welcomed by a gang of sneaking radicals, in the good old loyal city of Toronto? No! No! Forbid it heaven! Forbid it every principle of honour! By the memory of our fathers, who filled bloody though honourable graves rather than surrender their civil and religious freedom to a tyrannical and bigoted sovereign ... we publicly and solemnly warn the individual who calls himself James Bruce [Elgin] and his rebel partizans, against any attempt to outrage and insult the feelings of the Loyalist of Toronto by making a party triumph of his visit to Toronto – that is if he or they should dare to come ... Think of that Britishers of Toronto. Consequently, let your eggs be stale and your powder dry! Down with Elgin! – Down with the rebels![51]

This was matched by another broadside in the following month from 'The Watcher':

AWAKE! TREACHERY! TREASON!

Men of 1837 and '38, the plot has leaked out. For the purpose of receiving Rebel-rewarding Elgin ... hundreds of armed cutthroats have been hired to pour into Toronto ... to massacre the loyal inhabitant and to destroy their houses and property ... therefore perfect your Organization. Arm! Arm! Arm! Forward from the country! Forward from the city![52]

Opposition of this kind made it essential that Elgin visit the city. As his secret adviser in Toronto noted: 'The time has come when His Excellency must go everywhere he chooses without hesitation. To pass Toronto would be too marked in any case and particularly after all the press has said about it and would be trumpeted as a concession to fear. That sort of impression going abroad would be very unfortunate and would beget mobs.'[53] So on 9 October 1849 Elgin arrived in Toronto. His proposed visit had set off great debates over the nature of the address to present him. Tory MP Henry Sherwood's was rejected as too favourable, especially by W.H. Boulton, while Alderman Denison's was rejected as too partisan. A compromise was reached by Alderman Samuel Thompson, whose address noted the great disagreements raging in Toronto but nevertheless pledged the city's loyalty to Britain and to the queen's representative.[54] The unity apparent in this compromise was not shared by all Torontonians. Although Elgin was guarded by Denison's cavalry company, a few eggs still managed to find the governor-general's carriage on his arrival. That evening a crowd of 200 gathered and marched, with torches and an effigy of Elgin, on Elijah's Hotel on King Street. After an initial skirmish with the police, who ordered the crowd to disperse, it regrouped at the hotel, where a larger body of constables and the mayor met them. Arrests were made and the crowd dispersed. With unusual alacrity, which left even the *Globe* and the *Examiner* praising the magistrates, thirteen men were charged with riotous assembly and assault and another three with ringing the fire-bell when there was no fire. The fire-bells, under the control of Orange fire companies, were the standard Orange call to arms. Among those arrested for bell ringing were a tailor and two young O'Briens, one the son of Colonel E.G. O'Brien, the proprietor of the *Patriot*, and the other his cousin, the son of Dr Lucius O'Brien, a professor at King's College and the editor of the *Patriot*. Among those charged with assault and riotous assembly were a tailor, a shoemaker, a labourer, a carter, a confectioner, a tinsmith, and an innkeeper, and two Orange council members, the infamous William Davis and John Carr, later Toronto Orange district master.[55]

These arrests continued the debate about whether effigy burning was illegal in itself. This debate came to a head when Chief Justice Robinson instructed a grand jury that the burning of effigies was definitely illegal. Robinson had argued:

There seems to be a growing diposition to manifest displeasure by burning in effigy. As the exhibitions are indecent and insulting and have a tendency to lead to tumult, it is proper that it should be understood that by the law of England, and the law of Upper Canada is the same, the burning or hanging of any person in effigy openly and publicly, even without a tumultuous assemblage, is a misdemeanour punishable with fine or imprisonment or both and is a kind of libel ... and where the object is to bring odium on the government and its measures, it becomes then seditious in its character and exposes those concerned in it to be punished for that offence.

Here we have the reigning monarch of the Compact's remnants making quite clear that plebeian political violence could no longer be tolerated.[56] Orange crowds battling 'Yankee republicans' in the guise of radicals in the 1830s or attacking the alleged disloyalty of the Reform alliance of the 1840s had served Compact Tory, and later Corporation, aims well. The arrival of responsible government, while still uncertain in 1849, would make such politics an embarrassing anachronism in the 1850s, especially when they threatened the Conservative alliance with the Lower Canadian *Bleus*.

The willingness of the Toronto magistracy to break up this riot, partially on this basis, was carried through at the following assizes, when the thirteen were actually tried and three were convicted. Defended by Orange Aldermen George Duggan and Richard Dempsey, the rioters continued to claim that they had done nothing illegal in trying to burn an effigy, that the police had had no right to interfere, and that the defendants had thus only engaged in legitimate self-defence. Here we have a defence of traditional plebeian political practice against the new constraints of a redefined public order. Duggan politicized the proceedings by claiming this was not 'a state prosecution but a state persecution.' A few days after their conviction and sentencing, Elgin intervened to have the three rioters released from jail.[57]

Later that fall in Toronto the British American League held its second meeting. Dominated by Orange leaders such as George Benjamin and Ogle Gowan, as well as Toronto Orange politicians such as Mayor Bowes, councilmen John Carr and William Davis, and aldermen Duggan, Denison, and Dempsey, the meeting finally broke with annexation. Instead it promoted the series of reforms that would represent a significant part of the new Liberal-Conservative consensus of the next two decades. Among the reforms promoted were a protective tariff, the extension of democratic institutions, and a broader British American union.[58]

Two celebrated cases involving Orangemen arose in 1850. In the first, John Hillyard Cameron, a rising Orange legislature star, came to the defence of Orangeman and former London MP Thomas Dixon, who had been removed from his office of justice of the peace. While failing to gain Dixon's office back, the case did embarrass the Baldwin ministry.[59] The second and more serious case involved a Brantford prosecution of local Orangemen under the Party Processions Act of 1843. Although there could be no doubt as to the nature of the 12 July procession, which included the traditional King Billy on horseback, the jury nevertheless refused to convict. Thus, in what was claimed to be the first prosecution under the controversial act, it became clear that it was probably impossible to find a jury willing to convict, no matter what the evidence.[60]

This led to the repeal of the Party Processions Act in August 1851. A petition earlier that year by Orange Grand Master George Benjamin had put the matter before the house,[61] but it was a motion of Toronto Tory MP, W.H. Boulton that managed to work its way through the house with surprisingly little opposition. Boulton, following Benjamin, argued that the act was unjust and unequal, and that it should therefore be repealed. He pointed also to the speech of Reformer John Ross (Baldwin's son-in-law) upon introducing the petition into the legislative council, when he credited the Orangemen with having proven their loyalty in 1849 and further argued that the act was totally inoperative, citing Hamilton and Slabtown (St Catharines) cases where juries had refused to convict even in the face of very clear evidence. Boulton then argued that the original legislation had been vindictive because of Orange opposition to Sydenham in the election of 1841.

Francis Hincks, now premier, eventually intervened in the debate to indicate that he had intended to remain silent and had not even decided whether to divide the house on the motion, but that speeches defending the Slabtown Orangemen went too far. Henry Sherwood picked him up on this, drawing out the point that the government obviously did not regard this as a crucial question and further reminding the house of Lord Metcalfe's withholding of the second piece of legislation in 1843 which would have banned the order. This too drew a response from Hincks, who asserted ironically that Metcalfe had actually written that legislation before his falling out with the Reform ministry. Support for repeal was indicated by John Hillyard Cameron and, more surprisingly, by William Lyon Mackenzie, who remembered how the Toronto Orangemen had at first supported him because of their hatred for the Baldwins. Since then, Mackenzie assured his fellow MPs, he had been on the order's hit list, but he still felt that they should be allowed to march. When the house divided, it was clear that this was not a party vote and the revoking of the act passed easily. Even the *Globe* acclaimed this action.[62]

What had happened between 1843, or even 1849, and 1851 to make such a great difference in attitude? The first Baldwin government could not do enough to remove the threat of the Orange Order. Yet the new Hincks Reform ministry of the early 1850s was only too willing to accede quietly to the order's acceptance as part of Canadian public life. The basic answer would appear to be that a new and different political consensus had been growing in the Canadas in the intervening decade, one that increasing numbers of Orange leaders had helped form. This consensus, emerging in the Draper ministry, had come under severe strain in 1849, but one is struck by the speed with which annexation, the most radical of the contending positions, was forgotten after that crisis. Signing the Annexation Manifesto proved no political impediment in the new Canadian political scene of the 1850s. The Hincks ministry captured the new consensus nicely, for Hincks himself was the author of the two key pieces of legislation that underlay the capitalist expansion of the decade: the Railway Guarantee Act and the Municipal Loan Fund Act. The retirement of Baldwin and Lafontaine cleared the way for a series of ministries in the 1850s that increasingly agreed on most developmental questions.[63] In Toronto this emerging business consensus can be seen in the election of Irish merchant John George Bowes as mayor and in the minor judicial appointments of George Duggan and George Gurnett. The fact that a Reform ministry could bring itself to make such appointments suggests much about the new consensus of the 1850s. As the Reform *Examiner* suggested, 'The lion and the lamb have lain down together.'[64]

Orange politicians were central to the development of this new consensus. They moved the Conservative party in that direction, in terms of both electoral style and policy. Take, for example, Ogle Gowan himself, when he sought the nomination in Leeds in 1851; the *Examiner* noted the 'curious mixture of radicalism and toryism,' which included platform planks such as an elected legislative council, election of all local government officials, household suffrage, and increased representation for urban constituencies.[65] While never personally acceptable to the élite, Gowan certainly helped to move the Conservative party from its high Tory roots and transform it into a party with democratic appeal. Although Sir John A. Macdonald usually receives full credit for these achievements, his colleagues from his early years in the assembly, such as Gowan, undoubtedly influenced him. Macdonald's own Orangeism, generally viewed purely as political manipulation, brought him into constant contact with the Orange mass base of his emerging popular Conservatism. There are other examples of the new Orange Conservative political leader. Both John Hillyard Cameron and William Henry Boulton, despite a Compact background, appear to be politicians of this type. Boulton, for example, introduced legislation in the 1851 assembly session to extend the democratic system and to make the legislative council elective.

The consensus did not extend over the entire spectrum of Canadian affairs, and July 1851 saw Toronto again disrupted by bitter sectarian wrangling. This time the issue was the clergy reserves, and on this issue not all Orangemen stood united.[66] Some, like Gowan, in the new consensus were willing to see the reserves eliminated with a division of the proceeds between the various denominations. This solution was anathema to High Church Tories such as Sherwood and Cameron. In the Orange Order itself this led to a later split. In July 1851 the immediate issue was a meeting in Toronto of the Anti–Clergy

Reserves Association. A first attempt at a meeting was broken up when a Tory mob invaded the hall and took control of the stage. One leader of the crowd, Alderman Dixon, was thrown off the stage by the Reverend Mr Esson, one of the Anti–Clergy Reserve organizers. Orangeman Dixon pressed an assault charge against the minister, only to see Police Magistrate Gurnett rule that this was a private meeting at which Dixon had no right to be present.[67]

Approximately two weeks later, the antis again scheduled a meeting at St Lawrence Hall. The supporters of the reserves meanwhile scheduled a counter-demonstration for the rear of the new city hall. The call for this meeting came from Aldermen Robinson, Medcalf, and Dixon, among others. Speeches from Dixon, E.G. O'Brien, and MP Henry Sherwood were followed by a call to visit the antis. An attack was then made on St Lawrence Hall but the group failed to gain entrance. To quell the seige, the Riot Act was read and the military called into action. In the aftermath of this riot the *Globe* indignantly attacked the magistracy for its failure to make any arrests. The mayor himself had been assaulted, but no charges were laid. For three hours the city was in the 'possession of the mob,' screamed the *Globe*, yet none could identify the participants. Perhaps, implied the *Globe*, High Bailiff Allen's Orangeism was interfering with his effectiveness as a policeman.[68]

During the general election campaign at the end of 1851, the events of the preceding years made themselves only too evident when it came time for the selection of Conservative candidates. Initially four Conservative candidates entered the field. The two incumbents, Henry Sherwood and W.H. Boulton, were joined by G.P. Ridout and Samuel Thompson. Their quasi-Reform opponents were Terence J. O'Neill, a Roman Catholic, and Frederick C. Capreol. With the spectre of a split vote before the Conservatives, the Orange Order intervened, supported Sherwood and Boulton, and then requested Thompson and Ridout to withdraw from the contest. The internal workings of the order here perhaps suggest nascent anti-Gowan sentiment, because Thompson was both an Orangeman and Gowan's partner at the *Patriot*. Moreover, Thompson had been very vocal in criticizing Sherwood for his attempt at peacekeeping in the Elgin 1849 visit to Toronto. Whatever the internal debate, Thompson agreed to withdraw, while Ridout refused to do so in an open letter to E.T. Dartnell, the Orange leader.[69]

In the subsequent election Ridout topped the poll, followed by Boulton and Sherwood, with the Reformers well behind.[70] Two years later, however, Boulton was unseated when he was found not to have satisfied the £500 property requirement for candidacy for the assembly.[71] In the resulting by-election Henry Sherwood faced Ogle Gowan in a clear fight between the opposing elements of Toronto Orangeism. Gowan, at a disadvantage in his new home, proposed a formal nominating meeting. Sherwood simply refused to compete and asserted he would run no matter what a nomination meeting decided. At his nomination meeting Gowan attacked the Compact lawyers as a 'cod fish aristocracy.' E.T. Dartnell and some other Orangemen then surprised many by endorsing and actively working for Sherwood. Dartnell differed with Gowan on the clergy reserves and on separate schools, where Gowan was willing to be moderate and allow Catholics their own schools. All this was part of Gowan's moderate Conservative attempt to build unity among all Irish and even to appease public opinion in Quebec, if this became necessary politically. With some of Toronto's diehards these policies did not go down easily, though Gowan had the support of Orange Corporation worthies such as Aldermen Armstrong and Dempsey.[72]

Despite his attempt to draw Sherwood into a real campaign and his continous appeal to the working classes of the city, Gowan could not defeat Sherwood at the polls. He was defeated soundly, 833–423, carrying only St John's Ward.[73] No doubt the split in the order damaged Gowan's chances greatly. This realization may have helped convince him of the necessity of regaining control of the grand lodge, for in June 1853 he challenged the Benjamin leadership and regained the position of grand master. The Benjamin forces regrouped and, screaming foul, refused to accept the election result, instead organizing a counter grand lodge. This schism in the order lasted until 1856. Most Ontario lodges, especially Toronto lodges, sided with Gowan. In 1855 he reported that only about one-third of the lodges paid dues to the Benjamin Grand Lodge. The split, which had probably originated in policy differences, itself intensified those disputes. Gowan continued to support a moderate Conservative approach which included an alliance with Quebec *bleus*, while Benjamin moved into an open alliance with George Brown's voluntarism and found himself accused by Gowan of fostering nativist and know-nothing sentiments. This last accusation was probably only Gowan's spite, for after the reunion of the grand lodges in 1856, accomplished by the resignation of the two rival leaders from the grand mastership, and the election in their place of George Lyttleton Allen (the former high bailiff of Toronto) Benjamin returned to the Conservative fold. That the Gowan forces were clearly dominant in 1856 was illustrated by the prominence of Gowan's two sons in the new unified leadership. Their dominance was again evident in 1858, when Gowan's son Nassau defeated John Holland, a Brown supporter, to become grand lodge secretary.

In addition to the costly split in the order and Gowan's inability to defeat Sherwood in the Toronto by-election, Orangemen faced other serious difficulties in the early and mid-1850s. A Green assault on a 12 July procession in Hamilton in 1852 led to the death of one of the Green assailants.[74] Although a grand jury acquitted the Orange defendant of any wrongdoing on the grounds of self-defence against an unwarranted assault, bitter feelings grew between the two communities. Thus in 1853 Toronto Orangemen marched with their Hamilton comrades on the 12th and they went prepared. Lodge records show that the lodges offset the cost of supplying the members who marched in Hamilton with arms for the occasion.[75] Although quiet prevailed, this incident was generally indicative of the new self-assertiveness of the Roman Catholic community in Ontario under Bishop Charbonnel, which was to manifest itself in ever-increasing pressure for separate schools.[76] This policy would continue under Charbonnel's successor, Bishop Lynch. This assertiveness also began to appear in the streets of Toronto where, on 4 July 1853, a march of the Hibernian Benevolent Society resulted in a fracas with an Orange carter. Later that month 40 or 50 Orangemen marched with arms and engaged in a skirmish with some Irish Catholics. They explained afterwards that they had mobilized to defend William Mack's Enniskillen Home Tavern, a major Orange meeting place. Rumours had circulated of an impending attack by Irish Catholic railway navvies from Georgetown.[77]

These political difficulties continued with the emergence of George Brown and the *Globe* as bitter anti-Catholics and strong proponents of a Protestant alliance. This is not the place for this story to be told fully other than to note that the standard biography of Brown significantly underplays the virulence of the *Globe* in this period.[78] One example must suffice. In defending the Orangemen's right to walk, the *Globe* described a Montreal 'romish' procession: 'The melancholy spectacle of crowds kneeling down on the street and worshipping an eye carried on the end of a stick, to represent the Almighty, and the host, or the alleged living reality of Our Saviour, carried in a box.'[79] This was from 1852, before the *Globe* had enthusiastically and totally embraced anti-Catholicism.

Thus although the Toronto Conservative machine had held the city in 1854, returning John Hillyard Cameron and John George Bowes over their Conservative opponents Henry Sherwood and George Ridout, things did not go so well in December 1857. George Brown agreed to run in Toronto in response to a draft petition that was signed by nearly 2,000 individuals, including an alleged 200 Orangemen. His opponents were initially John George Bowes and a rehabilitated W.H. Boulton, who on his return to Toronto early in 1857 after a number of years on the continent had been greeted by Gowan and Toronto Orangemen as a returning hero.[80] When it became apparent that Bowes would not poll well he stood aside for Compact figure and former mayor John Beverley Robinson, Jr, the son of the chief justice. Brown was formally nominated by dissident Orange leader John Holland and by militant Protestant master mariner Captain Bob Moodie, an enemy of the Robinsons, who called on the voters to turn out like men and Protestants. Defections among Orange voters must have aided considerably, for Brown actually led the polls, with Robinson following closely and Boulton trailing behind. There was considerable poll violence, but the *Globe* complained less than usual, for it was clear that Reform forces were ready and willing to do battle themselves on this occasion.[81]

The following year, in the by-election that followed from the intricacies of the 'Double Shuffle,' Brown found himself opposed by John Hillyard Cameron, who was to become grand master of the Orange Order the following year. A vigorous campaign ensued, as had become the norm in Toronto at the end of the 1850s, though in the 1840s Compact Tory candidates often did not deign to campaign, leaving that to their subalterns who simply arranged for free houses. The new campaigning included a full series of ward meetings for each side and even the occasional appearance at each other's meetings, although the latter was still often impeded by supporters' predilection to shout down the opposition—or worse. The election itself was reasonably peaceful, probably more so than the previous December's poll. There were still Reform complaints of Tory rowdyism and an assault charge against Tory Alderman (Captain Bob) Moodie for attacking a Reform supporter at a meeting. Nevertheless, Brown's easy majority, which included victory in five of the seven Toronto wards, made pursuit of the rowdyism issue unnecessary. Brown, who in 1857 had led Robinson by only 51 votes and Boulton by 164, on this occasion beat Cameron by about 150.[82] No doubt the broad-based perception that Brown had been victimized by the double shuffle helped him. Equally, one suspects that the Orange Order's strenuous attempt to impose discipline on its members' voting may have backfired when it became a public issue later in the campaign.[83]

In August the Orange district lodge had passed a series of motions in support of Cameron, though it had taken two meetings to get them through. In addition, it had added resolutions threatening the expulsion of any member who did not vote accordingly or revealed the injunction. Needless to say, when this secret circular was made available to the *Globe*, the paper made ready propaganda gains by exposing the 'tyranny' of the order. The public revelation and Cameron's subsequent defeat led to an investigation and then a trial in the district grand lodge. John Holland, prominent in Brown's 1857 campaign, and two other lodge masters were charged. Holland was eventually suspended for two years by an overwhelming 34–2 vote, with Gowan in the minority. Later that fall all other masters who had voted for Brown were also suspended for two years, although the vote was far closer on this motion, 18–9. While this fight continued for the rest of the year and for a time four lodges threatened to leave the order, the issue had run its course by early 1859 and the dissident lodges were back in the fold.[84]

The political problems of Toronto Orangemen continued in the late 1850s when George Brown's Municipal Reform Association also mounted a successful challenge to Tory control of the Corporation. While partially stemming simply from the growth of Reform sentiment in the city, this campaign also grew out of a series of specific issues that involved elements of the order and raised a serious threat to their power base in the police force and the fire brigades. This story had been unfolding throughout the period. On every occasion of street violence the *Globe* and other forces of order had condemned the city's police. Complaints went back as far as the Durham Club Riot of 1839 and had continued to mount throughout the following twenty years.

Reform of the local justice system had been under discussion for a number of years. Initially the Corporation had objected to what it viewed as blatant attempts to limit its patronage, especially its ability to grant tavern licences. In 1845, however, it acceded to similar legislation in return for a pledge that the appointment would be made only at its request. When in 1847 it requested such an appointment, it found itself asking the new Baldwin ministry to appoint its Orange comrade, the stalwart George Duggan. Not surprisingly, the Baldwin government proceeded slowly. Indeed, no appointment was made until after the new Municipal Corporations Act of 1849 which created a stipendiary police magistrate as well as a recorder's court. Both officers were to be appointed by the provincial government. This centralization of power was no doubt softened for the Corporation when in 1851 two Orange worthies – George Duggan and George Gurnett – became respectively the city's first recorder and first police magistrate. These reforms and the striking appointments of Orange partisans suggest that there was a new bourgeois consensus emerging in the 1850s. The judgments meted out over the next two decades by Gurnett and Duggan further demonstrate this fact. As their biographers note, both men shed their partisanship and were perceived by all to have administered the law 'fairly.'[85] The transformation of the local legal system, however, proceeded far more peacefully than the ensuing debate over the police.

While the police were always a controversial issue in Toronto, the problem became especially prominent after 1855. On two occasions in 1855, only weeks apart, the police force not only proved incapable of maintaining the peace but also demonstrated its unwillingness to prosecute members of crowds with whom it shared general sympathies and Orange associations. The first incident arose during a fire on Church Street. The city's fire department, like that of many cities in this period, was still based on volunteer companies which combined club and social functions with their more useful civic pursuit. Competition was often fierce between these companies, and on 29 June a fight broke out among the firemen attending the Church Street blaze. When the police intervened to break up the fight, they were in turn attacked and administered a sound thrashing, by all accounts. As the *Examiner* noted, there was 'a want of water, a want of method, and the Maine Law was much wanted.' In the heat of the moment, and no doubt smarting from their injuries, the police arrested four of their assailants. When the cases came to court the next week, however, the police constables almost had to be dragged into court to obtain their testimony which then turned out to be so vague that only one of the four defendants' cases was committed for later trial. This failure on the part of the police force was condemned, and the *Globe* reported that 'it is plainly asserted by those who have access to the best information that during the days which have been allowed to elapse since the fire, a compromise has been effected between the constables and the firemen, who are too much birds of a feather long to differ.' 'Utterly disgraceful to the administration of civic justice,' this case demanded the reconstruction of the force 'which thus proves itself utterly corrupt.' The *Examiner* echoed the *Globe's* demands.[86]

All of this was bad enough, but only ten days later the police force found itself again assailed for almost identical behaviour. The second riot stemmed from an incident at a house of ill fame on King Street, when a few Toronto rowdies attacked some members of the visiting Howe circus. The circus performers gained the upper hand in the battle and seriously injured a shoemaker and a carpenter, both members of the Hook and Ladder Company. Police sought the clown who had administered the beatings, but he disappeared. On the following Friday night, a large crowd attacked the circus, initially trying to pull down the tent. A battle ensued in which Joseph Bird, a tavern-keeper and one of the Church Street rioters of the 29 June altercation, was badly beaten by the circus men. Toronto fire bells then rang, summoning fire department cronies and a huge crowd as reinforcements. The new troops turned the tide of battle, especially when the Hook and Ladder Company's truck was immediately put to use to pull down the tent. The circus men fled for their lives and the crowd turned on their wagons, which were broken into, overturned, and burned. The mayor desperately tried to restore order and managed to rescue some of the injured circus men, but finally he had to call out the troops. The riot then ended before the military arrived. Police constables present throughout did little to restrain the crowd, and, when called on later to make charges, they again developed collective amnesia about who had participated in the riot. After extreme pressure was administered, 17 rioters were arraigned, of whom 13 were committed for later trial. This time the *Globe* editorialized about the 'additional disgrace' of the firemen's further involvement and demanded that the city council act to reform both the police force and the fire department.[87]

The debates and actions that followed these riots are especially instructive in terms of the underlying class conflict at issue here. In the riots and their aftermath, police and firemen behaved in ways that drew on working-class solidarities. As one critic noted, 'There are three classes in the city which thoroughly understand one another as hale fellows well met – the innkeeper, the firemen, and the police.' 'These Classes,' he continued, 'are fed by the Orange Lodges.'[88] Moreover, the circus crowd clearly acted as a community enforcer acting on unwritten codes of moral economy. Not too surprisingly, police and firemen appeared to share the same assumptions as the crowd. While none of this seems at first sight out of the ordinary, given the preceding fifteen years of riots in Toronto, something quite new was contained in the press response, speaking of course for the respectable citizenry, and in the ultimate actions of the city council. From these riots stemmed the first significant reforms of both the police and fire departments of the city, and in both cases the operative assumption that underlay the reforms was the perceived necessity to end political control of the institutions and professionalize them, thus eliminating their plebeian roots.

The fire department received the *Globe*'s initial attention. Finding it in general 'a disgrace to the civic administration' and based on 'utterly unsound principles,' the *Globe* reviewed the force's history. Organized initially as a volunteer force, in the old days it had provided excellent service and recruited first-rate men. In recent years, however, this had changed. The increase in insurance had led to less concern on the part of the propertied, and 'their places were filled by men of lower standing.' This in turn led to a small stipend being attached to volunteer service (£3), which in turn attracted more of the 'dissolute young fellows.' Yet the basis of organization was never changed to reflect its different class reality. The 352 volunteers were still allowed to control their own company membership and to elect their own officers and even the chief engineer. This, according to the *Globe*, meant that the officers had no control over the men. (So much for democracy!) All this led to fire companies getting 'into the hands of a few evil-disposed fellows who chose others as their colleagues, and elect whomever they please.' There was only one possible reform, a paid fire department.[89] A few weeks later the *Globe* returned to the subject and made its assumptions even more transparent: 'The Toronto system must now be put an end to. It has served its day ... It must pass away, and be replaced by a system suited to the times and to our rapidly increasing city ... Toronto has outgrown that system ... A paid company work in a totally opposite manner. It is a system of subordination, while that element is scarcely known under the voluntary arrangement.'[90] Thus under the rubric of being up to date, traditions of voluntary control must be swept away. Why? Because they were insufficiently 'subordinate.' Capitalist relations extended their tentacles yet further.

These goals were accomplished, and in that year a professional fire brigade was created. Yet only five years later, under the financial constraints of the economic crisis of the late 1850s, the council reversed itself and tried to revert to a voluntary basis. It expected that the officers, however, would still be paid by the city and also insisted that a city council committee maintain supervisory power.[91] The firemen reacted strongly to this proposal, which held nothing for them, and in June 1861 they paraded in protest with an effigy of Alderman Sproat, the architect of this plan. After a heated confrontation with the mayor and Chief Constable W.S. Prince in front of Sproat's house, the firemen marched on without burning their effigy, which was destroyed by Prince.[92] Shortly thereafter the city again began to release funds to the volunteer companies, and, when the economy began to recover the next year, it began hiring permanent firemen.[93] Thus the workingmen of the fire companies had adjusted to their new situation and commenced to fight on a new terrain when the city tried to worsen their situation further. Even after all these reforms, the fire department remained an Orange bastion throughout the century and still provided the Corporation's shock troops in late Victorian Toronto.

The police received even more criticism than the firemen for the two 1855 riots. A special investigation by city council led to strong criticism of the chief, Samuel Sherwood. The key element in the emerging critical consensus on the police was the need to remove the force from politics. The chief constable should be 'free of the contamination of our local politics,' wrote the *Globe*. Moreover, hiring of the force should be removed from the hands of the city council and given instead to a board of police commissioners composed of the mayor, the police magistrate, and the chief constable.[94] The investigating committee endorsed most of these suggestions, emphasizing especially the need for a trained, experienced chief. While city council agreed to commence a search for a successor to Sherwood, no other practical reform was implemented and the issue soon died out.[95]

The police, never far from the public eye in these years, became a major issue again in 1858. A 16 March St Patrick's Society dinner at the National Hotel, owned by Irish nationalist leader Owen Cosgrove, had ended in a serious riot which included an attack on D'Arcy McGee. During the procession of the following day, an Orange carter drove his cart through the line of march, and in the ensuing mêlée an Irish Catholic received a mortal stab wound. The subsequent furore continued for almost a month and led to a vigorous denunciation of secret societies by Police Magistrate George Gurnett (a former Orangeman) and even by the Tory *Leader*. Directly criticized first for refusing to testify and later for appearing to be in collusion with the accused Orangemen was Chief of Police Samuel Sherwood. Gurnett inveighed against 'other obligations than those which are due to the public and the laws of the land,' while the *Leader* editorialized about 'the dangerous state of society in which any considerable portion of its members enter into secret obligations which are liable to defeat the ends of public justice.' Things did not improve for the police when more shooting and rioting occurred on 12 July as well.[96]

The controversy became a major issue in the fall when Mayor W.H. Boulton tried but failed to unseat Chief Constable Sherwood. The specific issue revolved around Sherwood's release of a prisoner charged with bank robbery. The police committee of city council mildly censured him, but Boulton demanded his resignation. When the mayor failed to carry his council, he resigned instead. This created a complete breakdown in the Conservative ranks, which had been in the process of trying to find a mayoralty candidate to oppose the nominee of George Brown's Municipal Reform Association: Adam Wilson. A series of Tory convention meetings broke down in embarrassment as various choices declined nomination. Meanwhile Boulton defied the convention by declaring that he intended to run even without its support. It finally settled on former mayor John Beverley Robinson, Jr, but he too refused. The subsequent mayoralty race saw Wilson opposed by Boulton, who had lost his Corporation support, and J.G. Bowes, who was still suffering from his association with the '10,000 pound job.' Wilson triumphed easily, gaining almost 2,000 votes to the combined 1,500 of his opponents. Reform had triumphed in Toronto.[97]

Police reform became a central task of the new Reform majority. Provincial legislation had created a Toronto Board of Police Commissioners which first met on 1 December 1858 and was composed of the mayor, the recorder (George Duggan), and the police magistrate (George Gurnett).[98] The new board's structure reflected proposals that Reformers had been pressing since the 1841 commission on the Toronto election riot.[99] The emerging bourgeois consensus on the need for law and order and a 'professional' police force was evident even before Mayor Wilson joined the commission. At its first meeting the commission had decided that 'the present police force in the city should be reorganized at as early a day as practicable after full enquiry and mature deliberation.'[100] In its first month of activity it disciplined no fewer than eight constables and set out to revise all police rules 'with the view of increasing the efficiency of the force.'[101] With Wilson's arrival in mid-January it proceeded to fire the former deputy police chief in the name of 'the efficiency of the force' and began to seek a replacement for Chief Sherwood. It sought authorization from the city council 'to offer such a salary ... as would induce the most efficient person that the Metropolitan Police of England or elsewhere could afford to accept the office.'[102] This by then familiar bourgeois rhetoric about 'efficiency' was, however, only one innovation of the police commissioners. With Wilson's arrival, they proceeded to rule that no member of a secret society could join the force.[103] This led to a storm of Orange protest, because it was only too clear that such a prohibition was aimed directly at the order. A public meeting was held at St Lawrence Hall in which prominent Orangemen such as John Hillyard Cameron, Nassau Gowan, Francis H. Medcalf, and others inveighed against this new measure as reprehensible and an infringement of their rights as freeborn Englishmen.[104] A subsequent city council motion to reconsider failed by one vote. The district lodge condemned Alderman Joseph Reed, an Orangeman, who had cast the deciding vote in favour of the prohibition.[105]

The new commission reconstructed the force totally, choosing, avowedly without regard for party or sect, 58 constables. The new force included only 24 constables from the old, and 45 Anglicans, 5 Presbyterians, and 8 Roman Catholics received positions as constables.[106]

In 1860, after the defeat of the Reform council, the returned Tories voted to overturn the police commission's decision. In response to an inquiry from Police Chief Prince, in which he indicated that his constables now felt that they were free to join secret societies, the police commission asserted its independence and power: '[The police] are appointed by and hold their office at the pleasure of the Board of Commissioners of Police and the Board is the only authority which can make rules for their government. These are powers which have been conferred by Act of Parliament upon the Board and neither the Council nor any other body or person has the slightest right to interfere with the force in any respect. Number 50 rule which relates to secret societies must be observed as strictly now as at any time heretofore and any disobedience of it will be punished with instant dismissal.'[107] Although a modus vivendi was eventually worked out, the formal rule was upheld, as was the commission's independence of council.[108] The clause preventing member-ship in secret societies was entrenched in 1866 as part of the police constable's oath of office. Prince, drawing on his British army background, introduced military discipline and recruited many members of the force from the Irish constabulary. In late Victorian commentaries on the Toronto police, he is personally credited with creating the force that was proudly held to be 'equal to that of any city in the world.'[109] Nevertheless, Prince proved to be a controversial figure and was involved in a series of battles with city council over the next decade, including a celebrated battle in 1863 when he requested arms for the police to enable them to protect themselves against the Orange-dominated, armed militia.[110] The equally Orange-dominated council refused to grant this request.

While the council refused to arm the police for riot duty, Prince's major contribution to law and order in Toronto was undoubtedly the new attitude to crowd violence. The daily order book initiated by Prince on his arrival in 1859 is filled not only with careful preparations for the policing of potentially explosive political and ritual events but also with new attitudes to popular disorder. In late February 1859 the whole force was mobilized to police a St Lawrence Hall meeting, with a conspicuous deployment of constables outside while a supporting force was hidden in the hall's anterooms. Upon the meeting's end, Prince ordered 'the streets will be patrolled by three parties from each section for an hour.'[111] On St Patrick's Day, the whole force was placed on active duty 'from 9:00 until it is deemed necessary to dismiss them.'[112] Two weeks later officers received instructions to 'prevent distur-bances amongst the cabmen,' traditional Corporation retainers.[113] A special force of twenty-four was instructed to keep all crowds well away from the militia during 24 May celebrations, while for the 'Glorious Twelfth' the whole force was again called out and special plans were made to prevent crowds from gathering, to scrutinize the various lodges after the procession, and to arrest anyone firing guns in the street, a customary accompaniment of 12 July merriment. In addition, 'particular care must be taken to prevent cabmen or others driving through the procession,' and if 'any attempt of this kind [took] place ... the arrest of the party or parties must be the immediate result.'[114] Popular disorders of a more mundane type received similar attention: 'Young blackguards' disrupting 'services or class meetings' at the Elizabeth Street Missionary Church; taverns open after hours; the arrival in town of the circus. No disruption of the new bourgeois order evaded Chief Prince's vigilance.[115]

The specifics of the transformation wrought by Prince aside, what had been accomplished by Wilson and the legislative assembly reforms was the distancing of the police from their working-class roots. The emphasis on experience, recruitment abroad, and commission control all further removed police from the plebeian milieu of which the earlier policemen had been an integral part. Again here, as in the case of the fire department, the reforms had this intent but did not totally achieve their aims. The Toronto police would also continue to play ambiguous class roles. Nevertheless the general thrust of capital to create dependable class institutions had proceeded one step futher in Toronto.

The Toronto voters' flirtation with Reform, which Brown had heralded in 1859 as the final demise of the corruptionists, did not last long. Wilson personally gained a second term, but with a minority of supporters on council, and in 1861 the voters turned to an old friend, John George Bowes. He held the mayor's chair for three terms and was replaced for three more by Francis Medcalf, former Orange district master. During Medcalf's last term in office the legislative assembly, reflecting concern for urban property values, removed the direct election of the mayor from the people and returned it to the city council. This same legislative assembly also increased the property requirements for the exercise of the franchise to $600 leasehold and for holding office to $4,000 freehold or $8,000 leasehold, both qualifications being double the 1858 level.[116]

Adam Wilson was only one of the problems faced by Toronto Orangemen in 1860. During the royal visit of the Prince of Wales to Canada, his adviser and companion, the Catholic Duke of Newcastle, precipitated a major crisis in the colony by refusing to receive Orange addresses or to pass under Orange arches. The subsequent series of incidents, which involved the cancellation of visits to Kingston and Belleville when local Orangemen refused to concede, has been described elsewhere.[117] In Toronto there was a major debate within the Orange order. Toronto's Orangemen were urged by their Kingston brothers to maintain their rights as citizens to march. However, respectable Torontonians had been planning their celebrations for months. After heated and prolonged negotiations, Toronto Orangemen arrived at a face-saving compromise by which they decided to hold their own separate march. This motion finally carried in the district lodge by a vote of 50 to 29, but the minority were quite unhappy.[118] They continued to demand both 'arch and march' and no doubt were responsible for the ensuing double-cross. While the separate Orange march was peaceable and then dispersed to allow the members to greet the prince as private citizens without party regalia, the arch that was supposedly stripped of party slogans in fact carried a figure of King Billy. Thus Newcastle and the prince actually passed under an arch with Orange symbols despite the earlier guarantees. The furious duke blamed

Mayor Wilson and the city council and demanded an apology, which he received. An additional incident took place on the following Sunday, when the prince and the duke attended services at the Anglican cathedral. Newcastle ordered the carriage to take a longer route to avoid the Orange arch. An Orange crowd then gathered at the cathedral and prepared a display of banners, flags, and decorations and threatened 'to cut the trace and drag the Prince through the arch' as he left the service. When the royal party escaped through a side door the crowd's fury mounted. Later, when the duke went out for a walk, he was hissed and booed by a crowd that then burned him in effigy.[119] Though Toronto authorities and Orange leaders had managed to escape without a major incident, it had not been easy. Or as one of the many journalistic accounts of the tour noted, 'the Battle of Toronto' was narrowly avoided.[120]

The ingenuity of the Orangemen was not to be underestimated. Aurora's Loyal Orange Lodge (LOL) 693 won a final victory over Newcastle when it erected an arch over the Northern Railway line which the prince's party passed under on its way to Barrie.[121] Meanwhile one Toronto lodge, Nassau LOL 4, passed a motion of thanks to its comrades in the fire brigade who had marched in the formal procession for the royal party, 'on which occasion we were proud to observe the Orange rosette on the left breast of each Orange fireman in the procession.'[122] 'Arch and march' had been gained.

The royal visit turned into a major political crisis for John A. Macdonald and his ministry. It took serious fence mending to repair the Conservatives' damaged relationship with their Orange allies, who blamed the government for Newcastle's insult to the order. Critical motions, for example, were passed at the provincial grand lodge of Canada West meeting in Hamilton in late October: 'That the government of Canada ... were guilty of a gross dereliction of their duty as the responsible representatives of the people and are chargeable with the unfortunate occurrence which afterwards took place; and this right worshipful Grand Lodge feels it due to itself to declare that the Ministry have in consequence forfeited all claim to the confidence of the orangemen of Western Canada and that the proper constitutional mode of redress ... is by withdrawing from them the direct and indirect support of the Loyal Orange body.'[123] This motion failed to carry at the grand lodge meeting in Kingston the following January and was then repudiated in February at the provincial grand lodge meeting in Barrie. Through hard work, Macdonald had managed to repair the alliance.[124]

The rise to prominence of the separate school issue in the politics of the 1860s, and the emergence of a radical Irish Catholic nationalist grouping, the Hibernian Benevolent Society, kept sectarian issues at the centre of Toronto political life in the pre-Confederation years. The Fenian threat represented a natural rallying point for the Orange order and would eventually join 1837 as one of the central historical incidents in the elaborate, developing Orange mythology. As tension mounted in Toronto in the early 1860s, the city prepared for war – the Fenians surrepetitiously, the Orange militia openly. On the route that would lead to the Fenian Raid battlefields, there were a few Toronto skirmishes in 1863 and 1864. Such tensions were of considerable significance in the coming of the new Confederation. The degree to which tensions of this kind reinforced the fears of Reformers about urban order, however, remains an open question. Nevertheless, more may well have been at stake in the 1866 disfranchisement than simply a protest over property taxes. Many Irish workers would have lost their votes under the new schema. Equally notable, 'Old Squaretoes' Medcalf, Toronto's first mechanic mayor and the people's choice in the preceding three years, lost office under the new system when the council chose his opponent. In 1874, when Toronto voters were once again given the right to elect the mayor directly, they suggestively chose Medcalf.[125]

'The Irish Protestants,' Don Akenson has written recently, 'were like a cocked gun, always ready to go off.'[126] While the Orange order in Toronto successfully expanded beyond its basic ethno-religious constituency, the organization nevertheless epitomizes Akenson's suggestive simile. In Ontario's major city, the order provided rising bourgeois elements with their major antagonist. While the struggles of the 1840s and 1850s have generally been viewed by historians as purely religious and ethnic conflicts, they did not reduce so easily for the participants. Battles over the licensing of taverns, over the right to march, over the burning of effigies, over the nature and composition of the police force and the fire brigade, and even over schools and church lands may not at first sight appear to be class issues. Yet, as the Yeos have recently reminded us in writing about Victorian England, such conflicts involved 'struggles over time and territory. They were about social initiative, and who was to have it. They were about expected notions of what it is to be human and normal. They were struggles of substance in themselves. They were also struggles about *form*, the forms that association would take. When put together, they may be seen as struggles about the dominant styles and contours, constraints and opportunities of whole periods.'[127] They further exhort historians to penetrate beneath the results of appearances in developing capitalist society to discover the conflicts that often mask the class struggles of the period.

Applying such methods, what can we make of the Canada of the 1840s and 1850s? Perhaps three contemporary figures should be allowed to guide our conclusions. First, John Macaulay, one of the last active Compact members, observed in 1850 that 'the most alarming symptom which I observe in the country is the decay of old-fashioned loyalty, and a general want of respect for authority and station which once prevailed among us ... when, whatever were the failings of the much abused "Family Compact," we had a Government of Gentlemen.'[128] Macaulay spoke astutely. The new bourgeois hegemony did not aspire to the patrician values of his old Compact contemporaries, be they real or pretend.[129] Nor did it harness popular consent by authority and station.

Second, note George Brown's positive assessment of the achievements of Adam Wilson's first term as mayor of Toronto: 'Prior to Mr. Wilson's Mayoralty, the police was a mixture of incapacity and ruffianism. Now it is respectable in character and conduct, and thoroughly efficient in all respects.' 'Respectability' was a major value of the new bourgeois order, as was 'efficiency.' In this same assessment, Brown argued that Wilson's second major accomplishment was the dramatic reduction of tavern licenses from 460 to 267.[130] Order, efficiency, and temperance, a new trinity far removed from plebeian society, had become the touchstones of the new. And yet we need to proceed cautiously here, for plebeian society too was changing.

Our third speaker, Orange leader Ogle Robert Gowan, made the following observations at the celebration of the Battle of the Boyne in 1855, comparing the twelfth of old with the new: 'Then a few coarse straw hats and a few orange ribbons might have been borne by some drunken men staggering through the streets. But now the procession has that uniformity and respectability which in the eyes of their fellow subjects give a character to Orangeism.'[131] 'Uniformity,' 'respectability' – have we here evidence of the final 'incorporation' of the Orange order into the new bourgeois hegemony? The answer to that question is, of course, both yes and no. There can be no incorporation 'without the incorporating host being altered, as well as the incorporated guest.'[132] Orangemen, who had once been viewed as incorporated by the Compact, had ironically played a significant part in the bourgeois alliance that promoted the extension of democratic reforms and had articulated the demand for tariff protection as an industrial strategy for Canada. So, yes, they too had changed, but not totally and not without a process of struggle, of reciprocal gains and losses – a process of the composition, decomposition, and recomposition of class. Gowan, himself, to cite one final irony, ended his career as Toronto's inspector of licences from 1869 to 1874.[133]

Orangemen had enjoyed one certain privilege from the 1830s to the 1860s, which they shared with no other force in Canadian society. They had been universally condemned even by those whose policies came to depend on their support. Francis Bond Head, Arthur, Durham, Sydenham, Metcalfe, Russell, Elgin, Edmund Head, Newcastle, a list of British political figures who probably agreed on nothing else, all despised the Orange order. The Yeos have pointed to working people as recalcitrant, innovative, and intrusive.[134]

These adjectives convey much about the class significance of the Orange order in the 1840s and 1850s. For Orangemen, 'No Surrender' had many meanings.

NOTES

My thanks for research assistance to Jessie Chisholm, Doug Cruikshank, and Peter Delottinville. Useful comments on the first draft were provided by Michael Cross, Michael Frisch, Bryan Palmer, Nick Rogers, and Paul Romney. The latter saved me from a number of egregious errors and shared with me his intimate knowledge of early Toronto.

1 For suggestive articles on these questions, see Geoff Eley 'Rethinking the Political: Society History and Political Culture in 18th and 19th Century Britain' *Archiv fur Socialgeschichte* (1981) 426–57, and Geoff Eley and Keith Neild 'Why Does Social History Ignore Politics?' *Social History* v (1980) 249–71. A stimulating review essay, which raises important questions, is Bryan D. Palmer 'Classifying Culture' *Labour/Le Travailleur* 8/9 (1981–2) 153–83, especially 181–3. Especially useful during the revision of this paper were Paul Romney 'Voters under the Microscope: A Quantitative Meditation on the Toronto Parliamentary Poll Book of 1836' paper presented to Canadian Historical Association, Vancouver, 1983, and his 'A Man out of Place: The Life of Charles Fothergill, 1782–1840' unpublished PhD thesis, University of Toronto, 1981.

2 The literature on the Orange order has been recently strengthened by Cecil J. Houston and William J. Smyth *The Sash Canada Wore: A Historical Geography of the Orange Order in Canada* (Toronto 1980). While I have numerous points of disagreement with their analysis (and they with mine), they present much useful data, especially on the growth of the order in Ontario. A stimulating general view is G.F.A. Best 'Popular Protestantism in Victorian Britain' in Robert Robson ed *Ideas and Institutions of Victorian Britain* (New York 1967) 115–42.

3 Barrie Dyster 'Toronto 1840–1860: Making it in a British Protestant Town' PhD thesis, University of Toronto, 1970. This critique applies to a lesser extent to his excellent paper in this volume, which I read after writing this paper.

4 Dyster 'Toronto' 40

5 This analysis of class is indebted to E.P. Thompson 'Eighteenth-Century English Society: Class Struggle without Class?' *Social History* III (1978) 133–66; to Adam Przeworski 'Proletariat into a Class: The Process of Class Formation from Karl Kautsky's *The Class Struggle* to Recent Controversies' *Politics and Society* VII (1977) 343–401, quotation at 367; and to his 'Material Bases of Consent: Economics and Politics in a Hegemonic System' *Political Power and Social Theory* I (1980) 21–66. In the Canadian literature, useful attempts to begin the discussion of early class formation are: Bryan D. Palmer 'Kingston Mechanics and the Rise of the Penitentiary, 1833–1836' *Histoire sociale* XXV (1980) 7–32; his 'Discordant Music: Charivaris and Whitecapping in Nineteenth-Century North America' *Labour/Le Travailleur* 3 (1978) 5–62; and his attempt at a synthesis, *Working-Class Experience: The Rise and Reconstitution of Canadian Labour, 1800–1980* (Toronto 1983), especially chapter 1.

6 Data drawn from Canada *Census* for various years. For a stimulating revisionist look at Canadian Irish, see Donald H. Akenson 'Ontario: Whatever Happened to the Irish?' *Canadian Papers in Rural History* III (1982) 204–56.

7 On Toronto's industrialization, see Gregory S. Kealey *Toronto Workers Respond to Industrial Capitalism* (Toronto 1980) 3–34.

8 Paul C. Appleton 'The Sunshine and the Shade: Labour Activism in Central Canada, 1850–1860' MA thesis, University of Calgary, 1974. Also see Palmer *Working-Class Experience* 67–71, 316–20.

9 Strike data are drawn from Toronto press. See also the list in Palmer *Working-Class Experience* 316–20.

10 Ruth Bleasdale 'Class Conflict on the Canals of Upper Canada in the 1840s' *Labour/Le Travailleur* 7 (1981) 9–39

11 Houston and Smyth *The Sash Canada Wore* 8–37, and Hereward Senior *Orangeism: The Canadian Phase* (Toronto 1972) 13–39. See also William Perkins Bull *From the Boyne to Brampton* (Toronto 1936) 17–90. Two early, useful studies which provide much background on the order in politics are Violet Nelson 'The Orange Order in Canadian Politics' MA thesis, Queen's University, 1950, and W.J.S. Mood 'The Orange Order in Canadian Politics, 1841–1867' MA thesis, University of Toronto, 1950. Finally, for a stimulating re-examination of the Irish roots of Orangeism, see Peter Gibbon 'The Origins of the Orange Order and the United Irishmen: A Study in the Sociology of Revolution and Counter-revolution' *Economy and Society* VII (1972) 134–63. A similarly useful study of the other side is Tom Garvin 'Defenders, Ribbonmen, and Others: Underground Political Networks in Pre-Famine Ireland' *Past and Present* XLVI (1982) 133–55.

12 The warrant books and much other Orange archival material is held in the Loyal Orange Association Archives in Willowdale (henceforth LOAA).

13 Material drawn from Minute Book, Loyal Orange Lodge of British North

America (LOLBNA), District 2, York County, 1858–84, in LOAA. This paper will not engage in further demographic analysis of the order. For such a discussion, see Kealey *Toronto Workers* 98–123. While Houston and Smyth *The Sash* 101–11 quibble with my findings, I would argue that their evidence actually further augments the notion of the order as a plebeian, and later a proletarian, organization. In addition, this paper will also assume the discussion of internal organization and ritual that can be found in the same pages of *Toronto Workers*.

14 United Province of Canada, Legislative Assembly *Journals*, 1841, Appendix s, 'Report of the Commissioners appointed to investigate certain proceedings at Toronto, connected with the Election for that City.' Unfortunately, this lengthy report is unpaginated (henceforth Toronto Election Commission). For manuscript material from this investigation see Toronto Election Riot, RG5B33, Public Archives of Canada (henceforth PAC). On the 1841 election in general, see Irving Martin Abella 'The "Sydenham Election" of 1841' *Canadian Historical Review* XLVII (1966) 326–43.

15 Toronto Election Commission, Testimony of Peter Harkin, Tavern Keeper. Specific denials of Harkin's damming testimony are contained in *Journals*, 1841, Appendix oo.

16 Ibid, Testimony of No. 32, John Lindsay, boarding-house-keeper

17 Howard Angus Christie 'The Function of the Tavern in Toronto, 1834–1875' unpublished MPHE thesis, University of Windsor, 1974, 10. On the importance of the tavern in Toronto see also F.H. Armstrong 'Toronto in Transition, 1828–1838' PhD thesis, University of Toronto, 1965, 337–40.

18 Toronto Election Commission, Testimony of No. 41, John Eastwood, paper maker

19 Ibid, List of tavern licences, 1841

20 Ibid passim. For campaign details see the *Metropolitan* (Toronto) and the *Examiner* 27 February–13 March 1841.

21 Toronto Election Commission *Report*

22 Ibid and Elizabeth Gibbs ed *Debates of the Legislative Assembly*, 1841, 1008–10 and *Debates*, 1843, 438–9, 442 (henceforth *Debates*). For the legislative committee's report on the riot, see *Examiner* 27 October 1841.

23 Dyster 'Toronto' 64

24 *Globe* 9 December 1845

25 Ibid

26 *Examiner* 24 November 1841. Boulton's failure led to his resignation. Without doubt he failed because he was then fighting with the Orangemen. He had led the opposition to George Gurnett's quest for the mayoralty in 1841 by challenging his qualifications. See *Examiner* 20 January 1841.

27 Toronto Election Commission *Report*
28 John Garner *The Franchise and Politics in British North America, 1755–1867* (Toronto 1969) 100–2
29 *Debates*, 1843, 210, 398–408, 438–47, 456–7, 460, 733; quotation at 443
30 Ibid 164, 409, 497–511, 546–8, 662–3, 733, 1210
31 *Examiner* 8 November 1843
32 *Canadian Loyalist* (Kingston) 2 November 1843
33 *Victoria Chronicle* (Belleville) 31 October 1844; *Examiner* 16, 23 October 1844
34 *Examiner* 21 February, 17 July 1844
35 *Globe* 16 July 1844; *Examiner* 17, 24 July 1844. See also Samuel Thompson *Reminiscences of a Canadian Pioneer* (Toronto 1884) 183.
36 See, for example, *Globe* 31 July 1847, 15 July 1848, 14 July 1849. For the complex political history of the period, see Paul G. Cornell *The Alignment of Political Groups in Canada, 1841–1867* (Toronto 1962).
37 Dyster 'Toronto' 83
38 *Examiner* 23 October 1844. See also R.I.K. Davidson 'Monro, George' *Dictionary of Canadian Biography* x (henceforth *DCB*).
39 Hereward Senior 'Boulton, W.H.' *DCB* x
40 Hereward Senior 'Benjamin, George' *DCB* ix
41 *Examiner* 20 January 1847. See also Dyster 'Toronto' chapter 2 and 213–15.
42 *Globe* 29 December 1847; *Examiner* 22 December 1847, 3 January 1848
43 Useful accounts of the Baldwin act are Leo Johnson *History of the County of Ontario* (Whitby 1973) 172–7; C.F.J. Whebell 'Robert Baldwin and Decentralization, 1841–9' in F.H. Armstrong et al ed *Aspects of Nineteenth-Century Ontario* (Toronto 1974) 48–64; and J.H. Aitchison 'The Municipal Corporations Act of 1849' *Canadian Historical Review* xxx (1949) 107–22.
44 PAC Petition of Toronto Inhabitants to Lord Elgin, 2 May 1849, RG5 CI vol 261, 1016
45 *Globe* 24, 28 March 1849; *Provincial Telegraph* (Toronto) 29 March 1849; *Examiner* 28 March, 4 April 1849
46 *Globe* 5, 9 May 1849; *Examiner* 2, 9 May 1849
47 Sir Arthur C. Doughty ed *The Elgin-Grey Papers, 1846–1852* (Ottawa 1937) 410, 413
48 *Globe* 21 July 1849
49 Ibid 14, 19 July, 9 August 1849
50 Doughty ed *Elgin-Grey Papers* 415
51 Ibid 462
52 Ibid 475; *Examiner* 12 September 1849
53 Doughty ed *Elgin-Grey Papers* 468

54 Thompson *Reminiscences* 268–73, and C.D. Allin and G.M. Jones *Annexation, Preferential Trade and Reciprocity* (Toronto 1912) 208–12; *Examiner* 19 September 1849

55 *Globe* 22, 24, 26 January 1850; *Examiner* 10, 17 October 1849

56 *Globe* 12 May 1849

57 Ibid 24 Jamuary 1850

58 British American League *Minutes of the Proceedings of the Second Convention of Delegates* (Toronto 1849)

59 *Debates*, 1850, 411–20

60 *Globe* 7, 9 November 1850

61 PAC RG 4C1, vol 326, item 788, Petition of George Benjamin to Lord Elgin.

62 *Debates*, 1851, 847, 1419, 1441–7, 1500. See also *Globe* 19 August 1851.

63 Useful background is provided in J.M.S. Careless ed *The Pre-Confederation Premiers* (Toronto 1980).

64 Dyster 'Toronto' 230–3; *Examiner* 16, 23 October, 6, 27 November 1850, 1 January 1851. See also F.H. Armstrong 'Gurnett, George' *DCB* IX, and Barrie Dyster 'Duggan, George' *DCB* X 262–3

65 Hereward Senior 'Gowan, Ogle Robert' *DCB* X; *Examiner*, 1 January 1851

66 For the story of this complicated issue see Alan Wilson *The Clergy Reserves of Upper Canada* (Toronto 1968), and John Moir *Church and State in Canada West* (Toronto 1959) 27–81.

67 *Globe* 12 July 1851

68 Ibid 24, 26, 29 July, 2 August 1851

69 Ibid 27, 29 November, 2, 6, 9 December 1851; *Toronto Mirror* 12 December 1851

70 *Globe* 11, 13 December 1851

71 *Debates*, 1853, 260, 2330–1

72 *Globe* 5, 12, 19, 23, 26 April 1853; *Weekly North American* (Toronto) 21 April 1853; *Toronto Mirror* 8, 22, 29 April 1853. See also Foster J.K. Griezic 'An Uncommon Conservative: The Political Career of John Hillyard Cameron, 1846–62' MA thesis, Carleton University, 1965, 62–8.

73 *Globe* 28 April 1853

74 Ibid 17 July 1852

75 Harry Lovelock 'Reminiscences of Toronto Orangeism' in *Official Orange Souvenir. In Honour of the 212th Anniversary of the Battle of the Boyne* (Toronto 1912) 17; *Examiner* 14 July 1852

76 On separate schools, see Franklin A. Walker *Catholic Education and Politics in Upper Canada* (Toronto 1955), and Moir *Church and State* 129–80.

77 *Globe* 12 July 1853; *Leader* 27 July, 1 August 1853; *Mackenzie's Weekly Message* 28 July 1853. See also Robin Burns 'Thomas D'Arcy McGee: A Biography' PhD thesis, McGill University, 1976; Edward J. Doherty 'An Analysis

of Social and Political Thought in the Irish Catholic Press of Upper Canada, 1858–1867' MA thesis, University of Waterloo, 1976; Murray Nicholson, 'The Catholic Church and the Irish in Victorian Toronto' PhD thesis, University of Guelph, 1981; Gerald Stortz 'John Joseph Lynch, Archbishop of Toronto: A Biographical Study of Religious, Political and Social Commitment' PhD thesis, University of Guelph, 1980; Peter Toner 'The Rise of Irish Nationalism in Canada' PhD thesis, National University of Ireland, 1974; Daniel Colman Lyne 'The Irish in the Province of Canada in the Decade Leading to Confederation' PhD thesis, McGill University, 1960; and Jacques Gibeault 'Les Relations entre Thomas D'Arcy McGee et James G. Moylan, 1858–1865' MA thesis, Université d'Ottawa, 1971.

78 J.M.S. Careless *Brown of the Globe* I (Toronto 1959)

79 *Globe* 17 July 1852

80 *Leader* 24 January 1857

81 Careless *Brown* I 244–6; *Globe* 4, 15 December 1857; *Mackenzie's Weekly Messenger* 4, 11, 18 December 1857. For the full story of this election, see Barrie Dyster 'Captain Bob and the Noble Ward.' For an excellent, detailed breakdown of the vote, see *Leader* 29 December 1857.

82 *Globe* August 1858

83 Ibid 26 August 1858; Minute Book, Toronto District Lodge, 10, 18 August 1858, Orange Archives, Willowdale, Ontario

84 Minute Book, Toronto District Lodge, 7, 16, 28 September, 15, 19 October, 1, 16 December 1858, 11 January 1859

85 See note 65.

86 *Globe* 5 July 1855. See also *ibid* 2, 3, 4, 6, 7 July 1855; *Examiner* 4, 11 July 1855.

87 *Globe* 16, 19 July 1855; *Examiner* 18 July 1855. For interesting American studies of volunteer fire companies, see Bruce Laurie 'Fire Companies and Gangs in Southwark: The 1840's' in Allen F. Davis and Mark H. Haller ed *The Peoples of Philadelphia* (Philadelphia 1973) 71–88, and Geoffrey Giglierano, '"A Creature of Law": Cincinnati's Paid Fire Department' *Cincinnati Historical Society Bulletin* XL (1982) 78–99. On the importance of fires in nineteenth-century Canadian cities see John C. Weaver and Peter DeLottinville 'The Conflagration and the City: Disaster and Progress in British North America during the Nineteenth Century' *Histoire sociale/Social History* XXVI (1980) 417–49. A more peaceable view is offered in Bradley Rudachyk ' "At the Mercy of the Devouring Element": The Equipment and Organization of the Halifax Fire Establishment, 1830–1850' *Collections of the Royal Nova Scotia Historical Society* XLI (1982) 165–84. For Toronto background, see Armstrong 'Toronto in Transition' chapter 8.

88 *Globe* 21 July 1855

89 Ibid 3 July 1855

90 Ibid 27 July 1855

91 Jarvis 'Mid Victorian Toronto' 148–54

92 *Globe* 1 June 1861

93 Jarvis 'Mid Victorian Toronto' 154

94 *Globe* 19 July 1855

95 Ibid 24, 27 July 1855

96 Ibid 23, 24, 25, 27 March, 1 April, 13 July 1858; *Leader* 18, 22, 23, 24, 25, 27 March, 1, 2, 5, 6, 8 April, 13 July 1858. See also Toronto petition in PAC RG5 C1, vol 550, item 625.

97 *Globe* October–December 1858. For more on the Boulton-Sherwood struggle, see Dyster 'Captain Bob and the Noble Ward.'

98 Board of Police Commissioners, Minute Book 1858–1862, 1 December 1858, Toronto Police Museum. For a more detailed study of police reform, see the essay by Nick Rogers in this volume.

99 For a mid-1840s example of Reform attitudes, see *Examiner*, 1, 8, 15 October 1845.

100 Board of Police Commissioners, Minutes, 1 December 1858

101 Ibid 1, 2, 3, 4, 6, 7, 11, 18, 23, 27 December 1858; quotation from 11 December

102 Ibid 15 January 1859

103 *Globe* 17 January 1859

104 Minute Book, District Lodge, 4 February 1859; *Patriot* 2 March 1859; *Globe* 25 February 1859

105 *Globe* 28 June 1859; Minute Book, District Lodge, 29 June 1859

106 Jarvis 'Mid Victorian Toronto' 71–5

107 Board of Police Commissioners, Minutes, 24 January 1860

108 Rogers 'Serving Toronto the Good'

109 Conyngham Crawford Taylor *The Queen's Jubilee or Toronto 'Called Back' From 1887 to 1847* (Toronto 1887) 74–5. For the equally interesting stories of police reform in Montreal, see Elinor Kyte Senior 'The Influence of the British Garrison on the Development of the Montreal Police, 1832–1853' *Military Affairs* XLIII (1979) 63–8, and in Saint John, M.G. Marquis 'The Police Force in Saint John, New Brunswick, 1860–1890' MA thesis, University of New Brunswick, 1980.

110 Jarvis 'Mid Victorian Toronto' 89–90

111 Toronto Police Order Book, 1859–63, 24 February 1859, Toronto Police Museum

112 Ibid 16 March 1859

113 Ibid 30 March 1859

114 Ibid 23 May, 11 July 1859

115 Ibid 5 July, 21 March, 8, 9 August, and 12 November 1859

116 Gerner *The Franchise* 116–17
117 Recent accounts include: Sean Conway 'Upper Canadian Orangeism in The Nineteenth Century: Aspects of a Pattern of Disruption' MA thesis, Queen's University, 1977; Ann MacDermaid 'The Visit of the Prince of Wales to Kingston in 1860' *Historic Kingston* XXI (1973) 50–61; and J.D. Livermore 'The Orange Order and the Election of 1861 in Kingston' in Gerald Tulchinsky ed *To Preserve and Defend: Essays on Kingston in the Nineteenth Century* (Montreal 1976) 245–60.
118 Minute Book, District Lodge, 9, 15, 22, 30 August, 3, 5, 27 September 1860; *Globe* 30, 31 August, 1, 4, 5, 6, 8 September 1860
119 The Toronto events are described in: A British Canadian [H.J. Morgan] *The Tour of H.R.H. The Prince of Wales Through British America* (Montreal 1860) 156–74, and J.G.D. Englehart *Journal of the Progress of H.R.H. The Prince of Wales* (London 1860) 56–8. For Newcastle's own account, see John Martineau *The Life of Henry Pelham, Fifth Duke of Newcastle 1811–1864* (London 1908) 297–9. See also Kinahan Cornwallis *Royalty in the New World; or, The Prince of Wales in America* (New York 1860) 127–8. For a full description of events in Kingston and Belleville, see William Shannon *Narrative of the Proceedings of the Loyal Orangemen of Kingston and Belleville* (Belleville 1861). See also *Address Presented to H.R.H. The Prince of Wales During His State Visit to British North America, 1860* (London 1860). For a general view, see James A. Gibson 'The Duke of Newcastle and British North American Affairs, 1855–64' *Canadian Historical Review* XLIV (1963) 142–56.
120 Cornwallis *Royalty* 128
121 Conway 'Upper Canadian Orangeism' 119
122 Lovelock 'Reminiscences' 19
123 'Resolution Passed at a Meeting of the Provincial Grand Orange Lodge of Canada West, Head at Hamilton, Wednesday, October 24, 1860' broadside, University of Western Ontario Archives, London, Ontario
124 Conway 'Upper Canadian Orangeism' 134
125 Jarvis 'Mid Victorian Toronto' 62–5. See also C.P. Stacey 'Confederation: The Atmosphere of Crisis' and Bruce W. Hodgins 'Democracy and the Ontario Fathers of Confederation' in Ontario Historical Society *Profiles of a Province: Studies in the History of Ontario* (Toronto 1967) 59–72 and 83–91, respectively.
126 Akenson 'Ontario: Whatever Happened to the Irish?' 241
127 Eileen and Stephen Yeo 'Ways of Seeing: Control and Leisure versus Class and Struggle' 128–54 in Eileen and Stephen Yeo ed *Popular Culture and Class Conflict 1590–1914: Explorations in the History of Labour and Leisure* (Brighton 1981)
128 Robert L. Fraser 'Like Eden in Her Summer Dress: Gentry, Economy and

Society: Upper Canada 1812–1840' PhD thesis, University of Toronto, 1979, 222. See also S.F. Wise 'John Macaulay: Tory for All Seasons' in Tulchinsky ed *To Preserve and Defend* 185–202.

129 On the new hegemony, see A.W. Rasporich 'The Development of Political and Social Ideas in the Province of Canada, 1848–1858' PhD thesis, University of Toronto, 1970, especially 495–503.

130 *Globe* 24 December 1859

131 Ibid 13 July 1855

132 Eileen and Stephen Yeo 'Ways of Seeing' 141–2. Here they make use of a most effective metaphor, namely blotting paper, arguing that the 'absorbents are affected by what they absorb ... eventually there's more ink than blotting paper in which case a new medium is needed by those who wish to mop up.'

133 Senior 'Gowan' 313

134 Eileen and Stephen Yeo 'Perceived Patterns: Competition and Licence versus Class and Struggle' in Eileen and Stephen Yeo ed *Popular Culture and Class Conflict* 271–305

Captain Bob and the Noble Ward

Neighbourhood and provincial politics in nineteenth-century Toronto

Samuel Reid, aged 17, was knifed to death during an election in Toronto in 1855. The inquest was sensational. Alderman Robert Moodie, aged 37, died of consumption in Toronto in 1865. The funeral was spectacular. Between these two deaths Macaulaytown, the working-class neighbourhood in Toronto which the two men inhabited, became the prize to be won in city-wide elections. This is a study of the way neighbourhood politics spilled over into Toronto as a whole in the decade before Confederation. The knifing in 1855 resulted from a conflict between taverns and lodges on one side and the chapels on the other. The funeral in 1865 celebrated the achievement of a sectarian alliance between the two sides. It is also a study of the deference that two rich provincial rivals found they had to pay poorer voters if their investments and other schemes for urban and national development were not to be thwarted.

T HEY GAVE BOB MOODIE a grand farewell. He had inspired and organized many a cavalcade in Toronto, and he would have been gratified by this one. It took the funeral procession a quarter of an hour to pass a single point. The mayor of Toronto and the police magistrate were pallbearers, together with past grand master Ogle Gowan, the supreme grand secretary of the Orange Order, and two officers of the Manchester Unity of Odd Fellows. The city council and a thousand beribboned lodge brothers accompanied the hearse, and other citizens fell in behind them. There were sixty-six carriages; the gentry, too, was there in force. 'Four hours before,' said the *Globe*, 'all the adjacent streets were filled with spectators and large numbers of vehicles.' After a Presbyterian service in his home on Colborne Street the procession threaded its way to St James' Cemetery on the slopes above the Don River where three more services were read, one Anglican, one Orange, one Odd Fellow. 'The streets were one mass of heads along the route, and windows and places were there was standing room were crowded.'[1]

How did an alderman, tavern-keeper, and mariner command such attention? He was only 37 years old (certainly cause for grief at early passing). How had there been time enough to build such a reputation among townspeople of every rank? His death had not been unexpected, though consumption (the word doctors used to describe the disease) stirred deep emotion in the nineteenth century.[2] The funeral took place on a Sunday, which was the only day of the week on which wage earners were free from work. It was early June 1865. Summer had come late. As recently as 12 May the thermometer had fallen to eighteen degrees Fahrenheit, and there was ice again on the ground on the 23rd. Instead of lining the dusty streets families on one of the first temperate Sundays of the year might be expected to relax by the lakefront or under the trees in one of Toronto's parks.

Admittedly, a trip to the island was impossible. Bob Moodie had been skipper of the excursion steamer *Firefly*. No passenger boat moved on the bay that day. There was still College Avenue (roughly the University Avenue of today), a long shady stretch of grass leading up the slope to the broad park around the university. The dead man's memory, however, lingered there as well. No cross-street interrupted the avenue between Queen and Bloor streets; wheeled traffic moving between east and west in the upper half of the city must make a long detour. In 1859 the city council had decided to continue Agnes Street over the avenue, thus cutting this promenade in two. (The year 1859 was the only term during the last decade of his life for which Moodie had failed to gain election to council.) Paling fences were built to flank the proposed road-bed, with gates permitting pedestrians to go from one side of the Agnes Street extension to the other. Three nights after unknown protestors had torn these gates off their hinges, aldermen angrily debated a motion to revoke the plan:

About this time a rush of three or four hundred persons was made into the gallery and space outside the bar of Council. A good deal of shouting and stamping and falling upstairs and wearing of hats and other unusual demonstrations ensued. Then a deputation appeared at the bar consisting of Captain Moodie, Mr George Platt and Mr John Wilson who wished to be heard against the continuance of the College Avenue obstruction ... Captain R. Moodie said it was high time that the citizens should look to their rights. They wanted justice and were bound to have it. In this country Jack was as good as his master. And they appeared there that evening to protest against the members of that Council putting money in their own pockets at the expense of the city. What good was this street opening to the citizens at large? Was it justice to the 60,000 inhabitants of Toronto that this street should be cut through and their fine Avenue disfigured for the accommodation of four members of that Council?[3]

Council voted there and then to pull down the fence and cancel the Agnes Street contract, upon which Moodie and the mayor drove to College Avenue to pacify several hundred people who were throwing stones at the palings. It re-established Moodie as champion of popular liberties. He never lost an election again.

But why should the Liberal, puritan, sabbatarian *Globe* report the Sunday funeral of an Orange innkeeper so fulsomely? Almost a decade earlier, George Brown, the paper's publisher, had vied with the Tories for Moodie's support. When Brown stood for the parliamentary seat of Toronto in December 1857 he brought young Moodie on to the hustings to second his nomination. In a few crisp words the *Globe* presented all it believed voters should know of the endorsement: 'What I want to see [Moodie was reported as saying] is national and sectarian feeling done away with. I want to see no Englishman, no Irishman, no Scotchman, but all united to put down those who have trampled on our rights ... Come up to the polls and vote like men and Protestants.'[4]

At the parliamentary elections of 1858 and 1861 Moodie switched his support back to Conservative candidates, but by the time of the 1863 election he was in alliance with George Brown again, waging a belligerently Protestant campaign. Brown's candidate for mayor in January 1864 was Orange Grand Master Francis H. Medcalf, who defeated a more conventionally Conservative rival by 2,267 votes to 2,122. In St John's Ward, Moodie's home territory, Medcalf received 605 of the 848 votes cast, which ensured his margin of victory across the whole city. In 1865 Medcalf took five-sevenths of all the votes in the city; the tally in St John was 790 to 71.[5]

The *Leader*, an opposing newspaper, wrote a brief obituary of Bob Moodie five months after that election: 'He was a man of ardent temperament and had great power over those who acknowledged his lead.'[6] Who was this man? And who acknowledged his lead?

In answering these questions we shall also bring to light the interests and ambitions of much richer men than Moodie and his following. Within his ward large landlords sought to advance their concerns: the squire John Beverley Robinson, Jr, the contractor John Bugg, the former slave Wilson Abbott. Across the city railroad directors (such as Robinson), contractors, lawyers, merchants, tavern-keepers, and property owners in general contended for control of city council. And at the provincial level the candidacies of Robinson, George Brown, and others were financed by, and served to promote, their landed estates, shareholdings, and distributive networks. In return for permission to pursue the politics of enterprise, Moodie's Toronto expected Torontocentric sectarianism from wealthy aspirants to office.

According to the family headstone, Robert Moodie had been born in Ireland in the late 1820s, as had his brother James.[7] They must have reached Canada in infancy because Robert traced his career as a defender of the province's British integrity back to the turmoil of 1838 when, as a nine-year-old cook's mate on the steamer *Cobourg*, he had rolled cannonballs across the deck to the gunners so that loyalists could defeat rebels and Yankees at the battle of Prescott, along the St Lawrence. The *Cobourg*'s cook had been Francis P. Johnston, who later kept a tavern on Elizabeth Street in Toronto, around the corner from Moodie's own home. Johnston chaired the meeting of 'coloured voters' in Moodie's Tavern, to which Bob told this heroic tale of his childhood.[8] Perhaps Johnston was himself black, which could explain why the city council always rejected his nomination as ward assessor or custodian of the polling place whenever his municipal representatives put his name forward.[9]

Robert and James seem to have been brought up on the river and lake. Official records usually called them 'sailor' or 'mariner.'[10] On the assessment roll for 1853, the first year in which St John was a separate ward, Robert owned his home in Teraulay Street (the name given then to Bay Street north of Queen), a vacant house on one side, and a vacant lot on the other. In 1854 he owned six houses, James living next door as his brother's tenant. By 1856, his first full year on council, he held eight houses on the west side of Teraulay Street, declaring an annual rental of £140, a taxable income of £250, personal property of £15, and a dog at home; he was also building two houses on Avenue Street worth £90 annually, between properties belonging to James Lukin Robinson and John Beverley Robinson, Jr. Down in the harbour rode his two-storey side-wheel steamer *Firefly* which began running to the island in 1855. In 1854 there is mention of a steam ferry called *Bob Moodie*, and in 1857 the *Lady Head*; in the latter year Moodie apparently introduced the earliest tugboat into Toronto Bay.[11]

For many months each year the bay was clogged with ice. Sailors had to turn their hands to other work. By the second half of the 1850s Moodie's Bowling Alley and Tavern on Teraulay Street flourished as a social and political centre, while in the summer of 1856 James Moodie leased a bowling alley opposite the wood market on Front Street, repaired, painted, and papered it, and opened there a saloon with tables served by waiters.[12] In the last days of 1857, less than a week after Councilman Robert Moodie had helped win a seat in Parliament for George Brown, council overwhelmingly approved the lease to James Moodie of five acres of Toronto Island for building a hotel and pleasure grounds.[13] The following April the storm that permanently swept away the sandbar connecting the island to the mainland also demolished Quinn's Hotel (John Quinn attended the same lodge as the Moodies and co-operated with them as a ferryman).[14] Freed of all competition, the brothers advertised that the *Firefly* would take people every evening in the summer to 'a Quadrille Party in Moodie's Magnificent New Ball Room,' admission to which was free.[15]

During the winters of 1855–6 and 1856–7 (at least) Robert worked for the Grand Trunk Railway, then under construction, managing 'a small propellor' that carried stone to build the embankment along the line and lakefront.[16] When his close friend John Hutchison was mayor in 1857, he secured a contract to pump out stagnant water lying between the tracks and the bay.[17]

Once Bob Moodie became politically formidable, jobs and leases might be won easily enough. Once he had gained a foothold as landlord and boatowner the accumulation of more land and more vessels would follow, for the period until 1857 was one of continental prosperity. Toronto grew fast. Housing and entertainment were both in great demand. Anyone who provided either earned a good income and might be able to borrow heavily against the future. This explained how an established proprietor increased his assets, but it could not explain how a former cook's mate came into possession of the *Firefly* in the first place, or how he collected sufficient town lots by his mid-twenties to qualify for public office and thus step on to this escalator. Apart from his own exuberant account of the battle of Prescott, Moodie's life before his municipal career remains obscure.

Conviviality was the stock in trade of the master of a bowling alley, a saloon, a pleasure ground, a ferry boat. Hospitality and electioneering merged imperceptibly into each other. The *Firefly* sailed often on moonlight or holiday excursions, sometimes free of charge to the group being treated.[18] Even following his regular timetable, however, Captain Moodie could make himself generally known to the complete cross-section of society that trod his decks. No mere tavern-keeper could hope to match his access to the women, children, and teetotal men of Toronto.

A satirical weekly wrote of a short, square-built, deep-chested man, clad in a pea-jacket, walking with a nautical gait, his nut-brown face surrounded by a rugged beard and close cropped hair.[19] This portrait agrees with other descriptions: a stocky jaunty figure, bearded as befitted a sailor (beards were just then becoming fashionable with the young), gregarious, garrulous. Hostile reports dwelt on his rough speech, his belligerence, his tobacco chewing and spitting, but even writers who labelled him 'Capting Bob' might temper condescension with good humour. On the declaration of the municipal polls each January, as soon as the successful candidate for mayor had spoken, the crowd would call for Bob Moodie, a tribute not only to the size of the entourage that followed him those icy nights into St Lawrence Hall but also to the gusto with which he regaled them all.

Moodie's entourage haled from 'the noble ward of St John,' the most recently gazetted of Toronto's seven divisions. If he had not himself bestowed the epithet 'the noble ward,' he was certainly its most enthusiastic popularizer. The epithet impudently asserted the boisterous, plebeian, clannish qualities of public life there. St John had been set apart in December 1852, being the congested eastern half of the most populous ward in the city, St Patrick, which had until then covered the entire quadrant of Toronto north of Queen Street and west of Yonge. St John had Yonge Street for its eastern boundary and College Avenue, 660 yards away, along its western side; it extended one and a quarter miles north from Queen Street to the city limits at Bloor.[20] The core of the ward was the neighbourhood known as Macaulaytown. Over the first dozen years of its independent existence, Moodie worked to mobilize its residents into an electoral force with which every aspirant for the mayoralty or for Parliament must reckon.

Queen and Yonge streets, which bordered St John's Ward, were two of the three high roads into the city. A busy ribbon of workshops, stores, hostelries, and stables developed along them. Behind their intersection the working-class village of Macaulaytown grew during the 1830s, some of the population serving the high roads' traffic and the rest settling there because of the cheaper land and housing on what had begun as the outskirts of the town. As the traffic increased and Toronto expanded, Macaulaytown became more densely peopled. Vacant lots disappeared under wood and brick.[21]

By superficial calculation, St John was the poorest of the seven wards. It had the lowest rateable value per capita at the end of the 1850s, $25 per head, by comparison with $110 for St George on the western lakefront, and $38 for what was left of St Patrick. Even St David in the northeast, which included Cabbagetown, was assessed at $30 per head.[22] The value of property nearer the lake was swollen by the presence of warehouses, factories, and public buildings, by wharfs, markets, and railways, while St David included expensive blocks along King Street, and St Patrick, less congested where it was built up and with large areas not yet subdivided, had a lower ratio of people to rateable land. The poorest people of all tended to live furthest from work (on the far fringes of St Patrick or St David), or in back alleys near the large employers of casual labour by the waterfront and market square. Thus Macaulaytown, a long-established precinct behind the road junction, was undoubtedly working class, generally poor, but not as impoverished as some other sections of Toronto.[23]

St John's Ward held many workplaces, but few that employed large numbers. Its rateable value per capita was not inflated by much wealthy business. The ward's workers and the ward's residents tended to be the same people, its electorate relatively unleavened by substantial entrepreneurs, either as neighbours or as absentee employers. Despite the existence of a franchise tied to property (an annual value of £8, freehold or rental, in the late 1850s), its non-electors were less distinct in their interests from those of the electors than they would be in precincts where boarding-houses or shanties on the one hand (haunts of the unenfranchised), and villas or factories on the other, were more common. Male non-electors tended to be workmates or relatives of men who had the vote. The skilled and semi-skilled workers of St John could dominate polls and public meetings less challenged by people above or below them than could be the case elsewhere in the city.

St John was relatively homogeneous in a third way. Only 18.9 per cent of the population in the northwest quarter of the city in 1851 had been Catholic; the proportion had been 28.2 per cent for the rest of Toronto and 34.5 per cent for St David, the ward with the next lowest average rateable value. More than half the Protestants, here as elsewhere in Toronto, called themselves members of the Church of England or the (Anglican) Church of Ireland. But in the northwest the proportion of Methodists was highest (17.5 per cent, compared with 12.9 per cent for the rest of the city), as was the proportion of Presbyterians who were not affiliated with the Church of Scotland (14.6 per cent of the district's population). Most of Toronto's small Baptist communion lived here too.[24] Nowhere, in other words, were there more Protestants, and in no other ward did so large a proportion of Protestants reject the churches established in England, Ireland, and Scotland and worship instead in nonconformist chapels. St John was united by its Protestantism, yet more evenly split than elsewhere between 'chapel' and 'church.'

There were, of course, some large land-owners and landlords interested in the ward. Much of the northern section was owned by 1854 by Dr Alister M. Clark, a railway and bank director, for whom there is little evidence of involvement in neighbourhood politics, though he can be tentatively identified as an Anglican Tory.[25] Clark's estate was described on the 1856 assessment roll as vacant land, but it was already platted by Clarendon Place, Surrey Place, and Grenville, Grosvenor, Breadalbane, and St Albans streets, and included twenty-four empty lots facing Yonge Street.

There were remnants, too, of the old Park Lot aristocracy. At the founding of the town of York sixty years earlier, park lots, fronting what became Queen Street, one-eighth of a mile wide and 1¼ miles deep, were granted to provincial dignitaries. Three of these grants made up the whole of St John. They belonged, from east to west, to the Macaulays, the Elmsleys, and the Robinsons. When John Simcoe Macaulay married Ann Elmsley in 1825, the boundary between those two parcels was shifted to give the husband the combined Queen Street frontage, which he subdivided to make Macaulay-town. After a series of humiliating electoral defeats, Macaulay abandoned Canada for England in 1843. His agent sold off 'the grass parks of Teraulay' over the next ten years, including the northern section that came into Dr Clark's possession. Macaulay's brother, a judge, lived on Yonge Street and retained valuable vacant land there, but was precluded by office from playing an active role at elections. Captain John Elmsley owned undeveloped acres further up Yonge Street, but his conversion to Catholicism limited his influence among his Protestant neighbours.[26]

It was the third park lot family, the Robinsons, that still strove to assert a squirely prerogative over the residents. Chief Justice Robinson's second son and namesake, John Beverley, Jr, had been alderman for the old undivided St Patrick, which he continued to represent after its partition at the end of 1852. Whenever he canvassed for mayor he demanded all the votes from St John as well. 'My brother and I,' he told the council on one of these occasions, 'are the mainstay of the labourers in that ward' and have created much of its housing. 'The Mayor's brother erected the buildings spoken of,' a jaundiced alderman conceded, 'but the fact is they are only shanties.'[27] That brother, James Lukin Robinson, was returned unopposed as alderman for St John at its very first poll in January 1853, but resentment aroused by the automatic assumption of Robinsonian rights and Lukin's dismay at the unruliness of council deterred him from ever standing again. He was a shy prudent man who withdrew gladly into the quiet enjoyment of company directorships and husbandry of the family's real estate.[28] John Beverley, however, continued to insist that St John's representatives defer to him as benefactor and squire, a pretension that Robert Moodie would spend part of his career opposing adamantly.

John Beverley was the antithesis of his brother – robust, extroverted, inordinately eager for acclaim. Thanks to the talents and verve of his wife, the daughter of a judge, a renowned hostess, and a fine singer who had the sublime self-confidence to insist on singing for Jenny Lind, Robinson dispensed hospitality to upper- and middle-class couples and became patron of the city's genteel entertainment. Husband and wife also became patrons of the city's sportsmen. People with fallible memories thought of Robinson as the best boxer and cricketer of his generation, which simply reflected his ability to keep his name before the sporting public long after he and his rivals retired from contest. His achievements in the ring and on the cricket field were more accurately represented by the results of the Toronto Athletic Games of 1841, when he placed second in four different events. John Beverley Robinson, Jr, was a natural occupant of second place whose family name, wife's accomplishments, deep purse, and animal energy combined to advance him above others more gifted than himself.[29]

Second place, however, is only one step from first. In Toronto, where there were two aldermen for every ward and two local members of Parliament, running second still won a prize. Wily men cultivated this rich patrician, who was so transparently keen to please. They wanted him compliantly to fill a back bench behind their ministry or to act as a makeweight on their company board. The Robinsons and their relatives by marriage owned a great amount of rural land. They were deeply interested in promoting railways that would run across their estates and increase their price vastly. A referendum in Toronto in June 1850 had rejected by more than three to one a campaign managed by Robinson and his brothers-in-law to commit the city to investing £100,000 in the projected Northern Railway. Citizens rightly trusted neither the motives nor the competence of these heirs of the Family Compact. The businessmen who ultimately did put together the Northern, the Great Western, and the various sections of the Grand Trunk nevertheless found a prominent place on their boards for Robinson in particular, recognizing the prestige and wealth that the Compact possessed. And Robinson co-operated fully. The location of railway stations on family land was one of many consequences. The railway interest and Robinson's ambition converged on Moodie in the second half of the 1850s, and, as we shall see, three sensationally bitter elections resulted.[30]

Although John Beverley Robinson, Jr, claimed St John's allegiance, he was never rash enough to stand there himself. The men who won seats beside his brother Lukin at the ward's initial poll represented forces far removed from patrician Toryism. Alderman Ogle Gowan was the elder statesman of the Orange Order, Councilman John Bugg a leader of Primitive Methodism, and Councilman Robert Dodds a Baptist;[31] when Dodds resigned before the end of the term, his place was filled by William Hall, carpenter, Ulsterman, and Methodist.[32] The chapel vote was strong in St John, stronger by far than the Compact's following, and at least as strong as the Orange lodge. Chapel-goers had consistently supported the Reform party against the Tories, who were shunned as advocates of church establishment. The chapel vote accompanied John Bugg and his friends as they moved from Reform to Liberalism in the political transformation of the 1850s.

In 1854 Bugg's successful running mate was William Rowell, a builder, but one of Rowell's brothers, Joseph, was Bugg's more constant municipal companion. A blacksmith and wagonmaker, Joseph Rowell owned his workshop and adjoining properties on Queen Street, close to its junction with Yonge, a location that brought much business. Being a successful artisan, a small landlord, and a lay preacher, he qualified for leadership among chapel-going workingmen – but only in John Bugg's shadow.[33]

Bugg threw a very large shadow indeed. He was a burly, hearty man, a Yorkshire carpenter who had become a builder and lumber merchant in Toronto and accumulated, alone or with a partner, substantial parcels of land from the Macaulay estate.[34] His home and lumber yard stood at the centre of the ward. As one of the largest landlords, employers, and contractors, Bugg had much to gain from election to council. He was technically St John's senior representative, having served already as councilman for St Patrick. Seniority mattered, for the first item of council business after each election was appointment of a select committee to nominate members of standing committees. The custom had developed, to limit dissension, that the senior representative of each ward (and no other) should sit on this select committee. Each year, then, Bugg could ensure that he was nominated his ward's member of the board of works, the basic instrument for patronage and performance at neighbourhood level. Subsequent council minutes rarely showed Bugg moving or seconding a motion except where it pertained to the returning officer and polling place for St John.[35] Apart from the patronage involved, a sympathetic returning officer and landlord of the polling place enhanced the chance of election. Maintaining an unbroken sequence of re-election was crucial to secure one's position on the nominating committee and on the board of works. There were times when questions were asked about sales of lumber to the city, or the disposition of road gangs, but colleagues around the table were reluctant to follow up allegations of conflict of interest lest the inquiry extend impartially to them as well.[36]

Bugg and Moodie contended for years for political control of the ward. A Primitive Methodist such as John Bugg found few friends in taverns, lodge rooms, or firehalls. Although Joseph Rowell was captain of Number 3 Engine Company,[37] the firehall was as much Bob Moodie's territory as the lodge and tavern. The halls were clubhouses for boisterous young men, with opportunity to drink while waiting for the excitement and danger of a blaze. St

John's volunteer company was an Orange preserve. Catholic Irishmen claimed that they shuttered their windows whenever St John's fire bell rang, particularly on days of procession such as 17 March, Corpus Christi, and 12 July.[38]

Jingoism might ring the bell as readily as sectarianism. On the night of 12 July 1855 a fight broke out in Maryanne Armstrong's speak-easy between local revellers and the clown of a travelling circus. The outnumbered stranger used his professional skill to wound two of his assailants severely. The next night a crowd searched for 'the damn Yankee son of a bitch.' Instructed by the hook and ladder company, the crowd set the circus wagons alight and pulled the tent down on the performers. Joseph Bird of the hook and ladder company was injured in the melee and carried to his tavern on Queen Street. Two of the alleged ringleaders, William Hopkins and William Dunwoodie, claimed they had visited Bird's bedside before they obeyed the clamour of St John's engine house bell and set off for the glow on the horizon. But Hopkins had early in the night been asked to stop breaking up the wagons by Constable Keary (called 'a damned Papist' for his pains), and the mayor and the chief of police agreed that Dunwoodie had been urging the crowd to take the Yankees prisoner until, on the mayor's insistence, Dunwoodie used his acknowledged influence over the rioters to restrain them.[39]

The named participants in the circus riot were Bob Moodie's close friends. His own brother James was brought before the police court, but discharged without penalty. Many of the ward's political meetings were held at Bird's Tavern. Hopkins, a tailor, had been the master of Lodge 301 when it received its warrant in 1844, and he was still master. Moodie was a member of 301 (which had assumed the name of Lodge Temperance); Hopkins would be a constant political ally and would stand surety for Caroline Moodie when she was appointed executor of her husband's intestate affairs.[40] And Dunwoodie, cabinet-maker, master of Lodge 212 on Yonge Street, chaired electoral meetings on Brother Moodie's behalf.[41]

A few months after the circus riot, Dunwoodie became a hero to Protestants across the province. A convention of Irish Catholics living in the United States had been held in Buffalo. Harassed as they were by Know-Nothing nativism, the delegates resolved on a scheme of emigration to Canada. Their friends in Toronto applauded this decision at an excited public meeting, which Dunwoodie attended in order to denounce the scheme from the floor. His brave but quixotic intervention was lauded soon after by a meeting of several thousand Irish Protestants who crammed St Lawrence Hall in protest against the threatened invasion. He was called to the platform of that second gathering: 'If there are any descendants of the brave boys of

Derry,' he cried, 'they ought to throw themselves heart and soul into this movement.' Many testimonials of approval reached Dunwoodie, including an address from Lodge 212 which thanked him for standing against those who were 'devising means of flooding Protestant Upper Canada with the rebellious offscourings of the United States.'⁴² Sectarian and national slogans were fused in this address.

It was with the backing of ardent artisans like these that Robert Moodie stood for licence inspector in St John in 1854. The man he beat by 271 votes to 260 was a fellow Orangeman, James Spence, carpenter, builder, small landlord. Spence was almost twenty years older than he was and far more respectful of the Compact families; his name had led the long requisition from humbly born electors who had begged James Lukin Robinson to represent them the year before, and he would continue to support the Robinsons even when Moodie turned against them. Spence inspired feelings of loyalty in turn. He became, for example, licence inspector the next year when Moodie stood for councilman; sixteen months later the grateful innkeepers of St John gave him a silver hunting watch and appendages 'as a token of esteem and respect ... for his impartiality and assiduity in the discharge of his duty.'⁴³ Less happily, it was Spence's own nephew who died one election night believing he was avenging physical injury done to his uncle.

This violent election took place in January 1855. It was Moodie's first attempt at council. The Reformer Joseph Sheard stood for one of the aldermanic positions, Bugg and Joseph Rowell stood together for the two councilman's seats in St John. A ticket formed to oppose them: Richard Dempsey for alderman, Robert Moodie for councilman, and James Spence for licence inspector. Dempsey, a lawyer, had sat for six years as an alderman in another ward and was deputy grand master of Ogle Gowan's branch of the Orange Order. The Orange ticket advertised nightly meetings in inns around the ward, a congenial and characteristic form of campaigning.

The two days of election were exceptionally rowdy. Sheard, Rowell, and Spence all suffered injury. A judicial inquiry found Dempsey and Moodie to be beneficiaries of the violence and of the ballots of eight unregistered voters. Dempsey had come second to the city's member of Parliament, John Hillyard Cameron, but only four votes ahead of Sheard, so the judge ruled that Sheard should take the second position. Moodie, who had run behind Bugg, led Rowell by over 100 votes. He, too, was unseated, and an election was called for the vacancy. He stood again. He genially conceded that 'the recent election for your ward having been declared void (as regards myself) on the ground of violence and intimidation,' Rowell's request for strong police supervision of the polling station was totally reasonable. Rowell won the return contest by 10 votes.[44]

In the mean time a sensational inquest, stretching over a week, had been held into the death of Spence's nephew, Samuel Reid.[45] On the night the poll closed Spence got into a fight near his house and was cut badly. Reid went with a friend to a druggist for sticking plaster and on the way home down Elizabeth Street set upon two men whom he thought in the dark to be his uncle's assailants. One of these men cried out 'Murder,' pulled a knife from his pocket, and severed an artery in Reid's thigh. Reid bled to death.

The killing angered the neighbourhood. Hundreds of people went hunting for suspects, rounding people up. At least eight men were arrested, exhaustively cross-examined by the coroner and by Dempsey (representing the bereaved family), and then discharged once the owner of the knife was traced by the name on its handle. Reid's 14-year-old cousin dramatically approached one (innocent) suspect, put her hand on his breast, identified him as the culprit, and fainted. Proceedings took place in city hall to hold the crowds; the hall was packed every day.

This tragic scuffle in the wintry dark tells us more about Macaulaytown than that its politics were aggressive and its family loyalties passionate. The dead man was barely 18 years old. Although a non-elector, he took an active part in the election. He belonged to the Orange Order and to the local fire company, whose members were summoned to his funeral. He and his companion earned their living as carters, a common occupation near the intersection of Queen and Yonge streets. Carters needed a licence from city hall. As recipients of council patronage they could be both recruited and disciplined as council dependants. The licence ensured an income that could raise a man to the ranks of the enfranchised. Carters, too, were sufficiently mobile to swell an alderman's demonstration. As many of them operated from the market square beside city hall or from the nearby wharfs, they could be marshalled readily. When they wanted diversion after hours they could go upstairs to the gallery of the council chambers and cheer or jeer the civic debaters. Opponents of Tory or Orange majorities complained that carters were used as a claque for councillors, to pack meetings, overrun polling places, and dispirit contrary voters. Robert Moodie's career, as we shall see, included the defence of carters' rights against companies or technology that threatened their livelihood.

The inquest also revealed what suspects and witnesses did with their evenings. Some men had come from a shooting gallery, one of them went on to a dancing school. Some attended a meeting of the Bootbinders' Society. A simple lad had been off to look at a sheep that had been killed by dogs in a butcher's yard and to look at the dogs, too. The knife's owner (later acquitted by a jury on his plea of self-defence) was a stone cutter employed building the observatory, who had taken his brother (down from Esquesing over the New Year's break) for a quiet drink after work before going to a schoolmistress's house for a party. One man, Joseph Butler, had been arrested because he was a renowned partisan for Bugg and Rowell, but he was able to prove that he was picking up a coat from a tailor's house at the time of Reid's death and had then gone on to choir practice at a Methodist chapel; indeed, Butler had called at Spence's house earlier, offered to take the injured Spence to the apothecary, left him his own muffler, and, in Spence's words, 'showed greater kindness to me than usual.'

The election in 1856 was a quiet one. The rival tickets shared the seats: Bugg and Dempsey were chosen aldermen, Moodie and Rowell were chosen councilmen, and Spence retained the post of licence inspector. The Orangemen had canvassed thoroughly, Dunwoodie chaired the meeting which opened the campaign, Francis Johnston took the minutes, and James Spence moved the main motion of support for Moodie.[46] There was no doubt of his return. But within weeks he was the centre of another controversy – the Grand Trunk Railway's removal of him from Toronto during the mayoral election.

Until 1859 the mayor of Toronto was chosen by members of council from among their own number. In 1856 Alderman John Beverley Robinson, Jr, from St Patrick insisted that it was his turn to be mayor. There were four wards to the west of Yonge Street and only three to the east, yet every mayor since 1851 had sat for the east end. Robinson demanded the vote of every representative west of Yonge Street. Jonathan Dunn, fellow alderman from St Patrick, an old butcher who had been on council for twenty years, nominated him in such a grudging, jocular, even insulting fashion, that it seemed obvious he was under pressures he detested but could not resist.[47] Robinson's rival, John Hutchison, merchant, came from the eastern lakefront. Bob Moodie lived west of Yonge Street but sailed his steamer from the eastern lakeshore; the Yonge Street division meant little to him. Hutchison, moreover, belonged to the Orange Order,[48] while Robinson haughtily asserted proprietary rights over the votes from St John. It was known that Moodie supported Hutchison.

Robinson unabashedly represented the railways on council. Council had the right to appoint a director to the board of the Northern Railway; the Northern Railway coolly informed council that Alderman Robinson filled that position already.[49] During the winter of 1855–6 Moodie was working for the Grand Trunk. Three days before the mayoral election he was ordered to

Montreal, ostensibly to advise on the purchase of a little steamer for the company. He left Toronto in the custody of a superior officer of the railway who exercised a double power over him because he was grand tyler of the Orange lodge. This expulsion from Toronto was a blatant attempt to affect the outcome of the mayoral ballot. In Moodie's absence Robinson defeated Hutchison by four votes, basically the west's majority over the east.[50]

A year later Robinson demanded a second term. He even thought of running his brother, Lukin, in St John, but it would have been senseless, given the loyalty of chapel and Orange to Bugg's and Moodie's slates of candidates respectively. The new council met at noon to select a mayor. With one three-hour break it sat until 2:45 a.m. without result, adjourning to the next evening. The absence of four representatives from the eastern ward of St David immobilized the municipal politicians; the returning officer there had abandoned the poll when rioters stormed the polling station and demolished its porch. Robinson, as retiring mayor, had refused to issue a writ for a fresh election; in consequence it looked as if the four western wards would swamp the two eastern wards represented around the table. Councilman Moodie and Alderman Alexander Manning filibustered through the afternoon and night, suggesting that council itself fill the vacancies in St David from among the candidates at the abandoned election. Robinson's opposition berated the presumption that the Family Compact had a lien on the mayoralty. Moodie in addition berated the arrogance of a man who had him expelled from Toronto twelve months before and who believed he owned the 'Noble Ward.' On the second night, after a massive petition from St David had been presented, an exhausted council co-opted four of the candidates from that ward. All four voted for Hutchison, who gained the chair by 14 votes to 13.[51] Bob Moodie's victory was sweet.

There was more at stake than a single year's spoils, though this was part of the prize. Robinson's mayoral campaign was managed (as his parliamentary campaigns would be) by Alderman John Worthington, perhaps the largest building contractor in Toronto; his teamsters were an effective squadron on election day.[52] Moodie's filibuster for Hutchison was shared by another contractor, Alderman Manning, whose contentious municipal career would stretch into the 1880s.[53] Robinson belonged to the railways. All three railway companies demanded rights of way along the front of the city and investments or concessions from the city as well. Hutchison's brother-in-law led the lobby of water-lot owners who, in fighting for compensation against railway encroachments, might be seen by some people as fighting also for public access to the lake. A steamboat captain such as Moodie, although seasonally employed by the Grand Trunk, valued the bay more highly than the rail.

There had been a victory procession from St John's Ward to city hall only a fortnight before he prevented Robinson's second term; the banner carried before it read: 'Presented to Captain Robert Moodie by the captains and shipowners of Toronto, for his independent conduct in the City Council for the past two years.'[54]

These urban power struggles spilled over into provincial affairs in 1857. A general parliamentary election was held at the end of that year. Robinson was the candidate in Toronto of the Liberal Conservative ministerialists. Moodie seconded the nomination of George Brown, the Liberal antagonist. Moodie had come to see in Brown virtues far transcending mutual detestation of Alderman Robinson.

Militant Protestantism typified North American politics in the 1850s. The Know-Nothings won victories in the United States. Liberalism became increasingly sectarian in western Canada. It was an article of faith that popery threatened both liberty and material progress. Partisans pointed to starving Ireland, Spanish and Austrian repression, the pope's forcible reaction to reform and unification in Italy, and political turmoil in France as proof that Catholicism blighted the lives that it touched. North American Protestants were convinced that the perennial cold war for men's souls was being waged more aggressively than ever before by a reactionary Catholicism. This feeling was sharpened in Canada by the electoral power of the *Canadiens*.[56]

Two issues in particular focused this hostility for many Torontonians in the mid-1850s. One was the new legislation for separate schools, whereby an explicitly Catholic system of education was funded from provincial revenue. In one of his first acts as councilman, Moodie moved that council petition the legislature against the support of separate schools. Aldermen Robinson and Worthington tried to prevent the motion being put. George Brown led the attack in the legislature for which the motion called.[52] Antipathy toward separate schools would bring Brown and Moodie together in 1857 and again in 1863.

The second issue concerned the seat of government.[58] The capital of Canada moved every four years; between 1855 and 1859 it was in Toronto. This meant that townspeople could attend parliamentary debates, of which reports and analyses would appear in the next morning's paper. Lobbying and demonstrations could be mounted while matters were still under consideration. Such immediacy heightened political fervour. Politicians appeared on the streets as flesh-and-blood heroes and villains. George Brown's newspaper, the *Globe*, promoted and dramatized his comprehensively sectionalist and Protestant version of events. In 1856 the legislature voted to locate the capital permanently in Quebec City, the heart of enemy territory, and to spend money on new quarters there. Brown fought that battle in Parliament, too. The Liberals fanned local feeling about the seat of government by calling a tumultuous meeting during the summer of 1856 at which Brown demanded the dismissal of the ministry and the dissolution of Parliament. He crowed in a letter: 'Our St Lawrence Hall affair was a great victory. The Compact never got such a beating ... Only fancy W.B. Robinson [the mayor's uncle] standing pleading piteously before a Toronto audience for a hearing, and the Editor of the *Globe* interfering for him!' His paper summed it up with brutal terseness: 'The whole affair was a magnificent demonstration of the feeling of Protestant Upper Canada against the vile tyranny which has been so long imposed upon her by her priest-led yoke fellow of Lower Canada.'[59]

Orangemen such as Moodie, Dunwoodie, and Hopkins thrilled to such rhetoric. Lodge brothers in the audience had swelled the cheering, despite the appeals of Ogle Gowan (the senior Orange politician) who climbed on the platform beside W.B. Robinson in an attempt to defend the Liberal Conservative ministry. The Orange Order was fundamentally split. Gowan, Dempsey, and other traditional leaders remembered the hostility shown by Liberals and the *Globe* toward Orangeism, and they saw sense in separating Protestants and Catholics from school days onwards. But many in the ranks, younger men particularly, detested the use of public funds and the threatened loss of the capital. The *Globe* on its side stopped calling Orangemen thugs as it used to do and renamed them patriots misled by cynical time-serving officers. It switched from contempt for the glorious Twelfth of July to fulsome description of it, saying of the order: 'Its fundamental principles, fairly carried out, are all conducive to the growth of constitutional liberty and the best interests of religion.'[60]

Brown represented a rural riding where he had business interests. But he enjoyed, in the *Globe*, a huge investment in Toronto too and, thanks to the *Globe*, an electioneering vehicle there. Being returned for the capital would cement his claim to leadership over his party colleagues. So he stood for the city, nominated by the young grand secretary of the loyal Orange lodge and seconded by Captain Moodie, whose exuberant speech from the hustings was quoted in the opening paragraphs of this essay. It was a two-member constituency: Brown got 2,361 votes, John Beverley Robinson, Jr, 2,319, and William Henry Boulton 2,197. 'The opposition candidate owes his success,' said the hostile *Leader*, 'to the superhuman exertions of Bob Moodie, his guide, protector and friend.' More than two-thirds of the 842 electors of St John cast a vote for Brown; many of them had spat upon Liberal canvassers in the past. The Loyal Orange Prentice Boys of Derry thanked Captain Bob for 'the great victory which we as Protestants achieved, chiefly through your instrumentality'; in reply he invoked the principles 'for which our fathers bled and died' and described George Brown 'ever on the watchtower, guarding our sacred liberties from the attacks of the Church of Rome.'[61]

Boulton's unsuccessful campaign revealed how good a hater Moodie could be. Moodie had tried to yoke Brown and Boulton together. Boulton had been the Orangemen's friend in earlier years as mayor and parliamentarian. He was also Robinson's cousin, however, and he hoped by neutrality to gain the second vote of both his rivals' supporters. Finding himself lagging after the first day of polling (and already quoted as supporting separate schools) he threw himself into coalition with Robinson on the second day. Moodie had stigmatized Robinson as little better than a Catholic; Boulton's alleged apostasy, following his alleged opportunism on the first day, meant (so Moodie shouted characteristically) that he could never be trusted by honest men again. Less than a year later came the reckoning. Boulton, then mayor, clashed with the chief of police. Alderman Moodie moved, successfully, that council support the chief of police. The mayor in consequence submitted his resignation. Moodie forced its acceptance through council. Boulton never held high office again.[62]

The Protestant alliance between chapel and lodge, forged in Brown's campaign, was intense but short-lived. John Bugg and Bob Moodie stood, unopposed, as aldermen on a common ticket. More astounding still, Bugg, the longest-serving representative for the ward, nominated Moodie to the ward's seat on the board of works, the key committee of council, on which the senior member invariably placed himself to control day-by-day patronage. Moodie reciprocated by moving that James Spence not be appointed assessor of rates for St John, and neither should other old friends who had stayed with Robinson receive any post in the gift of council. But he was also being wooed furiously from the other side. It was Alderman Worthington (Robinson's campaign manager) who moved council's approval of James Moodie's lease on Toronto Island for a hotel and pleasure ground – this less than a fortnight after the election.[63] Robinson's men no longer treated him as an underling, but as a powerbroker to be won back.

Brown seemed to take Moodie for granted once he had served his purpose. On St Patrick's Day, Alderman Moodie was found looking on while a crowd stoned a hotel at whose dinner D'Arcy McGee was guest of honour. Brown's association with his fellow Liberal McGee galled Moodie, who had severed friendships for the sake of a single-mindedly Protestant champion. Brown not only failed ever to consult him, he claimed, but he also went back on a pledge to promote incorporation of the Orange Order by voting with McGee against it. Moodie added that Brown's parliamentary alliances imperilled Toronto's case for the seat of government. By April Alderman Bugg and Alderman Moodie were enemies on council again. By July, Robinson, Worthington, and Moodie walked arm in arm into Liberal meetings to disrupt them.[64]

Robinson consequently thought he held the upper hand when George Brown unexpectedly had to stand for re-election in August (as a result of forming a two-day government, the one that was ousted by the Double Shuffle). As the city's other member, he believed he should choose the anti-Brown candidate. Instead Moodie, no more deferential than before, drafted a candidate himself, a former cabinet minister and eminent Conservative, thus pre-empting Robinson. This man was John Hillyard Cameron, soon to be Orange grand master for British North America. Cameron suited Moodie well, for he was as sectarian as Brown and a critic of the temporizing ministry that Robinson supported. Moodie had locked Robinson effectively out of the election, but he also lost ground himself, for Cameron failed, though narrowly, by 2,516 votes to 2,660. In St John, Bugg's candidate led Moodie's by 80 votes. Not all of those who had followed him in support of the Clear Grit publisher in 1857 swung away with him in 1858. What would appear, to fervent practising politicians such as aldermen and worshipful masters, as hypocrisy and betrayal in Brown could be invisible or trivial in laymen's eyes. Some people now called Moodie 'turn-coat Bob.'[65]

'Moodie who, a year ago, reminded one of Ceccio del Vecchio of Bulwer's *Rienzi*, and who seemed to have the city at his feet; to be almost in the position to dictate who should represent the city in parliament, cannot now be elected councilman for the ward which, last year, he represented as alderman. Verily, humbug has its day.'[66] Thus the *Leader* gleefully reported his defeat by John Bugg and a Reform sweep of council in 1859. In that year of economic depression cries of retrenchment displaced many sitting council members. There had been much talk of petty corruption, some of it touching Moodie with his waterfront contracts, his brother's hotel on the island, and the preference given his bosom friend, the tailor William Hopkins, in tendering to provide coats for the police force.[67] But Bugg was a notorious contractor also. The struggle in St John lay basically between chapel and tavern and was tipped by Moodie's affront to the admirers of too many provincial politicians at once.

The Reformers lasted one term only. They did not keep rates down and in limiting tavern licences they tampered with many people's pleasures. This was the year when Captain Bob led the rush upstairs into the council chambers that reversed the decision to construct a road and fence across College Avenue, a decision that Bugg outspokenly defended, as it would have enhanced his property values and business. In 1860 tavern triumphed over chapel. The victory parade down the slope from Macaulaytown featured John Bugg in effigy, seated in an ass-drawn cart.[68]

Moodie realized he must survive in his own ward if he hoped to sway the province as a whole. Bugg was the immediate threat, and behind him stood George Brown who was thus an electoral as well as a moral impossibility. A truce with Robinson might recapture every last Conservative, Orangeman, and anti-Grit. It made sense for Robinson in turn to speak fair to Moodie, who had shown a great talent for thwarting his plans. By the time Robinson sought re-election to Parliament in 1861, Moodie had an honoured place in his entourage and (audaciously) counselled people against fanning old prejudices of race and creed. The city was now divided into two single-member electorates. Robinson won the west with the help of St John; Brown lost the east as crowds from the Noble Ward swarmed across Yonge Street to make a clamour at the hustings and intimidate Liberal voters at the polls.[69]

Then confessional issues came roaring back into politics. Separate schools and the seat-of-government issue both split the legislature again in 1863, an election year. Robinson had absented himself from the crucial votes, Brown (back in the house) had not. 'Like a hog on ice,' in the *Leader*'s contemptuous phrase, Moodie joined Brown's camp again. A mass meeting in Moodie's bowling saloon urged 'Mine Host' to stand himself for the western seat against the pusillanimous Robinson. 'He was,' he admitted, 'a man of the people. He had not been an Honourable's son, with a silver spoon in his mouth.' But he had neither sufficient education nor sufficient means, he went on, whereas the Liberals had called out a self-made man, the Methodist merchant John Macdonald, who would support 'good Protestant principles, and was prepared to stand by the rights of Upper Canada and justice to Toronto.' So a deputation of 100 people trooped from Moodie's saloon to Macdonald's warehouse and presented a lengthy requisition. At the hustings for Toronto West, Moodie was nominated as well as Macdonald. This allowed the alderman from St John, his proposer, and his seconder all to deliver speeches in praise of Macdonald, who also had a proposer and a seconder, and then to withdraw Moodie's candidacy in Macdonald's favour. The same tactic, to demonstrate and mobilize the range of interests that backed the Protestant and Liberal candidate, was used in Toronto East. The *Leader* reported ruefully that 'the Capting' and the preachers triumphed in both halves of the city.[70]

Moodie and Brown campaigned together in the two municipal polls remaining before Captain Bob died. John George Bowes, standing for a seventh term as mayor, was an unrepentant sponsor of separate school legislation. He must be humbled. Hence Moodie and Brown ran against him Grand Master Francis Henry Medcalf, an old ironfounder who almost never spoke except to extol the empire and to damn the Fenians. He presented himself as a bluff workingman. The artisans of Macaulaytown voted for him, three to one, making the difference between victory and defeat. The following year they supported him ten to one. When this second result was known, his friends from the Noble Ward bundled the mayor into a four-horse sleigh, filled other sleighs with bandsmen playing *The Protestant Boys*, and drove down to St Lawrence Hall in a volley of celebratory pistol shots. The grudging *Leader* estimated that between six and eight thousand people gathered there on that winter's night to hear the speeches and to give three cheers for Queen Victoria, three for King William III.[71]

Brown by now had realized that it was Bugg who could be taken for granted (who else but the *Globe*'s candidate would Bugg's chapel followers support?) and Moodie who must be wooed. Moodie rallied the swingers – and the shock troops. With Brown's imprimatur he won more and more votes from Bugg within the ward. (In 1865 Bugg stood for alderman after five years' absence from council – the result was Moodie 635, James E. Smith 536, and Bugg 388). When chapel and tavern agreed on a Protestant candidate for the city the ward became an irresistible force, every last favourable voter coming forward confidently, the opposition deterred from the polls, and a massive bloc of ballots thrown onto the scales. Moodie delivered a unified vote from Macaulaytown and thus delivered the city.

What generalizations can we draw from all this about Canadian urban politics in the middle of the nineteenth century?

Samuel Reid's death on election night reflects the importance of youth, of kinship, and of the non-electors in the politics of the Noble Ward. Robert Moodie was only in his mid-twenties when he won office. Robert Griffith, councilman between 1858 and 1860, was no older. James E. Smith began his long career as St John's representative in 1857, at the age of 26. In so many jobs at that time, income peaked in the early vigorous years, not rising with seniority.[72] Conditions of work and domicile for poorer people particularly could be harsh. The medical knowledge and facilities available to them might not palliate those conditions. A politician, unless he possessed unearned income as Robinson did, must stick at his trade while developing his career. Young men stood the pace best, a pace that burnt out candidates early. Nowhere was this more likely than in a working-class constituency. Middle-class voters valued business talents or sheer social standing, but workers tended to require evidence also of generously distributed energies in the streets and the neighbourhoods. They were less easily impressed by performances in the committee room, in the courtroom, or at the public dinner-table – all profitable places of resort for merchants and professionals.

Municipal affairs imposed their own strains. Elections took place in the dead of winter and involved face-to-face canvassing. The ballot was open. A successful candidate nerved supporters to take time from work, to venture into the cold, and to declare a preference publicly. Henchmen who got out the vote could also be mobilized by an energetic organizer to block or intimidate the would-be voters for rivals. It took stamina and high spirits to visit throughout the year firehalls, lodges, saloons, meetings – places where bands of enthusiastic imprudent young men could be tapped for maintaining electoral momentum whenever needed. Young non-electors, who did not own or rent property, responded best to candidates who shared their boisterous leisure.[73] Griffith, an ornamental painter, designed banners for many processions.[74] Smith, a rich wholesale grocer, was captain of No 2 Fire Company and held office among the Freemasons.[75] Moodie, as we have seen, moved from bowling alley to foredeck and back again, inspiring parades, invading public meetings, talking incessantly. He was able to furnish two crowds for outdoor gatherings – one around the platform to drown out unworthy speakers, one to wave hands and banners from high ground to impress the undecided.[76] Victorian journalists translated most speeches into orotund prose, but whenever Moodie leaped on a table or wagon his headlong unequivocating delivery took control of even the most conventional reporter's pen.

It was the experience of George Washington Plunkitt of Tammany Hall that relatives formed the initial following of any aspiring statesman.[77] This was as true for Macaulaytown as for New York. At least three Rowells acted in ward matters. At least four Griffiths filled positions in the Orange Order, and one of them became both a local grand secretary and assessor of city rates.[78] Given his common surname, James E. Smith's family network is harder to identify, but his father was described as a person through whom young James's judgment could be swayed;[79] a 26-year-old wholesaler with a residence in suburban Brockton was hardly a self-made man. As for Moodie, brother James had been handed the lease for a pleasure ground on the island, and Francis Johnston, cook on the steamer *Cobourg* when little Bob was cook's mate, worked for him electorally inside St John. Relatives shared the burden of organization. They also guaranteed that the candidates were neighbourhood boys.

As each man brought his own associations, Moodie found it impossible to duplicate or absorb his colleagues' constituencies. Griffith, for instance, represented those second-generation Orangemen for whom chapel-goers were allies and not aliens, hence he stayed with Brown and Bugg when Moodie turned away.[80] Smith was a second-generation businessman, the council nominee to the board of the Northern Railway, who supported John Beverley Robinson, Jr, even when Moodie crusaded against him.[81] Their followings might overlap with Moodie's, but they were far from identical with his.

The black vote stayed independent of Captain Bob as well. Most of Toronto's black population lived in Macaulaytown.[82] Its composition mirrored that of the ward as a whole, largely working class but with a few professionals, employers, and landlords. Wilson R. Abbott, a former slave, was one of the largest property owners in St John and sometimes headed delegations or petitions of the ratepayers at large, irrespective of race.[83] The black community was also overwhelmingly Protestant. Although a great number were Methodists and Baptists, they celebrated each Emancipation Day (the anniversary of the end of slavery in the British Empire) at a service in the Anglican cathedral. Quite consistently many blacks preferred the Tory gentry, who represented the emancipating empire, over the city's Reformers, who were suspected of sympathy for the United States, where slavery was still legal.[84] Those Liberals who formed the Canadian Anti-Slavery Society won over some of the black chapel folk, but Wilson Abbott, a member of its original committee, soon left the society, and its committee became a white man's preserve. Abbott and others detested George Brown as a hypocrite. He had refused to employ a black printer, they said, and curried favour from explicitly racist parliamentarians.[85]

Moodie realized that a black vote counted as much as a white vote, but found that Macaulaytown's blacks supported Robinson or Brown for reasons beyond his control.[86] Nevertheless, black opinion coalesced toward Brown in the 1860s. In 1860 Chief Justice Robinson ruled that a fugitive slave should be returned to Missouri for trial for the murder of his master; the obloquy of the decision rubbed off on Robinson, Jr, while Brown and his associates organized a large meeting of protest. During the Civil War, Liberal support for the North contrasted with support from some Tories for the South. Defence of Protestantism made Brown even more appealing than Robinson, so that by 1865 the black vote, like nearly all others in St John, had swung the way Bob Moodie did.

What did Moodie offer his constituents? At one extreme he fought the ward's battle over sewerage. Councillors from older precincts beside the lake wanted St John's ratepayers alone to bear the cost of sewer extension to their ward; Alderman Moodie just as forthrightly argued that it should be a charge on the city as a whole.[87] At the other extreme he defended the people's recreation and brought theatre to public life. In 1859 (the year he fought to retain the greensward of College Avenue) the Reform council added to its unpopularity because of what became known as the 'gaol guzzle,' a champagne lunch to lay the foundation-stone of the Don Gaol. The single expense of which citizens approved had been the $50 Moodie obtained for gas to power a balloon in which he was the passenger. No one could begrudge him this daring piece of spectacle, a political opponent said, because 'Capting Bob was a treasure.'[88] The one entertainment he detested was the circus, a Yankee device for taking shillings from the poor[89] (competing, he did not bother to add, with saloons, bowling alleys, ferry boats, and pleasure grounds).

In this Moodie voiced populist dismay at outsiders or innovators making money at townsmen's expense. This showed most clearly in his concern for carters' rights. The carters swelled his parades and filled the gallery for his speeches. The Great Western Railway entered a contract with Hendrie and Shedden, a cartage company, that deprived other operators of the lucrative business of the station yard; runners on the trains and platforms sold tickets for Jones and Co's omnibuses. In the summer of 1857 Moodie presented a petition from cabmen and carters against these monopolies, many of whose workers were Yankees (it was alleged). Later that evening a crowd of cabmen and carters tried to demolish Jones and Co's fleet; the Canadian Rifles and the volunteers were called out, arrests were made, and six of the 'Omnibus Rioters' sentenced to prison at the following assizes.[90] In 1860 a projector from outside Toronto sought the council's franchise to run streetcars in the city. Moodie and a master carter were almost the only councillors to oppose the scheme. They believed that it would reduce traditional employment further still. Moodie made an additional prediction, in which the shrewdness of a practising politician anticipated urban historians by several generations: streetcars would allow the rich to live beyond the city and leave the poor behind to pay the rates.[91]

If we conclude that Moodie was a populist, protecting people's pockets and pleasures, how far can we describe him also as a class-conscious politician? 'In this country Jack was as good as his master,' he proclaimed in defending the College Avenue park. 'He had not been an Honourable's son, with a silver spoon in his mouth': this during his recurrent campaign against Robinson. But he too had become a landlord and shipowner. He could support Robinson when it suited, while the candidates he espoused just before his death, the Honourable George Brown, John Macdonald, MP, and Mayor Medcalf, were all substantial employers of labour who left flourishing businesses to their children. The Captain's probate speaks only of $550 worth of personal estate and effects, although admittedly his wife was licensee in her own name of a fine hotel.[92] When Moodie in 1863 directed support to Macdonald, whom he praised as a self-made man, he said that he himself had neither the education nor the money to be a member of Parliament (apart from the property qualification and the cost of canvassing, the post was unpaid and Parliament sat in another city). It was a realistic assessment of the conditions for success. Unless he were a practising lawyer or journalist a man needed inherited wealth or income earned through the labour of others to be able to afford to sit in Parliament away from his home town.

The issues that swung the Noble Ward behind a provincial candidate were not ostensibly class issues, anyway. This is not to say that class issues did not exist, simply that they were not yet sharply articulated at the provincial level. The legislature was no place for a workingman. In such a vacuum sectarianism and jingoism fused in campaigns against francophone or Fenian Catholics. Disputes over the spending of provincial revenue, particularly spending in or withdrawal from Toronto, assumed sectarian and jingoistic forms. The local Liberal leadership moved swiftly to exploit these enthusiasms. By fighting the good fight for Protestantism and the empire, Jack could feel himself to be as good as his masters, as long as the masters were Protestant and anglophone. If they were not, Jack asserted his superiority over them and sought to drag them down from their high seats. Thus he could disparage any unworthy section of the ruling class, distance himself also from what became a Catholic underclass, and yet not challenge the established order of classes at all. Protestant and anglophone masters found this behaviour far more acceptable than any explicitly class-conscious movements that might otherwise have come out of Macaulaytown.

NOTES

1 *Globe* 9, 12 June 1865; *Leader* 12 June 1865; *Irish Canadian* 14 June 1865
2 Susan Sontag *Illness as Metaphor* (New York 1978)
3 *Leader* 5 August 1859, also 5, 12 April, 2, 3, 4 August 1859; (Petition) To Mayor ... of Toronto, 12 August 1859 (Monster Broadsides, Metropolitan Toronto Library); *Grumbler* 6 August 1859
4 *Globe* 15 December 1857
5 *Irish Canadian* 6 January 1864, 4 January 1865
6 *Leader* 9 June 1865
7 Lot 122, Section s, St James' Cemetery, Toronto; obituary of James Moodie, *Leader* 28 November 1859
8 *Globe* 9 August 1858

9 City of Toronto Archives (hereafter CTA), Minutes of Toronto City Council (hereafter Minutes), 4, 18 February, 1, 22 December 1856, 15 February 1858

10 CTA, Assessment Rolls, St John's Ward; Archives of Ontario (hereafter AO), Surrogate Court RG22, York County, Series 6–2, Documents of administration of estate of Robert Moodie, 26 June 1865

11 Mike Filey *Trillium and Toronto Island* (Toronto 1976) 9–12, picture of *Firefly* p 17; *Canadian Merchants Magazine* (May 1857) 148–153, (July 1857) 327–8

12 *Leader* (advertisement; hereafter ad) 16 December 1856

13 *Ibid* 29 December 1857

14 Filey *Trillium* 9, 11; *Leader* 17 April 1856, 14 July 1857

15 *Globe* (ad) 25 June 1858

16 *Ibid* 19 January 1856

17 *Leader* 10, 15 April, 24 December 1857; Minutes, 31 May 1858

18 *Grumbler* 19 June 1858, 12 May 1860; *Globe* 3 August 1858; *Leader* 15 June 1863

19 *Grumbler* 13 November 1858; cf 12 May 1860.

20 *The Municipal Manual for Upper Canada* 5th edn (Toronto 1855) 163

21 Henry Scadding *Toronto of Old* (Toronto 1873) 307

22 These calculations have been made from statistics in *Globe* 15 March 1860.

23 These generalizations are consistent with the calculations and maps in Peter C. Goheen *Victorian Toronto, 1850 to 1900* (Chicago 1970) 115–55.

24 Calculations from *Census of 1851*; see also *Census of Canada, 1665 to 1871* IV (Ottawa 1876).

25 *Globe* 26 July 1851, 30 March 1852, 12 December 1860; *Canadian Merchants Magazine* (September 1857) 551, 555

26 AO, Elmsley-Macaulay Papers; Metropolitan Toronto Library (MTL), T.A. Reed, Memoranda re the Crown Grants of Park Lots in the City of Toronto, typescript, 1926; Edith G. Firth *The Town of York, 1796–1815: A Further Collection of Documents of Early Toronto* (Toronto 1966); Barrie Dyster 'Macaulay, John Simcoe' *Dictionary of Canadian Biography* (DCB) VIII (forthcoming); Henri Pilon 'Elmsley, John' DCB IX; Barrie Dyster 'Toronto 1840–1860: Making It in a British Protestant Town' PhD thesis, University of Toronto, 1970, 155–8

27 *Globe* 20 January 1857

28 AO, Robinson Papers; MTL, Jarvis-Powell Papers, S.P. Jarvis, Jr, to his mother, 23 August 1854; *Globe* (ad) 23 February 1856, 26 June, (ad) 11 August 1860; *Reminiscences of Charles Durand of Toronto, Barrrister* (Toronto 1897) 410; W.H. Pearson *Recollections and Records of Toronto of Old* (Toronto 1914) 77–8. The Robinsons are 'Landholder 1' in figure 17 in Goheen *Victorian Toronto* 134.

29 Dyster 'Toronto 1840–1860' 136–9

30 Ibid 301–15
31 Membership of city council can be found in Minutes and in an appendix to
J.E. Middleton *The Municipality of Toronto: A History* (Toronto 1923).
32 C. Blacket Robinson *History of Toronto and County of York, Ontario* 2 vols
(Toronto 1885) I 58–9
33 Assessment Roll; *Leader* 20 February 1856, 9 February, 23 March 1857;
Minutes, 20, 27 October 1856
34 *Grumbler* 6 August 1859; Robinson *History of Toronto* II 17; Mrs R.H.
Hopper *Old Time Primitive Methodism in Canada* (Toronto 1904) 99–100
35 *Globe* 19 April 1853; Minutes, 19 February, 17 December 1855, 18 March, 1,
22 December 1856, 7 December 1857
36 Minutes, 15 December 1856, 9, 14 April, 1, 3 June, 10 August, 9 November
1857; *Globe* 20 May, 24 June, 20, 24 July 1857, 4 December 1860, 3 January
1861; *Leader* 24 July 1857
37 CTA, Toronto City Council Papers, Petition of officers of the fire brigade,
8 October 1853
38 *Leader* and *Globe* 14–18 July 1857; *Mirror* 16 July 1858; *Irish Canadian* 1, 8
June, 14, 21 December 1864
39 *Leader* and *Globe* 16 July–1 August 1855
40 L.H. Saunders *The Story of Orangeism* (Toronto 1960); Loyal Orange Association of British North America, Annual Report of the Proceedings of the Grand
Lodge 1846, 1849; reports of demonstrations against Governor-General Elgin
in *Examiner* and *Globe* October 1849; *Globe* 4, 5 July 1855, 14 July 1856, 14
July 1857, 13 July 1858, 13 February 1860; *Leader* 4, 7 July 1855, (ad) 9 April
1856, 14 July 1857, 10 July 1858; Documents of administration ... of Robert
Moodie
41 *Leader* (ad) 21 December 1854, (ad) 19 December 1855, (ad) 9 April 1856; *Globe*
14 July 1856
42 *Mirror* 8 February 1856; *Leader* 11 February, 18 March 1856
43 *Globe* 9 January 1851, 8 January, (ad) 18 December 1852, 5 January 1854, 2
May 1856; *Leader* 15 June 1861; Robinson *History of Toronto* I 152
44 CTA, Toronto City Council Papers, Mandamus re election in St John's Ward,
17 February 1855; Minutes, 19 February 1855; *Globe* (ad) 19 December 1854,
3 January, 13 February, 2 March 1855; *Leader* (ad) 28 February, 1, 2
March 1855
45 *Leader* and *Globe* 3–10 January 1855
46 *Leader* (ad) 19 December 1855, 9 January 1856
47 *Ibid* 22 January 1856
48 *Globe* 11 March 1857
49 *Leader* 24 March 1857

50 *Globe* 14–22 January 1856; *Leader* 22 January 1856

51 Minutes, 7, 19 January 1857; *Globe* 7, 8, 14, 20, 21 January 1857; *Leader* 20, 21 January 1857

52 *Commemorative Biographical Record of the County of York* (Toronto 1907) 87; *Globe* 10 July, 10 August 1858

53 *Commemorative Biographical Record* 115; Desmond Morton *Mayor Howland: The Citizen's Candidate* (Toronto 1973)

54 *Leader* 7 July 1857

55 J.M.S. Careless *Brown of the Globe* 2 vols (Toronto 1959, 1963)

56 Dyster 'Toronto 1840–1860' 333–459; Ray Allen Billington *The Protestant Crusade, 1800–1860* (Chicago 1964); J.M.S. Careless *The Union of the Canadas, 1841–1857* (Toronto 1967)

57 Minutes 3, 25 March 1856; *Globe* 26 March 1856; Careless *The Union of the Canadas* passim

59 Public Archives of Canada, Buchanan Papers, G. Brown to I. Buchanan, 26 July 1856, 2542–3; *Globe* 24 July 1856

60 *Globe* 2 July 1857; see also 1 February, 21 June, 13 July 1855, 14 July 1856, 11 March, 14 July, 10 December 1857.

61 *Leader* 24, 29 December 1857; *Globe* 27 January 1858; see *Leader* and *Globe* throughout December.

62 B. Dyster 'Toronto 1840–1860' 374–8; Minutes, 1, 8 November 1858; *Leader* 2, 9, 19 November 1858

63 Minutes, 15 February 1858; *Leader* 29 December 1857, 12 January 1858

64 *Leader* 18, 25, 27, 29 March, 1, 6 April, 10 July 1858; *Globe* 10 July 1858

65 Careless *Brown* I 263–85; *Globe* 6, 10 August 1858; *Leader* 17, 27, 31 August, (letter from J.B. Robinson) 3 September 1858

66 *Leader* 6 January 1859

67 *Grumbler* 12 March 1859

68 *Leader* 4 January 1860; see also note 3, above.

69 *Leader* 15, 19, 29 June 1861; *Globe* 29 June 1861; Careless *Brown* II 43–6

70 Reverend Hugh Johnston *A Merchant Prince: Life of Hon. Senator John Macdonald* (Toronto 1893); *Globe* 29, 30 May, 2, 3 June 1863; *Canadian Freeman* 4, 18, 25 June 1863; *Leader* 9, 24 June 1863

71 *Leader* 4 January 1865; see also note 5, above.

72 Michael Katz *The People of Hamilton, Canada West* (Cambridge, Mass, 1975) 160–3

73 There is a discussion of the role of non-electors in English elections in J.R. Vincent *Poll Books: How Victorians Voted* (London 1967).

74 *Globe* 13 July 1855; *Leader* (ad) 9 January 1856

75 *Globe* (ad) 20 December 1855, 14 July 1857, 4, 11, 18, 19 May 1860; *Leader* 6 June 1860

76 *Leader* 15 June 1863

77 W.L. Riordon *Plunkitt of Tammany Hall* (New York 1963) 7–10

78 *Annual Report of Proceedings of the Grand Lodge of the Loyal Orange Association of British North America* 1856; Minutes, 18 February 1856; *Leader* (ad) 21 December 1854, (ad) 9 April 1856; *Globe* 13 July 1855, 14 July 1856

79 *Globe* and *Leader* 20 January 1857

80 Minutes, 26 April 1858; *Grumbler* 21 August 1858

81 *Globe* 20 January 1857, 24 January 1860; *Leader* 10 June 1863

82 Benjamin Drew *A North-side View of Slavery* (Boston 1856) 94; Mrs Agnes Dunbar Chamberlin 'The Coloured Citizens of Toronto' Women's Canadian Historical Society of Toronto *Transactions* No. 8 (1908) 10–12; Daniel G. Hill 'Negroes in Toronto, 1793–1865' *Ontario History* LV (June 1963) 90

83 Minutes, 18 September 1854, 1 October 1855, 4 May 1857; *Globe* 24 July 1857, 23 June 1858; *Leader* 24 July, 4 August 1857

84 John Macgregor *Our Brothers and Cousins* (London 1859) 49–50; *Mirror* 25 December 1857; *Globe* 9 August 1858, 19 December 1860; *Leader* 13 October 1860, 15 June 1861, 19 June 1863

85 *Leader* 12, 19, 21 December 1857

86 *Globe* 15 December 1857, 3 August 1858, 3, 4, 5 January, 27 June 1861; 1 January 1864; *Leader* 21 December 1857; *Grumbler* 21, 28 August 1858

87 Minutes, 20 April, 27 July 1857, 22 August 1858; *Leader* 28 July 1857, 3 April 1860; *Globe* 24 January, 3 April, 18 May 1860

88 *Globe* 2 January 1860

89 *Grumbler* 26 June 1858

90 *Mirror* 21, 28 August, 11 September, 29 November 1857; *Leader* 20, 21 August 1857

91 *Globe* 2, 30 October, 1 November 1860; *Leader* 1 November 1860

92 Documents of administration ... of Robert Moodie

NICHOLAS ROGERS

Serving Toronto the Good

The development of the city police force 1834–84

T HE DEVELOPMENT and changing role of urban policing in Western industrial societies have attracted increasing attention in recent years, particularly in America and Britain where the police have found themselves at the centre of a political controversy over their responsibilities and accountability under the law. Although a good deal of research in Canada has been devoted to the RCMP and to private law enforcement agencies, municipal forces have not been subjected to the same critical scrutiny. In the case of Toronto, historians have tended to assume that the development of a city police force, 135 strong by 1881, was a natural concomitant of urban expansion, forgetting that the very notion of a policed society and the form it might take were not divorced from questions of ideology, political partisanship, and class. Just as in Victorian Britain, police reform in Toronto was not unproblematic. Given Toronto's sectarian politics it could hardly have been so. Rather, it was the product of changing and sometimes competing political and social forces, the determining presence and influence of which must be recovered if one is to understand both the organization and role of the early force.

Prior to 1834 responsibility for the police was vested in the hands of the Home District magistrates appointed by the lieutenant-governor. The radicals in York objected to this arrangement on democratic grounds and especially because it gave the Family Compact a virtual monopoly over police appointments. They were quick to seize upon any incident that exposed police inefficiency or partiality. Even when it was proposed to put the organization of the force on a more representative footing under Henry John Boulton's plans for incorporation, radicals remained sceptical, largely because they feared the police would continue to be an instrument of Toryism. 'The Police system of this town is most infamous,' wrote Francis Collins in the *Canadian Freeman*, 'but corrupt and deficient as it is, it is still preferable to a Corporation chiefly composed of, and directed by the 'reptile band' of officials at Little York.'[1] An annual election of magistrates by secret ballot, he believed, was eminently preferable to guarantee some accountability.

Radicals appear to have had few initial reservations, however, about the organization of the force under the final incorporation act of 1834. The size of the force was small, comprising five full-time constables under the direction of the high bailiff and subject to annual review. Every year a committee of council received nominations for the so-called permanent positions and also for the periodic recruitment of specials, although the size and duties of the force were in large part determined by two other committees, those of police and prisons and finance and assessment, the recommendations of which were discussed and voted upon by the whole assembly. So committed was council to controlling police appointments that in 1835 it hesitated to give the mayor the discretionary power to suspend constables for dereliction of duty.[2] Even three years later, in the immediate aftermath of the rebellion of 1837, when the government proposed to recruit special constables under George Gurnett's supervision to police Toronto, the council was techily suspicious about any infringement of its powers.[3]

Despite the Rebellion and the government's intervention, city council did not expand or reorganize its police force. In fact, for a time the number of permanent constables was reduced to four. It was not until 1843 that a select committee recommended that the force be increased to eight constables, divided into two divisions, one based at the market house and the other at a station at the junction of York and Lot streets. Under this arrangement two constables remained on duty at their stations from 8 a.m. to 2 a.m. the following morning, while the others spent nine hours on the beat noting infractions of city by-laws and intervening in 'all breaches or threatened breaches of the peace.'[4] In addition, constables had to report to the high bailiff when they came off duty and to the sitting magistrates of the police court at 6 p.m. For this exacting round of duty, some 18 hours in the station alternating with 13 on the beat, constables were paid £80 a year plus a £5 clothing allowance. This base salary could be supplemented by various fees and perquisites, rewards for arrests, for example, or gratuities for attendance at some special social function. But these incidental allowances were never regularized and on occasion gave rise to disputes between the high bailiff and the constabulary over their distribution.[5]

The permanent force remained exceptionally small until the mid-1850s, when it first passed the fifty mark and was organized into five districts, each with its own station and lock-up. Yet it faced mounting criticism. Its early critics were, predictably, the Reformers. In the aftermath of the rebellion of 1837 they were dismayed by the way in which successive Tory councils viewed the force as a source of political patronage and openly exploited it for partisan ends. Constables were marshalled to break up a Reformist meeting at Davis's Temperance Tavern just north of Toronto in October 1839.[6] In the following year the 'Corporation bullies,' led by City Inspector William Davis and constables John Wallis and Francis Earls, successfully disrupted another. And in the Toronto general election of 1841 the constabulary connived at the violence inflicted upon Reform supporters. One witness recalled how he was confronted on his return from the hustings 'by four men in the yard, from one of whom I received a blow ... in the head. I had not gone far till I was surrounded by a number of these inhuman monsters and dragged to the street where I was beaten and mangled till covered over with my own blood, the constables standing all the while.'[7] In the ensuing provincial inquiry the police were roundly condemned for their partiality, particularly the special constables, some of whom, it transpired, had been recruited by one of the Tory candidates. As long as the police were dependent upon a partisan corporation, the commissioners concluded, they would be 'employed as political instruments'; an 'efficient Police force' they went on, 'should be appointed, directed and governed by authorities remote from, superior to, and independent of local bias or interference.'[8]

This recommendation, which in principle reflected the aims of the Metropolitan London Police Act, was not, however, implemented. Perhaps the newly formed ministry of Robert Baldwin found it difficult to reconcile the measure with the broader aims of representative government and local autonomy. Instead, the government sought to tackle the issue indirectly, through an assault upon Orangeism. The commission of inquiry into the 1841 riots had disclosed that a substantial section of the police had been recruited from the Orange lodges through the agency of the high bailiff, George Kingsmill, and other municipal politicians. Representing the trinity of crown, Protestantism, and empire, Orangeism had become the central ideological buttress of Tory loyalism outside the Family Compact since 1836, when its electoral presence was first felt. It was this conjunction of forces, the intermeshing of local patronage with strong sectarian loyalties, that sharpened the political role of the Toronto police in the post-Rebellion years. 'Orangeism' claimed the commissioners, 'has become the watchword and symbol of the party which supports the Corporation, and is the most efficient, if not indispensable recommendation to civic favour or employ.'[9]

The measures passed by the Baldwin ministry to eliminate Organeism were compromised by the British government, which refused to ban secret societies in Canada, but the prohibition of political processions did take effect, and for eight years, until its repeal in 1851, Orangemen were legally denied the right of public assembly. In practice, this act proved difficult to enforce, particularly in the smaller townships, and did nothing to curb the presence of Orangeism as a force in Canadian politics. Nor did it disengage local politicians and in turn the police from the Orange Order.

In 1844 six of Toronto's ten aldermen were known to be Orangemen, and from 1845 the order enjoyed a near-monopoly of mayoral office.[10] Moreover, roughly half of the police force, including at least two high bailiffs, were recruited from Orange ranks. Given these links, it was hardly surprising that the police roll in curbing sectarian demonstrations was severely compromised. This was well illustrated in 1849 when the police were implicated in the violent public protests over the Rebellion Losses Bill and William Lyon Mackenzie's return to Toronto. A public inquiry was called for, but, as the *Globe* noted, 'nothing was more remarkable in the Council discussion than the careful avoidance of all reflections on the city constables.' Reform pressure, however, did force the magistracy to adopt a more circumspect approach to the question of public order. In a subsequent demonstration against the Rebellion Losses Bill, the mayor, George Gurnett, did call upon military aid to protect property. In October 1849, when Lord Elgin visited the city, the police dispersed an Orange crowd parading the governor-general's effigy, much to the relief of the Reform press, which commended 'the promptness with which this riot was knocked on the head.'[12] For the first time in over a decade, under the watchful eye of the Reformers, the magistracy and police had risen above partisan loyalties.

There was no guarantee, however, that this state of affairs would continue. Effective police intervention depended a great deal upon the disposition of the civic authorities, particularly upon the leadership of the high bailiff and his influence over the rank and file. In October 1849 the police chief, George Allen, was not prepared to allow his own Orange affiliation to compromise the impartiality of the force, although he was careful to emphasize the 'trying and arduous circumstances' under which the police had to act and mentioned, almost apologetically, that the conduct of the police force 'might not afford that satisfaction to all parties which they desired it to do.'[13] These equivocations, which almost certainly reflected the tensions within the force about its role in suppressing Orange demonstrations, were to be heightened by subsequent developments. In 1851 came the repeal of the Party Processions Act and the revival of Orange parades in Toronto. Meanwhile, the massive influx of Irish Catholics after the Famine – one resident in four was

Catholic, according to the census of 1851 – was transforming the social dimensions of the city. Sectarian rivalry threatened to become the order of the day with clashes between Orange and Green. These animosities were further intensified by the growing fear that the government was undermining the Protestant ascendancy of Upper Canada in its efforts to appease Catholic opinion in Quebec, principally through the distribution of clergy reserves and concessions to separate schools. Although these issues divided Protestants and complicated party alignments in Toronto, they did nothing for religious harmony. Rather, they increased the likelihood of an extremist Protestant backlash against a visibly expanding Catholic minority. In this context the very viability of an Orange-dominated police force in a sectarian city was called into question.

The incidents that ultimately triggered the campaign for police reform did not revolve around sectarian tensions. And the Orange loyalties of the force were not central to the debate, although they were never far from the surface and formed an important subtext. The events that pushed the issue of police organization into the public limelight occurred in 1855, when the force proved unwilling to deal with two riots and showed the utmost reluctance to bring their perpetrators to justice.[14] In June the police intervened ineffectually in a dispute between rival fire brigades on Church Street and subsequently scrabbled their testimony in court. In the following month they allowed a large crowd with the aid of the firemen of the hook and ladder company to demolish the tent of a visiting American circus – an act of retaliation against the circus clown and other performers who had been involved in a bawdy-house brawl the previous night. Again the police proved extremely reluctant to testify, and it was only after a full-scale municipal inquiry that the ringleaders were prosecuted.

Trivial as these incidents appeared, at least from a political perspective, they raised a number of issues about the way in which local patronage and neighbourhood-cum-sectarian loyalties could pervert the course of justice. The firemen, like the police, were heavily recruited from the Orange Order, and pressure had been clearly brought to bear to conceal their identity. The fabric of influence and dependence that sustained the organization of the police had made it very difficult for the pusillanimous chief of police, Samuel Sherwood, to enforce discipline. As he himself complained at the inquiry, his attempts to instil discipline in the force had been continually undercut by patronage. 'So long as it is under the present organization and the men depend upon the Council for putting them in and putting them out, it will never be a force.'[15]

The special committee in charge of the inquiry into the Church Street and circus riots recommended Sherwood's dismissal. City council did not endorse this, but it did make the first tentative steps toward delegating police authority to a more permanent and arguably less partisan board. The lead was taken by the mayor, George William Allan, a lawyer whose business interests and administrative experience pushed him to the forefront of the negotiations surrounding the construction of the railways and esplanade in Toronto. An advocate of development, he argued that an efficient force could be created only if it were divested of its current 'social and politicial ties' and subjected to the management of a body distanced from municipal politics.[16] He suggested that the London Metropolitan Police Force should be approached for a suitable chief and that the organization of the force should be taken out of the hands of the council and vested in a triumvirate of police magistrate, recorder, and chief of police. In other words, the police should be removed from partisan politics and appointed by a permanent body of officials along the lines of Sir Robert Peel's proposals for the British capital. Although the finer details of this recommendation were not set out, the recommendation itself marked a break with the representative system of police management that obtained in Toronto and in many American cities.

The proposals were accepted in principle by both Tories and Reformers on the Toronto council.[17] The debate in the *Globe* reveals that there was some disagreement about whether a new police chief should be recruited from London or one of the other British cities rather than from the home population. Aldermen Charles Romain and John Smith, for example, believed that the former chief of police, George Allen, should be invited to reapply. But there was no vocal opposition to the notion that the police should be disengaged from council politics, neither from Orange-Tories nor from Reformers, who ten years earlier might have defended the principle of police accountability to elected representatives. This prevailing consensus reflected the changing priorities of municipal politics: the growing insistence upon efficiency and order in a rapidly expanding Toronto; the need for a disciplined force to tackle the problems of immigration, drunkenness, rowdyism, and petty crime, which were beginning to attract great public attention. Above all, politicians wanted a police force attuned to the new image of Toronto as a prosperous commercial metropolis of the west and an appropriate seat of government.[18] Civic pride and commercial development dictated that the police force be put at a greater distance from Toronto rowdyism, even if this meant some re-evaluation of its relationship with the Orange order.

The debate on police reform was sharpened by subsequent events. In the spring of 1856, as the Toronto council drafted its proposal for the reorganization of the police, the government of the United Canadas introduced legislation for a province-wide police force. Based on the recommendations of a provincial commission the previous year under the leadership of Sir Allan MacNab, the bill sought to amalgamate the existing municipal forces into one large force of 350 constables and 150 sub-constables controlled by a government-appointed police commissioner. Such a step was necessary, claimed Attorney-General John A. Macdonald, because the municipal authorities had shown themselves unable to handle large-scale public disturbances. He therefore proposed 'to cut the Police Force off from all local influences and prejudices,' as Sir Robert Peel had done in both London and Ireland.[19] Municipalities would no longer be responsible for their forces, but they would have to foot part of the bill, some two-thirds of the cost. Only where extraordinary forces were required to police the construction of public works would the municipalities gain some respite from the cost-sharing enterprise.

Despite the fact that the government bill also sought to disentangle the municipal police from local politics, it predictably met with considerable opposition in Toronto. Many regarded it as an unwarranted interference in municipal affairs and were disturbed by its political implications. The *Globe* feared that it would transform the police into another source of political patronage, giving the provincial government 'a power over the liberties and privileges of the people which we do not think it safe to entrust to them.'[20] Others feared that it would provide yet another pretext for Quebec domination of Upper Canada. *Mackenzie's Weekly Message* even characterized the bill as 'the new dodge of a Roman Catholic Police from Lower Canada to take the place of our Protestant city police.'[21] And many more were disturbed by the expense of the new force, which they believed would be exorbitant, oppressive, and detrimental to cheap, efficient municipal government. These arguments proved persuasive, for when Toronto city council debated the measure in April, it roundly denounced it by nineteen votes to three.[22] Only well-known Conservatives such as John Beverley Robinson Jr and John Hillyard Cameron gave verbal support to the bill.

In the event the government's police bill was abandoned. It was one of the legislative casualties of the ministerial crisis of 1856 that culminated in the resignation of Sir Allan MacNab in May. The new Taché-Macdonald administration, beset by Upper Canadian sectionalism, was not prepared to take up the issue again, and this left the field open for the city's counter-proposal, which finally received royal assent in 1858 as an amendment to the Municipal Corporations Act of 1849. Under this amendment responsibility for the police was vested in a board of commissioners that was responsible for all appointments and discipline within the force. The commissioners comprised the mayor, the police magistrate, and the recorder, thus ensuring a link between the commission and the municipalities. Indeed, the recognition of local interests, so conspicuously absent in the provincial police bill, was buttressed in other ways. City council had the power to determine the number of constables to be employed in the force and controlled its financing, with the act simply stipulating that the council had to provide 'a reasonable remuneration for and to the respective members of the Force' and to 'pay for all such offices, watch-houses, watch-boxes, arms, accoutrements, clothing and other necessaries as the Board may from time to time deem requisite and require.'[23] The act thus sought a judicious balance of central and local power in its reorganization of the police. While the police board was not responsible to the council in its day-to-day management of the force, it could not afford to ignore it. It had to establish a working, harmonious relationship with the city's elected assembly.

Such a relationship was not forged overnight, and it took some time for the new arrangements to start working smoothly. The commissioners' plans for a visible, efficient force did not always square with the council's desire for municipal economy, an issue of the utmost importance in Toronto circles following the financial scandal of the 10,000 pound job. In its first meeting with council, the police board argued the case for a constabulary of 60 men, believing a ratio of one policeman to 800 inhabitants to be necessary. But the politicians reduced this number to 50 (excluding the officers) and two years later reduced it by a further 10.[24] The commissioners fought the latter decision and successfully persuaded council to agree to a gradual diminution of the force. But their subsequent efforts to restore it to its former strength were resisted until the 1870s, when council agreed to finance a larger force to oversee the new licensing laws and to enforce stricter observance of the Sabbath. Even then the board did not get all the men it desired and was unable to convince council to grant more than 4 per cent of the municipal budget toward police expenditures.[25] Not until 1880, in fact, did the police budget make up more than 5 per cent of the total, and by this time the proportion of police to inhabitants was roughly 1 to 1,200. The 1859 target was never achieved.

Municipal politicians remained imperious about their right to determine the size and funding of the police force; they were also quite prepared to impose upon the commissioners' jurisdiction. The old practice of politicians defending supporters within the force continued, and the early years of the board saw a number of aldermanic interventions on behalf of dismissed constables, including one from Captain Bob Moodie, the Orange representative from the working-class district of Macaulaytown within St John's Ward.[26] In some instances, extreme pressure was brought to bear. Such was the case with Sergeant-Major John Steacy, a well-respected Sabbatarian who was fired from the force for general incompetence and for attending the Reform convention of 1859 when he was supposed to be on duty. It was widely suspected that the new police chief, Captain William Stratton Prince, had engineered his dismissal for personal reasons, and a petition of 250 prominent citizens was drawn up calling for a public inquiry. Inevitably the matter was raised in city council. The commissioners, in reply, baulked at the prospect of a public inquiry and reminded council that they were 'constituted by the law of land' to be 'the only judges of the case.'[27] They did, however, provide a lengthly explanation of their decision to dismiss Steacy and through the tactful intervention of Mayor Adam Wilson averted a confrontation with the city.

If the commissioners quickly enforced their right to discipline the police without outside interference, they faced a tougher battle over their proposals to exclude Orangemen from the force. Since the mid-1850s this had been on the agenda, but while many Toronto politicians deprecated the violence of Orange demonstrations and the influence that the order could bring to bear on the operations of the police they had consistently evaded the issue of proscription. This was because the electoral presence of the order was considerable. In the political flux of the 1850s, when the forces of western sectionalism and anti-Catholicism cut the order loose from its traditional moorings, it became a source of support for both parties. Rather than force a confrontation with this powerful organization, many civic politicians hoped that the order's own efforts to instil greater respectability within its ranks would absolve them from tackling the issue of police-Orange relations. This explains why, in the first discussions of reform in 1856, Toronto council rejected the proposal to ban all members of political or secret societies from the force.[28]

When the police board was established, however, the issue was again raised. Flushed by its success at the polls, the Reform council of 1859 urged the new commissioners to exclude all members of secret societies.[29] When the board agreed, a storm of protest was raised. At an Orange meeting convened by District Master John Carr, prominent civic politicians fulminated against the decision. John Hillyard Cameron saw the move as a flagrant violation of British liberties and urged that pressure be brought to bear on the provincial government to repeal the regulation. Others urged electoral retribution. 'We would show to Mr. Brown and his clique of small potatoes,' claimed one, 'that he was not the man for Toronto.'[30] In the new year, however, when the Tories regained a majority on council, the Reformist recommendation was reversed, much to the displeasure of the *Globe*. On a motion from the Orange alderman James E. Smith, the former resolution was declared 'uncalled for and unnecessary' and 'membership of a secret society or particular church' was deemed 'no cause for objection for the force.'[31]

The commissioners continued to assert that the decision to ban members of secret societies was theirs and theirs alone. They refused to be bound by any of council's resolutions and insisted upon proscription. On the advice of Mayor Adam Wilson, a leading light in the Municipal Reform Association, they none the less agreed to interpret the regulation in a liberal fashion, banning only those members who were actively engaged in secret societies.[32] This compromise suited all parties, save for a minority of sectarian die-hards. It allowed all to save face without a protracted legal and political battle. And it was consonant with the general drift of respectable opinion in Toronto, which was more interested in the discipline and efficiency of the police force than in its composition. Even the *Globe* could live with this decision, provided that the police force was disengaged from the rougher elements of the working class.[33] Consequently, Orangemen continued to be enlisted in the Toronto police force, though they were obliged to declare their affiliations upon entry. There was always the possibility, of course, that they would be dismissed if their loyalties to the order interfered with their duties, but since many of the police commissioners in Victorian Toronto were themselves Orangemen, the limits of tolerance were wide.

Orangemen, then, continued to be admitted to the force. In 1859 it was estimated that there were at least twenty members of the order on the books, and in the next two decades their numbers may even have proportionately increased. Certainly the *Irish Canadian* thought so, for in 1885 it complained that the police department was still 'the refuge ... for many whose only credentials are the sign and the password.'[34] As late as the 1920s, in fact, the Orange presence on the force was considerable, constituting roughly one-third of the new recruits. Even so, this element of continuity in police personnel was not replicated in other ways, for a conscious effort was made to distance the post-reform police from working communities, to sever those 'ties of blood and friendship'[35] that had hitherto bound its members to local neighbourhoods, had implicated them in partisan politics, and had arguably provided a licence to rowdyism. Following the British rather than the American model, the Toronto commissioners sought to create an impartial force standing outside local networks, circumscribing its discretionary powers of action, and, through the police chief, closely regulating its activities.

This was attempted first through new and more stringent recruitment procedures. Only those constables who could write a coherent account of their activities and were regarded as 'very deserving, sober, steady men' were retained in 1859.[36] This ruled out a substantial number of the old force, more than half when one adds those who did not trouble themselves to reapply. The Descriptive Roll of February 1859 shows that only 26 of the 65 officers and constables listed had previous experience in the Toronto police.[37] They were joined, significantly, by a flood of new recruits from Britain. No less than 19 had served in one of the British forces, the majority in the Irish Constabulary, and a further eight had been active in the army. One man was brought in from the Australian police, and two from local Ontario constabularies. The remaining nine were rookies, with no army or police experience to their credit at all.

The first eighteen months of the new force brought a series of dismissals, principally for drunkenness, and a pruning of the constabulary under the financial constraints imposed by council. But this did not alter the overall composition of the police in any significant way. Under the new chief of police, Captain Prince, a former officer in the light infrantry, more army men were recruited, bringing the total of policemen with army experience to 13.[38] But no attempt was made to increase the number of admissions from the local civilian population, and the commissioners did not strive to build a force with an ethnic or religious affiliation proportionate to the city's population as a whole. Indeed, the number of Catholics in the force declined, from 13 to 8, even though one-quarter of Toronto's population was of that denomination. In contrast, the number of British recruits, especially Protestant Irishmen, remained disproportionately high. In sum, the commissioners sought to build an experienced force, which by training and outlook would respond to paramilitary discipline and remain distant from the working-class population, or at least its rougher elements. As Chief Prince declared in his annual report of 1869, a policeman 'should be in the prime of manhood, mentally and bodily, ... and of a general good character, in order to command a moral as well as an official influence over those among whom he may be required to act, and subject to the most rigid discipline.' He should be, he continued, 'far above the class of labourers and equal, if not superior, to the most respectable class of journeymen mechanics.'[39]

There was no guarantee, of course, that the new force would meet these requirements, even those members who had previously been called upon to police alien populations and been subject to military discipline. Some of the British recruits, in fact, failed to live up to expectations and were dismissed for habitual drunkenness and insubordination. The rigorous invigilation of police conduct therefore continued, and officers were pressured to report cases of misconduct on duty and any other circumstances that might compromise the reputation of the force. The commissioners took a dim view of the discovery that two former British soldiers on the force had frequented brothels, an act that brought 'the character of the force into disrepute' and was not only a 'gross breach of discipline' but showed 'a great want of decency.'[40] They also condemned Constable Sprale for 'living beyond his means and contracting debts and borrowing money in such a manner as would be likely to interfere with the independent discharge of his duties.' Constables were supposed to lead exemplary lives, both on and off the beat, whether in uniform or not. 'The practice of drinking,' in particular, was thought 'so disreputable and calculated to lower the efficiency and respectability of the Police Force' that it would result in instant dismissal.[41] The Toronto force had to be seen to be disciplined and moral.

In order to implement this policy the commissioners passed a number of regulations designed to insulate the force from popular influences and to establish its own esprit de corps. Greater attentiveness was paid to drill and dress, and all articles of personal clothing such as coloured mufflers were expressly banned.[42] Contacts with the press were also formalized, and police stations were discouraged from fraternizing with local journalists who dropped in to pick up the latest news. Instead, officers were commanded to observe 'those rules of order, secrecy and discipline which are so essential to a well organized body, without the necessity of a newspaper puff as an incentive to the proper performance of their duties.'[43] In addition, a police barracks was set up for the single constables to minimize their informal contact with the population. When this practice had to be discontinued for financial reasons, the bachelors on the force were advised to board together in a 'respectable lodging house as they will find it more comfortable and more independent than scattered and mixed with people through the Division.' On no account could they board in taverns or saloons or 'be seen lounging and talking about Bar Rooms and public houses.'[44] In a similar vein, constables were ordered not to fraternize on the beat, either among themselves or with the street population. To enforce this, the commissioners instituted a card system that obliged the men to clock in at various points on their daily rounds.[45]

There is no doubt that the rank and file chafed at some of these regulations and resented the power that they gave to the more overbearing officers on the force. Particular exception was taken to the card system, which many felt prevented them from investigating infractions of the law and subjected them to humiliating reprimands from officers. These grievances surfaced in 1872, when the dismissal of several respected members of the force triggered demands for the suspension of the chief and his two principal supporters, Sergeants William Ward and Patrick Cummins. At a meeting at St Lawrence Hall at which forty-three members of the force were present, a public inquiry into the firings was demanded in conjunction with the suspension of Prince and company, in whom the force expressed no confidence. Several strictures were also passed against the commissioners for consistently siding with Prince over police grievances and denying the force a fair hearing. 'If men who were engaged in working on the streets for a dollar a day knew what the members of the Toronto police force had to endure,' declared one constable, 'they would rather continue to work on the streets until they were as grey as badgers.'[46] So embittered was the force, in fact, that until its demands were met it seriously contemplated a strike.

The commissioners, in reply, dismissed the whole force, much to the alarm of city council, whose high regard for the chief of police was far from unanimous. Since his appointment, Captain Prince had not escaped censure, partly because he had consistently flaunted the powers of the board on questions of discipline, and partly because he had gained a reputation for arrogance and arbitrariness. As one constable had complained some years earlier, Prince 'might be a very good military man, but he was no man for the police force.'[47] Even so, the commissioners refused to back down, and within two weeks police resistance crumbled. Most of the constables were reinstated, but at least sixteen were not.

The 1872 episode revealed that the police rank and file did not always take kindly to Prince's brand of regimen and resented the degree to which the force was run on paramilitary lines with little discretionary power for the man on the beat. Discipline had often been enforced at the expense of morale. Under the more relaxed leadership of Major Frank Draper, a barrister and officer in the Upper Canada Company of the Queen's Own Rifles, this situation changed. Assuming command in 1874, when Prince retired to become the warden of Toronto Prison, Draper ensured that the police force was aware of its growing responsibilities, particularly in the area of moral reform, and yet remained sensitive to its needs. He was instrumental, for example, in establishing a life insurance and disability fund that guaranteed the force some security against the hazards of daily duty. He built up the social aspects of police life, providing the force with gymnastic equipment in the form of clubs, dumbells, parallel and horizontal bars, and pistol-shooting contests. He also set up a bagatelle and billiard room at headquarters and a library, where policemen could browse through 700 volumes of 'useful and instructive literature.'[48] How extensively these facilities were used it is impossible to say, but the evidence suggests that they achieved the desired aim of enhancing police solidarity and forging a perception of its role as a 'muscular Christian' force. The Toronto policemen of the mid-1880s won respect for their 'soldierly bearing' and physique; they were also commended for their reforming zeal. As an 1886 report noted: 'The religious and temperance elements are by no means unrepresented in the ranks: not a few occupy important official positions in connection with city churches, and many are enthusiastic Sabbath School workers. A Police Bible Class has been in existence for many years, and the weekly meetings are attended by large and constantly increasing number.'[49] The report added that there were probably more temperance advocates in the force than in any comparable institution in the country. The police force of Toronto the Good had been born.

By the 1880s, then, Toronto had a professional police force, which in middle-class eyes compared favourably with its counterparts south of the border. Suitably equipped with batons, handcuffs, and pistols and suitably drilled, it seemed a far cry from the 'uniformly slovenly' force of the pre-reform era and a genuine advance upon the 'anything but martial-looking patrolmen of the American cities.'[50] Unlike those forces, it was also segregated from the mainstream of working-class life. Policemen in Toronto tended to live close to one another in the more respectable quarters of the city, and a substantial proportion were recruited from outside.[51] Despite the dramatic growth of the native-born population, only 28 per cent of the force were Canadian in 1881. The rest were British, principally Irish Protestants, and often drawn directly from British forces. Given the composition of the force and its relative distance from working-class communities, one needs to ask whether the popularity of the force was as unanimous as its middle-class supporters claimed and what role it fulfilled in the rapidly expanding commercial and industrial metropolis of Ontario.

The Toronto police force of the mid-Victorian era fulfilled the expectations of its architects in one important respect. It was no longer embroiled in municipal or provincial politics. The old charges of police corruption and partiality, which had formed the staple of Reform rhetoric in the 1840s and early 1850s, disappeared in subsequent decades. The police commissioners enforced the 'no politics' rule in the force and threatened any constables or officers with dismissal if they openly canvassed at election time. They assured the constables that it was 'in a great measure owing to the members of the Toronto police force keeping aloof from Election matters that they have gained for themselves that high opinion which the respectable portion of the public entertain for them.'[52] Such emphasis did not go unheeded, and there is no evidence that the police acted as an electoral phalanx or connived at the habitual violence of the hustings. Non-partisanship remained the policy of the era. Police neutrality was not extended to the left in subsequent decades, particularly in the 1920s, but that is another story.[53]

The Toronto police force also sought to disengage itself from the sectarian violence that characterized Protestant and Catholic anniversaries after 1850. Following the circus riot of 1856, the police were anxious to rebuild a reputation as an impartial force and avoid the imputation that they were sympathetic to Orange rowdyism. Indeed, the tolerance of Orangeism within the force was to a large extent conditional upon its willingness to suppress sectarian disturbances. Consequently, it arrested rioters on St Patrick's Day in 1858 and again on the anniversary of the Battle of the Boyne on 12 July.[54] The police also restrained Orange militancy during the visit of the Prince of Wales in September 1860, although they made no attempt to remove the transparency of King Billy from the arch that greeted the heir apparent, much to the disgust of his Catholic companion, the Duke of Newcastle.[55] This indiscretion aside, respectable opinion in Toronto was satisfied with the force's role in curbing sectarian rivalry and commented favourably upon its interventions. This task was greatly helped by the efforts of both Orange and Catholic hierarchies to keep youthful societies in line and to domesticate local festivals with orderly processions and sometimes indoor celebrations. By the 1870s, Orange and Green anniversaries were quite respectable affairs, with well-organized parades, defined routes, and spectators of all classes and ages; including, so the *Globe* reported in its description of the 1870 Orange day, large numbers of 'the gentler sex, who showed in the colors of their *toilette* sympathy with the cause.'[56] What violence there was tended to occur on the periphery of the main celebrations, or even days later, when the youthful bands of the Orange and Green broached on each other's territory with songs and airs calculated to inflame tempers.[57] These ritualized encounters were often quite predictable, both in time and place, and were not especially difficult to contain. The police moved promptly to frustrate the regular Orange descents upon the Catholic quarter of Queen Street West, which centred on Owen Cosgrove's tavern. They kept a sharp eye out for the impetuous and impromptu marches of the Young Britons and Young Irish down the main thoroughfares, the symbolic appropriations of space for their respective orders.[58] And they cracked down on Stanley Street, where rough, bohemian Catholics were noted for their Hibernian passions, bad whisky, and lawlessness.

There were occasions, of course, when sectarian violence proved more difficult to contain, when respectability gave way to demagogy, forcing the police to deal with licensed crowds. Such was the case in 1875, when the Catholics planned a series of pilgrimages to their churches to celebrate the papal jubilee. The first visits passed without incident, but the more ostentatious procession of late September, coming in the wake of the Guibord affair in Montreal and the first Catholic provincial council in Toronto, occasioned disturbances.[59] The 7,000 people in the procession were heckled on their way to the cathedral, and skirmishes between Catholics and Orangemen broke out during the second phase of the parade, as it wound its way to St Mary's on Bathurst Street, forcing the police to bring in reinforcements to maintain order. This upswing of violence prompted some Orange lodges to campaign for a ban on the final pilgrimage on the grounds that it violated the Lord's Day and was openly provocative. At a general meeting convened by Mayor Medcalf, a leading Orangeman, this position was not endorsed; indeed, the violence between pilgrims and Protestants was deplored, but Orangemen made it blatantly clear that Catholics 'had no right to obtrude publicly their sectional peculiarities upon the majority'[60] and that they would be responsible for further disorder. To the Young Britons present, this was a licence to riot and they responded accordingly. On 3 October, with troops in readiness in case of a major disturbance, the police had to protect the parade from angry demonstrators at the intersections of Queen and Yonge streets and of Victoria and Adelaide. That night they intervened to prevent the destruction of Cosgrove's tavern, the major rendezvous for Toronto Fenians. Although the *Leader* believed the force used its pistols too freely in these disturbances and shot indiscriminately at fleeing spectators, most newspapers commended the police for their restraint.[61] The *Mail* found it admirable that a predominantly Protestant police force had acted so impartially. So, too, did the Catholic community, which subscribed money to a police benevolent fund. 'Let it not be said in future,' wrote the *Irish Canadian*, 'that we have a Police Force who wink at crime or shirk their duty in the most trying emergency.'[62]

Three years later this judgment was put to the test. On 17 March 1878, the American Fenian O'Donovan Rossa visited Toronto to deliver a lecture to local Hibernians. Again tempers ran high, and the police had to form a deep cordon around St Patrick's Hall to ward off angry Orange demonstrators. Later that evening they were called in to protect Cosgrove's and also Collins's tavern further west. A large number of people were wounded in these affrays, including several policemen, who 'stood the showers and revolver firing with singular coolness,' one newspaper reported, and 'behaved throughout with great intrepidity and prudence ... using their batons only in their repeated charges on the mob.'[63] Whether this was true or not, the police interventions were bolstering the reputation of the force as a bulwark against sectarian violence. Despite its Orange membership, it was no longer seen to be an instrument of the order.

By the 1870s, then, the Toronto police had been disengaged from its old partisan stance and had begun to win the admiration of the press for its suppression of public disturbance. Yet important as this activity was in enhancing the public image of the police and shaping the debate over reform, it did not constitute its major function. The force's role in curbing popular protest was never as pronounced as it was in some British cities, or as pressing, as contemporaries were well aware. This point was made repeatedly in the public discussion of the government's police bill in 1856. Toronto did not need a large, highly centralized force adept at riot control. A more modest force, shorn of its former political affiliations, would ably perform that task.

What Toronto required, and what ultimately determined its size and tenor, was a force that would serve as an efficient 'instrument in curbing the immorality of society.'[64] As the annual crime statistics show, this constituted the force's main responsibility. During the early reform era the Toronto police did not have to deal with a major increase in property crime. Burglaries and robberies represented an insignificant proportion of the total offences handled by the police.[65] The same was true of petty theft or larceny, which formed some 6 per cent of the prosecutions in the 1860s and 1870s, rising to nearly 11 per cent by 1880. By this time public anxiety about the level of property crime was beginning to increase and the detection services of the force were augmented. Even so, the per capita level of property crime, including fraud and receiving stolen property, had scarcely risen, amounting to seven offences per 1,000 inhabitants in 1862 and eight per 1,000 in 1880. These were insignificant compared to the levels that prevailed in large British cities.

If property crime was not a major concern, arresting drunks, prosecuting prostitutes, and clearing the streets of troublesome youths undoubtedly were. The crime statistics reveal that the police spent the bulk of their time dealing with such offences. Indeed the prosecution of the 'drunk and disorderly,' which included periodic raids on bawdy-houses and the apprehension of street-walkers, was the major preoccupation of the Victorian police, constituting from 40 to 55 per cent of the offences listed in the annual statistics. Together with common assault, the second major offence, it represented roughly 60 per cent of the total crime reported in Toronto in any one year.

No doubt readers will express little surprise at this. After all, such offences have traditionally formed the staple of the magistrate's court and the routine business of the police. Nevertheless there is evidence to suggest that the Toronto police, egged on by respectable opinion, saw moral reform as its particular vocation. To begin with, the force strove to curb the more unruly aspects of popular culture, prohibiting bonfires, restraining weekend revels, banning squibs and firecrackers, and curbing the activities of 'mischievous urchins' who sought to soil the crinoline dresses of respectable ladies on national holidays.[66] The police also acted assiduously to disperse 'all assemblies of boys' who heckled church-goers; several complaints of such plebeian banter were made to the police board by aldermen and other influential citizens. In addition, they regularly enforced the Sabbatarian laws, arresting those playing skittles and baseball and clamping down on Sunday trading.[67] Infractions of the licensing laws were not tolerated. Constables were encouraged to keep a sharp eye on the more rowdy taverns and to prosecute after-hours drinking, and while there was some resistance to this policy in the early days of the reformed force,[68] it most certainly subsided in the wake of mounting pressure from temperance societies. By the 1870s police enforcement of the licensing laws was more rigorous and comprehensive than hitherto. New beats were established to crack down on illegal groggeries. Such was public confidence in police action that it looked to the New Year's prosecutions of drunkenness in the police court as an index of the moral standing of the city. Thus the *Globe* reported in January 1870: 'The city appears to have settled down into an unusual state of sobriety after the holidays and elections. The promoters of the temperance cause have reason to hope that the millenium of temperance is at length about to dawn upon our once alcohol imbibing city.[69]

Thus there are grounds for seeing the police as the domestic missionaries of Toronto, buttressing the efforts of moral reform agencies to clean up the city and imbue it with the values of work, religion, and respectability. The efforts of the police to restrain plebeian revelry and instil habits of sobriety and industry in the working class undoubtedly appealed to respectable Torontonians who wished to distance the city from its pioneer past and to establish a moral ethos consonant with the new industrial and commercial order. But what was the response of the populace at large to police activity? To what extent did the rougher elements of the working class resist police authority? And what was the overall effect of police intervention in everyday life on police-community relations? It is these questions that we must now address.

Such questions are not, unfortunately, easy to answer. The police records themselves tell us far more about the organization of the force than they do about its relationship with the community. In so far as they reveal anything at all about the public view of the police, it is a middle-class view, of those citizens whom the board would respect. The sentiments of the subaltern classes have to be reconstructed through indirect sources, from the odd snippet of information in the newspapers or from the criminal statistics. These sources suggest in the first instance that the population that bore the brunt of police vigilance was the marginal poor (rather than the organized working class), especially the Irish immigrant.[70] Casual labourers, prostitutes, and vagrants constituted at least half of those brought before the courts, and within the criminal population as a whole the Irish were disproportionately highly represented. Throughout the mid-century decades the percentage of Irish men and women prosecuted by the police remained roughly twice as high as the percentage of their numbers within the total population. The same was not true of other major immigrant groups, still less of native-born Canadians.

Most of these Irish were Catholics who arrived in Toronto in vast numbers after the Famine. Unemployed and desperately poor, bringing with them patterns of sociability that did not square with the dominant ethos of Victorian Toronto, they were the inevitable targets of police action. Lacking the collective resources of other groups and receiving little solace from the church, which used its charitable resources to moderate their wakes and instil notions of self-help, thrift, and decorum within their ranks,[71] they were powerless before police discrimination. How resistant the Irish Catholics were to police intervention one can only guess. Certainly they strongly resented the official prohibition of their shebeens, for registered assaults on the police took an upswing during the drive against unlicensed dram-shops and the Irish were disproportionately represented.[72] In all probability it was not until the 1880s, when the Irish Catholics became more attuned to the rhythms and expectations of industrial life, that they accorded the police a begrudging acquiescence.

Compared to the Irish Catholic population, other sectors of the working class appear to have had better relations with the police. The older working-class neighbourhoods could count on aldermanic protection in their relations with the police, and if the force proved too officious, pressure was brought to bear both in and outside the police court.[73] Where policemen were resident in the ward such constraints could be considerable, particularly if the constable concerned was an Orangeman, for there seems to have been an unwritten code of honour that policemen affiliated to the order should not arrest fellow members.[74] The geographical segregation of the force, however, and its growing occupational identity, counteracted such tendencies as the century progressed, so that no area of the city could gain immunity from policing. In any case, such immunity was not considered desirable. A cursory perusal of the 'Police News' in the *Globe* and other papers suggests that working people were not averse to calling on the police to take action on private quarrels. One is struck by the frequency with which constables were called in to deal with cases of nuisances and common assault, even wife-beating, despite the fact that the force was officially advised 'not to interfere unnecessarily between a man and his wife who are quarrelling ... unless it is absolutely necessary to prevent serious violence to either party.'[75] Interventions were sometimes resented. In some households the Toronto police were nicknamed the 'new Peelers' after Sir Robert Peel's unpopular force.[76] But such resentment was far from universal and by and large was based on pragmatic rather than ideological considerations. The working class might baulk at the police's morality drives and its curtailment of youthful revelry; such resentments surfaced during the papal jubilee riots of 1875 – for the *Globe* reported that 'the full anger of the roughs ... seemed dictated rather by a dislike of the officers of the peace than to the processionists.' Even so, the more respectable element of the working class was prepared to avail itself of police services where necessary, particularly with regard to prosecutions for larceny and assult.[77] There was little resistance within the working class as a whole to the notion of a policed society.

Three themes are worth emphasizing in the development of Toronto's police force. The first, and most obvious, is the growing presence of the police in civilian life through the accretion of responsibilities in a rapidly expanding, complex city. In 1834 the police force resembled the parish watch of old England. It was small, localized, and marginal; without auxiliaries it could not fulfil even its peace-keeping responsibilities at election time, still less a political crisis such as the rebellion of 1837. Fifty years later it was a professional force, 159 strong, equipped with a telegraph service and a detective agency, and also with a range of social services such as a library, a recreation room, an insurance fund, and a few voluntary societies that provided both security and a sense of occupational identity. Disciplined and drilled, it proved capable of dealing with large-scale riots and with the enforcement of a growing array of city by-laws. In this sphere, particularly with respect to licensing, the police had assumed new responsibilities, just as they had with respect to the prosecution of interpersonal suits in the lesser courts.

But the development of the force should not simply be measured quantitatively, in terms of the growing volume and range of police business and the sophistication of organizational forms. In a more profound sense the police had become integrated into the authority structures of Victorian

Toronto, alongside schools, charities, prisons, asylums, and benefit societies.[78] Whereas the early force had served as an intermittent check on
lawlessness and was constrained by its size, by its links with the community,
and by the easy-going, indulgent attitude of the authorities, the mid-century
police were called on to discipline in new ways. It became the coercive agency
of moral reform, the task force for the new respectability. To be sure, the
dominant forces in Victorian Toronto could not always agree on the form
police reform should take. But they were always unanimous about the force's
function as a vanguard of 'improvement,' active in the campaign against
ruffianism, drunkenness, and immorality. So central did the role of the police
become that the state of the police force itself became an index of the moral
condition of society.

If the police force was to fulfil its task, it had to be disengaged from its old
affiliations. As an instrument of hegemony it had to be seen as impartial. This
was effected in two ways. First, it was encouraged to insulate itself from local
neighbourhoods, to segregate itself from the working class and develop its
own occupational solidarity. After 1858 Toronto policemen were deliberately
recruited from outside, from British forces where the tradition of police
autonomy was deep-rooted. In many respects this violated the representative
principle to which many Reformers were initially committed, but, as in Britain
so in Toronto, the imperatives of moral improvement held sway. Whatever
virtues Reformers saw in the American system of police organization, where
accountability was determined by more democratic procedures, they were
tarnished by the experience of early Toronto politics. A more centralized,
paramilitary force seemed more appropriate to the task at hand.

The problem of detaching the police from the Orange order proved more
vexatious and intractable. The more progressive Reformers, certainly those
such as John O'Donoghue who represented the Catholic constituency,
would have liked to ban all members of secret societies from the force. But
Conservative resistance and the political exigencies of the day made this an
impossibility, at least as a practical policy. The result was that the Orange
presence on the force was openly tolerated on the implicit assumption that it
would not embroil the force in party politics. This policy was respected. It
satisfied the Reform party, which wished to create a non-partisan force
without alienating the Orange electorate. And it allowed the Conservatives to
court Catholic ranks without abandoning their traditional constituency. It
also aided the Orange Order's own quest for respectability without any loss
of prestige. Police reform, in other words, was the product of a complex
resolution of forces. Without challenging the prevailing configurations of
power, reform strengthened the hegemonic authority of the police and, by

extension, the quest for moral reform. No longer a political weapon in the struggle for municipal power, the police could make a significant contribution to the making of Toronto the Good.

NOTES

I should like to thank Cynthia Patterson and Nicole Tellier for their research assistance and the Social Science and Humanities Research Council of Canada for funding the project. Thanks also to Greg Kealey for sending me an early draft of his essay 'Orangemen and the Corporation,' above. Without it I should have been lost in the thicket of mid-century Toronto politics.

1 *Canadian Freeman* 1 January 1829, cited in E.G. Firth *The Town of York, 1815–1834: A Further Collection of Documents of Early Toronto* (Toronto 1966) 279
2 City of Toronto Archives (hereafter CTA), Minutes of City Council (hereafter Minutes), 1835, items 174, 202
3 Ibid, 1838, items 149, 163
4 Ibid, 1843, item 108
5 Ibid, 1843, item 173
6 *Examiner* 11 November 1841
7 Ibid 2 December 1840, 24 March 1841
8 Ibid 11 November 1841
9 Ibid
10 Cecil J. Houston and William J. Smyth *The Sash Canada Wore: A Historical Geography of the Orange Order in Canada* (Toronto 1980) 157–9
11 *Globe* 28 March 1849
12 *Examiner* 17 October 1849
13 *Globe* 23 October 1849
14 Ibid 16 July 1855; *Examiner* 4 July 1855
15 *Globe* 24 July 1855
16 Ibid 24 July 1855; Minutes, 1855, item 574
17 Minutes, 1855, item 574
18 See council debate in *Globe* 27 July 1855.
19 *Leader* 29 March 1856; *Globe* 29 March 1856. See also *Report of the Commissioners Appointed to Investigate and Report upon the Best Areas of Re-Organizing the Militia of Canada and upon an Improved system of Police* (Quebec 1855).
20 *Globe* 31 March 1856

21 *McKenzie's Weekly Message* 11 April 1856
22 *Globe* 15 April 1856
23 Province of Canada *Statutes* 22 Victoria cap 99 clause 380
24 *Globe* 5 February 1859
25 Police expenses, as a proportion of total civic expenditure were as follows: 1859: 3.7 per cent; 1870: 3.4 per cent; 1875: 4.2 per cent; 1880: 5.2 per cent.
26 Police Museum, Minute Book of the Board of Police Commissioners (hereafter Police Minutes) 1858–1862, 3 December 1858, 4
27 Minutes, 1860, Appendices 8 and 9; *Globe* 7 February 1860
28 *Globe* 3 June 1856
29 Ibid 5 February 1859
30 Ibid 25 February 1859. See also *Canadian Freeman* 4 March 1859.
31 *Globe* 28 June 1859, 14 January 1860
32 Ibid 28 June 1859, 31 January 1860
33 Ibid 28 December 1858
34 *Irish Canadian* 12 November 1885
35 *Globe* 27 December 1858; for a useful comparison of British and American police forces, see Wilbur R. Miller *Cops and Bobbies: Police Authority in New York and London 1830–1870* (Chicago 1977).
36 Basil Jackson 'To Serve and Protect: The Remarkable and Exciting History of the Metropolitan Police Force,' typescript, n.d., CTA, p 47
37 Minutes, 1859, Appendix 7
38 Ibid, 1860, Appendix 187
39 Ibid, 1869, Appendix 9
40 Police Minutes 1858–1862, 31 July 1861, 177–8
41 Ibid 1868–1878, November 1877, 456; *Toronto Police Force: General Orders and Regulations* (Toronto 1878) 39–40
42 Police Museum, Order Book 1860–1863, 64
43 Order Book 1859–1860, 50–2. See Minutes, 1864, items 155, 156.
44 Order Book 1859–1860, 88; Order Book 1860–1863, 262
45 *Globe* 10 May 1872. See also Gurnett's address to the force, ibid 25 December 1858.
46 Ibid 10 May 1872; *Daily Mail* 10 May 1872
47 Police Minutes 1858–1860, 16 June 1860, 77–8
48 Minutes, 1878, Appendix 35
49 Jackson 'To Serve and Protect' 62
50 C.C. Taylor *The Queen's Jubilee and Toronto Called Back from 1887–1847* (Toronto 1892) 49; *History of Toronto & County of York* (Toronto 1885) 305
51 These conclusions are drawn from an investigation of the published roll of the 1881 force, in conjunction with Might's city directory. For the roll see Minutes, 1882, Appendix 12.

52 Order Book 1860–1863, 242–3, 249

53 Michiel Horn 'Keeping Canada "Canadian": Anti-Communism and Canadian-ism in Toronto 1928–29' in *Canada: A Historical Magazine* III 1 (September 1975) 35–47

54 *Globe* 18, 23, 25, 27 March 1858

55 Ibid 4–12 September 1858

56 Ibid 13 July 1879, 14 July 1873

57 See *Globe* 11 July 1876, 13 July 1877; *Daily Mail* 13 July 1877.

58 *Daily Mail* 19 June 1877; *Globe* 29 July 1873. On Stanley Street, see *Globe* 14, 16 July 1857, 13 July 1870.

59 *Globe* 27 September 1875

60 Ibid 2 October 1875

61 Ibid 4 October 1875; *The Nation* 8 October 1875. For a good summary of the press response see Martin Galvin 'Catholic and Protestant Relations in Ontario 1864–1875' MA thesis, University of Toronto, 1962, chapter 4.

62 *Irish Canadian* 6 October 1875. See also ibid 20 October 1875.

63 Ibid 20 March 1878. Two policemen, Constables Johnston and Worth, were severely wounded. See Minutes, 1879, Appendix 35.

64 *Globe* 15 April 1856

65 These conclusions are based on the crime statistics given by the chief of police in his annual reports to council, 1862–80. For an English comparison see David Jones *Crime, Protest, Community and Police in Nineteenth-Century Britain* (London 1982) chapter 5.

66 *Globe* 17 May 1872; Order Book 1859–1860, 120–2, 490; Order Book 1860–1863, 69, 106, 211, 218, 351–3, 361

67 *Globe* 6 May 1872, 13 May 1872, 2 April 1856 (with headline 'A Caution to Sabbath Breakers')

68 Order Book 1860–1863, 237

69 *Globe* 8 January 1870

70 See the criminal statistics for 1870–3, where occupations are given (see note 65, above).

71 Murray W. Nicolson 'The Irish Catholics and Social Action in Toronto 1850–1900' *Studies in History and Politics* I 1 (fall 1980) 30–55

72 These conclusions are based on an examination of the annual criminal registers and the Register of Criminals for 1876 and 1878 in CTA.

73 Minutes, 1867, item 401; *Evening Colonist* 26 September 1859

74 *Globe* 5 February 1859, 'Police Court,' the case of Henry Wray

75 See, for example, ibid 27 December 1858, 16 January 1870, 14 May 1872, 22 May 1877.

76 Ibid 29 January 1859. For domestic disputes see *Toronto Police Force: General Orders and Regulations* 1st edn (Toronto 1878) 10.

77 Of the 86 cases of larceny mentioned in the Register of Criminals for January 1878, 83 were prosecuted by or with the aid of policemen. Similarly, most of the assault charges made in August 1879 were prosecuted by the police rather than by private individuals (50 to 41). Twenty-three years earlier the great majority of prosecutions for larceny and assault brought before the Police Court were private. See *The Leader* 1 May–9 June 1856.

78 This was revealed during the semi-centennial celebrations. Not only did the police occupy a prominent position in the Municipal and Historical Day parade, but the police stations were also listed among the sights of Toronto, alongside the court house, the asylum, and the central prison. See the *Globe* 28 June, 1 July 1884.

J.M.S. CARELESS

The first hurrah

Toronto's semi-centennial of 1884

BEFORE TORONTO'S SESQUICEN-
TENNIAL of 1984 came the centennial salute of 1934, and, before that, the
semi-centennial of 1884, when for the first time it celebrated its civic growth,
the first fifty years of being a city. What was it like, that initial public hallelujah
of 100 years ago, when the citizens honoured Toronto's past, lauded its
present, and hailed its future? It might be instructive as well as interesting to
find out. Not that there are profound conclusions to be drawn. The one
general conclusion that comes readily to mind is that the city has skilfully
managed to prepare its recurring fifty-year festivities in times of economic
gloom, whether the recession-depression of the early 1980s, the Great
Depression of the 1930s, or the severely strained times of 1884. In the two
earlier cases, depression did prove to be a prelude to succeeding stages of
striking city growth; and the festivities themselves at least diverted attention
from existing troubles. We should trust that history will go on repeating itself.

Beyond that, the circumstances in which the events of 1884 took form show
other analogies with those of our present occasion. There was worry over
jubilating when so many were in need, concern about extravagance when the
civic budget was so tight. Otherwise, the differences are quite revealing. This
was a much smaller, Victorian, and very British city in the 1880s, flag-waving
imperialist though no less ardently Canadian in national hope. It was
'Toronto the Good' in that age (and liked the reputation), not 'Toronto the
Pleasure Dome'; the city of homes and churches, not of high-rise and airport
hotels. And yet it was Toronto, then as now. History may repeat or not, but it
does continue. Similar forces then affected and moved the citizens; the city
shaped them, as they shaped it, 100 years ago as well as today. The

semi-centennial affair in Victorian Toronto can thus tell the present populace something of themselves as well as of their own town's past. And it is in that broad (if inevitably hazy) sense that it is really worth looking at the high doings of 1884.

Let us look at the stage and the actors – the people – before the play unfolds. Toronto in the early 1880s was a prominent lake port and railway town going through rapid industrialization. Its role as capital of Ontario gave it political leadership of a wide and productive section of Canada; southern Ontario had thriving, heavily populated farm land and substantial local commercial centres. Toronto's radiating railway network linked and focused this most advanced of Canadian regions. Toronto's wholesale sector dominated much of the area, competing vigorously against inroads from still larger Montreal. And Toronto's expanding factories and outreaching finances now supplied goods or services not only to Ontario, but to Canadian areas beyond. Here was a notable record of economic development since the city's incorporation in 1834. From an aspiring little Lake Ontario port town it had grown to a controlling regional hub and was heading onward to become a national metropolis, once railway lines had spanned the west, which the Canadian Pacific Railway would do in 1885. Times might look bad, even as that rail line was thrusting westward in 1883–4, but there was much to anticipate, and a great deal to acclaim already.

From under 10,000 residents in 1834, the city's population had risen to around 86,000 by 1882 and was climbing rapidly as massing industries gathered in workers; the annexation of neighbouring suburbs began in 1883. The citizens of this community of the 1880s were in majority Canadian-born, but overwhelmingly of British descent, products of long-continuing immigration from Great Britain. According to the census of 1881, the largest element were of English origin, more than 34,000, to 32,000 Irish (both southern Catholic and northern Protestant) and nearly 14,000 Scots.[1] Those with non-British origins were few in number, including about 2,000 of German background, 1,200 French, 124 Jews, and 103 Italians. In religion, the Church of England again was largest, with almost 31,000 adherents to 15,700 Roman Catholics, 15,200 Methodists, and 14,500 Presbyterians. The Catholics (chiefly Irish) formed a substantial minority, but the city was predominantly Protestant; and the sizeable numbers of Protestant Irish had made the Orange order, derived from Northern Ireland, a powerful factor both in lower-class society and civic politics. Clashes between Orange and Green remained an unruly feature of Toronto life, while religious allegiances still divided a very church-conscious citizenry. However, the 93 per cent

preponderance of British stock produced a high degree of cultural homogeneity. Language and ethnic differences played relatively small parts in this
late Victorian community.

Certainly there were class separations – including those of residential
neighbourhoods – between an upper class of big merchants, bankers, and
entrepreneurs, a middle class of rising industrialists, building contractors,
professionals, and shopowners, and the wage-earning masses, among whom a
broad new union organization, the Knights of Labor, was gradually taking
shape. The hard year of 1884, however, saw a declining phase in labour strife,
though waves of strikes occurred both before and after that year.[2] Otherwise,
the uniformities in British background and community outlook seemed to
hold sway. They showed in the city's reverence for the crown and eager pride
in empire. That very year, the vast British imperial domain would be caught
up with the African Nile expedition to rescue General Charles Gordon from
foes in the Sudan: for empire (and Toronto), Fred C. Denison resigned as
alderman to command Canadian voyageurs sent to the Nile.

The city appeared sure of its destiny in an English-dominated Canada, in
the continent-wide Confederation that major Toronto politicians had worked
earnestly to build. Yet it still kept a wary eye on the power of the United States
across an open Lake Ontario water boundary. Twice in the War of 1812
American forces had crossed to raid and ransack the early town. In 1837
rebels, fired with pro-republican radicalism, had descended on the city, and,
though they were quickly dispersed, their American sympathizers had kept
up border skirmishes for a year more. Within closer memory was the Fenian
Raid of 1866 over the border into the nearby Niagara area. Though
Torontonians traded readily with American neighbours and welcomed
American techniques and capital, they suspected that useful friends might still
turn menacing again. Hence, in the preaching of hands across the border,
there was always a strain of doubt in this defensively British and Conservative
city: doubt not felt in happily flying the guardian Union Jack.

This, too, was implicit in the celebrating mood of 1884, as was the
enthusiastic singing of a near–national anthem, *The Maple Leaf Forever*,
written by Toronto's own Alexander Muir in 1867. It was a very British
anthem, nevertheless, that had General James Wolfe planting Britannia's flag
on the 'fair domain' of Canada, and 'entwined' the rose, thistle, and
shamrock. It left out the French fleur-de-lis, which did not loom large in the
city's consciousness except as associated with Quebec Catholicism, another
highly suspect outside force to Protestant Toronto. At all events, *God Save
the Queen* still reigned, as did the great Victoria herself. In the national
capital, Ottawa, her loyal adherent, Sir John A. Macdonald, ruled, soundly

backed by Toronto's majority Conservative opinion, its Orangeism, and its economic interests, which had aligned themselves with Macdonald's National Policy of protection, which had in turn profitably stimulated the city's own recent industrial growth. As a provincial capital, Toronto was the seat of the no less enduring Ontario Liberal government of Oliver Mowat; there was a considerable city Liberal minority, and the cautious, 'good business,' and duly loyal regime of Mowat could be tolerated by the city's Tory majority.

The city of 1884 occupied most of the low lakeside plain where it had begun, beside the sheltered harbour of Toronto Bay – spreading from the Don River westward toward the Humber River, and inland, where a sudden rise led to higher plains above. Already, though, Yorkville Village north of the old Bloor Street city limit had been annexed in 1883; and Riverside east of the Don and Brockton Village reaching west to High Park followed in 1884, the first extensions of the original civic limits set in 1834. A filling city was spilling over its boundaries and taking in adjoining suburbs that wanted its services, as it did their revenue. Newer residential areas were also rising, from the working-class west end to high-class, north-central Rosedale. Older areas close to the downtown core had become crowded and run down, gathering places for poor and immigrants, as in central St John's Ward (later, just 'The Ward') or the east end, near the Don. This shabby world was sharply different from that of the mansions on upper Jarvis Street, or near Queen's Park beside the University of Toronto. Yet in its central area this Victorian city also displayed some admirable buildings: stately, classical Osgoode Hall, home of the lawyers; the ornate, pillared Custom's House; tall Gothic churches such as the Anglican St James', Catholic St Michael's, and Methodist Metropolitan, or the newer 'Norman-Scottish' Presbyterian St Andrews'. There were a Grand Opera House, a pinnacled Union Station, big banks, a monumental 'Second Empire' Post Office, and, most recent, the Manning Arcade of 1884, a well-proportioned modern office block.

King Street remained the main business thoroughfare, as it long had been; but Queen was rising, especially near Yonge, where the aggressive merchants Timothy Eaton and Robert Simpson were building large stores and centralizing retail shopping. Yonge Street, moreover, was Toronto's main north-south artery, leading north into country markets; and lower Yonge, near to the harbour and railway station, was the focus of large wholesale firms that also spread out their warehouses on Wellington and Front streets. A horse-drawn streetcar line ran up Yonge to Yorkville from the 1860s. But if electric streetcars were nine years distant from the Toronto of 1884 (though an amusement attraction that year at its annual late-summer exhibition), the horse car had linked up the downtown core, thrust several lines east to the

Don or up to Bloor, and on the west had reached the Exhibition Grounds, out west of King, and to Brockton via Queen and other streets.[3] The citizens in the semi-centennial year could thus move easily, if not speedily, by public transport from residential districts to downtown parades, could mass for celebrations in Queen's Park and the Horticultural Gardens by Jarvis Street, or travel out to galas in the spacious Exhibition Grounds and down to fireworks at the harbour.

The harbour area itself was close to being a public mess of rampant private enterprise, scarcely to be hindered by Victorian laissez-faire city administrations. Dock facilities were going up and falling apart at about the same rate; silt, refuse, and sewage surged around the thrashing steamboats and graceful schooners that were the life of the port. Along the waterfront ran the main converging railway lines vital in linking Toronto transport to Montreal, New York, and Ottawa, north to the Muskoka lumber realm, and west across the province to Detroit and Chicago. They could also pour in country people for its celebrations and hotel trade. Yet their tracks imposed a barrier between the citizens and the bay, a belt of dingy wasteland that offered only inconvenient, wearing level crossings through its traffic. Railways might be building an industrial city; but they also gathered smoking factories along their tracks around the eastern and western ends of the waterfront – drab industrial stretches where only those who could do no better lived with the soot, smells, and noise.

Victorian Toronto would blithely regard all this as 'progress,' while its booster publications proudly displayed arrays of belching smokestacks, ungainly factory establishments, and the whiskered worthies who commanded them. Here was another reality of the city of 1884. While zealously upholding law and order, it was spreading disorder in unregulated industrial expansion and unplanned development, urban misery only partially relieved by public, church, and private charities. Fortunately, the possessors showed some degree of social conscience – yet their undoubtedly rich and advancing Toronto had much on the debit side. It was widely gaslit, and electric-arc street lights were introduced in May 1884; but the streets themselves, apart from wood-block pavement on main roads, were only gravel or simply well-manured mud. The city had a plentiful public water-supply, though the product was barely drinkable. It had just launched an active public health office but did little about main drains that poured raw sewage into the harbour from which came drinking water. Its major crime rate was reasonably low, yet lower-class drunkenness and resulting assaults were so apparent that a vehement temperance crusade was rising in response. All in all, Toronto the Good had its black spots. On balance, however, it had ample reason to crow after fifty years of growth, and, good times or bad, it meant to do so.

The resolve to celebrate was no sudden decision. As early as 1882 a special committee of city council led by Mayor William B. McMurrich, a keen exponent throughout,[4] had been set up to consider designs for marking Toronto's fiftieth anniversary. Discussions continued into the winter of 1883–4 under a succeeding mayor, Arthur Boswell. A popular, handsome, well-connected lawyer aged 46, Mayor Boswell made an ideal front man for grand public affairs and enjoyed them heartily.[5] In his opening meeting with the new council in mid-January 1884, he proclaimed that this should be 'in all future time a red-letter year in the history of the Queen City.'[6] Meanwhile, however, a correspondent writing to the Toronto *Globe* complained about a committee progress report that excluded from the proposed celebrations a music festival urged by the influential *Globe* – 'because they could not spare more than two or three thousand dollars.' 'Pitiable,' said the unknown reader Musicola, who went on to deplore the 'parsimonious spirit' typical of the civic fathers, here being injected into the very celebration 'at which the city is to display its character and resources to guests from far and wide.'[7]

The *Globe* itself soothed the writer's indignation, replying that the city would surely rise to the occasion, while adding, 'We should like to see the whole Semi-Centennial idea now take upon itself a greater measure of activity.'[8] Toronto had traditionally been tight-fisted when civic works other than of the practical kind were called for – and often even there as well. There was little room for public gestures in the utilitarian minds of most Toronto aldermen. Drawn largely from conservatively cast lawyers, contractors, and junior merchants, their mandate was to keep down the tax rate, interfere as little as possible with private property rights, maintain social order, and provide just enough municipal services and a modicum of welfare. As a result, city government could scarcely be accused of extravagance and not often of corruption – blatant, anyway. It was a comfortable comradeship of old hands and learning apprentices with notable ties to the Orange order that channelled voting strength from below, in return for civic jobs to the accredited. Yet there was little bossism, plundering, or special dealing (other than for real estate favours) among this staid political in-group. It gave fairly sound, if limited and uninspired, municipal rule. Could it rise to the occasion, or would penny-pinching prevail?

There was good cause to count the cost. The economic downturn signalled by the collapse of the western land boom in 1882 had widened into a general slump in 1883, and 1884 would be no better. The export trades stayed depressed, Toronto's harbour receipts were down as well; sales were off, businesses were folding, and unemployment was rife in the city. Even at the end of the anniversary year, President H.W. Darling of the city's board of trade had to report, 'It would be gratifying if we could say ... the temporary check on our progress which began in 1882 had come to an end, but the record of failures ... forbids this.'[9] Clearly, it was not a good year for lavishing public or private money.

All the same, public and private enthusiasm was mounting as the spring neared, to be expressed in a first round of celebrations on 6 March – the anniversary date of Toronto's incorporation as a city in 1834. But it had been deemed to fall in too chilly a season for public jubilating, and so only brief official ceremonies were planned to commemorate the date, with the real festivities left for summer weather. Accordingly, Mayor Boswell held a civic reception at the forty-year-old city hall on Front Street: a new one was wanted, but funds were the problem. There was a fifty-gun salute at noon, and in the afternoon, to mark the event more lastingly, the lieutenant-governor opened the new free library.[10] So began the Toronto Public Library system, by taking over the book stock and building of the former Mechanics Institute, a privately subscribed body. The public schools were let out for the afternoon, and, though businesses did not close, the main streets were decorated with flags and streamers, while church and school bells rang. It was a not inauspicious beginning to the semi-centennial. The Toronto *Mail* of 6 March, heralding the city's fiftieth anniversary, thought it 'not too much to expect that ere another fifty years roll by her [Toronto's] fame will be worldwide and her influence felt beyond the seas.'

From this time also, the pace of preparations accelerated for the main events in the summer. Public committees had been set up to organize proceedings and were composed of both politicians and leading private citizens: an executive committee chaired by William McMurrich and including Mayor Boswell, a reception committee under Boswell, and a score of others.[11] Membership read like a roll-call of Toronto's élite: the crucial finance committee contained George Gooderham, president of the Bank of Toronto; James Austin, head of the Dominion Bank; Edward Gurney, Jr, of the big stove manufactory; and William Mulock, MP, wealthy jurist and future federal minister. The reception committee boasted Edward Blake, Oliver Mowat, Senator David Macpherson, the powerful Conservative railway contractor, and his no less formidable business associate, Casimir Gzowski, plus Toronto's Anglican bishop, Arthur Sweatman. The military display committee was commanded by Colonel George Taylor Denison, the city's police magistrate and chief authority both on empire and on cavalry tactics. The grounds committee displayed the opulent Honourable George W. Allan, but also the rising labour union figure Robert Glockling: class, party, and sectarian divergences were to be submerged in common citizenship. Similarly, the arrangement committee featured Catholic Vicar-General Rooney, along with various Protestant ministers, Conservative Alexander

Morris, a former federal cabinet member, and the strong Liberal John Macdonald, Toronto's wholesale 'merchant prince.' Finally, in a bow to the intelligentsia, the memorial volume committee held Canon Henry Scadding, dean of city history; G.M. Rose, leading publisher; John Charles Dent, editor-historian; and Dr William Canniff, author and public health reformer, now city medical officer.

If any selection could make the plans succeed, this high-calibre assortment should do so. In April, council even squeezed out $10,000 for the celebrations and named a committee of 10 aldermen (out of a total membership of 36) to take charge henceforth of the city's side of the project, working closely with the citizen groups.[12] It was finally announced that the events would take place in the six days from 30 June to 5 July, a propitious midsummer period that included both Canada's national Dominion Day and 4 July for American tourists. During May and June arrangements went on feverishly – inviting visiting dignitaries, securing bands, bunting, and firework set-pieces, ensuring that parade routes would be kept open[13] and that speeches would be profusely delivered. Citizens, moreover, raised funds of their own (though real totals are hard to fix) and cheerfully gave unpaid labour and services. The city's $10,000 – plus $1,000 given in 1883[14] – might seem paltry today, but the annual salaries of Toronto's chief officials, from mayor to health officer (aldermen were unpaid) amounted to $21,170 – a partial, but revealing index.[15]

At length, everything was as ready as it could be, when 30 June dawned amid beautiful sunny weather. As the *Memorial Volume* subsequently described it: 'In all the glory of a bright summer morning, with flags and banners floating merrily from housetops and windows, with sounds of music from east and west and all around, the 'Semi-Centennial Week' was ushered in.'[16] Under cloudless skies lake breezes cooled the sun's heat, as citizens thronged the streets to admire the decorations. Yonge and King streets led in their wealth of display, though Queen came close, and streets of private residences were hung with boughs, bunting, and Chinese lanterns for the dark. The evergreens and flowers, the flags everywhere, demonstrated the ordinary inhabitants' desire to do their own commemorating. Scarlet tunics of militiamen and ladies in light-hued summer dresses added still more colour, while 'from nearly every coat depended a Semi-Centennial medal or souvenir or fluttered the silk badge announcing the wearer to be an official.'[17] Incidentally, sterling silver souvenir pins cost $1 and up, and gold cost from $8 to $24.[18]

The events of Municipal and Historical Day got under way at noon, when at city hall the civic fathers entertained former mayors and council members, with the mayor of Philadelphia among the guests.[19] That afternoon the first grand procession was held. It moved triumphantly down Yonge Street, headed by mounted city police, resounding bands – from the Queen's Own Rifles to the Massey Manufacturing Company's – and Grand Marshal Henry Piper, a burly alderman astride a splendid horse. Toronto's notables all trundled by in carriages, beaming; the council, the fire and gas committee, Orators of the Day (no connection), the public and separate school boards, and members of the semi-centennial committees and of the York Pioneers. Firemen, 'gorgeous in gleaming helmets, red and blue shirts and bouquets,' were cheered as they marched;[20] but the main attraction was the historical tableaux, a long succession of emblematic floats. They ranged from 'Early Settlers,' 'Landing of Governor Simcoe,' and 'Incorporation of Toronto,' to 'Toronto the Queen City,' showing modern progress festooned with telegraph wires and poles, and 'Toronto Welcomes All,' presenting persons in different national costumes as an early salute to ethnic variety. 'It was such a spectacle as one may not hope to see on more than one occasion in a lifetime,' said a somewhat ambiguous verdict.[21]

The parade circled ponderously but happily through the downtown (with Toronto's old hand-drawn, hand-pumper fire engine of 1834 a particular crowd favourite) and eventually wound up at the Exhibition Grounds well on in the afternoon. There Sir Daniel Wilson, president of University College, gave the main oration. But while he said the city's history was unwritten (his own knowledge ran from ancient rocks to about Henry VIII), he pictured its future as unbounded in 'the greatest, noblest country on the face of the earth.'[22] That evening, a fancy dress ball lasted into a hot night at the pavilion in the Horticultural Gardens, although more popular were the firemen's torchlight parade and the glowing illuminations of business offices and homes 'in glorious red, white and blue,' colours of the patriot flag, the Union Jack.[23] Crowds wandered the streets surveying the scene, especially the triumphant arch over King and Yonge – 'Toronto 1834 and 1884,' depicting a log building on one face, and solid masonry on the other.

Next came Military Day, 1 July. Under a blazing sun relieved only through boating and steamboat excursions on the shimmering bay, the festivities featured foot races out at the athletic grounds in Rosedale and a great meet of 'wheelsmen,' the cycling enthusiasts of the time. The bicycle craze was strong in Toronto (where roller-skating was just being introduced as well), and multitudes saw the cyclists parade and race their high-wheeled 'steeds' for Canadian championships. But the chief spectacle was that of the military forces, properly honouring Canada's national birthday. From campgrounds at the old Garrison Reserve (now Stanley Barracks) by the harbour entry, militia units marched up into Queen's Park for a grand review, held in scorching temperatures that toppled over many participants as well as others among the thousands jamming the park to watch. There were the cavalry of the Governor General's Body Guard, with their mounted band, the horse artillery, the fusiliers, the foot guards, and the grenadiers, dazzling in scarlet, blue, and gold; there were the green of the riflemen, the flash of brass helmets, and always bands, bands for the soldiers of queen and country. Toronto's Queen's Own, well over 500 strong, moved smartly and trimly. Colonel William Otter was especially praised for the efficient training of the men he led. Next year, he would be leading troops to march on Battleford, Saskatchewan, in the Northwest Rebellion, where many of those now drilling would follow. But this was a day of pomp and glory, not bullets and death. Despite the overpowering dusty heat, and 'moving masses of struggling, sweating humanity,'[24] all agreed that it had been a magnificent treat, a high point in the celebrations. Night brought a concert in the cooler Horticultural Gardens by a thirty-five piece band from the Heintzman piano company, followed by an elaborate firework display. Big balloons floated up firing out rockets (the firemen must have looked on anxiously), and it was after 1 a.m. before the show was over.

Trades and Industrial Day followed, representing labour's time on stage. Again there was a massive parade: four miles of marching ranks of workingmen with banners and badges, lines of wagons, tableaux, and bands – including the Ontario Bolt Company's, Dominion Organ's, and the 'Coloured Band.' The Brotherhood of Carpenters, the Bricklayers' Union, the Knights of St Crispin, and other organized trades led the way, while delegations from the Massey Company, engine and metal works, sewing machine and corset plants, Gooderham and Worts Distillers, and Consumers Gas were among the host that followed. Perspiring in the heat, the united workers were undoubtedly glad to reach the Exhibition Grounds and a picnic with their families. A rather different assemblage of 'the fashion and culture of the city' gathered in the Horticultural Gardens Pavilion that evening to hear Haydn's oratorio *The Creation*, nobly sung by a choir of some 300. They 'rose to the sublime,' in fact.[26]

United Empire Loyalists Day, 3 July, remembered the city's loyal past – and more, commemorating the 100th anniversary of the Loyalists' arrival in what was to be Upper Canada, Ontario's predecessor. The Loyalist centennial was a far wider feature of 1884 than Toronto's own anniversary. Hundreds of descendants of United Empire Loyalists now gathered in the city for combined celebrations and crowded a fervent meeting at the pavilion directed by Dr Canniff, authority on early Upper Canadian settlement and of solid UEL stock himself. The Honourable George W. Allen spoke, as did Colonel Denison. There was loyalist poetry and song, and *The Maple Leaf*

Forever; then an afternoon garden party for all the UELs on the lawns of government house. The Toronto press waxed eloquent on the historic contribution of Loyalism; though the keenly Conservative *Mail* thought the Liberal *Globe* not enthusiastic enough.[27] Elsewhere, a great afternoon lacrosse match (then the city's reigning sport) was held at the Rosedale Athletic Grounds, between the Toronto First Twelve and a champion Caughnawaga Indian team that had played before Queen Victoria at Windsor Castle. And in the evening there was the Grand Harbour Parade, starting at 10 o'clock, after another pavilion concert, Gounod's *The Redemption* by the Philharmonic Society under F.H. Torrington. Scores of steamers, tugs, and rowboats lit with coloured lanterns moved across the bay. The waterside and boat-houses were similarly strung with lights, and over all arched rockets and roman candles, as the waters sparkled back their brilliance. 'Professor Hand's' set-pieces did not come off as well, however, and it was judged that the illuminated boats had the best part in Toronto's honouring of its historic port life.

But now the spell of clear, hot weather broke, and 4 July proved literally a wash-out. It was billed as Benevolent Societies Day, when nearly 10,000 were expected to parade, from the Masonic lodges, St George's, St Andrew's, and Irish Catholic societies to the Knights of Phythias and Odd Fellows, their numbers swelled by fraternal delegates from Rochester and other American centres as well as Ontario towns. Crowds gathered as usual in the morning, under darkly massing clouds, but when the threatened downpour burst, they scuttled for shelter and home, and the procession was postponed till the following morning. Many out-of-town visitors departed, as the rains drummed on; but enough stayed to be entertained at a large luncheon in the Exhibition dining hall by the semi-centennial committee. This was 'conducted on strictly temperance principles, nothing but tea, coffee and lemonade being used.'[28] Small consolation; but it *was* Toronto the Good.

The last day, Educational Day, was also marked by showers, but not enough to spoil the climactic events. Around noon, and further delayed by sudden torrents, a somewhat disorganized procession of benevolents finally moved off, and later its members competed for prizes in drill contests at the Exhibition Grounds. Far more noteworthy, however, was the excited gathering of school children in Queen's Park and their own parade through town to the athletic grounds. Toronto had reason to be proud of its public educational system, at least by standards of the time. The city had over 17,500 pupils enrolled in 1884, generally in good facilities and with a well-qualified teaching staff – again for the time.[29] It was in the forefront in North America in instituting kindergartens, pushed by the energetic inspector of schools, James L. Hughes.[30] Now Hughes's cherished pupils, and the city's future, would be on public display. Under his marshalship, and accompanied by fife and drum, close to 4,000 children marched – 800 of them from the state-aided Catholic separate schools. At the Rosedale grounds they performed drills and gym exercises before a large, admiring audience. And at night 600 pupils of public and separate schools presented a music festival in the Horticultural Pavilion, 'united in singing the praises of the city they lived in, and of the country they claimed as their own.'[31] The young girls, 'dressed in white centred on and above the stage, reminded one of the heavenly choirs.'[32] Perhaps this was sentimentally effusive, if quite Victorian. None the less, here was still an effective climax for the citizen audience of the day, who thus had seen its celebrations of Toronto's semi-centennial move plainly from past history, through present, to the future. One day washed out or not, it seemed a warmly satisfying achievement, a real rejoicing throughout.

It was over now. The fires faded from the dunes of Toronto Island, the captains and the kings departed – the visiting firemen and the Knights of Pythias – but the pride in city, country, and empire remained. Apart from those who had criticized the celebrations' cost or gloomily expected the worst kind of foul-up, some had also scoffed at their pretensions. The Toronto *Week*, an ably critical literary periodical, printed the following appraisal of the semi-centennial at its close:[33]

> If coloured lights and fiery flags
> Or men tricked out in gaudy rags
> Can glorify a city,
> Then this must be most richly blessed,
> Or like a child that's overdressed,
> Excite her sisters' pity.

Still, few Toronto residents of whatever social rank would likely have agreed.

What did it all signify? The Victorian city's bent for choral music had been amply demonstrated, its insistent sense of being an imperial garrison, and its English-Canadian moral and cultural uniformities. So had its prevailing economic growth, despite depression: the evident affluence, the rising industrial numbers, the effective transport system that brought countryside and neighbouring townsfolk flocking in by rail line or lake steamer; city hotels and bars (where lemonade was seldom chosen) had surely had an excellent business. The stores gave semi-centennial week bargains, while the sizeable Golden Lion even featured free concerts in its show rooms, and a roof-top balloon ascent.[34] And city politicians and top citizens had obviously worked in common accord to make this truly a red-letter year. Mayor Boswell, as chief magistrate, had been a congenial and active embodiment of civic leadership, though he meted praise to others open-handedly. Perhaps, indeed, both he and other city politicians had been led to take a broader view of civic affairs than they had usually done before. At any rate, it is worth observing that a trend to a positive city administration under a strong mayor, which did more than just sustain order and restrain taxes, was only a year or two away. Possibly it started here, in the grant of $10,000 for mainly social purposes and in the engagement of no-nonsense aldermen with things other than road repairs or hotel licences. In the event, the semi-centennial splurge also produced the valuable historical work by Scadding and Dent, *Toronto Past and Present*, as its memorial account.[35]

It is not necessary to find deep meanings and consequences in this first Toronto anniversary episode. It was a passing social moment, a short, bright relief in a sombre, grinding year. It was fun. It was fully shared and enjoyed, not just by dignitaries but by the whole community, the lively crowds, and the sturdy marchers, whether militiamen, workers, Odd Fellows, or children. It was indeed a time to laud the present and hail the future. The semi-centennial *Memorial Volume*, in closing the record of the preceding fifty years, pronounced optimistically on Toronto of 1934: 'The sun will then rise upon a densely packed population extending from the Humber to Scarboro' Heights, and from Mount Pleasant Cemetery to the Bay. It may very well be that Toronto's population will then number more than a quarter of a million, and that Bloor Street will be a central and main business thoroughfare.'[36] We have the advantage of our 100 years' of hindsight when judging this declaration. It does not, however, affect one further memorial pronouncement: 'It ought never to be forgotten by any Torontonian that he is a citizen of no mean city.'[37] That, in sum, was the essential confidence behind Toronto's first hurrah.

NOTES

1 See *Census of Canada, 1881–2* 1 (Ottawa 1882) 174–5 and 276–7 for the following figures in this paragraph.
2 G.S. Kealey *Toronto Workers Respond to Industrial Capitalism 1867–1892* (Toronto 1980) 320–2
3 L.H. Pursley *Street Railways of Toronto, 1861–1921* (Los Angeles 1958) 9
4 H. Scadding and J.C. Dent *Toronto Past and Present, Historical and Descriptive, A Memorial Volume for the Semi-Centennial, 1884* (Toronto 1884) 302

5 Victor L. Russell *Mayors of Toronto* 1 (Toronto 1982) 109–10
6 *Globe* 22 January 1884
7 Ibid 21 January 1884
8 Ibid 22 January 1884
9 *Annual Report of the Toronto Board of Trade* 1884 (Toronto 1885) 18
10 *Daily Mail* 7 March 1884
11 For these committees and their members see Scadding and Dent *Toronto* 302–7.
12 City of Toronto Archives (hereafter CTA), Minutes and Proceedings of the
   Council of the Corporation of the City of Toronto (hereafter Minutes), 1884,
   15 April, item 105, and item 52
13 Ibid, 23 June, item 615
14 Ibid, Appendix, p 6
15 Ibid, Salary expenditures for 1884
16 Scadding and Dent Toronto 307
17 Ibid 309
18 *Globe* 28 June 1884.
19 For events of this day see Scadding and Dent *Toronto* 309–14; also the official
   program, *1834–1884, Semi-Centennial Celebration* (Toronto 1884), and *Globe*
   and *Mail* 30 June–8 July 1884. The same sources apply for the account of the
   following days' events, beyond other specific references.
20 Scadding and Dent *Toronto* 312
21 Ibid 310
22 Ibid 315
23 Ibid 316
24 Ibid 319
25 Ibid 323
26 Ibid
27 *Mail* 5 July 1884
28 Scadding and Dent *Toronto* 326
29 Toronto Board of Education *Annual Report of the Inspector of the Public
   Schools of the City of Toronto for 1884* 9.
30 *Centennial Story, the Board of Education for ... Toronto, 1850–1950* (Toronto
   1950) 88–9
31 Scadding and Dent *Toronto* 329
32 Ibid
33 *Week* 10 July 1884
34 *Globe* 28 June 1884
35 CTA, Minutes, 1884, 29 December 1884
36 Scadding and Dent *Toronto* 268
37 Ibid 330

PART TWO

The triumph of consensus

Servicing the modern city 1900–30

THE TENDENCY of Canadian historians has been to view the growth of government in the twentieth century from the vantage point of the federal Parliament and the provincial legislatures and to underestimate the contributions of the municipal councils. While the upper levels of government emerged as the principal architects of the so-called welfare state during and after the Second World War, municipal government had already laid the groundwork for a positive social and economic role for the state in the pre-war era. Indeed, the increasing number of Canadians who became urban dwellers, particularly in the first three decades of this century, looked first and foremost to municipal government to provide those essential services and amenities that made their communities more accommodating places in which to live and work. Certainly Mayor Horatio C. Hocken of Toronto was conscious of the importance of municipal government in his address, 'The New Spirit in Municipal Government,' to the Canadian Club in 1914: 'Municipal government is so close to the people that it deals with their everyday needs, almost every hour of the day, and surely that form of government which touches at so many points and which has to do so much with our comfort and happiness as a community must be considered of the very first importance.'[1] Hocken's claim could be dismissed as reflecting the self-serving optimism inherent in civic boosterism if it were not for the impressive performance of his own city in providing for the social and economic welfare of its citizens between 1900 and 1930.

In his monumental history of Toronto, Jesse E. Middleton notes: 'Approaching the last decade of the Nineteenth Century, Toronto found itself no longer a compact little city, but a straggling big one, outgrowing its civic services as rapidly as a small boy outgrows his pantaloons.'[2] The metaphor was still appropriate at the turn of the century, as the city's population had increased scarcely 20,000 during the 1890s and the nature and scope of its public services had changed relatively little. However, after 1900 the budding adolescent acquired not only a finely tailored pair of pants but also an extensive wardrobe. The annual reports of the city treasurer are testimony to the willingness of civic authorities to spend increasing sums of money to provide a wide range of services.[3] As shown in Table 1, the total annual current and capital expenditures of Toronto grew from almost $5.6 million in 1900 to almost $82.5 million in 1930.[4] Of course, some of this fifteenfold increase in civic spending can be accounted for by a threefold increase in the city's population (from 208,040 in 1901 to 631,207 in 1931).[5] More difficult to calculate is the extent to which inflation would exaggerate the increase in public expenditures, but even the most conservative estimates would place the value of the 1930 dollar at about half that of the 1900 dollar.[6] Therefore, it can reasonably be asserted that civic spending per capita in constant dollars expanded by about two and a half times from 1900 to 1930. A further indication of the city's investment in the development of public services is the rise in the net debenture debt from $15.4 million in 1900 to $158.4 million in 1930. The amount of dollars spent may not necessarily reflect the effectiveness of a public service, but it does provide valuable insight into the scope of governmental activity; and, besides, quality of service is difficult to achieve without quantity of funds.

This remarkable growth in public expenditures extended to the whole realm of municipal services, which can be arranged into twelve categories representing, by 1930, 97 per cent of the annual expenditures of the city of Toronto.[7] These can be collected into three distinct groups of services. The first group, designated as physical and protective services, encompasses roads and local improvements, sanitation, police protection (including administration of justice), and fire protection. These are considered to be the primary functions of local government because they are most directly related to the servicing and improvement of property and to the maintenance of property values.[8] The second group of services, designated as public utilities, includes the waterworks, the Toronto Hydro Electric System, and the Toronto Transportation Commission. These enterprises are not regarded as essential to the servicing and improvement of property, through they do tend to enhance property values. The basic rationale for these services is that they tend to benefit all city dwellers and can be operated more economically and efficiently as non-profit public enterprises. The third group, designated as social, cultural, and recreational services, consists of parks and recreational facilities, schools, libraries, health, and social welfare (including subsidized housing). Even though it can potentially benefit all city dwellers, public spending for these services tends to be more contentious because they seem to have only a marginal, if any, effect on property values.[9]

The largest single expense in the civic budget of 1900 was for the construction and maintenance of roads, sidewalks, bridges, and other related local improvements. Although more than one-quarter of the entire budget (exclusive of debt charges) was being allocated to these public works, taxpayers and civic politicians were less inclined to question the wisdom of such expenditures.[10] R.O. Wynn-Roberts, a noted civil engineer and analyst of the early-twentieth-century municipal scene, insisted 'that judicious expenditures of public money on streets and highways is a lucrative investment,' particularly when one considers 'the economy effected in the cost of transportation,' which in turn 'has its influence on the cost of the specific material or goods, and also on the cost of living.' He went on to argue: 'Well-paved and clean streets ... because they are seen by all ... constitute a measure of successful administration, foresight, and judicious expenditure of ratepayers' money. The converse is equally true, for unsightly, dirty streets are powerful factors in the demoralization of the people.'[11] The positive effect that paved roads could have on property values in a thriving commercial area or a populated residential district offered added justification for public expenditure.[12]

Despite the considerable attention already being given to road development by 1900, the Toronto street commissioner, John Jones, admitted 'that there yet remains room for a great deal of improvement in this direction, there being far too many worn out and unimproved roads for a City of the size and importance of Toronto.'[13] Toronto had almost 260 miles of roads, but only 30 miles were paved in asphalt, which was becoming known as 'a better class of pavement.'[14] In fact, half of the existing asphalt roads had been undertaken within the past three years, and the advent of the automobile after 1902 would be a further inducement to this kind of paving. By 1930 the city could boast of 571 miles of streets, 483 miles (or 91 per cent) of which were paved in asphalt.[15] Increasingly mindful of its metropolitan stature, Toronto was also contributing almost $250,000 per annum to the improvement of roads and highways leading into the city by 1930, as compared to nothing at all in 1900. Another major advance was the concrete sidewalk. In 1900 the city had 429 miles of sidewalk, 400 miles of which were constructed of wooden planks four to six feet in width; by 1930 there were almost 900 miles of concrete sidewalks.[16]

TABLE 1

The current and capital expenditures of Toronto 1900–30 (in thousands of dollars)

Service		1900	1910	1920	1930	Factor of increase 1900–30
Highways*	current	353	592	1,335	2,013	
	capital	675	1,423	3,142	8,699	
	total	1,028	2,015	4,477	10,712	10
Sanitation	current	195	670	1,996	2,361	
	capital	15	549	705	653	
	total	210	1,219	2,701	3,014	15
Police protection†	current	324	713	2,008	3,284	
	capital		31	28	152	
	total	324	744	2,036	3,436	11
Fire protection	current	182	386	1,984	2,640	
	capital		66	60		
	total	182	452	2,044	2,640	15
Waterworks	current	198	367	1,633	1,607	
	capital		796	560	1,292	
	total	198	1,163	2,193	2,899	15
Toronto Hydro	current			1,964	8,941	
	capital		747	491	1,905	
	total		747	2,455	10,846	
Transit‡	current	1	3	1,951	9,009	
	capital	105	314	368	1,491	
	total	106	317	2,319	10,500	100
Education	current	626	1,397	5,405	8,840	
	capital	188	505	1,412	2,532	
	total	814	1,902	6,817	11,372	14
Libraries	current	28	66	247	472	
	capital			48	181	
	total	28	66	295	653	23

The streets of 1930 were also brighter than those of 1900. By the turn of the century, 900 gas lamps still dotted the parks and streets of Toronto, but the 1,200 electric arc lights were more luminous and cheaper to operate and thus represented the wave of the future.[17] (The last gas lamps disappeared in 1911.) More adequate street lighting was deemed essential to a modern, expanding city in order to reduce loss of life and property damage caused by traffic accidents and to reduce crime, since a brightly lit street was assumed to a less comfortable haven for criminals.[18] By 1930 the number of street lights had

TABLE 1 (*Continued*)

Service		1900	1910	1920	1930	Factor of increase 1900–30
Parks and recreation§	current	66	387	868	1,510	
	capital	—	309	1,141	2,006	
	total	66	696	2,009	3,516	53
Public health	current	42	90	884	954	
	capital	—	38			
	total	42	128	884	954	24
Welfare‖	current	82	229	993	2,540	
	capital	—	90	396		
	total	82	319	1,389	2,540	31
Debt charges#		1,918	2,602	6,501	16,401	9
Total	current	4,544	6,738	27,440	63,501	
	capital	1,046	4,802	8,037	18,954	
	total	5,590	11,540	35,477	82,455	15

*These figures include local improvements, since a very high percentage of these expenditures is for roads and sidewalks and only a small amount is for sewers.
†These figures include the administration of justice.
‡These figures include in 1900 and 1910 payments to the Toronto Railway Company, in 1910 and 1920 the operation of the Civic Car Lines, and in 1920 and 1930 the operation of the Toronto Transportation Commission.
§These figures include for all years the operation of the Canadian National Exhibition, and for 1920 and 1930 the Royal Agricultural Winter Fair.
‖These figures include housing – $402,000 in 1920 and $38,000 in 1930.
#These figures include principle and interest payments.
SOURCES: *Treasurer's Reports* 1900–30; Toronto Hydro-Electric System *Annual Reports* 1920–30; Toronto Transportation Commission *Annual Statement* 1930

increased to nearly 56,000, which had prompted J.P. Bickell, registrar of motor vehicles in Ontario, to remark: 'Toronto ... is considered one of the best lighted cities on the continent, with street lights placed approximately 100 feet apart on both sides of most streets.'[19] Altogether (including debt charges) $16.6 million, or 20 per cent, of the civic budget (still the largest single expenditure) was devoted to ensuring that the streets of the city were cleaner, safer, and more serviceable than they had been three decades before.

The general physical environment of the city was further enhanced by the extension of sanitation services, including the collection and disposal of garbage, street watering and snow removal, and the construction and maintenance of sewers and sewage disposal facilities. By 1900 Toronto was long past the days when garbage was burned in backyards or fed to the hogs, although such practices had not completely disappeared. Garbage was collected semi-weekly and disposed of in two crematories built in 1893 and 1896. The total cost of garbage collection and disposal in 1900 was almost $84,000; by 1930 it had risen to more than $1.1 million. The greater cost was mostly attributable to the replacement of the horse and wagon by motorized trucks. Moreover, since the city had doubled its size through annexation of suburban areas (from 17 square miles in 1900 to 34 squares miles in 1930), it was necessary to organize the city into twenty-four districts averaging 900 acres each to ensure efficient collection in every area. Likewise, street watering to reduce dust on the main thoroughfares and snow removal had entered the motorized age which, along with the need for wider coverage, increased the cost of such operations from about $110,000 in 1900 to $825,000 in 1930.[20]

In 1900 Toronto had over 232 miles of storm and sanitary sewers, and only recently were houses starting to have private drains installed by the city's public works department to connect with the main sewers.[21] Unfortunately, the main sewers were discharging directly into the lake or the watercourses that emptied into it, thus contaminating the city's water-supply and triggering periodic epidemics of typhoid fever. In 1908, after more than a decade of heated public debate, city council passed a by-law authorizing the expenditure of $2.4 million for the construction of high and low interceptor sewers to convey raw sewage to a new treatment plant on the north shore of Ashbridge's Bay.[22] After this project was completed in 1913, city funds were directed toward the construction of trunk and local sewers to stimulate development of the newly annexed areas. North Toronto was the last area serviced with sewers, in 1925, and in 1929 a separate treatment plant was completed there. Thus, by 1930 there were 678 miles of sanitary sewers and 65 miles of storm and relief sewers, with private drains to the street line being installed by the city as a matter of course in all new buildings. The total expenditure on sewers and sewage disposal in 1930 was almost $1.7 million (including debt charges), as compared to slightly more than $25,000 in 1900.[23]

Promoting a better physical environment also involved greater public expenditures for the protection of persons and property. The growth in the area and population of the city naturally increased the size and workload of the police force. The force expanded from 295 men in seven divisions in 1900 to 1,002 men in twelve divisions by 1930. However, the nature and scope of police work, and hence the budget, was most profoundly affected by the appearance of the automobile. The automobile compounded the problem of traffic control in the downtown area, already congested with street railway cars, carriages, bicycles, delivery vans, and wagons (some even driven by children). In the first decade of the century traffic control was assigned to a mounted detachment of eight men. It did not take long for speeding automobiles to become a danger to public safety as owners eagerly sought to show off the capabilities of their new vehicles. Chief Constable Henry J. Grasett complained in 1908: 'The over speeding of automobiles is of such common occurrence, and so difficult to prevent, that decided steps should be taken by the use of motor cycles or other means to compel observance of the speed limit.'[25] In 1912 a traffic squad, equipped with motorcycles, was formed to impose a speed limit of 15 miles per hour, and the first motor-driven patrol wagon was introduced the following year. Police mobility was further improved by the regular use of the automobile after 1917, and by 1930, 81 automobiles, trucks, and motorcycles were part of basic police equipment.[26]

Even in 1919 Chief Grasett was uttering a now familiar complaint: 'The parking of motor cars in the down town districts has developed into a nuisance, and obstruction to business is becoming serious ... In fact the streets are becoming an open air garage.'[27] So, a time limit was imposed on downtown parking in 1920, adding to the growing list of police duties. Constables were also required to operate manual traffic-regulating signals at busy intersections (starting in 1921) and to serve as crossing guards for school children (starting in 1922). The growing use of automatic traffic signals after 1925 diminished these duties somewhat but added to the equipment cost of police protection. Other technological advances included brake-testing equipment (which found that 81 per cent of all vehicles tested in 1928 had defective brakes); the Gamewell Patrol and Signal System, complete with teletype and private automatic telephone exchange system, which allowed constables to communicate with headquarters from patrol boxes located at 282 street corners throughout the city; and one-way radio equpment in the squad cars (by 1935), which allowed officers to receive instructions directly from the station up to 100 miles away.[28] The new duties and technology were indeed increasing the cost of running a police force, but this was the price that a modern city had to pay.

Urban growth and changing technology were also increasing the cost of fire protection. By 1900 the Toronto fire brigade, consisting of 185 men at sixteen stations, had already entered the 'advanced age of mechanical and scientific progress,' in the judgment of John Ross Robertson.[29] Prominent among its equipment were five horse-drawn steam-engines and a water-tower, a hand-raised aerial turntable ladder that extended 75 feet (one of the longest of its kind), a life net (used for the first time in 1895), and twenty horse-drawn wagons of various kinds. A cause for concern, however, was dependence on the domestic water system, which provided a pressure of 45 to 80 pounds per square inch, sufficient only for buildings up to four storeys. The great fire of 1904, which burned for two weeks and destroyed $10 million worth of property in the downtown business district (Front and Bay streets), led to a reassessment of the needs of a modern fire department.

In addition to increasing the size of the force and building new stations to service the newly annexed areas, the civic administration in 1909 invested over $700,000 for the installation in the downtown section of a high-pressure water system that could provide upwards of 300 pounds pressure per square inch.[30] By 1915 the ponderous, slow-moving steam-engine pumps were being replaced by faster motorized trucks with greater pumping capacities. The motorized vehicles with motor pumps were also more economical because they could take the place of three wagons and several horses. The last of the old steamers was phased out in 1921. Another major innovation was the truck with power-raised combination aerial ladder and water-tower, with a main ladder reaching 100 feet. The twenty-four-hour-a-day shift was abandoned in favour of the double platoon system in 1918, which itself added nearly 200 men to the force.[31] By 1930 the force encompassed 686 men at thirty-three stations housing fifty-seven units of motor-driven fire-fighting apparatus.[32] Edwin Guillet noted in 1934: 'Insurance companies rate the Toronto fire department among the best on the continent.'[33]

Besides expanding these traditional functions of municipal government, the city of Toronto had by the 1920s become engaged in services usually considered to be within the realm of private enterprise. For half a century the virtues of public versus private ownership of services that directly or indirectly affected the entire population of the city had been debated. Gradually, as the desire of franchise-holding utility companies for maximum profits clashed with the city's concern for efficient services, public ownership prevailed in the provision of water, electricity, and streetcar transportation.[34]

The battle for a municipally owned waterworks had been won in the early 1870s, and yet by 1900 it could hardly be called an efficient public utility, at least as far as James Beaty, a civic-minded businessman and former mayor, was concerned: 'The impure quality of the water frequently introduced into the houses and, necessarily, into all domestic uses – drinking, cooking, washing – demands immediate consideration ... The health of the citizens is of the first importance, and it is menaced by the unsanitary water. The uncertainty and inadequacy of the supply for fire purposes brings home to every property owner the necessity of demanding a radical and permanent change in the system.'[35] The disastrous fire of 1904 had prompted civic action on a high-pressure water system for fire-fighting purposes. City council had also allocated $750,000 for a new water filtration plant on Toronto Island, although the facility was not completed in time to avert a serious typhoid epidemic in 1910.[36] The major advance occurred in 1925, when council passed a by-law authorizing the expenditure of $14.3 million for the extension of the waterworks to meet the needs of a rapidly expanding population as well as new commercial and industrial enterprises. When completed in 1932, the extension provided the city with a duplicate system, including a second filtration plant in the east end and new watermains leading from the new plant. The Toronto waterworks now pumped 23.3 billion gallons of chlorinated water annually through more than 700 miles of watermains to some 140,000 customers, certainly a vast improvement over the primitive and restricted service of 1900, when 8.1 million gallons of contaminated water were pumped through 258 miles of watermains to about 43,000 customers.[37]

Toronto went into the hydroelectric power business in 1907 when city ratepayers by a large majority approved a by-law permitting city council to enter into a contract to purchase power from the recently formed Hydro-Electric Power Commision of Ontario. The following year another by-law authorized the council to spend $2.75 million to construct a distribution plant to serve the entire city.[38] Administered by a special commission, the Toronto Hydro-Electric System began operations in 1911, though in the first decade of its operation it had to compete with the privately owned Toronto Electric Company, which had provided electric power to the city on a limited scale since the mid-1880s but which refused to sell out to the public utility. The competition proved to be rather one-sided, since the system initially set its rate schedule for its 25,000 customers at about one-half that of the private company; and after a decade of operation the public utility rates were less than one-quarter of those charged by the private utility company. In 1920 the Toronto Electric Company was purchased at a cost of $6.4 million, for which the system received an almost obsolete distribution plant which was soon dismantled and scrapped.[39] By 1930 almost $40 million had been invested in the Toronto Hydro-Electric System, which served 180,000 customers and charged rates that were among the lowest in North America.[40]

Growing dissatisfaction with the Toronto Railway Company prompted the city's gradual involvement in public transportation. By 1900 the company serviced the city with a completely electrified system consisting of 85 miles of track extending to the city limits (as far north as Yorkville, as far east as the Don River, and as far west as High Park). Even though the company had over 200 streetcars in operation, carrying over 36 million passengers per year, critics such as Professor S. Morley Wickett of the Unversity of Toronto had some reservations, which would soon provide the impetus for public ownership: 'The service, though good, would have been much more popular if the company had been ... more active in developing suburban traffic.'[42] The company, however, with the backing of a ruling by the Judicial Committee of the Privy Council in London, refused to extend service beyond the city limits as they existed in 1891, when the city had awarded the company a thirty-year franchise. Accordingly, with the annexation of the suburban districts, the city made a more concerted effort in the direction of public ownership with the formation of the Toronto Civic Railway in 1910. The public enterprise operated, at a substantial deficit, 22 miles of track along Danforth, St Clair, Bloor (west of Dundas), Gerrard, Greenwood, and Lansdowne. With the rolling stock of the financially hard-pressed company becoming obsolete and run down, and with service deteriorating rapidly, especially in the downtown core, the ratepayers in 1917 voted overwhelmingly in favour of operating the street railways as a public utility.

The establishment of the Toronto Transportation Commission (TTC) in 1920 ushered in a dynamic era in public transit development. From the Toronto Railway Company the TTC purchased 138 miles of track (at least half of which had to be completely rebuilt) and 832 cars (of which only about 350 were still serviceable) for $11.5 million.[43] In the first five years of TTC operation, over $44 million in city debentures were issued to finance the extension of services (as far north as York Mills, as far west as Mimico, and as far east as Scarborough), the replacement of deteriorated or outmoded track and the laying of new track, the rebuilding of older vehicles and the purchase of new streetcars and buses, and the building of new shop facilites. The TTC also took over the operation of the Toronto Civic Railway. By 1930 the TTC system encompassed over 250 miles of track and almost 1,300 vehicles and that year serviced about 200 million passengers over twenty-six different routes. At an average of a little more than 6 cents (with free transfer privileges), TTC fares were among the lowest on the continent.[44] Indeed, with the operation of the TTC, the Toronto Hydro-Electric System, and the expanded waterworks, Toronto had become a model of successful public ownership of utilities.

Undoubtedly, civic administrators in the first three decades of the twentieth century were preoccupied first and foremost with economic development, particularly with keeping property values on the rise and attracting more businesses to Toronto. Yet there was also increasing concern for the potentially debilitating social, moral, and physical effects of urban concentration on the individual, as Mayor Hocken pointed out:

Municipal government has ceased to be a matter of construction and maintenance ... The chief problems we have to deal with are not the construction of sewers and sidewalks and that kind of thing. These things have to be done, and a few years ago they constituted the whole sphere of municipal government. But we have got a long way past that and the problems we have to deal with now are problems affecting human welfare, problems of prevention, the problems looking to the betterment of the people of cities ...

In Toronto we describe the kind of work I am trying to talk about as 'Welfare Work.' It is work that looks to the serving of those human instincts which when properly provided for make a healthy, moral, and intelligent community.[45]

This 'New Spirit in Municipal Government' was to be reflected in Toronto's budget: by 1930 almost $22 million, or $35 per capita (as compared to $1 million, or $5 per capita, in 1900), was spent on parks and recreational facilities, schools and libraries, and health and welfare services.[46]

At the turn of the century Toronto parks were still commonly referred to as 'public walks and gardens,' and there were 21 such areas, covering a total of 1,152 acres and costing about $35,000 per year to maintain.[47] As late as 1909, according to Mayor Hocken, 'there was not a supervised playground in Toronto ... and all that people got out of a park was the privilege of sitting on a bench and looking over the green-sward.'[48] But as cities such as Toronto became more congested with people and automobiles, and the leisure time of the predominantly industrial work-force increased, the arguments in favour of greater public investment in parks and recreational facilities became more compelling. The noted British town planner Thomas Adams pointed to both the economic and social benefits to be derived by a city:

The provision of parks and playgrounds, if the land is purchased at a reasonable cost, does not add materially to the tax burden of the community. The increased value these open spaces give to adjacent land counter-balances the cost of acquiring them ...

The greatest benefit from the parks will, however, be derived from the increased health and, consequently, greater efficiency of the population. Parks are a better investment than hospitals and asylums, and if we do not spend money on the one we shall be compelled to spend it on the other in greater degree than is needed if we exercise proper judgement and foresight.[49]

Child welfare advocates were especially hopeful that supervised parks and playgrounds would benefit less privileged children by keeping them off the traffic-laden streets, by improving their physical and moral outlook, and by combating the idleness that often led to delinquency and crime.[50] So by 1930

Toronto had 80 parks, covering almost 2,200 acres, along with 60 supervised playgrounds, 291 tennis courts, 78 baseball diamonds, 66 skating rinks, 48 football and lacrosse fields, among numerous other athletic and recreational facilities. The total annual civic expenditure for maintaining and developing this service was almost $3.7 million, more than 100 times the amount spent in 1900.[51]

Public investment in schools and libraries was also seen as a stimulus to social and moral improvement. By the end of the nineteenth century the city had a well-established and rapidly expanding elementary education system that led even social critic C.S. Clark to conclude: 'Toronto stands ... in the front rank of all cities on the continent for the excellence and extent of its system of public schools'[52] In 1900 there were 51 public schools having an average monthly attendance of almost 24,000 pupils and operating at a cost of $27 per pupil.[53] With the growth of the city, the number of public schools by 1930 had increased to 102, with a registration of almost 83,000 pupils and an operating cost of over $92 per pupil.[54] The higher operating costs were partly attributable to the erection of larger and more lavishly equipped buildings which stood as monuments to educational progress. As well, the public schools became linked with the public health and child welfare movements. The school was a logical place to conduct the campaign to inculcate personal hygiene practices that would contribute to the development of a healthier community, because children were the parents and taxpayers of the future.[55] After 1910 medical and dental inspection of school children by a public health nurse became a regular feature of the primary system. The system also came to include an 'open air school' and two 'Forest Schools,' the latter designed to enhance the health, education, and morality of underprivileged tubercular children. By 1930 there were 150 classes for almost 3,300 pupils who were crippled, deaf, or blind, as well as 50 classes for mentally retarded children. Toronto was a leader in the field of special education, spending about $500,000 annually.[56]

But the development of secondary education had perhaps a more profound impact upon the civic budget. In 1908 the city had only 3 collegiate institutes and 1 technical school, with a total enrolment of about 3,000 pupils. Technological advances in business and industry were demanding more skilled labour, and increasingly those students who 'dropped out' before completing high school found themselves unemployed or trapped in low-paying jobs. Two provincial enactments, the Industrial Education Act of 1911, which offered substantial grants toward the building and equipping of technical schools, and the Adolescent Attendance Act of 1919, which raised the age of compulsory schooling from 14 to 16 years, proved to be a boon to secondary education. And no modern and progressive secondary school was complete without science laboratories, industrial and carpentry shops, libraries, gymnasiums, and other facilities for extracurricular activities. In the 1920s extracurricular activities were viewed no longer as luxuries but rather as a necessary part of the socialization process and the advance toward responsible adulthood.[57] Nevertheless, all these added dimensions to the education system proved to be expensive items in the civic budget. In 1930 each of the more than 41,000 pupils in the city's 20 secondary schools (including 4 commercial schools) cost the taxpayers $150.[58]

The public library was a more modest but no less significant adjunct to educational development. Toronto had been the first municipality in Ontario to establish a free public library, in 1883, and by 1900 it had expanded to include a central reference library and six branches. The whole system had almost 120,000 volumes, with an annual circulation of well over one-half million serving over 21,000 registered card-holders.[59] The system received much-needed financial support in 1903 when Andrew Carnegie donated $350,000 for the building of a new central library, on condition that the city contribute at least $35,000 annually for its maintenance and for the establishment of branches when needed.[60] Some economy-minded civic officials were reluctant to make such a financial commitment for this amenity. However, the rising concern for education and morality in the rapidly expanding city stimulated civic support for public libraries. By 1930 the library system consisted of the central reference library (the largest in Canada) and sixteen branches; the system's half-million volumes had an annual circulation of almost 3.2 million to upwards of 250,000 registered card-holders. When civic authoities agreed to spend $430,000 to build a new wing to the reference library (at College and St George streets) in 1930, Andrew Carnegie's money was not required.[61]

Civic administrations in early-twentieth-century Toronto were concerned not only with the moral and intellectual well-being of the citizens, but also with their physical health. To be sure, Toronto was a healthier place to live in 1900 than it had been when Dr William Canniff was appointed the city's first medical health officer (MHO) in 1883. An adherent to the sanitarian school of preventive medicine, Canniff had instituted regular annual inspections of homes, schools, factories, dairies, and slaughterhouses in order to discover and remove 'nuisances' that could lead to disease. Dr Charles Sheard, who became MHO in 1893, added a bacteriological approach to disease control by establishing a city laboratory to undertake periodic testing of the quality of tap water, ice, milk, and food that Torontonians consumed. The medical health department also operated the Riverdale Isolation Hospital, which by 1900 had about seventy-five beds to treat patients suffering from communicable diseases such as diptheria, typhoid and scarlet fever, measles, and smallpox.[62] Although Toronto's death rate from these diseases was not as bad as the rates in some larger North American cities, an editorial in the *Globe* in 1912 titled 'Barbarian Toronto' was adamant that the prevailing standards of health still left much to be desired.[63]

During his tenure as MHO from 1910 to 1929, Dr Charles Hastings managed to convince civic authorities that a healthy and productive worker and taxpayer was 'the most valuable asset' of municipalities and 'that money used for public health work ... gives them a larger return than any other investment.'[64] During the First World War he also appealed to patriotic sentiment by citing the findings of medical examining boards of the Allied nations that upwards of half of potential recruits were 'physically unfit for service at the front.'[65] As a result, by 1930 the budget of the department of public health (as Hastings renamed it) exceeded $1.60 per capita, as compared to about $0.20 per capita in 1900.[66] With the additional funds, Hastings transformed the department into a model of an efficient and effective public health bureaucracy, eventually employing over 500 medically trained personnel, certainly a far cry from the rudimentary operations of three decades earlier, which had employed a staff of ten sanitary inspectors.[68] He divided the city into nine districts, each with its own MHO, who reported to the central office. The department's work was organized into twelve divisions, the most noteworthy of which were public health nursing, medical services, and dental services. These three services, inaugurated in the first five years of Hastings's tenure, were instrumental in extending health care to children of primary-school age in particular and the underprivileged in general. Along with the Riverdale Isolation Hospital, which was expanded to 450 beds, the three divisions encompassed almost three-quarters of the city's entire health budget by 1930.[69] When Hastings left the department, Toronto was recognized internationally as a leader in public health.

Included within the department of public health was the division of social welfare, the formation of which in 1921 was symptomatic of the growing civic responsibility for the relief of poverty and destitution. Until the early twentieth century the main thrust of civic relief efforts was confined to subsidizing private philanthropy, which in 1900 in Toronto included 30 charitable institutions and 7 hospitals and homes caring for indigents.[70] A special committee investigating the state of poor relief in the city in 1908 reflected the prevailing notion of civic responsibility: 'There seems to be a mistaken idea abroad that for some reason ... the Corporation is responsible for the care of those who are destitute ... It cannot take the place of private benevolence, nor relieve citizens of their private duties and obligations. It ought, however, to aid and encourage all wise philanthropic efforts.'[71] The final sentence would seem to indicate that the civic administration was willing to enter into a partnership (albeit not an equal one) with voluntary organizations to guard against a haphazard and inefficient allocation of funds. The appointment of a full-time salaried relief officer in 1893 to co-ordinate private charity and to oversee the distribution of public assistance had been a significant step toward a more active role for municipal government in the field of social welfare.[72] The recurrence of mass unemployment in 1907–8, 1913–15, and 1920–2 accelerated that process. These crises not only necessitated a considerable increase in civic grants to private charitable institutions – particularly the House of Industry, which was primarily responsible for administering outdoor relief – but also revealed the inadequacy of the traditional approach to poor relief in a modern urban and industrial society.

In 1912 city council appointed a social services commission to act as a central bureau supervising the work of all philanthropic organizations receiving funds from the city. The appointment of the commission reflected the desire of the civic administration to exert greater control over the distribution of poor relief in the interests of more business-like efficiency and economy.[73] However, the commission's general preoccupation with guarding the public purse, and particularly its slow response to the distress caused by the unemployment crisis in the winter of 1920–1, drew considerable criticism. The Reverend Frank N. Stapleford, general secretary of the Neighbourhood Workers' Association (the main social work agency in Toronto), complained: 'Toronto's welfare work is not a system – it is a disorganized heap.'[74] He and others, such as Alderman James Phinnemore, called for the abolition of the commission and for social services to be administered by a civic department responsible to council. Accordingly, the commission was replaced by a division of social welfare, which over the next decade built up a permanent staff to provide care and assistance for needy families within their own homes, to serve as a clearing-house for social information and requests for public assistance, and to issue grants to private charitable institutions (including the House of Industry, which continued to administer outdoor relief).[75] Under the division's auspices, the city was spending over $4 per capita in 1930.[76] The gradual bureaucratization of Toronto's social services was completed in 1932 with the establishment of a department of public welfare in response to the heavy demands for unemployment relief created by the Great Depression.

Meanwhile, the city made a brief attempt to provide low-cost public housing. Hastings's investigation of Toronto slums in 1911 brought to the forefront the dismal state of housing in some areas of the city and the need for reasonably priced accommodation.[77] Accordingly, in 1913 the city agreed to guarantee $850,000 worth of bonds issued by Toronto Housing Company Ltd, a private enterprise endeavouring to provide cheaper rental units. After some initial problems the company did manage to operate 334 five-room apartments, though this was far short of the anticipated objective.[78] The city became more directly involved in public housing in 1918 when it appointed the Toronto Housing Commission. To relieve the post-war housing shortage the commission used $948,000 of civic funds to build 240 attractive dwellings for which the purchaser paid 10 per cent cash and the balance in monthly payments of approximately $24 over 20 years. The project was financed with an issue of 20-year debentures at $6\frac{1}{2}$ per cent interest. The city in turn charged the occupants only 5 per cent and thus incurred a slight annual loss in the project. This project was of limited success because the average workingman had difficulty raising the down payment or meeting the monthly payments, and so the commission decided to get out of the housing business in 1920.[79] Large-scale public housing enterprises had to wait until after 1945.

Toronto's early efforts in the field of social welfare are modest by post-1945 standards, but when viewed in the context of their own time they can be considered significant. Early-twentieth-century society and government had a broader concept of 'welfare' than would succeeding generations; the term was associated with any governmental activity that promoted health, happiness, and prosperity. In other words, welfare related to the whole positive role of the state. Civic authorities in Toronto believed that they were looking after the social and economic welfare of their citizens by providing them with improved health services, more public libraries, better-equipped schools, more parks and playgrounds, cheaper and more extensive public transportation and hydroelectric power, cleaner water, more up-to-date fire and police protection, regular garbage collection and snow removal, and more serviceable roads and sidewalks.[80] Did not massive expenditures on these services create jobs, enhance business prospects, improve the physical and intellectual capacity of the individual, and generally make the community a more desirable place to live and work? Mayor Hocken certainly thought so when he referred to his city's 'welfare work'; and Controller J.O. McCarthy concurred: 'The possibilities and duties of Social Service upon Municipal Departments are growing year by year ... The Municipal Government is in the light of today responsible for the physical, mental, and spiritual well-being of the people.'[81]

The 'New Spirit in Municipal Government' does not seem to have been confined to Toronto, as indicated by an editorial in the *Canadian Municipal*

Journal in 1920:

All municipal councils in Canada are the elected representatives of the citizens not only for the material administration of their respective municipalities, but are the actual trustees for the general social and economic welfare of their respective communities. No longer are the duties of our municipal councils confined to just the collecting and spending of local taxes in the sense of the term commonly understood. Rather the spending of taxes today is based on principles which in themselves underly the social as well as economic development of the community. This gospel, now generally accepted by our municipal councils has been preached for eighteen years by the Union of Canadian Municipalities, and the eight Provincial Unions, as is evidenced by the reports of their annual convention, and through this journal.[82]

In providing for the social and economic welfare of their communities, municipal politicians and administrators were not usually motivated by a benevolent spirit or socialist conviction. More likely they would be concerned with sound corporate management, which invariably appealed to the interests of the propertied classes on whose votes and taxes municipal administration depended so heavily. Too frequent outbreaks of communicable diseases such as typhoid fever might well discourage business investment and civic growth, a concern that dovetailed conveniently with the emphasis of public health reformers on the health benefits of pure water and effective sanitation measures. Businessmen also approved of improvements in public transportation, which allowed greater ease of access to the workplace for their work-force. Yet the benefits accruing to the propertied classes tended to 'trickle down' to the lower echelons of society as well. That enhancing the lot of the less privileged might have been more a by-product than a prime motivation should not detract from the positive social role of municipal government in the pre–Second World War era.[83]

Not everyone, however, rejoiced over the expanding role of municipal government. For example, J. Herbert Hodgins, a well-known writer on municipal finance, lamented the 'crippling taxation' which he attributed to 'the paternalism which is creeping into our civic life.'[84] He was particularly critical of Toronto's civic administration for becoming too preoccupied with 'fads and frills' in education, recreation, health, and other social services. By the late 1920s the city was allocating over 45 cents of every tax dollar (as compared to about 28 cents in 1900) to cover the cost of social, cultural, and recreational services.[85] Not only did such expenditures weigh heavily on the civic budget but also they undermined the whole rationale of the municipal tax structure. The backbone of the municipal tax structure in Ontario has always been the real property tax (levied on the assessed capital value of all lands and buildings in a locality), because it was originally assumed that the most costly functions of local government were usually related to the servicing of property. However, the socially oriented services that were now rising steadily in cost had relatively little bearing on the value of real estate.[86] Other business and civic-minded men such as Thomas Bradshaw, a former city treasurer, and Horace L. Brittain, of the Bureau of Municipal Research, expressed their concern for the rapidly rising costs of municipal services by preaching the virtues of 'balancing the budget' and 'pay as you go.'[87] Indeed, the rhetoric of fiscal conservatism was so strong in the 1920s because municipal officials were all too willing to violate its sacred dictums. In retrospect, these critics of municipal expansion were foreshadowing the fiscal crisis of the 1930s.

During the Great Depression the dynamic role of municipal government was undermined by fiscal misfortunes beyond its control. The recurrence of mass unemployment reaching upwards to 30 per cent of the labour force and remaining abnormally high throughout the entire decade left the civic administration overwhelmed with relief costs by virtue of its traditional but anachronistic responsibility to care for the poor. While the federal and provincial authorities belatedly recognized the distinctly national character of the unemployment crisis and assumed about two-thirds of municipal relief expenditures, the city of Toronto still had to pay out almost $30 million in relief benefits between 1930 and 1940 in addition to its normal social service costs. At the same time, municipal administrations faced a heavy burden of fixed debt charges as a monument to past expansion. To make matters worse, municipal governments had to try to meet these financial obligations with a limited and regressive tax structure that had necessitated a greater reliance on borrowing in the first place and now could not withstand the strain of declining incomes and construction activity. As a result, 40 municipalities in Ontario (including 10 of the 12 suburbs of Toronto) were driven into bankruptcy and receivership by 1935, while numerous other cities, towns, and villages hovered on the brink of financial collapse.[88] Although Toronto's civic administration managed to remain solvent, fiscal restraint and sizeable budgetary cutbacks in both essential services and amenities became the order of the day. Moreover, municipal financial operations in Ontario became subject to stricter provincial supervision and control by the newly created Department of Municipal Affairs. The legacy of the 1930s for municipal government was greater fiscal dependance and demotion from a primary to a secondary role in the evolution of the welfare state.

Municipal government would never again reach the pinnacle of prestige, authority, and affluence that it had on the eve of the Great Depression. Nevertheless, this demise should not obscure the formidable contributions of municipal government in promoting a positive social and economic role for the state. The extensive state intervention at the federal and provincial levels that began in the 1940s was significant in establishing what could be termed 'national minimums' in the realm of social services and economic development. Yet, as the experience of Toronto in the first three decades of the century demonstrates, municipal government had already raised the standards for the level of public service that a modern urban society could expect.

NOTES

1 Horatio C. Hocken 'The New Spirit in Municipal Government' Canadian Club, Ottawa *Addresses* (1914–15) 85
2 Jesse Edgar Middleton *The Municipality of Toronto: A History* I (Toronto 1923) 337
3 Toronto *Annual Report of the City Treasury Department* 1900–30. (After 1915, when the city treasurer became known as the commissioner of finance, the title of the annual report changed accordingly.) The reports were published annually and are hereafter cited as Treasurer's Report.
4 The figures for expenditures and revenues cited in the text or listed in Table 1 may not necessarily correspond to the figures that appear in the annual Treasurer's Report for two reasons. First, the method of classifying services changed over time. In 1900, for instance, there was a greater tendency to maintain accounts on an item-by-item basis, whereas by 1930 the accounts were consistently maintained on a departmental basis. For the purpose of accurate comparison I have tried to establish uniformity in the classification of services on the basis of the criteria used in 1930. This has necessitated a recalculation of the figures for 1900 and 1910 and to a much lesser extent for 1920, and in some cases rather arbitrary decisions had to be made as to category. Second, the method of accounting also changed over time. Up to about 1915, city accounts were maintained on a cash basis, that is, revenues for the fiscal year were recorded in the accounts as they were received and expenditures as payment was made. This method makes it difficult to distinguish capital expenditure and revenue from current ones since they were generally lumped together. Where it is possible I have tried to make a distinction. After 1915 the treasurer began using an accural method of accounting in which revenues are recorded as they are earned and expenditures as they are incurred. Then it becomes possible to distinguish

between capital and current expenditures and revenues since these figures are listed separately. Neither of these irregularities in bookkeeping is serious enough to alter the central argument of this study.

5 All figures on the population of the city are based on the *Census of Canada*, particularly for 1901 and 1931. Any per capita figures used for 1900 and 1930 are based on the expenditures or revenues of those years and the population figures of the following year.

6 M.C. Urquhart and K.A.H. Buckley ed *Historical Statistics of Canada* (Toronto 1965) 291–305. There are still no accurate figures available on the changing purchasing power of the Canadian dollar between 1900 and 1930, but a sense of the rate of inflation can be derived from calculations of the consumer price index, the wholesale price index, and the cost of living index presented in this study.

7 The remaining 3 per cent are comprised of general administrative costs and miscellaneous expenses. These costs are included in the total capital and current expenditures listed in Table 1, but they are not listed separately in the table discussed in this study.

8 Civic Advisory Council of Toronto *Municipal Finance* (Toronto 1950) 28

9 Ibid 6, 28

10 Treasurer's Report 1900, xxiii–xxvii. The figures for expenditures on individual services in 1900 do not include debt charges. The debt charges are cited in the Treasurer's Report in aggregate terms, but there is no indication as to how the debt charges are distributed among the various services. By 1920 the treasurer is indicating the specific amount being spent on debt charges for each service. Therefore, it is possible, for 1930, to cite the total cost of a service including debt charges, but, for 1900, only the maintenance cost of a service can be cited.

11 R.O. Wynn-Roberts 'Public Roads and Streets' *The Canadian Municipal Journal* x 6 (June 1914) 251

12 E.A. James 'How Good Roads Affect Land Values' *The Municipal World* XXVII 4 (April 1917) 35

13 Toronto *Annual Report of the City Engineer*, 1900, 2–4 (hereafter City Engineer's Report)

14 City Engineer's Report, 1898, 4–5

15 Treasurer's Report, 1930, 63

16 City Engineer's Report, 1900, 2–3; see also Edwin Guillet *Toronto from Trading Post to Great City* (Toronto 1934) 115–16

17 City Engineer's Report, 1900, ix

18 'The Cost of Inadequate Street Lighting' *The Municipal Review of Canada* XXII 3 (March 1926) 89

19 J.P. Bickell 'Motor Vehicle Development and Ownership' *The Municipal World* XXXVI 4 (April 1926) 77; see also Treasurer's Report, 1930, 27–8, 71

20 'Toronto's Garbage' *The Canadian Municipal Journal* x 9 (September 1941) 375;

George W. Dies 'Snow Removal in the City of Toronto' *The Municipal Review of Canada* xx 10 (October 1924) 387; Treasurer's Report, 1900, xix, xxvii; Treasurer's Report, 1930, 5

21 City Engineer's Report, 1900, 5

22 City of Toronto Archives (hereafter CTA), Minutes of the Proceedings of the Council of the Corporation of the City of Toronto (hereafter Minutes), 1908, Appendix B 446–8

23 William McCourt 'Outline History of Roads in Toronto' manuscript, CTA, 1975, 53; Treasurer's Report, 1900, xxiii, xxv; Treasurer's Report, 1930, 21, 65

24 Minutes 1900, Appendix C 23–8; Treasurer's Report, 1930, 48

25 Minutes, 1907, Appendix C 24. See also Basil Jackson 'To Serve and Protect: The Remarkable and Exciting History of the Metropolitan Toronto Police Force' manuscript, n.d., CTA, 143–8.

26 Jackson 'To Serve' 149–53; Treasurer's Report, 1930, 48

27 Minutes, 1919, Appendix C 26

28 Jackson 'To Serve' 159–67, 499; Treasurer's Report, 1929, 55; Treasurer's Report, 1930, 48; 'Toronto Will Have Police Radio' *The Municipal Review of Canada* xxix, 4 (April 1933) 23

29 John Ross Robertson *Landmarks of Toronto* II (Toronto 1896) 563–5; City Engineer's Report, 1900, ix; see also Guillet Toronto, 215–16

30 Middleton *Toronto* I 369; *History of the Toronto Fire Department* (Toronto 1923) 42–6

31 *History of the Toronto Fire Department* 49–81

32 Treasurer's Report, 1930, 45

33 Guillet *Toronto* 206

34 Paul Rutherford 'Tomorrow's Metropolis: The Urban Reform Movement in Canada, 1880–1920' Canadian Historical Association *Historical Papers* (1971) 207–8; John C. Weaver 'Tomorrow's Metropolis Revisited: A Critical Assessment of Urban Reform in Canada, 1890–1920' in Gilbert A. Stelter and Alan F.J. Artibise ed *The Canadian City* (Toronto 1977) 394–403

35 James Beaty *Civic Relief* (Toronto 1896) 37–8

36 Minutes, 1908, Appendix B 437–8. Like the sewage treatment plant, the water filtration plant was approved in 1908 but not completed until 1913.

37 Treasurer's Report, 1930, 65–6; City Engineer's Report, 1900, viii, 66

38 E.M. Ashworth *Toronto Hydro Recollections* (Toronto 1955) 19–23; see also E.B. Biggar *Hydro-Electric Development in Ontario* (Toronto 1920) 98–100; Middleton *Toronto* I 366–7.

39 Ashworth *Toronto Hydro* 20, 44; Middleton *Toronto* I 367

40 Toronto Hydro Electric System *Annual Report*, 1930; Treasurer's Report, 1930, 71

41 S. Morley Wickett 'The Municipal Government of Toronto' in S. Morley

Wickett ed *Municipal Government in Canada* University of Toronto Studies, History and Economics, 2 (Toronto 1907) 43. This article was originally written in 1902. See also City Engineer's Report, 1900, xi

42 Wickett 'Municipal Government' 43

43 Guillet *Toronto* 147–8; see also *Wheels of Progress: A Story of Toronto and the Development of Its Public Transportation* (Toronto 1940) 15–63; John F. Bromley and Jack May *Fifty Years of Progressive Transit: A History of the Toronto Transit Commission* (New York 1973) 9–43; Treasurer's Report, 1929, 66

44 Treasurer's Report, 1930, 73–4; Toronto Transportation Commission *Annual Statement* 1922–30

45 Hocken 'The New Spirit' 85

46 Treasurer's Report, 1900, 1930

47 City Engineer's Report, 1900, x

48 Hocken 'The New Spirit' 87

49 Thomas Adams 'Parks and Playgrounds in Cities' *The Canadian Municipal Journal* XIV 11 (November 1920) 348; see also 'Do Parks Pay?' *The Canadian Municipal Journal* VIII 4 (April 1912) 132

50 Hocken 'The New Spirit' 87–8; see also Robert M. Stamp *The Schools of Ontario, 1876–1976* (Toronto 1982) 68

51 Treasurer's Report, 1930, 22, 27–8, 47; Treasurer's Report, 1900, xxi

52 C.S. Clark *Of Toronto the Good* (Montreal 1898) 79

53 Honora M. Cochrane *Centennial Story: The Board of Education For the City of Toronto, 1850–1950* (Toronto 1950) 99

54 Treasurer's Report, 1930, 43–4

55 Stamp *Schools* 66–9

56 Treasurer's Report, 1930, 43–4

57 Cochrane *Centennial* 120–4, 142–65; Stamp *Schools* 79–84, 97–121

58 Treasurer's Report, 1930, 43

59 City Engineer's Report, 1900, x; H.C. Campbell 'Reading for All: The Origins and Growth of the Toronto Library, 1883–1968' unpublished manuscript, CTA, 1981, 28–31

60 Middleton *Toronto* 1 368

61 Campbell 'Reading for All' 43–5; Treasurer's Report, 1930, 53

62 For a fuller treatment of public health developments in Toronto in the late nineteenth and early twentieth centuries see Heather A. MacDougall ' "Health is Wealth": The Development of Public Health Activity in Toronto, 1834–1890' PhD thesis, University of Toronto, 1981, and Heather A. MacDougall 'The Genesis of Public Health Reform in Toronto, 1869–90' *Urban History Review* x 3 (1982) 1–10.

63 *Globe* 2 April 1912

64 C.J. Hastings 'The Value of Health to a Municipality' *The Municipal World* xxxv 10 (October 1925) 202
65 Ibid 201
66 Treasurer's Reports for 1900 and 1930
67 For a fuller treatment of Hastings's work see Paul Adolphus Bator 'Saving Lives on the Wholesale Plan: Public Health Reform in the City of Toronto, 1900 to 1930' PhD thesis, University of Toronto, 1979, and Paul Adolphus Bator '"The Struggle to Raise the Lower Classes": Public Health Reform and the Problem of Poverty in Toronto, 1910–1921' *Journal of Canadian Studies* xiv 1 (1979) 43–9
69 Treasurer's Report, 1930, 21, 60–1
70 Treasurer's Report, 1900, 128–34; see also Stephen A. Speisman 'Munificent Parsons and Municipal Parsimony: Voluntary vs Public Poor Relief in Nineteenth Century Toronto' *Ontario History* LXV (1973) 33–49.
71 Minutes, 1908, Appendix A 1596
72 James Pitsula 'The Emergence of Social Work in Toronto' *Journal of Canadian Studies* xiv 1 (1979) 38–9; see also Richard Splane *Social Welfare in Ontario, 1791–1893: A Study of Public Welfare Administration* (Toronto 1965) 114–16.
73 Toronto *Social Service Commission Report Dealing with the Origins, Duties, Growth and Work since November 1912* (Toronto 1921)
74 *Toronto Star* 7 December 1920, 1, and 9 December 1920, 8
75 Treasurer's Report, 1920, 61
76 Treasurer's Report, 1900, 128–34, and Treasurer's Report, 1930, 21
77 Charles J. Hastings *Report of the Medical Officer Dealing with the Recent Investigation of Slum Conditions in Toronto Embodying Recommendations for the Amelioration of the Same* (Toronto 1911)
78 Treasurer's Report, 1928, 60; the efforts of the Toronto Housing Company are discussed at greater length in Shirley Spragg 'The Toronto Housing Company: A Canadian Experiment' paper, Queen's University, Kingston, n.d. (deposited in CTA).
79 Treasurer's Report, 1928, 50; see also Michael J. Piva *The Condition of the Working Class in Toronto – 1900–1921* (Ottawa 1979) 136–8.
80 By the 1920s most of these services were designated as 'Common Welfare Services' in the Treasurer's Report.
81 J.O. McCarthy 'The City Problem' *The Canadian Municipal Journal* x 8 (August 1914) 314
82 'Social Services and the Municipal Councils of Canada' *The Canada Municipal Journal* xvi 1 (January 1920) 10
83 For a more critical view of municipal social policy in Toronto see Piva *Condition*, especially 61–86, 113–42.
84 J. Herbert Hodgins 'Can We Cut "Frills" off Civic Finance?' *The Municipal*

Review of Canada xx 11 (November 1924) 425–6, 441, 446; Hodgins 'Playing Hopscotch with Our Taxes' *The Municipal Review of Canada* xx 12 (December 1924) 480–1

85 Treasurer's Reports for 1900 and 1928–30

86 Civic Advisory Council *Municipal Finance* 6; see also J. Harvey Perry *Taxes, Tariffs, and Subsidies: A History of Canadian Fiscal Developments* 1 (Toronto 1955) 79–80, and H. Carl Goldenberg *Municipal Finance in Canada A Study Prepared for the Royal Commission on Dominion Provincial Relations* (Ottawa 1937) 94–6.

87 Horace L. Brittain 'A Dollar's Worth for a Dollar,' *The Municipal World* xxxi 10 (October 1921) 218; Thomas Bradshaw 'Municipal Finance' Ontario Municipal Association *Proceedings* (Toronto 1934) 81–5

88 Thomas Bradshaw 'The Maintenance of Public Credit' *The Canadian Chartered Accountant* xxvi (1935) 123–8; Roger E. Riendeau 'A Clash of Interests: Dependency and the Municipal Problem in the Great Depression' *Journal of Canadian Studies* xiv 1 (1979) 50–8

PATRICIA PETERSEN

The evolution of the board of control

Toronto began life as a city with a form of government similar to the one that the British Parliament had designed for its cities in the Municipal Corporations Act of 1835. In the simple structure set up for Toronto all legislative and executive powers were 'vested in the Mayor, Aldermen and Common Council of said City.'[1] Most of the routine administrative work was allocated to standing committees, composed of council members, which council set up during the year; the authority to pass by-laws and determine expenditures, however, still belonged to council.

Toronto city council, from the outset, had difficulty regulating the work of the committees, despite its authority over them, and it found it especially difficult to control committee expenditures. Today it is common practice, if not required by statute, for city councils in Ontario to pass by-laws appropriating money for certain expenses before the work incurring that expense is done. In this way councils can control every item of city expenditure. This was not so in early-nineteenth-century Toronto: Toronto's act of incorporation did not require an appropriation by-law for every expenditure and council would often authorize work with no prior allocation of funds. In fact, very often council did not know, until it received the bills, just how much the work would cost the city. In 1835, for example, the market committee asked council to hire a carpenter to raise by six inches the floor under the butchers' stalls in the St Lawrence Market. Council approved the request and referred it to the building committee to contract for the work. Neither the market committee's report nor council's direction to the building committee suggested a possible limit to the cost of the work. Council did not see the item again until the finance committee, months later, presented it with a bill for £75.[2]

For larger items of city expenditure, such as improvements to roads and sidewalks, council did make appropriations, but, in practice, council proved to have very little control over city spending. Again, there was nothing in the act of incorporation that required those who spent the funds to remain within the original amount appropriated. To take another example from 1835, several ward committees that council had established to spend the appropriations for sidewalk and road improvements exceeded the total funds appropriated by 50 per cent. As the work had already been done, council had no choice but to pay the bill.[3]

It is easy to see how these loose financial practices indirectly transferred council's spending authority to its committees. In the early years, when the city had very little money at its disposal, this arrangement proved only occasionally problematical. Toronto's first council was so strapped for funds that at its first meeting one alderman suggested 'each member of council loan the corporation £25 for one year.'[4] By 1860, however, the city's annual expenditures had risen to $900,239, and council's patience with committee spending was wearing thin. In the 1860s, council began to amend the procedural by-law purposely to reassert its authority over spending. 'No committee,' one amendment pointedly reminded the aldermen, 'shall ... enter into a contract or incur or authorize any expenditure, without having obtained ... the previous authority of Council.'[5] Even with these amendments and with the growing predominance of the finance and assessment committee, council was still unable to obtain the control it wished over its committees. To that end, in 1877, on the recommendation of Alderman James Beaty, city council created the city's first executive committee.

James Beaty, QC, head of the Toronto law firm Beaty, Snow and Smith, was serving his first term on Toronto council when he made his proposal. 'A thorough economist,' Beaty had become dismayed with the city's inability to keep expenditures within appropriations: city expenditures had exceeded appropriations by $135,000 in 1875 and by $90,000 in 1876. This, Beaty argued, was 'most disgraceful to a city of the standing of Toronto.'[6] According to Beaty, the problem lay in the fact that Toronto council, despite all its amendments to the procedural by-law, still did not know exactly what its committees were spending during the year, and this only facilitated the 'continuation of the baneful practice of building up deficits.'[7]

Beaty asked that council abolish the finance committee and replace it with an executive committee composed of the mayor and a number of aldermen, 'not to exceed one member from each ward.' These aldermen would be appointed by council. The new executive committee incorporated within its jurisdiction all the functions of the old finance committee: it was responsible for the city accounts, the annual financial statement, and the estimates. It had additional powers, however, that gave it the authority to supervise the work of the other standing committees. Beaty's proposal required all standing committees to report every decision that involved an expenditure of money to the executive committee and further gave the executive committee a veto over these decisions. The standing committees could appeal to council any veto by the executive committee, but this appeal could be sustained only by a two-third vote of council.

Beaty was aware of at least one suggested reform to local government in the United States and mentioned this in introducing his proposal to council: 'In New York City ... a committee of twelve men had been appointed to enquire into these matters ... and the first of their findings was that a Board of Finance should be organized having the same powers which [I have] suggested the Finance Committee ... be given.'[8] The Tilden Commission had been established by New York governor Samuel Tilden in 1875 to recommend a structure of city governments in the state that would control excessive spending and prevent a recurrence of corruption, particularly of the kind that had just been revealed in New York City. The commission proposed that all financial matters in city government be the responsibility of a board of finance. The board alone would decide how the city spent its money through its exclusive authority to prepare the estimates, levy taxes, and determine the city debt. The city's legislative body, city council, had no say whatever in these matters; financing the city had been removed completely from its jurisdiction. Members of the board of finance were directly elected by those residents of the city who met certain property qualifications, for the commission reasoned that 'the assembly which votes taxes should be elected by those who contribute toward taxes imposed.'[9]

Beaty's solution to Toronto's problem was quite different from this, despite what he had said at council, and much more congenial to the existing structure of city government.[10] The new executive was, in fact, very similar to the other standing committees of council. It was composed of council members who were appointed by council; it was not a separately elected body like the board of finance of the Tilden Commission. Further, like Toronto's other standing committees but very much unlike the board of finance, it was subordinate to city council because it had to report all of its decisions to council for approval. But then Beaty was not interested in curtailing the financial powers of city council, which was clearly the purpose of the Tilden Commission's report, but rather in promoting 'some plan ... by which it could no longer be said of the Council of Toronto that they exceeded their appropriations without knowing it.'[11]

Though the executive committee had some of the characteristics of the board of control, to be established much later, it had considerably less power. First, the committee's veto over spending was more limited, since it could be used only if requests for money contradicted city by-laws or exceeded either appropriations or estimates, and it was council that, by a majority vote, determined estimates, appropriations, and by-laws. Second, and even more disruptive of the executive committee's authority over the standing committees, it had been created by a council by-law and was thus a creature of council. It was, therefore, within council's authority to abolish the executive committee or rescind any of its powers.

The executive committee apparently did little to aid Toronto on its road to efficiency: complaints of aldermanic interference in department affairs and ward influence in city spending persisted and eventually led to two major but unsuccessful attempts during the 1880s to make the executive committee more independent of council. The first attempt occurred in 1880, just three years after the committee had been created. James Beaty, then mayor of the city, proposed in his inaugural address that the committee be restructured to consist of the mayor and nine aldermen elected at large for three-year terms. This would, Beaty argued, 'rid us of the ward and grabbing influences which have clung to us for the past twenty-five years' and, he hoped, also 'bring out as candidates our best citizens.' Toronto council did not agree with the mayor and rejected his proposal. Most of the aldermen were afraid that under this scheme Torontonians would elect inexperienced men 'unfitted for the work of supervising the work of the committees composed of more experienced men'; others felt that it would be too difficult for the candidates for the committee to canvas the whole city for votes every year; and two aldermen disliked Beaty's scheme because it 'had been copied from the Yankees.' The city should reject it for this reason alone: 'the records of Chicago and New York should be a warning to Toronto.'[12]

In 1889, Alderman E.A. MacDonald produced another plan meant to strengthen and consolidate executive power in city government. MacDonald proposed a board of commissioners for the city composed of the mayor and six commissioners elected at large for three-year terms; his intention was 'to provide for the more efficient administration of the affairs of the City.' The board, it was hoped, would stop 'aldermanic interference with officials' because 'it made these officials responsible to the commissioners only.' Some aldermen liked the plan, if only because 'the present system [was] so cumbrous and unworkable that nothing could possibly be worse,' while others were horrified. 'Send that on to Council ...' Alderman Denison raged, 'That piece of Yankee legislation! ... I hope I never will see the day when such legislation will receive our approval.'[13] To Denison's delight, council did not approve the plan but referred it to a special committee created to review various methods of reform. This committee was reconstituted in 1890 with MacDonald as chairman and eventually presented its recommendations to council in October 1890. There was no mention of MacDonald's board of commissioners in the committee's report.

Apparently there was very little debate at council on the few recommendations this special committee did make. Two proposals for change (on the mayor's veto and on the office of president of council) that might have been labelled 'Yankeeisms' were rejected. The only alteration council did accept was the reduction in number of wards for the city from eight to six. It seemed that council was no closer to introducing executive government at the close of 1890 than it had been in 1880; therefore, in an effort to make some change before the end of the year, Alderman Alfred McDougall presented council with a draft by-law detailing his idea for a restructured executive committee and requested that the by-law be placed on the municipal election ballot 'for endorsement.'[14]

McDougall's plan was intended to reflect the cabinet system of government. Council would be the city's parliament; the board of control would be the cabinet and would consist of the mayor, still elected at large, and the chairmen of council's standing committees, which McDougall proposed to reduce to three. The most important feature of the plan was the requirement that the mayor appoint the chairmen of the three standing committees; this meant that it was the mayor who, like a prime minister, chose the executive body of government. 'I believe,' McDougall stated in defence of his plan, 'the Executive ought to be held directly responsible for the business of the city ... I propose to give him an opportunity of choosing his advisors at the beginning of the year.'[15]

McDougall's plan was not as radical as the schemes proposed by Beaty and MacDonald – for one thing, council could implement it without an amendment to the Municipal Act – yet council baulked. Most aldermen disliked giving the mayor authority to choose the members of the board, and they therefore replaced his power to appoint committee chairmen, as McDougall had suggested, with the power to nominate only. Council retained authority to approve those nominated. To further reduce the potential for concentrating power in the mayor's office, council added to the by-law the proviso that 'the Mayor may in his discretion leave the nomination and appointment of the chairman of any committee to the members thereof.' These amendments satisfied a majority of the members of council, and the by-law was placed on the municipal ballot in January 1891. The changes obviously statisfied the citizens of Toronto also, and they approved the by-law by a vote of 10,356 to 3,461. In late February council submitted the by-law to the provincial government, and the usually reserved *Globe* was confident that, with such resounding public support, it would 'probably pass ... pretty much as it [was] drawn up by the city.'[16]

The *Globe*'s optimism notwithstanding, the provincial legislature did not consent to the city's request. It probably would have passed the city's by-law (after all, it had permitted Toronto to place the question of a board of control on the municipal ballot) had it not been for the intense lobbying against it; lobbying which, like the criticism of some Toronto aldermen, objected to increasing the power of the mayor, however slight this increase might have been. Opposition came from many people prominent in the city's political life: eight aldermen, three former aldermen, a former mayor, and from the Toronto *Telegram*, certainly the most vocal critic of the plan. Under McDougall's by-law, committee chairmen would be paid a salary of $2,000 annually; aldermen in 1890 earned no money for performing their duties. The *Telegram* feared that this salary would entice a clique in council to use the appointment power as patronage and 'pay party debts with public money.' 'That McDougall enormity – is not an Act,' the *Telegram* fumed, 'it is an axe supplied by a Liberal government to civic statesmen ... who will use it in the annihilation of Liberals who are not useful to machine politicians of their stamp.' 'Civic Reform, oh Civic Reform,' the paper moaned in an early editorial, 'What crimes are contemplated in thy name?'[17]

Most of the other daily papers did not seem much bothered by the by-law. The *Mail* found nothing in it 'to doom Toronto ... to be ground under the heel of despotism'; the *News* thought the scheme 'the most sensible one yet presented.' Even the *Globe*, never eager to see the structure of Toronto government tinkered with, was willing to give the board a try, but still left those of its readers wishing to make more structural changes with this warning to ponder: 'Constitutions moulded with the greatest care have in the heat and stress of usage taken a form quite different from that which their framers intended.'[18]

From out of all this brouhaha, the opponents of the by-law emerged victorious. Twice the private bills committee of the provincial legislature debated the by-law: the first time it approved the change; the second time, after the by-law was referred back from the house as requested by some committee members who wished to reconsider it, the committee rejected it. The enemies of McDougall's by-law had convinced enough members of the committee to change their votes. The number of those who spoke against it had, by the second meeting, increased enormously; yet this was not the only thing that demonstrated to committee members the folly of their original decision. Intense lobbying had also convinced the Liberals, the party in power, to oppose the by-law. As the *Globe* reported: 'The whips had been floating in and out of the [Committee] room during the sitting in a way that is not customary in committees ... and had [then] taken their places with a definitiveness which indicated that their work was done.' 'It was,' the paper curtly remarked, 'a party vote.'[19]

The failure of Toronto's petition in the Ontario legislature may have killed McDougall's board of control, but some members of Toronto council, joined by a number of citizen groups, continued to wrestle with the question of reform and to believe that the key to better government lay in a strong executive board. Warring Kennedy, candidate for mayor in 1894, still preferred a board of control, but to avoid the objections raised by McDougall's board 'he would have the three controllers elected by the people instead of being appointed by the mayor.'[20] Alderman Hallam, in an open letter to the *Globe* two years later, also declared for a board of control because, he argued, the city's legislators were 'totally unfit'[21] to administer city government. Defence of a strong executive body was taken up outside council by the Civic Reform Conference, organized in 1893 by Dr E.J. Barrick, president of the Ratepayers Association. Delegates to the conference included members of the Toronto Board of Trade, the Ratepayers Association, the Toronto Trades and Labor Council, and two Toronto aldermen. The conference devised an election platform demanding the separation of legislative from executive functions 'as far as possible' and, for the next two years at least, publicly endorsed any candidate for municipal office who supported this change. It was not until late 1895, however, that city council again acted on structural reform.

On 19 December 1895, council approved almost unanimously a by-law creating a board of administration for the city.[22] This board was smaller than the board of control McDougall had proposed and had considerably fewer powers. The only voting members of the board of administration were the mayor and the chairmen of the works and executive committees; the city engineer, city solicitor, and city treasurer were on the board but only as advisers. The board's only function was to tender and contract for public works; it did not prepare the estimates or administer the civil service. The feature of McDougall's board that had drawn so much blood, the nomination by the mayor of board members, was not a part of the board of administration; committee chairmen, including the chairmen of the works and executive committees, would be appointed, as usual, by their respective committees.

Several things had occurred in Toronto in the two years preceding that seemed to demonstrate that council was, if not 'totally,' at least partly 'unfit' to provide the city with the services it needed, and these prompted, no doubt, council's decision. Perhaps the most startling of these occurrences was the release, by January 1895, of two reports by County Court Judge Joseph E. McDougall into the activities of Toronto aldermen. The first report revealed that several aldermen had tried to sell their votes on street lighting questions to the Toronto Electric Light Company, one of the three firms seeking to install lights in the city. The second report, which council had authorized because McDougall had uncovered more corruption than expected, was 'a long and depressing chronicle of malfeasance stretching back to 1891.'[23] McDougall's findings did not help council's image. 'The Council of 1894,' the *Globe* wrote, 'will be remembered in civic history as the Council of the boodle investigation,' regardless of whatever else it had accomplished. Council hoped that the board of administration would correct this form of corruption. It concentrated responsibility for public works in a small body of men, thereby removing 'one of the chief temptations of civic life'[24] from most members of council.

The board of administration had a very short life: six months later, in April 1896, the provincial government amended the Municipal Act, making it mandatory for all cities in the province with a population of more than 100,000 to establish a board of control.[25] As Toronto was the only city in the province with this many people, it was the only city affected by the legislation. The authority of the new board did not differ from the authority proposed in 1890 for McDougall's board; it prepared the estimates and administered the civil service, and its decisions in these matters could be overruled only by a two-thirds vote of council. The board, therefore, superseded not just the board of administration but the executive committee as well. Like its predecessors, moreover, the board had to report all its decisions to council for approval; yet the board was more independent of council because it was a creature of provincial statute, not council by-law, and therefore could be abolished only by the province. More importantly, it was mandatory for the city. Council was forced to establish a board of control and bestow on it specific powers as defined in the Municipal Act. However, the board consisted of the mayor and three aldermen who were nominated and appointed by council, which meant that council could still meddle in board policies. With council choosing three of the four members of the board, it would be difficult to argue that this new executive was greatly protected from 'aldermanic interference.'

The provincial government had initiated the change without waiting for a petition from Toronto council. As a matter of fact, council formally opposed the bill creating the board, wishing it to be held over to the next session of the legislature' as it [was] such a radical and far-reaching proposal.'[26] What made the board so radical was obviously not its constitution, which was very much like the structure of the old executive committee, but rather the fact that the province was making it mandatory – and for one city in the province. In the eyes of the majority on council, the bill was much too arbitrary.

Not all members of council, however, agreed with this formal position. Robert J. Fleming had opposed McDougall's board of control because of the clause giving the mayor extra powers; but now, as the city's mayor, along with Alderman McDougall he argued for the bill before the municipal committee of the provincial legislature. Both believed it to be 'in response to public demand.' Others on council and outside of it praised the board particularly because it reflected cabinet government: 'The introduction into civic affairs of the idea long applied in Parliament itself, that a small committee, call it a cabinet ... can far more efficiently act in an administrative capacity than can a large body, the direct duty of which is the legislation.' This principle could make the board of control 'a capital piece of municipal machinery.'[27]

But the board of control still did not satisfy a majority of Toronto politicians. The most frequent complaint was the method by which board members were chosen, because a particularly large number of aldermen were now spending more time lobbying for a position on the board than seeing to their aldermanic duties. Lobbying skills rather than governing ability had become the criterion for board membership. Electing controllers at large, the *Globe* argued, 'would greatly improve the personnel of the Board of Control.'[28] Some years later, Toronto council would agree. In 1903 it petitioned the provincial legislature to make the change, and the province acceded to the city's request.

That the board of control was a form of government indigenous to Toronto is clear. It was the product of a series of manoeuvres within the city's committee structure, and one could find traces still of the old finance committee in it, even though the two structures differed greatly. In all the changes council made to its executive, however, the notion of executive responsibility remained constant. The executive branch of government was to be accountable to the legislature for all its actions. In British and Canadian governments this is achieved in two ways. First, the executive must always have legislative approval to act; second, members of the executive must also be members of the legislature. Despite numerous alterations to the Toronto executive, these two characteristics were always present. None of the city's executives ever had the authority to act on its own; it was always subordinate to council. Moreover, its members continued to be members of council as well. Any plan that went contrary to either of these, such as MacDonald's board of commissioners, was flatly rejected.

Executive responsibility in this form did not exist in the major proposals put forth by American municipal reformers. It was not present in the Tilden Commission's board of finance, which Beaty spoke of in 1877. That board was quite separate from the city's legislative body, and purposely so. This was also true of other American plans. The scheme most favoured in the United States in the late nineteenth century was the strong-mayor system created in 1880 by Brooklyn politician Frederick Schroeder and promoted for a short time in the 1890s and early 1900s by the reforming National Municipal League. In this type of system the executive was quite clearly independent of the legislature. The mayor possessed some authority that he could exercise without the permission of city council; further, he was not a member of council. The plan, in fact, closely resembled the structure of American state and federal governments. The link between executive and legislative branches of government that existed in Toronto was absent in the United States, and it was this link that kept Toronto government 'British' and 'good,' a fact that Alderman F.S. Spence, on council when the board was created, was to note a few years later: 'The present system had been derived from the old English views of responsible government, whereas the Americans had destroyed its effectiveness by divorcing the two functions of legislation and administration ... A Board of Control, with a safety-valve in the form of an Aldermanic body, is virtually the only practicable form of government.'29

NOTES

1 *Statutes of the Province of Upper Canada*, 1834, 4 William IV, cap 23 sec 21, City of Toronto Act of Incorporation
2 City of Toronto Archives (hereafter CTA), Minutes of Toronto City Council (hereafter Minutes), 1835, items 203, 335
3 Ibid, items 236, 338
4 The aldermen did not loan council any money; Mintues, 1834, meetings, Saturday, 12 April 1834.
5 Minutes, 1862, By-law No. 378 sec XI subsec 88
6 *Globe* 15 May 1877
7 *Telegram* 14 May 1877
8 *Globe* 15 May 1877
9 *Report of the Commission to Devise a Plan for the Government of Cities in the State of New York*, presented to the Legislature, 6 March 1877, New York State Assembly Documents 1877, No. 68, 26
10 Minutes, 1877, By-law No. 793
11 *Telegram* 15 May 1877

12 Minutes, 1880, Appendix 1793, 22; *Globe* 20 January 1880; *Telegram* 30 January 1880 (three quotations); *Globe* 2 February 1880

13 Minutes, 1889, report No. 5 of the Legislation Committee, Appendix A, items 1693, 1697; *Telegram* 19 November, 16 October, and 9 November 1889

14 Minutes, 1890, items 1326, 1346; *Globe* 9 December 1890

15 *Globe* 24 December 1890

16 *Journal of the Legislative Assembly of the Province of Ontario*, 1891, 176; Minutes, 1891, item 1426; *Globe* 3 January 1891

17 *Telegram* 16 January, 15 April, and 2 January 1891

18 *Mail* 28 April 1891; *News* 15 April 1891; *Globe* 15 April 1891

19 *Globe* 29 April 1891

20 Ibid 23 December 1893

21 Ibid 29 October 1895

22 Minutes, 1895, item 912; By-law No. 3374

23 The quotation is from Christopher Armstrong and H.V. Nelles *The Revenge of the Methodist Bicycle Company* (Toronto 1977) 135. The chapter titled 'The Redemption of the City' explains the events that forced the province to act. CTA, Evidence and Reports, In the Matter of the Investigation before his Honour Judge McDougall, pursuant to resolutions of city council dated 8th October 1894 and 13th November 1894

24 *Globe* 21 Decmeber 1894, 29 October 1895

25 *Statues of Ontario*, 1896, 59 Victoria cap 51

26 Minutes, 1896, items 271–2, and Appendix A 87

27 *Globe* 25 March 1896; *Telegram* 31 March 1896

25 *Globe* 15 January, 15 December 1902

29 Ibid 1 December 1914

CHRISTOPHER ARMSTRONG and H.V. NELLES

The rise of civic populism in Toronto
1870–1920

Sometimes a great notion seizes a city. So it was in Toronto at the turn of the century that the ideas we will call civic populism infused municipal politics for a generation. The majority of Torontonians came to believe that certain essential services could be most economically, efficiently, and honestly supplied by public rather than private undertakings. And Toronto went further, sooner, toward realizing this goal than any other major city in North America.

Not only was the idea of public enterprise new, but so also was the gospel-like fervour with which it was espoused. Just a few years earlier the notion had been the scorned property of a handful of political radicals and municipal mavericks. Now it was a commonplace. What brought about this change of heart? Toronto was no less capitalist than any other city: it aspired, after all, to become a better Chicago. The citizens of Toronto obviously shared the prevailing liberal capitalist ideology. Nevertheless, a key portion of the business élite, the solid bourgeois ratepayers, and the leading trade unionists all supported a movement for public ownership of utilities. Torontonians came to this conviction gradually; they were not suddenly seized by an idea but rather seized upon it as a solution first to one problem, and then another. From one confrontation to the next the notion acquired greater legitimacy, although the campaigns for public ownership did not reach the same conclusion in every case. But if the idea that utilities were public had a spiritual home in North America, that home would be Toronto.

Cities are in the business of supplying services: roads, bridges, markets, protection for life and property, public order, and social amenities. What services are provided and in what way vary greatly from time to time and place to place. Demography, incomes and their distribution, technology, and the political milieu interact in a specific social context to determine who gets what and at whose expense. Obviously what a city can do for its citizens changes over time. So, too, does the notion of what it ought to do. Roads of widely varying quality, for example, have been provided and maintained, some built by the state and paid for out of taxation, others constructed by private enterprise and paid for by tolls. During the early decades of the twentieth century Toronto was in the forefront of those cities pushing out the frontiers of what municipal government ought legitimately to provide. In doing so, it acted not upon abstract principles so much as in vigorous response to practical problems.

Why was the municipal government more inclined to experiment with public ownership? An American tourist visiting the city around 1900 would have found the bitter conflicts between city council and the gas, telephone, street railway, and electrical companies all too familiar. What would have been novel and perhaps a bit startling to him, however, would have been the extent to which the municipality seemed prepared to move beyond negotiation and litigation to open competition with private companies.[1] Why should this have been so? What was it about the city and its politics that explains this adventurousness?

By the 1890s most North American cities were entering a new stage in their relations with the private companies that supplied their gas, transit, electrical, and telephone services. When these companies had first appeared earlier in the century these services had not been deemed essential. Pure water, bright lighting, speedy transportation, and efficient communication had once been luxuries; in compact, close-knit towns they were not really necessary. They became utilities as towns grew into cities, as technology changed and as incomes rose to make such services more widely affordable. In short, the utilities became the infrastructure for large, modern, urban communities. At first the suppliers had been regarded as ordinary commercial enterprises, and it was assumed that competition or a simple contract would be sufficient to safeguard the interests of the city, the company, and its customers. In some places the improbability of an adequate rate of return on the investment made the provision of such services something close to an act of public charity for which the citizens showed due gratitude. But in the course of time the tendency toward monopoly (the phrase 'natural monopoly' being invented to describe these services), mass use, and dependence and the sheer size and financial power of these companies rendered competition and contracts wholly ineffective as guarantors of adequate, reliable, and inexpensive services. Instead, municipal politicians by the late nineteenth century sought to hammer out detailed franchise agreements that would bind the utilities closely and even force them, in some cases, to share the profits they earned with local governments.

Differences over the interpretation of franchises almost invariably ended in litigation. As the courts brought to these disputes a narrow interpretation of contract and an exaggerated respect for the rights of property, aggrieved cities and angry ratepayers soon turned to their legislatures to create regulatory tribunals to enforce some broader conception of the public interest in determining rates, levels of service, and sharing of revenues. This third stage in the relations between the cities and their utilities, regulation by commission, is the point at which Toronto parted company with most other North American jurisdictions.[2] In Toronto public ownership became for a time the preferred instrument of regulation. Civic populism made the substance of Toronto politics as distinct from that of other North American cities as its geography, architecture, and social composition.

This account of Toronto's early experiences with the suppliers of these services will show the mood of rather casual optimism that prevailed at first but later soured as conflicts developed over rates and service. The outcome was a period of intense negotiation between 1887 and 1891 that produced new and, it was thought, ironclad agreements that would control the gas, telephone, electric, and street railway companies and even require them to share their revenues with the citizens. In a surprisingly short time in each case, however, these franchises created an unprecedented uprising of populist feeling against the utility companies as spirited as that of North American farmers against the trusts and the 'goldbugs' at the very same time. The result was the city's takeover of two of the utilities, after a period of competition between public and private enterprise, and attempts to regulate the other two. Civic populism, the politics of public ownership, and the visual vocabulary that this movement developed form the subject matter of this essay.

By the 1880s the rather loose arrangements that the city had worked out with its gas, water, and street railway companies around mid-century had broken down completely. In 1841 the city authorized Albert Furniss, the proprietor of the Montreal Gas Light Company, to operate a gas and water company using the city streets. Dissatisfaction with the service provided by Furniss led city council to charter a competitor, the Consumers' Gas Company, in 1848, which soon acquired Furniss's gasworks. A third company was chartered in 1853 but never operated. It was hoped that the discipline of competition would produce better service at lower prices, but as a precaution the city also acquired from the legislature in 1854 the authority to construct its own gasworks.[3]

In 1860, when Alexander Easton offered to build a street railway in Toronto similar to the one he had previously laid out in several American cities, council tried a different approach. First it called for public tenders for street railway service in order to obtain the best deal. Second, it offered to grant an exclusive thirty-year franchise in return for an annual licence fee and an agreement that the company would pave and clear the roadways along its tracks. If the company flourished, the city's roads would be improved at no direct cost and the licence fees would relieve the burden on the taxpayers.[4]

The debates over these early franchises reveal that while the citizens understood that the city might provide these services itself, it was generally agreed that it was better to leave them to private entrepreneurs. The heavy capital investment required would be an onerous burden for the ratepayers. And the risks were high. Furniss's water company got into difficulties and twice had to be repossessed by him from those to whom he had sold it. The street railway fell into receivership in 1869 and limped along for many years thereafter. Even the Consumers' Gas Company had its difficulties in the depression after 1857. Thus there was almost a whiff of noblesse oblige about those willing to undertake the supply of these conveniences to the city.[5]

That was not the only odour that surrounded these undertakings. The water-supply was tainted with sewage from the bay and the hydrants had so little pressure that they were practically useless for fire-fighting. There were fewer complaints about the quality of gas, which was a relatively expensive commodity that only commercial establishments and the well-to-do could afford to install, but in 1874 the proprietor of the Rossin House asked for a reduction in his bill on the grounds that 'There was [sic] several nights we had but little gas and much of the time it was very thin and poor. In fact, you have charged us for air instead of gas.'[6] Yet as the city grew and incomes rose these services became more and more important. As an overgrown village was transformed into a recognizable city and even began to spawn its own suburbs, these amenities became necessities. After twenty years of prodding and bullying the water company to try and improve its service, city council decided in exasperation in 1870 to construct a larger waterworks of its own. By then the city could borrow the money itself and the ratepayers were prepared to approve the investment. Henceforth water for sanitary and fire-fighting purposes was a municipal responsibility, and that meant that the city shouldered the inevitable criticism when water pressure dropped or the tap-water was filled with germs.[7]

During this period gas and public transportation began to undergo the same transformation from social amenities to absolute necessities. The street railway was an important catalyst in the transformation of town into city by making it physically possible for the growing population to spread out into the suburban housing developments beyond easy walking distance from downtown. As the population sorted itself according to class in this newly enlarged space, the street railway became a principal means of transporting Toronto's citizenry to and from work.[8] So, too, gas replaced candles and oil lamps in public buildings, shops, and the parlours of the wealthy. Gas rates fell by 75 per cent between 1850 and 1886, permitting middle-class and even humbler homes to secure service. Widespread literacy helped sustain demand for better lighting at night. Thus the street railway, the gas company, water-supply, and sewage moved from the margin of politics in the old commercial town to the very heart of municipal concerns in the emerging industrial city.

Dependence on gas lighting and streetcars had two related effects: complaints about service grew more numerous and insistent and the utility companies became notoriously profitable. Knowledge of these profits – often wildly exaggerated in the telling – heightened public indignation, bringing pressure to bear upon municipal politicians to seek redress. Previously these private activities had not seemed in conflict with the general, public interest. Indeed, much earlier there would have been no service at all without public-spirited initiatives by private individuals. But under the changed conditions of the 1870s and 1880s private ownership seemed almost inevitably to conflict with emerging public needs. The owners sought to maximize profits, and the users wanted cheap and reliable service. As the demands of consumers intensified, the operators dragged their heels or openly defied municipal authorities. The many saw themselves enriching the few and resented it.

Relations with the gas company became strained whenever it came time to renew the city's street lighting contract. The city itself was the biggest single user of gas and saw the contract as the cornerstone upon which the company's profits rested. Ratepayers as well as consumers had an interest in driving a hard bargain with the company to secure lower rates. Conflict also arose over the company's sweeping powers to dig up the streets. Particularly in the early 1880s the company was inundated with complaints over the quality of gas produced by the new Lowe system. As one disgruntled user wrote to the general manager, 'The consumer is not of much consequence to a wealthy company.' While gas rates fell they did not come down nearly fast enough, in the opinion of most people. As the gas company's profits rose during the 1880s antagonism focused on its attempts to mask this by building up a large reserve fund.[9]

The street railway attracted even more bitter public obloquy. Apart from failing to run enough horsecars or supply transfers, the company also did not meet its obligations to maintain the pavement around its tracks. Ceaseless wrangling resulted from the mid-1870s onward. As strap-hangers lurched in cramped (and often unheated) cars or waited eternities in the snow, Senator Frank Smith, the prominent liquor and grocery wholesaler who acquired control of the Toronto Street Railway in 1881, amassed huge profits, at least so the city's newspapers held. The *Telegram* explained in 1890, 'How Wealth Is Picked Up On The City's Thoroughfares,' and the *Mail*, not to be outdone in sensationalism, ranted, 'MILLIONS IN IT: Vast Stores Of Wealth Piled Up By Toronto's Horsecars.'[10] The extent of public hostility toward Smith and his gold mine was revealed in 1886 when the carmen went on strike. City council, the major newspapers, and a large portion of the citizens heartily supported the rioting strikers and their allies – hardly the usual state of affairs in a labour dispute in late-nineteenth-century Toronto.[11] As if to demonstrate that he had no scruples, Smith tried to sneak a bill through the provincial legislature during the strike that would have extended forever the franchise due to expire in 1891.

By the mid-1880s, therefore, the gas and street railway companies had entered a new and dangerous phase of their relations with the city and their customers. The old arrangements had clearly failed. Citizens were exerting great pressure to improve and cheapen service. Competition could not be counted on to discipline private enterprise, because Toronto, unlike a number of other North American cities, never had rival undertakings to challenge its local monopolies. Changing technology was bringing new and desirable services into being – electric lighting, electrified trolley cars, and the telephone. As the provincial secretary of Ontario had warned the gas company about its unsatisfactory service in 1880: 'Some Members [of the legislature] would also appear to think it necessary that some interference on behalf of the public is called for.'[12]

When the opportunity arose Toronto politicians were thus persuaded that more vigorous regulation of local utilities was necessary. And, as it happened, such opportunities presented themselves between 1887 and 1891. One obvious and drastic solution was public ownership: Manchester, for instance, had had a civic gasworks since 1817. Most Torontonians, however, simply refused to believe that public ownership would work. Any public enterprise must surely be beset by the twin evils of corruption and inefficiency. As the city's lawyer commented about the proposal to take over the street railway: 'With the many masters that must of necessity be introduced in the case of civic control, it will be made the dumping ground of incapables, the failures and the needy relatives, who will be hourly applicants for the fat and easy places that must be found for them.'[13] Instead, many citizens thought that the answer lay in compelling the companies to enter more tightly drawn franchise agreements that would force them to fulfil the needs of their customers.[14] Between 1887 and 1891 much energy was expended by municipal politicians on trying to corral the companies on acceptable terms.

Consumers' Gas seemed, at first glance, to be strongly placed to resist any such pressure, for it had a perpetual right to supply gas in the city under its 1848 charter. True, that charter was not an exclusive one, but the size and cost of its plant constituted a formidable barrier to entry for any rival. The city's only means of influence over the company was to lobby the provincial legislature whenever Consumers' Gas requested changes in its charter. In 1887 Consumers' Gas applied for an increase in capitalization from $1,000,000 to $2,000,000, with the intention of offering the new stock *pro rata* to the current shareholders at par, the proceeds to be used to build a new gas plant. In addition, this was an opportunity to distribute some of its bountiful profits to its shareholders since the stock was currently trading at nearly 200 per cent of par. Mayor William Howland exerted his influence with the provincial government and succeeded in blocking this. The new legislation required that in exchange for the increase in the company's capital any additional surplus if earned would be applied to reducing gas rates to all consumers.[15] The city believed it had put in place a mechanism that would require the company to share its continued prosperity with the citizens by reducing the cost of service.

The strategy of using agreements as a mechanism for exerting control over utilities was also employed by the city to regulate its electricity companies. In 1883 the Toronto Electric Light Company had been incorporated to supply arc lighting and soon took over much of the street lighting downtown. In 1889, Toronto Incandescent Electric Light was founded to use the patents held by Thomas Edison. The two firms were complementary rather than rivals, as arc lighting was suitable for large outdoor and commercial spaces, incandescent bulbs for residences. With the two companies each putting up wires and poles (not to speak of telephone lines), the city became convinced that it must exercise some control over the use of its streets and require the utilities to place their wires in underground conduits, at least downtown. To gain the right to use public thoroughfares the companies were required to sign 'Underground Agreements' that bound them to install conduits in exchange for the use of the city streets over a thirty-year period. At the end of that time the city would have the right to acquire their plants if it wished, at a price to be arbitrated. In order to prevent the exploitation of consumers by a monopoly, the city added provisions that these agreements were to be voided if the electrical companies amalgamated with each other.[16]

The city also tried to gain control over another utility through a franchise agreement. The Bell Telephone Company of Canada had been incorporated by federal charter in 1880 and began serving Toronto in 1882. That same year it procured a charter amendment from Ottawa declaring that all its works were for the 'general advantage of Canada,' which, as it turned out, rendered it largely immune from provincial and, hence, municipal control. None the less, the city remained able to exert a certain amount of authority over the company by threatening to license a rival company to string its wires through the streets. In 1891 a new Toronto Telephone Company approached the city. Charles F. Sise, the president of Bell, was apparently determined to retain his local monopoly, partly because he suspected that the newcomers were merely hoping to secure some rights in order to sell them either to Bell or to a menacing CPR syndicate. He therefore offered the city an exclusive franchise that gave council an opportunity to bring the company under its control. In exchange for a five-year agreement to license no other phone companies, Sise offered to reduce rates and to pay over to the city 5 per cent of the company's gross receipts annually. Rates would not be increased during the term of the franchise without the city's consent. After a great deal of frantic lobbying and haggling, city council approved the arrangement, which was signed in September 1891.[17]

The expiration of the street railway franchise in 1891 seemed to most Torontonians a heaven-sent opportunity to escape from the poor service offered by Frank Smith's company and at the same time to replace the creaking horse car with speedy electric trams. So unpopular was the existing company that in May 1890 the ratepayers voted by a margin of 5,385 to 427 to have the city purchase it when the franchise expired. A majority of council, however, regarded public ownership only as a threat to be used 'to burst up any combine amongst intending purchasers of the franchise.' The aldermen were convinced that a new agreement regulating fares, routes, and paving and requiring the successful bidder to pay over to the city a percentage of gross receipts would ensure that this vital utility would in future serve the public rather than just its proprietors.

In the event, the process of awarding the franchise took so long that the city was compelled to take over the system and operate it for several months, but, despite profits of over $1,000 per day flowing into the treasury, only a fringe of radicals, socialists, single-taxers, and the like favoured civic ownership. The new thirty-year franchise was finally awarded to a syndicate headed by H.A. Everett, George Washington Kiely, and William Mackenzie. The

THE STREET RAILWAY BONANZA.

BURDENED CITIZEN—"Gee Whittaker! If that was only pouring into the city treasury I wouldn't have to carry quite so much of a load!

ABOVE *Grip* 15 November 1890

OPPOSITE *Grip* 25 April 1891

A PITEOUS APPEAL.

" Won't some private speculator please take this gold-mine? The City Council won't work it as a civic department, as they're afraid they can't trust their own honesty ! "

decision was controversial because of rumours of bribery of aldermen that had been circulating throughout the summer of 1891, but by September the by-law was passed and the new Toronto Railway Company set about the task of electrifying the system which was completed by 1894.[18]

By the early 1890s the city of Toronto seemed to have moved a long way toward regulating and modernizing its vital utilities through franchise agreements. The gas company was now required to reduce its rates should it continue to earn such substantial profits. The electrical companies had been compelled to place their wires underground downtown and were forbidden to amalgamate with one another. The city now possessed the right to purchase their plants at a price to be arbitrated when these agreements expired in 1919. In return for an exclusive five-year franchise the telephone company had lowered its rates and agreed not to alter them without the consent of council. The much-reviled street railway had passed into new (and, it was hoped, more responsible) hands to be electrified, while the city could anticipate a substantial income from its percentage of the gross receipts as a steadily increasing population boarded the trolleys. From now on the utilities would serve the public and not vice versa.

During the extended debates over the franchises between 1887 and 1891 it was clear that many Torontonians accepted the proposition that a city might own its utilities. Of course, a number of well-known enthusiasts for public ownership, such as Phillips Thomson of the *Labor Advocate*, the Single Tax Association, and the Trades and Labour Council, argued that the city should own and operate all its utilities. But the majority of citizens had concluded that city government, as then constituted, was ill-equipped to operate efficiently such technologically complex capital-intensive systems. Twice in the 1890s Torontonians had the chance to pronounce upon the question of public ownership: in 1891 council returned the street railway to private hands as rapidly as possible, and in 1895 the ratepayers rejected a municipal lighting plant. The spectre of rampant patronage, the taint of corruption, the likelihood of overstaffing, and the possibility of higher taxes to cover the cost of the investment and any deficits incurred inclined the cautious voter and alderman to stick with strictly regulated private enterprise instead of public ownership. Having drawn up the franchise agreements with painstaking care, the civic authorities seemed to have the upper hand: the interests of the corporation, the consumer, and in some cases even the employees of the utility companies seemed to have been looked after. At last peace would reign between the city and its utilities.

It was not to be, of course. Friction continued with the gas company and the street railway as though nothing had changed at all. As early as 1888 an accountant for the city reported that unless the new gas company charter were changed to reduce the amount that was being set aside for repairs the total reserved would never reach the sum that would trigger a reduction in gas rates. This proved to be only the start of a decade and a half of bitter wrangling between Consumers' Gas and the city, as the company went on salting away large sums and spending them on the maintenance and improvement of its plant so that it was never compelled to cut rates, though rates were several times reduced by the company of its own volition. The 1887 charter provided that the city might inspect the company's books at the end of each fiscal year, and the every autumn this became the occasion for stinging criticisms of the company. In 1891, for instance, the company was denounced for using its reserves 'improperly' and attacked for investing reserve funds in its own business. Management was charged with using money extracted from gas consumers to finance expansion rather than selling new stock (any premiums above par realized on stock sales now had to be added to the reserve funds and might trigger rate reductions). The company denied any wrongdoing, arguing that its actions were perfectly legal. [19]

In 1892 the city petitioned the provincial legislature to have the charter amended, but it was made clear that both parties would have to consent to alterations in an arrangement so recently arrived at and the company showed no disposition to agree. It had received excellent legal advice when drafting the 1887 charter and for the time being was quite prepared to stick to the letter of the law despite angry criticisms. When the courts were resorted to they found in the company's favour. J.R. Johnston, a gas user, brought suit against the company in 1894, claiming that he was overcharged. Johnston was victorious in the trial court, and the city decided to provide financial assistance to him to fight an appeal by the company. Its legal advisers, however, were confident that their position would eventually be upheld and they proved correct. In 1898 the Judicial committee of the Privy Council in London refused even to hear the grounds for an appeal by Johnston, sustaining a verdict favourable to the company in the court of appeal. This was but the first in a series of unsuccessful legal battles by the city against its franchised utilities. The courts interpreted such agreements very narrowly and with great respect for proprietary rights, and the city had little luck in convincing them that the spirit of the agreement ought to rule. [20]

The gas company found itself in a particularly strong position because it possessed a perpetual franchise. Threats to take over the company did not have to be taken very seriously, because under a piece of provincial legislation passed in 1877 the company had to give its consent to any takeover and the city would be required to pay for all its 'rights, franchises, privileges and easements' in addition to the plant itself. The city's auditor pointed out that these might be valued as high as $17,000,000, even if the gasworks were worth but one-tenth as much. Although the local press might fume against this 'legalized robbery,' it was a powerful weapon in the company's arsenal. In 1898 a new auditor appointed by the city to examine the company's books reported that the oft-repeated charges of improprieties in handling reserve funds were equally unlikely to stand up in court, and the idea of suing was dropped.[21] At the same time, the company's shrewd management did make occasional offers of concessions to take the steam out of these attacks. In 1895, for instance, discussions were held with the city about linking gas rates inversely to the level of corporate dividends on a sliding scale, as had been done in Britain. Or the company offered to hand over a fixed percentage of its profits to the city in exchange for 'free control of our own affairs.'[22] No agreement could be reached, however, as the aldermen still hoped to make the company adhere to the spirit of the 1887 arrangement. The friction continued.

Relations between city and street railway remained just as acrimonious, just as litigious, and just as unproductive as ever. There was a disagreement about whether to use batteries or the trolley system to electrify the lines. The company refused the city access to its books, which was necessary in order to calculate the city's share of the gross receipts. And there was interminable bickering about paving the streets. But perhaps the most serious disagreement concerned suburban extensions. The 1891 franchise seemed straightforward enough: the city engineer would receive petitions from ratepayers, and if a favourable report from him were endorsed by two-thirds of council the company would be ordered to construct new routes. But William Mackenzie, who dominated the company, preferred to confine his profitable system to the heavily travelled inner-city routes. And in 1898 his lawyers advised him that the city had no right to order him to build lines outside the limits of the city as they had existed in 1891 when the franchise was obtained. After 1904 Mackenzie steadfastly refused to make any extensions beyond these boundaries, hardly surprising since he now controlled all the electrified suburban lines and preferred to channel the traffic along them and collect another fare at the city limits. In 1908, when the city tried to force his hand by refusing to grant him any more inner-city lines unless he agreed to suburban extensions, he took it to court, and in 1909 and 1910 the Judicial Committee of the Privy Council upheld his right both to refuse suburban extensions and to be granted new lines downtown.[23] Again the city seemed to have been outwitted in the franchise negotiations, and the courts refused to help rectify things.

Relations with the electrical companies seemed to go better, at least at first. Competition from the gas company led to significant reductions in the cost of electric street lighting in 1891. Rate cuts for domestic lighting were announced in both 1892 and 1893, again apparently occasioned by falling gas prices. None the less, some citizens began to toy with the idea of a municipal street lighting system. One prominent businessman, who admittedly hoped to provide the machinery of the civic plant, supported the idea, and the Conservative *Mail* endorsed Liberal George Bertram's ideas: 'There is a strong tendency against the disposal of public franchises to private organizations ... The city has no wish to allot to private companies franchises that it can work on its own account ... What the longest-headed citizen says is: If these things are to be done and they come within the scope of civic action, let us do them ourselves as a city. A company comes along and offers electric energy at a cent a horsepower per hour. But if the city, by a plant of its own, can produce electric energy at half that figure, it is plainly to its interest to decline the company's offer.'[24] Evidently support for public ownership had begun to spread beyond the small circle that had endorsed it at the time of the street railway debate in 1891. Yet it was far from being the view of the majority. In June 1895 ratepayers rejected by a margin of 4,940 to 798 a by-law to authorize $277,000 worth of debentures to build a municipal street lighting plant. City council promptly approved a new five-year contract for street lighting with Toronto Electric Light.[25]

The events of the next few months, however, increased enthusiasm for public ownership. Until 1894 Toronto Electric Light had supplied only arc lighting, but in that year it entered the incandescent field, although its system was inferior to the Edison one provided by the Incandescent company. The result was more rate-cutting and a scramble by both to extend their pole lines for fear that the city might decide to ban duplication of the systems on the same streets. It appeared that competition was having a salutary effect and could be expected to continue to do so, since the 1889 'Underground Agreements' prevented the companies from amalgamating. This situation proved too good to last. Seeing their undertakings endangered by rivalry, Henry Pellatt of Toronto Electric Light and Frederic Nicholls of the Incandescent company got together in 1896 and decided to unite. Since they had many shareholders in common this did not prove difficult: the Incandescent plant was valued at $919,350 and its shareholders either sold out or accepted Toronto Electric Light shares in exchange. To provide a defence against the charge that this voided the 1889 agreements, the two companies retained their separate legal existence under a single management. At the same time the companies held out a carrot in the form of a rate reduction of 33 per cent. In his inaugural address to council in 1896 Mayor Robert J. Fleming urged the aldermen to 'definitely and emphatically inform corporations doing business with and having agreements with the city that they must live up to their agreements in every particular, and no violation of these agreements will be allowed upon any considerations.'[26] Despite this tough talk, however, the city failed to act; the matter was allowed to drift and the companies consolidated their operations.

Not until 1901 did the city's legal advisers recommend launching a suit to nullify the 'Underground Agreements,' but when the suit was brought the companies claimed that the failure of the city to act sooner constituted a condoning of their actions. The case dragged on through the courts, all of which found for the companies, until 1905, when the Judicial Committee of the Privy Council refused the city leave to appeal. Once again, regulation through franchising and enforcement by the courts had failed to protect the interests of the public in the eyes of Torontonians.[27]

The telephone company created similar problems. When its exclusive franchise was due to expire in 1896 the city demanded lower rates and a higher percentage of gross receipts to renew it. Bell Telephone, by then feeling quite confident of its position in the Toronto market, without serious competition in sight, refused. Instead, it simply applied to Ottawa under its federal charter for an increase in the Toronto rates and began charging higher rates to new subscribers. When the city protested to the federal government, the ministers of justice and of railways replied laconically that an 1892 statute that required cabinet approval for telephone rate increases 'is legally ineffective so far as subscribers are concerned, and that proceedings to restrain the Company from increasing the rents charged to subscribers would be unsuccessful.' Outraged, city council rounded up 140 other municipalities to sign a petition demanding more effective regulation, but Bell proved an effective lobbyist with Sir Wilfrid Laurier's government and nothing resulted.[28]

In an effort to force the company to come to terms, in 1900 the city engineer was ordered to prevent Bell from erecting poles on the city's streets without his approval. Under its federal charter and provincial legislation the company claimed the right to place its poles wherever it wished. The city therefore took the company to court in 1901, but once again the Judicial Committee of the Privy Council ruled against it, holding in 1904 that the company's federal charter took precedence over all municipal and provincial regulation. Not only could the municipality not control the placing of poles upon its streets, but also the company was not obliged to pay it any compensation for their use.[29] Franchising had again failed to provide a means to control a utility, and the courts had again found against the city.

Thus by the early twentieth century the hopes of civic politicians that vital utilities could be made to serve the public through franchise agreements had been dashed. The agreements made between 1887 and 1891 with each of the utilities had failed to operate as expected. And the seemingly endless disputes between the comanies and the city had done much to create a feeling of anger, frustration, and determination not to give up the fight. Here lay the source of the gospel of civic populism that captured widespread public support during the next two decades. Local politicians concluded that if the private companies could not be bent to the public's wishes by contract then more drastic remedies must be tried. These Toronto politicians had been taught a lesson: public ownership was the only absolutely sure means of municipal control over utilities.

One of the reasons that civic populism gained such widespread support was that local business leaders as well as politicians saw themselves as badly treated customers of the utilities. In the case of gas and electricity the municipal corporation was a major consumer of energy for street lighting. Businessmen needed lighting, telephone service, and public transportation to move themselves and their employees about the city. If the cost of such services were unduly inflated in order to earn monopoly profits for utilities magnates, that harmed everyone, other businessmen included. Competition had failed to discipline the market as it did in many other businesses, and there were no substitutes. Expensive and inadequate services were also thought to hobble the city in the desperate struggle to attract new industry, and so civic populism fused with local boosterism.

Not everyone, of course, agreed on just how essential a given service was to the city's inhabitants at any moment. When Toronto took over its water-works from a private company in 1873, the council's fire, water, and gas committee was soon thinking about doing the same to the gas company on the grounds that it was 'a private corporation ... managed wholly in the interests of its shareholders.' The gas company, however, was quick to reject any similarity between the two services; there was 'a very plain and obvious distinction between the supply of water and that of gas, the one being an article of necessity and the other of comparative luxury, and that regulations which could properly be made and justified on sanitary and other grounds respecting a water supply are not applicable to a supply of gas, and that rates which would properly be imposed and willingly paid by all classes of the community for the former, would, if imposed for the latter, be regarded as a grievous burden by those who are not gas consumers and who form a large part of the ratepayers of the city.'[30]

In time some utilities entrepreneurs did come to accept that a degree of regulation might be acceptable, but none was prepared to agree to public ownership. Theodore N. Vail, the organizational genius behind the American Telephone and Telegraph empire (of which Bell Telephone of Canada formed a part) explained his philosophy as follows:

To the extent that anything of a utilitarian nature is adopted by or assimilated into the habits of the public and contributes to their comfort, convenience or even generally to their profit, it should become an object of *sufficient government regulation to prevent the public convenience being made the cause of private exaction*; the distinction between what should be furnished in whole or in part by the government and what should be regulated by the government being whether *the necessity is absolute* and the thing is indispensable to the life, health and well-being of the individual and consequently of the community.[31]

By the turn of the century in Toronto, however, many businessmen and politicians were prepared to go much further. Stout free-enterprisers who would strongly have decried any extension of public ownership in their own sectors nevertheless felt that their dependence on certain utilities was so great and the present service so unsatisfactory that public ownership might be justified, if no other means could be found to rectify the problem.

That point of view arose not solely out of unhappy experiences with utility companies, although as we have seen those were not lacking. It came from a growing conviction that certain kinds of business interests corrupted and debased politics and public life and had to be brought under control. Richard McCormick has suggested that this recognition dawned on many Americans about 1905 and helped to spark the Progressive movement, one of the objectives of which was municipal ownership of public utilities.[32] Alerted by the muckrakers in the United States, whose revelations they consumed as enthusiastically as any American, Canadians, too, became convinced that they were beset by 'rings' and 'trusts' whose malevolent influence held sway over the workings of government. And it was to combat this that Torontonians developed their brand of civic populism and sought greater public control over their utilities.

When the citizens of Toronto sought evidence that 'business corrupts politics' they had not far to seek. The political life of their city had been rent by a major scandal during the mid-1890s involving malfeasance by the local utilities. The whole affair started over the street lighting contract, up for renewal in 1894. Early in October city council's fire and light committee recommended that Toronto Electric Light's contract be extended for another five years. Then the *Evening News* published allegations that a number of aldermen had been seeking bribes to secure their votes on the contract. Judge Joseph E. McDougall was quickly appointed by council to investigate.

McDougall soon discovered the charges to be all too well-founded. The chairman of the fire and light committee was found to have approached the management of Toronto Electric Light on no less than three occasions, seeking money that was to be used to secure the votes to award the contract to the company. When the bids were made public and the company's was revealed to have been the lowest all along, the details of the extortion attempt were leaked to the press, apparently by management. Thus far the blame lay more with the aldermen than the company, though it had been somewhat laggard in making the whole affair public. But the testimony at the inquiry produced a flood of allegations that this was but one of many municipal contracts in which corruption figured. City council hastily extended McDougall's mandate to probe these other charges.

Further witnesses revealed a pattern of corruption stretching back to 1891. The entire process of letting the street railway franchise had been fraught with dishonesty. Fearful that its bid might not be accepted, the Kiely-Everett-Mackenzie syndicate had imported from Cleveland one Baruch Mahler, nicknamed the 'Clean Skater.' Armed with $40,000 of syndicate money he glided among the aldermen letting it be known that there was a payoff for voting the right way. Soon he had a number of councillors eating out of his hand. In the end $30,000 was spent, and well spent too from the syndicate's point of view, since the street railway committee of council accepted its tender by the narrow margin of eight votes to seven. And that was not the end of the matter: in the fall of 1891 local representatives of the Edison General Electric Company were busy bribing more aldermen to make certain that Edison motors were purchased to power the new trolley cars. In 1893 there was further bribery by the street railway company in connection with the letting of the contracts for paving the streets along the tracks. And the whole shabby chronicle was capped by the revelation that during the McDougall investigation a Pinkerton detective had been set to trailing commission counsel Wallace Nesbitt, presumably in the hope of finding something that could be used against him.[33] Bemoaning 'THE WAVE OF BOODLING,' the *Mail*'s editorialists predicted: 'When the Toronto historian of the distant future begins his chapter on the city during the last decade of the nineteenth century he may refer to the period as the boodle era, and if he is loyal he will weep copiously while he writes.' J.W. Bengough had been proven entirely correct when he had warned:

Boodle for contractors
If they get a public job,
Boodle for officials
Who the people help to rob.

...

Boodle for the civic rings,
Whoever may be mayor,
Boodle, boodle, boodle, boodle
Boodle everywhere.[34]

The most important consequence of these unpleasant revelations was a drive to reform the structure of local government. The aim was to strengthen the executive so that individual aldermen did not play such a large role in making policy and spending money. In 1896 the city got a board of control, chosen from among the council, which had special responsibilities for letting contracts and drawing up spending plans. Their recommendations could not be overturned by council without difficulty. Although staffed at first by familiar faces rather than newly elected reformers, the board at least promised a check on the repetition of the shameful events of the early 1890s. When the controllers began to be elected on a city-wide ballot in 1904 their authority was further reinforced. Thus scandal taught a moral lesson about the corrupting influence of utilities on the body politic, raised public suspicion about the motives and methods of these monopolists, and equipped Toronto with a form of municipal government that was much better adapted to dealing with the problems facing the modern city. At least in theory, the men who sat on council would never again be like those about whom E.E. Sheppard of *Saturday Night* had once moaned: 'What is the use of building a viaduct if we elect a City Council which has barely enough sense to pound sand or alert honesty enough to prevent contractors from stealing the furniture out of City Hall?'[35]

Civic politicians in these years had plenty of opportunities to learn their lessons about the difficulties of controlling privately owned utilities, as we have seen. Corruption, bad service, and regular defeat in the courts gradually converted them to the gospel of civic populism. A continuity of personnel greatly facilitated this process of 'political learning.'[36] From 1896 through 1922, when the city at last secured complete control of both electricity supply and public transportation, a total of 160 men were elected as mayor, controller, or alderman. Over the whole period on average they served on council for a little more than four years each, so that most of them had a chance to acquire a vivid understanding of the problems that the city faced with its utilities. During the period of most intense conflict, between 1902 and 1908, one finds that members had longer-than-average tenure. After 1901 the average experience of councillors was well over five years each and reached a peak of six years in 1906. Not all municipal politicians became ardent proponents of public ownership, but influential veterans of civic affairs such as Frank Spence, Horatio Hocken, and Tommy Church took the lead in the fight against the companies. With public opinion aroused by unsatisfactory service, the vote-getting possibilities of the issue of public ownership were not lost on astute politicians, who quite naturally welcomed the opportunity to present themselves as the fearless guardians of the public interest.[37]

Public ownership, it must be reiterated, had once been a radical solution, the property of socialists, but these men were no socialists. (The only exception was James Simpson, a perennially unsuccessful candidate for controller in this period who attained office only once.) Had the dogma been the exclusive property of Toronto's socialists it would not have made much headway. What was remarkable about Toronto in the North American context was the way in which the acceptance of public ownership of utilities sprawled across class and occupational boundaries. The demands for public telephones and public power, for instance, were backed by both the board of trade and the Trades and Labour Council, although not always for the same reasons. Public ownership was acceptable precisely because its goals were limited, and because workingmen, shopkeepers, and manufacturers alike visualized themselves as helpless victims of ruthless monopolists. These inter-class alliances for the specific purpose of helping consumers and, above all, the moral fervour that this crusade acquired lead us to associate this urban movement for economic and social reform with its contemporaneous rural counterpart, populism.[38]

Despite the effective propaganda of the civic populists, by no means all of Toronto's utilities passed into public ownership. The gas and the telephone systems remained firmly in control of private interests although they had to make certain concessions to quell the uprising. Why did the campaigns succeed in some cases and not in others? To repeat: this was not a crusade for municipal socialism. Only special circumstances convinced the majority of Torontonians that ownership of utilities was essential. When a less drastic remedy promised a degree of control without ownership Torontonians would settle for it if that would ensure that consumers would no longer be unduly exploited. The first of the utilities to come to terms with the civic government in this way was the oldest, the gas company.

Consumers' Gas remained a target for severe criticism by municipal politicians throughout the 1890s, despite the fact that the courts persistently upheld the legality of the company's behaviour under its 1887 charter. In 1901 a proposal to build a municipal gasworks was approved by the voters by a margin of 14,355 to 6,801. Mayor Oliver Howland argued that there was 'nothing in principle to prevent our acquiring this kind of semi-communal service. They are as appropriate as waterworks and in a sense almost as appropriate as highways. They are simply an extension of the ordinary municipal sphere of action.'[39] Yet the city had to face the fact that it had either to purchase the company's expensive plant (with a book value of $2,685,000 in 1900) or else duplicate it. And the company would sell only at a price agreeable to it, which meant paying a large additional sum for goodwill.

Rising demand for gas, however, was once more forcing the company to consider increasing its authorized capital to expand its plant. In negotiations in the fall of 1901 the company agreed to limit the size of its reserves, to lower rates, and, most significantly, to permit the city to purchase its shares. Here was a means of coming to terms with the municipal government by offering a share in the ownership of the company without acquisition. For the city the deal promised both falling gas rates if reserves continued to mount and a means to exercise close supervision over the firm's affairs without the expense and difficulty of a complete takeover. By the end of 1901 only a few details were left to be ironed out and city council had approved the arrangement; but the new council elected in 1902 rejected it and the idea was dropped. Once again the city embarked on a challenge to the company over the handling of its reserves and once again the courts found for the company.[40]

Demand for gas continued to increase, and eventually civic politicians were persuaded to agree to amendments to the company's charter. Following the initiative of 1901 the company agreed to limit reserve funds to $1,000,000 plus the premiums on any stock sales. The city was given the right to a seat on the board of directors provided it purchased $10,000 par value of stock, which it did in December 1904. Thereafter the mayor was an ex officio director, privy to the company's affairs.[41] Although complaints about gas rates continued to be heard, this compromise ended the serious antagonism between city and company. Rising profits now ensured the lower gas rates that the 1887 charter had failed to deliver. When the company's capital stock was expanded again in 1909 the board of control moved to limit its reserves further. Mayor Joseph Oliver suggested that the general manager be invited to meet privately with the controllers to explain why he considered a larger reserve essential. When he did so the proposal to limit the reserves was promptly withdrawn, something unimaginable prior to 1904.[42] Coming to terms with the city by offering it a small share in the equity of the company was sufficient to purchase comparative peace for Consumers' Gas.

Bell Telephone was equally prosperous, equally well-managed, and equally difficult for the city to corral. When its exclusive franchise with Toronto expired in 1896 the company refused to renew it on the terms sought by the city. Its federal charter and the declaration of its works for the general advantage of Canada placed it to a large extent beyond municipal control, and, unlike the situation with the other utilities, the city could not look to the province for aid. Efforts to persuade Ottawa to regulate the telephone industry bore little fruit because of effective lobbying by Bell.

In 1900 the city engineer was ordered to prepare estimates of the cost of setting up a municipal phone system, but the council elected in 1901 lacked enthusiasm for this idea. The investment required would be large and there remained the question of whether or not subscribers would install two phones if Bell continued to compete. The council decided that it was more prudent to let another private company take these risks. Negotiations dragged on until 1904, and a contract had almost been signed when the decision of the Judicial Committee of the Privy Council made it clear that Bell Telephone could not be controlled by city regulation of its poles and wires. With its guns spiked, the city was compelled to resume negotiations with Bell in 1905 in the hope of securing rate reductions.[43]

The city's only other recourse was to try and pressure the federal government to act. In his inaugural address as mayor in 1900, E.A. Macdonald had urged Parliament to take over all long-distance telephone and telegraphs lines, a suggestion endorsed by council in March. Thereafter, Toronto played a leading role in a noisy campaign by local governments, operating through the newly organized Union of Canadian Municipalities, to secure federal control of trunk lines, which would permit municipal and independent telephone companies to link up with one another. W.F. 'Billy' Maclean, who was the maverick Conservative MP for East York as well as proprietor of the Toronto *World*, introduced a private member's bill on this subject at every session beginning in 1902.[44] But Sir Wilfrid Laurier's cabinet showed little disposition to accede to these demands, preferring to listen to Bell Telephone's well-placed lobbyists. When the towns of Port Arthur and Fort William (which had a municipal phone system) sought to install an instrument in the local railway station, Bell invoked its long-standing exclusive agreement with the CPR. The matter was referred to the board of railway commissioners which decided that this breach of Bell's monopoly would require the towns to pay it compensation for loss of business. In view of the outcry against this decision, however, Postmaster-General Sir William Mulock, Toronto's cabinet member, announced the appointment of a select committee of the House of Commons to investigate the telephone industry. Before this body, Mayor Thomas Urquhart aired the city's grievances against Bell and demanded that municipalities have the right to purchase Bell's local exchanges where they wished to do so. The committee, however, produced no report, and it soon became clear that the cabinet did not intend to act to facilitate public ownership. To diffuse complaints Prime Minister Laurier did place all federally chartered telephone companies under the regulatory authority of the board of railway commissioners in 1906.[45] While this might not satisfy Torontonians completely, it did provide them with a forum to argue their case.

In 1907 the board reviewed all of Bell's rates but made no changes. At later hearings Toronto appointed counsel to make its case for lower rates, but city politicians were never entirely happy with the results. In 1914 the board of control recommended that Adam Beck be asked to study the possibility of setting up a public telephone system through Ontario Hydro which could operate the trunk lines while municipalities supplied local service. With Hydro's broad legal powers, pole lines, and rights of way and the financial backing of the province, such a challenge to Bell's monopoly would have been formidable. Beck, however, replied uncharacteristically that he did not think Hydro had the necessary authority. As late as 1919 Mayor Tommy Church was still hopeful that Beck would act, for he complained of Bell, 'This grasping company has paid [an] 8 per cent. [dividend] for 33 years. They have a monopoly. They pay nothing for the use of our streets and have [a] $14,000,000 reserve [fund] ... They propose to take nearly a mill on the dollar out of Toronto as the increased rates will extract nearly $5,000,000 from this City ... Toronto is left alone to fight out this rate increase, and it is high time that Parliament acted to check this raid on the public of this monopoly.'[46] Despite such fervent populist rhetoric the advent of formal regulation by commission had largely sapped broad-based public support for public ownership of telephones in eastern Canada. While some politicians might fulminate against Bell Telephone its management found a comfortable haven for its local monopoly in the legitimacy of a formal regulatory process. The refusal of the federal government to act rendered Toronto powerless to capture this local utility.

Civic populism's greatest triumphs were scored over the electric and transportation enterprises of William Mackenzie. He proved to be a lightning rod for reformist sentiment because of his growing reputation as a greedy monopolist who bore much responsibility for the corruption of the political process as well as for supplying poor service at high rates. With a target such as that, the public power movement was able to weld together a coalition that crossed class lines and to secure the all-important backing of the provincial government which enabled it to emerge victorious in its struggle. Had it not been for the movement's ability to call on the province at critical moments the outcome of this campaign might well have been quite different.[47]

The first proposal to set up a municipal street lighting plant in 1895 was overwhelmingly rejected by the ratepayers. The existence of rival electrical companies (combined with competition from gas) seemed to guarantee that there would be no undue exploitation of consumers, but that situation was markedly altered by the amalgamation of the electric firms in 1896. The city engineer was soon directed to investigate the cost of a municipal generating plant once more, and in 1898 council called tenders for such a plant. Without costly specifications, however, these tenders proved useless for estimating the funds required for construction and the bids had to be returned. On four different occasions city council asked the provincial government for legislative authority to enter the electrical business but did not receive it. Moreover, in 1899 the Municipal Act was amended by the addition of the 'Conmee clause' requiring municipalities to buy out existing utilities before competing. The city had no success in procuring the repeal of this clause over the next few years.[48]

The news that a syndicate composed of Mackenzie, principal owner of the street railway, and Henry Pellatt and Frederic Nicholls of the Toronto Electric Light Company had been granted a franchise to develop hydro-electricity at Niagara Falls provided a powerful spur to populist sentiment in 1903. Mayor Thomas Urquhart hastened to 'point out to the Ontario government the effect of such a monopoly on the city of Toronto and its franchises': 'If these parties ... are granted the privileges of bringing power from Niagara Falls it will be done by the expenditure of a large sum of money, and the Government will thereby prevent itself and also the Municipalities from engaging in similar operations, because it will be argued that to do so will have the effect of destroying the capital which has already been invested in the enterprise. The time is certainly here, if it has not been here long ago, when public utilities should be owned and operated by the Government of the Province or by the Municipalities.' Unfortunately these arguments fell on deaf ears at Queen's Park. The Liberal government of George Ross did not prove sympathetic to the cause of public ownership and consented only to permit the establishment of a municipally funded investigatory commission to examine the feasibility of a public co-operative to distribute electricity.[49]

The city voted to support the Ontario Power Commission, but what proved crucial in the long run was the adoption of the rhetoric of civic populism, born at the municipal level, by the Conservative party of Adam Beck and James P. Whitney. Early in 1905 the Conservatives won control of the provincial government, and Premier Whitney quickly declared that the water-power of Niagara 'should be free as air, not only to the monopolist and friend of government as it used to be, but every citizen under proper

Toronto World 2 October 1909
Going right thru
Teamster Whitney – 'It was for tying up at that place so often that George Ross lost
his job.'

Toronto World 27 February 1907
'Mort!'
Jack Canuck – 'Get to the ladders with your hods, Gentlemen.'

Toronto World 12 January 1908
A Killiswat

Toronto World 22 March 1908
King Canute Mackenzie commands the sea to go back.

Toronto World 10 February 1907
David and Goliath
David: 'He's providing me with plenty of stones for my sling.'

Toronto World 12 December 1907
When the lightning struck
Mr. Nicholls: 'Help! Fire!! Police! Help!'

Toronto World 29 December 1907
A wise resolve
The Civic Bunny – 'My, it does look nice, but I think I'll girdle that sapling a little
before I reach for the Cabbage.'

Toronto World 27 December 1907
An unsatisfactory encounter
The Hungry 'Tagger' – 'Say, Blamed if 'taint full of slivers.'

condition should be free to utilize the powers that the Almighty has given to the Province.' Beck, who was chosen to head a new Hydro-Electric Power Commission of Enquiry, added, 'It is the duty of the Government to see that development is not hindered by permitting a handful of people to enrich themselves out of these treasures at the expense of the general public.'[50] And within a few months he had created the Hydro-Electric Power Commission, a co-operative undertaking with credit backed by the province, which could purchase power at Niagara Falls and sell it to municipally owned distribution systems 'at cost.'

The public power movement that developed in Toronto after 1903 had the support not only of socialists and labour leaders but also of Toronto's board of trade and the local branch of the Canadian Manufacturers' Association. All agreed on the necessity of a public electrical distribution system to compete with the existing private monopoly, and the action of the provincial government made this possible in a way that the city could not have achieved on its own. Once Ontario Hydro came into existence, city council lost little time in approving Toronto's membership, and the issue was put before the ratepayers at the municipal elections in January 1907. The vote was 11,026 to 2,907 in favour of the city becoming part of Hydro. The province did not, however, grant the city's request for the right to expropriate the Toronto Electric Light Company in the spring of 1907. Plans were therefore made to build a distribution system to compete with the company's.[51]

The city's evident determination led Sir Henry Pellatt to abandon his defiant stance at long last and seek a compromise with the mayor in the fall of 1907. He suggested that the city either buy the company outright or else acquire an interest in it and place its own nominees on the board. Here was an arrangement on the model of the deal with the gas company in 1904, which offered protection for the public interest without going as far as public ownership. But by 1907 it was too little and too late. The behaviour of Pellatt and Mackenzie had convinced Torontonians that public ownership was the only guarantee of economical electricity. Council voted instead to seek final approval of the creation of a rival system, and the ratepayers again gave their assent by a margin of 15,048 to 4,551 in January 1908. Although negotiations between the city and the company about a takeover continued in a desultory fashion, no agreement was reached because the city absolutely refused to give up its plans to take power from Ontario Hydro. Having got the private monopolists at a disadvantage, the city insisted that the company would have to terminate its power supply contract with the generating company at Niagara Falls, which was also owned by the Pellatt-Nicholls-Mackenzie syndicate. These men, faced with the loss of their distribution system, balked at giving up their major power market to Beck's Hydro. All that they could do was to try and block the city's contract with Hydro, but once again Beck outflanked them, at a critical juncture calling on the province to pass a statute validating the contract.[52]

Nothing now stood in the way of the construction of a municipal utility, and it finally went into service in 1911. That spring, with the Toronto Hydro-Electric System almost completed, the city did offer to purchase all of Toronto Electric Light's $5,000,000 par value worth of stock for 125 per cent and to assume its bonded debt of $1,000,000, but the stockholders chose instead to sell their shares to the syndicate at 135 per cent of par. This seemed to end the city's interest in purchasing the company before its 'Underground Agreement' expired in 1919. Over the next few years the public and private enterprises competed, and, owing to aggressive rate-cutting promoted by Beck at the provincial level, Toronto Hydro had captured two-thirds of the local market by 1918. The company's business stagnated, with only about 25,000 meters connected to its lines and annual revenues estimated at a little over $1,000,000, while Toronto Hydro grew to over 70,000 meters by 1920, producing annual revenues of over $3,000,000. In the end the city decided not to take over Toronto Electric Light in 1919 when its franchise expired, on the grounds that the company was sure to demand a high price. Instead, civic authorities preferred to wait a couple of years until Adam Beck presided over the acquisition of all the utilities interests of Sir William Mackenzie. Then the local operations went to Toronto Hydro while Ontario Hydro took the generating and transmission facilities.[53] Once again, these municipal insurgents were able to call on the aid of the provincial government to give them greater bargaining power in dealing with private interests.

Thus in the case of electicity supply, civic populism triumphed by the end of the First World War. From its halting beginnings in the 1890s, when the ratepayers rejected a municipal street lighting plant, support for a takeover of the private company or competition from a civic undertaking grew. And this support crossed class and occupational boundaries. In part this militancy stemmed from the behaviour of the company's management, eliminating all competition in defiance of its franchise and later appealing to a friendly provincial cabinet to capture a valuable franchise at Niagara Falls over the city's objections. Torontonians had become convinced of the necessity of cheap electricity for lighting and power (a conviction, based on technological change, that made them less aggressive in dealing with the gas company) and absolutely determined not to let the Pellatt-Nicholls-Mackenzie syndicate hold the city to ransom.

The election of the provincial Conservatives to office in 1905 was vitally important in paving the way to victory for the populist cause. Toronto was not the only city interested in cheap power, and Adam Beck and James P. Whitney were able to forge a strong province-wide coalition on the issue. But what happened in Ontario contrasted sharply with what happened in the United States. Although Beck's Hydro-Electric Power Commission had all the authority of a state-wide regulatory commission, it chose not to function in that way. Instead, Beck remained sensitive to what local politicians wanted. He intervened at critical junctures to assist the municipal politicians in their struggles with the private utility because that suited his interests in his broader campaign to take over the syndicate's entire operation throughout the province. Ontario was thus spared the kind of contest over 'home rule' that flared up in many American cities and often left private utilities in being, regulated only by comparatively ineffectual state-wide boards.[54] In Toronto, civic populists could count on the help of the province when it was essential.

None of the city's franchised utilities became the focus of so much anger on the part of municipal politicians as did the street railway, also controlled by William Mackenzie. To him it was a solid little property which, if carefully nurtured, might generate a handsome flow of earnings to raise the price of the stock, distributed free to the insiders in the syndicate, to gratifying heights. To the citizens it was the vital link between their suburban residences and their work places downtown. A sense of grievance on the part of local citizens became acute as the suburbs stretched futher and further afield and it became plainer and plainer that Mackenzie had little intention of extending his lines to serve them. He preferred to operate high-volume downtown lines, and in 1909 and 1910 the Judicial Committee of the Privy Council upheld his right to refuse extensions beyond the 1891 city limits or to build new lines in the central area, ordered by the city.

Infuriated, city council decided to ask the ratepayers for authority to operate a civic street railway to serve the outlying areas, and in January 1910 the ratepayers approved this by a vote of 19,376 to 10,696. Then the city sought from the province the power to acquire the Toronto Street Railway before its franchise expired, by expropriation if necessary. And in an effort to force the company to bargain, the city began a study of a subway system that would permit it to compete directly in the central core. Construction began on the Toronto Civic Railway in the eastern and western suburbs in 1911, and by 1915 the city was operating seventeen miles of double-track line, but the system was-not integrated with the private company.[55] Having to pay two fares merely increased citizens' antagonism toward the Toronto Railway Company.

Meanwhile, negotiations with the company proved fruitless. Mackenzie apparently decided on a strategy of intransigence, of sticking to the last scintilla of his legal rights and working to extract the maximum possible profit from the company in the certainty that it would be taken over before long. The city's offer to lease its lines to the company to operate was rejected, and the company stubbornly refused to grant transfer privileges, connections, or running rights to the city's cars on its own lines. Mackenzie did offer to sell the entire plant to the city at a price to be arbitrated, but city council refused, countering with a proposal to pay only the amount of the actual investment in the undertaking plus a consideration for the unexpired period of the franchise. Considering Mackenzie too obstinate and unreasonable, municipal politicians were leary of entering into a deal too favourable to him, preferring to suffer until 1921.[56]

Some of the steam went out of the civic assault on the Toronto Railway Company when the voters rejected the notion of a subway up Bay and Yonge streets in January 1912. Nevertheless, intermittent negotiations with Mackenzie continued during 1913 and 1914. In fact, an agreement to take over the company was almost arrived at in 1914, but the outbreak of war created restrictions on the city's ability to borrow large sums of money in the British market to finance the deal. Moreover, at the 1915 elections council became dominated by a militant faction that objected to paying the high price sought by Mackenzie, preferring to wait him out.[57] So there the matter stood until 1921, when Sir Adam Beck arranged the 'Clean-up Deal' by which Ontario Hydro took over Mackenzie's electric companies and the street railway passed into the control of the Toronto Transportation Commission.

What fuelled civic populism in the case of Toronto's street railway was partly its importance to the city's development. When Mackenzie refused to extend his lines, council went ahead and filled the void, and once a civic car line was in operation there was every reason to extend it when the opportunity arose in 1921. Mackenzie's manner of negotiating also contributed to the outcome. He made it clear that he looked on the aldermen as votes to be bought (and with good reason). However, the major reform of the structure of civic government in 1896 (brought about by the scandals he and his agents had caused) made it much harder to buy and sell council. Yet Mackenzie steadfastly refused to make any accommodation that might have brought him peace. Instead he insisted on his legal rights. If he did sell, it would only be with handsome recompense for the value of the franchises so dubiously acquired and grudgingly operated. That kind of attitude ensured that the militants on council would stand in the way of any 'sweetheart' deal with him. When a settlement was almost achieved in 1914, the outbreak of war intervened and gave the opponents of the settlement a new lease on life. The style of management of the Toronto Railway Company was such as virtually to guarantee that only a complete takeover would satisfy the majority of local citizens.

During more than three decades the city of Toronto was locked in almost constant conflict with its utilities, first as a frustrated regulator, later as a competitor with certain private enterprises, and finally as itself an aggressive monopoly-maker determined to recapture all its lost territory in the field of electric supply and public transportation. The war saw furious verbal battles marked by occasional truces but more often by long drawn-out legal sieges. How did the civic populists sustain their quasi-religious fervour during the struggle, even when the city seemed to be no nearer to gaining its objectives? Their weapons in this fight were not just verbal but also visual, a series of pictorial images by which the proponents of public ownership sought to convey their message. This message was undeniably effective in political terms as an almost unbroken stream of votes on by-laws showed after 1900, but these images also helped to shape the very nature of the debate and to reinforce the sense of righteousness and virtue that came to imbue this crusade.

'Boss' Tweed of New York was one of the first municipal politicians to be seriously wounded by the jabs of a cartoonist's quill. In the 1870s Tweed complained about the relentless pen of Thomas Nast of *Harper's Magazine*, 'I don't care a straw for your newspaper articles; my constituents don't know how to read but they can't help seeing them damn pictures.' Tweed ended up in jail. Nast practised caricature not for its own sake but to preach and to persuade; he was a North American pioneer in the fusion of art with political and moral didacticism.[58] He had many notable Canadian emulators, including the redoubtable J.W. Bengough, whose scratchy pen sketches in *Grip* enlivened all levels of Canadian politics between the 1870s and the 1890s. Samuel Hunter of the Toronto *World* may be less well known, but he did much to limn the titanic struggle of a virtuous people against the scheming monopolists in Toronto during the first decade of the twentieth century. Every contest with the street railway or the light, gas, or telephone company was cast in the same rhetorical and visual terms by the civic populists. When, in late 1907, the voters of Toronto were confronted with the question of whether or not to authorize the city to create an electrical utility in competition with Toronto Electric Light, Samuel Hunter was at the height of his powers. Each day he churned out drawings setting forth the issues as he and his mercurial employer, W.F. 'Billy' Maclean, saw them. The cartoons from this campaign illustrate the iconography of civic populism in Toronto and help to explain how complex economic, legal, and financial issues were transformed into simple moralistic maxims.[59]

The central figure in the populist bestiary was, of course, a stock figure from Thomas Nast: the bloated, cigar-smoking capitalist complete with top hat, pince-nez, and spats. Clearly recognizable (and often labelled) in standard monopolists' garb were Frederic Nicholls, Sir Henry Pellatt, and William Mackenzie. In life, of course, their behaviour inadvertently did much to confirm the cruel caricature (though Pellatt's Casa Loma came later). In this world the capitalist lurks in almost every frame, scheming to divert the hard-earned incomes of workingmen and ratepayers into his ample pockets. To preserve their undeserved privilege these men were organized in a conspiratorial 'ring,' watering the stock of the companies they controlled and arrogantly defying the public and its elected representatives. Samuel Hunter played endlessly upon the symbol of the 'ring.' Rings appear as targets, ripples on water, life preservers, finger rings, boxing rings, Saturnian rings. So, too, Hunter rang the changes on the image of 'water': under thin ice, formed by snow melting under the rays of the sun of public ownership, watermelons to be carved up, rain, a full bucket beside the battered boxer's stool, and as sweet sap trickling from the forest of telephone, telegraph, electric, and trolley poles that crowd the city streets. Wherever the capitalist went, whatever he sought to do, he was faithfully served by a venal, grovelling press. In this case the journalistic villains abetting the electric ring included J.W. Flavelle, owner of the *News*, and Robert Jaffray of the haughty *Globe*. Yet despite their services, while William Mackenzie might command the waves to retreat like a feckless Canute, the rising tide of public opinion (water again) was about to sweep him irresistibly away, according to Hunter.

The people who supported public ownership appeared in several guises: as a watchful 'old man Ontario,' an evocation of the sainted shade of Oliver Mowat hovering in judgment over the present generation; as a clean-cut, hard-working mason building a better country, a veritable Johnny Canuck in breeches, scarf, rough-rider hat with trowel in hand; as Miss Canada, virginal and innocent but surrounded by designing suitors; or as Mr Toronto, a respectable, frock-coated ratepayer, striding purposefully past temptation. To these figures Hunter attached all the visual signs of virtue: modest dress, trim figure, patience, reasonableness, determination, and industriousness. And it is notable that Hunter chose these representative figures from all classes, accurately depicting the somewhat unusual nature of the public power movement. These paragons stood at the parting of the ways, eager to do what was right and good regardless of the demagogic influence of the ring and the dope dispensed by its hired flacks.

And in Toronto, Hunter made clear, the ringsters, however much they tried to ape the dangerous Tammany tiger, would meet their match in the vigilant citizens, honest politicians, and, naturally, the porcupines of crusading journalism. The cartoonist used a number of visual metaphors to suggest the transcendent power of an informed democracy. Public opinion struck like lightning, zapping the schemes of ringmaster Frederic Nicholls; it was the powder keg about to explode beneath an insouciant William Mackenzine. The public will was the knife that sliced through the straps, ropes, and ties with which the ring believed it had securely bound the electorate; and it was the sun – symbol of light and goodness – melting the monopolists' snowman. The people could also deliver a knockout blow to the champions of the ring. Adam Beck of Ontario Hydro (as the sun, the hired man, the Santa Claus of small power consumers and manufacturers, the gleam in the bunny's eye) and Premier James P. Whitney (woodsman, farmer, teamster hauling grain, and a rock standing against the storm) embodied the political power of an aroused and irresistible public opinion.

This, then, was the exaggerated, evocative, economical world of the caricature. Every day Billy Maclean's *World* doled out these messages transmitted by Hunter's firm, uncluttered line. From the theatre, literature, sport, and more mundane workaday experience, the cartoonist drew settings for his didactic yet humorous vignettes. The cartoon was quite literally a figure of speech. 'It is this freedom to translate the concepts and shorthand symbols of our political speech into metaphorical situations that constitutes the novelty of the cartoon,' the great art historian E.H. Gombrich once observed.[60] Cartoons condensed simplified, satirized, and personalized complex issues; they drew on a rich archive of literary, symbolic, and mythological memory and sometimes depended for their force on deep-seated fears and prejudices. The visual vocabulary thus provided a sketch of the political dialogue, and, in turn, the symbols subtly shaped public perception of the issues. With these pictures and their parallel editorial texts in their minds, the ratepayers of Toronto conceived public ownership as the solution to the vexing question of their utilities and went to the polls year after year, ready to authorize the city to fight the telephone monopoly, buy into the gas company, compete with the light company, or build its own street railway.

From 1900 onwards, therefore, public ownership of the city's utilities was always a hot political issue in Toronto. Scandal, poor service, corporate arrogance, and high rates all fuelled the increasing popular insurgency against these companies. Workingmen, social gospellers, temperance advocates, merchants, and manufacturers were united in this crusade. In the United States these municipal campaigns often turned into debates about municipal 'home rule' versus state-wide regulation of utilities.[61] After 1907 state regulation triumphed there in almost every jurisdiction, seriously hampering ardent local reformers and providing a safe, quasi-judicial haven for hard-pressed utilities operators. Instead of being taken over they often secured 'service-at-cost' contracts which guaranteed them a healthy return on their capital, generously estimated. Toronto not only enjoyed fairly complete home rule but it also worked with the full support of the province at certain critical junctures. The city normally received the legislation for which it asked. In 1905, for instance, city council called for repeal of the Conmee clause of the Municipal Act which prevented municipalities from setting up their own electrical works without offering to buy out existing concerns. The new Whitney government granted an exemption to any municipal electrical system using power purchased from Ontario Hydro. When Toronto Electric Light arranged a legal challenge to the contract that the city had signed with Ontario Hydro in 1908, Adam Beck quickly rushed through provincial legislation rendering these contracts immune from such suits. And in 1921 the city did not have to bargain with Sir William Mackenzie over the breakup of his utilities empire, but left it to Sir Adam Beck to arrange the 'Clean-up Deal' which destroyed the last vestiges of Mackenzie's integrated traction and electrical undertaking. Thus a combination of home rule and virorous pursuit of public ownership in the hydroelectric sector by the provincial government greatly facilitated the takeover of the private power system and the street railway by the city. The fact that Toronto was the capital and that Ontario's legislators were so close at hand undoubtedly aided the co-ordination of activities by the two levels of government.

Municipal politicians were also helped by the intransigence of Nicholls, Pellatt, and Mackenzie, who did their best to live up to their caricatures. Not only were they poor negotiators or opposed to negotiation altogether, but also they squandered what legitimacy private utilities possessed without realizing until too late what was happening. In other cities the managers of private utilities met this problem by broadening the base of their support among the business community. Here, too, Mackenzie and his associates failed. Rather than stand as a class against measures that might, in another context, have been regarded as socialistic, Toronto's businessmen were divided about the issues of public power and a municipal street railway, with the majority evidently favouring these innovations.

The extension of public control depended in part on technological developments. In the case of gas, for example, the city bought an interest in the company just like any other investor and in doing so obtained fuller information about its operations and more influence over its behaviour. This arms-length arrangement proved acceptable because there was a satisfactory substitute for gas in electricity, which proved to be a fairly effective regulator of rates. Similarly, substitution made gas a less vital source of illumination, even though the quantities consumed for other purposes continued to increase. The partial eclipse of gas by the new electrical technology helps to explain the relatively early truce arrived at in that sector, as well as the feverish intensity of the battle for cheap electric power.

The gas, electricity, and street railway companies were easier to capture because they all lay within municipal and provincial jurisdiction. The telephone company, however, escaped to a higher level of government where it rightly believed that regulation would be less dangerous. Theodore N. Vail was one of the earliest utility entrepreneurs to come to terms with regulation, and in his protégé, Charles F. Sise, civic populism in Toronto met its match. The board of railway commissioners presided beneficently over Bell Telephone's monopoly; in a case concerning the independent Ingersoll Telephone Company in 1911 Chief Commissioner Mabee held: 'When you have one telephone system and you have a public service commission or a controlling board with authority to compel that company to furnish instruments to intending subscribers, and to furnish proper service, with control over the rates that company shall charge, there is no necessity for an additional company exploiting that field. The exploitation of competing lines in towns and cities is simply a waste of capital and a cause of irritation in municipalities where duplicate lines exist.' And Mabee noted that regulators also had other responsibilities: 'There is capital invested there that it is just as much the duty of this Board to protect as it is to see that the subscribers of the Ingersoll system get long distance communication.'[62] This was an attitude typical of the state- or province-wide regulatory bodies that were created in most other parts of North America. In that sense the experience of Toronto in dealing with the telephone company represented the norm, and public ownership a distinct anomaly, so that municipalities usually found themselves fuming impotently on the sidelines while decisions were being taken about the provision of services essential to them.

Between the 1840s and the 1920s Toronto had changed dramatically from a commercial town into a sizeable industrial city. Of this transformation Michael Frisch has written, 'The taking on of each new responsibility, the planning of each new project in business or government, the crossing of each new threshold of debt or taxation, the abandonment of each out-moded social form – every step involved a more or less conscious rethinking of what was appropriate to the changing city, and each new development, institution, or assumption thus produced became part of the context against which subsequent questions were measured.'[63] Part of that process was the development of an abstract notion of what ought to be publicly controlled and what private. In Toronto this debate focused on the local utilities, where, it was felt, the ordinary rules of commerce could not apply.

The achievement of public ownership was thus not simply a triumph of virtue over vice, good over evil, as the cartoonist might have it. Rather, technological, locational, and political factors came into play in a particular time and place to legitimize the idea. Once the policy of public ownership had become intellectually respectable to the broad mass of voters, civic populists were able to exploit the feeling of indignation aroused by scandals and the displays of corporate arrogance. And they found among their fellow citizens a willingness to embark on bold experiments, which one of the executives of the street railway company had identified in 1898 when he wrote ruefully, 'I fear the spirit of mischief is Toronto's curse.'[64]

NOTES

1 See, by way of comparison, Melvin Holli *Reform in Detroit* (New York 1969), Clay McShane *Technology and Reform* (Madison, Wisconsin, 1974); David Thelan *The New Citizenship* (Columbia, Missouri, 1972).

2 Thomas McCraw, 'Regulation in America: A Review Article' *Business History Review* XLIX (1975) 160–83; Paul Garfield and Wallace Lovejoy *Public Utility Economics* (Englewood Cliffs, New Jersey, 1964); David Nord 'The Experts versus the Experts: Conflicting Philosophies of Municipal Utility Regulation in the Progressive Era' *Wisconsin Magazine of History* LVIII (1975) 219–36

3 Elwood Jones and Douglas McCalla 'Toronto Waterworks, 1840–77: Continuity and Change in Nineteenth Century Toronto Politics' *Canadian Historical Review* LX (1979) 300–23

4 Christopher Armstrong and H.V. Nelles *The Revenge of the Methodist Bicycle Company* (Toronto 1977) 27–9

5 York University Archives, Consumers' Gas Company, *Annual Reports*, 1849–1905; in our time this spirit of public benefaction by wealthy individuals remains attached to marginal franchises. See for example Barry Shenkarow's comment quoted in the *Globe and Mail* 26 May 1983: 'You can only lose so many millions of dollars before you say to yourself, "My civic duty has been exhausted."' Mr Shenkarow is president of the Winnipeg Jets hockey club.

6 See Consumers' Gas Company Archives (herafter CGA), Correspondence, 1874, G.P. Sheard to Consumers' Gas Company, 15 January 1874, for one of many such complaints.

7 Jones and McCalla 'Waterworks'; and Armstrong and Nelles *Revenge* 85

8 Michael Frisch *Town into City* (Cambridge, Massachusetts, 1972); Peter Goheen *Victorian Toronto* (Chicago 1970)

9 CGA, Correspondence, and City of Toronto Archives (hereafter CTA), Toronto City Council Minutes (hereafter Minutes), passim. For the complaint of Thomas Ferguson see his letters to W.H. Pearson, CGA, Correspondence, 1880, 26 May, 31 May, and 1 June 1880.

10 *Telegram* 1 May 1890; *Mail* 28 October 1890; Armstrong and Nelles *Revenge* 29–34

11 Desmond Morton *Mayor Howland* (Toronto 1973) 43–56; Gregory Kealey *Toronto Workers Respond to Industrial Capitalism, 1867–1892* (Toronto 1980) 201–6

12 CGA, Correspondence, 1880, Arthur S. Hardy, Provincial Secretary, to W.H. Pearson, 2 December 1980

13 CTA, Toronto City Council Papers, S.H. Blake to Thomas Caswell, 29 June 1891

14 *Grip* 20 November 1891

15 York University Archives, Consumers' Gas Company Minutebooks (hereafter CGA Minutes), 18 January, 25 October 1886; 1, 4, 18 April, 31 October 1887; CTA, Minutes, 1887, Appendix, Mayor's Message re Consumers' Gas Company, 17 March 1887; *Statutes of Ontario*, 1887, 50 Victoria cap 55

16 CTA, Minutes, 1889, Appendix. Mayor's Message re Underground Wires, 1 October 1889

17 Ibid, Appendix A, Report of the Committee on Works, 7, 19 May, 3 June 1891; Minutes, 1891, 12 June, 6 July, 27 July; Appendix C, Agreement between the City of Toronto and the Bell Telephone Company, 17 September 1891. The Toronto *World* gave this telephone franchise extensive coverage. See for example 1, 12 May and 13 June 1891.

18 Armstrong and Nelles *Revenge* 35–48

19 CTA, Minutes, 1891, Appendix C, Report of Auditor W.R. Huges re Consumers' Gas, 30 October 1891; CGA, Minutes, 16 November, 7, 21 December 1891

20 CGA, Minutes, 18 January, 1, 18 February, 1, 21 March 1892; CGA, Correspondence, memorandum to S.H. Blake re *Johnston* v. *Consumers' Gas*, 24 September 1894; Minutes, 18 April 1898

21 CTA, Minutes, 1896, Report of Auditor W.R. Hughes re Consumers' Gas and *J.T. Johnston* v. *Consumers' Gas*, 26 May 1896. The act in question was *Statutes of Ontario*, 1877, 40 Victoria cap 39 sec 14. CTA, Minutes, 1898, Appendix C, Auditor's Report on Consumers' Gas

22 CGA, Correspondence, Memorandum re Telephone Message from Larratt Smith, 23 October 1895; Minutes, 23 October 1895

23 Armstrong and Nelles *Revenge* 121–6; on the litigation over suburban extensions see, inter alia, CTA, Council Papers, Board of Control Report, 6 May 1904;

Minutes, 1906, Mayor's Message, 8 January 1906; Board of Control Papers, Box 19, Ontario Railway and Municipal Board File, 22 May 1907; Board of Control Papers, 11 January, 1 April 1910, Report on the Privy Council Decision. For an overview see Michael Doucet 'Mass Transit and the Failure of Private Ownership: The Case of Toronto in the Early Twentieth Century' *Urban History Review* III (1977) 3–33.

24 *Mail* 22 January 1895

25 Armstrong and Nelles *Revenge* 138–9

26 CTA, Minutes, 1896, Appendix C, Mayor's Inaugural

27 Ontario Hydro Archives, Toronto Electric Light Company Minutebook, 12 September 1901 and 12 February 1906; CTA, Minutes, 1901, Appendix A, Board of Control Report, 24 October 1901

28 CTA, Board of Control Minutes, 21 June 1900; Board of Control Papers, Box 4, T. Caswell to E.A. Macdonald, Mayor, 3 August 1900; see also Mayor Macdonald's furious rejoinder, CTA, Minutes, 1900, Appendix C; Bell Telephone Company Archives, Minutebook, 11 September 1900.

29 The disappointing progress of this case up through the courts can be followed in CTA, Minutes, culminating in the final outcome, registered in the Board of Control Minutes of 16, 18 November and 7 December 1904.

30 CGA, Correspondence, Petition of Consumers' Gas Company to Toronto Corporation, n.d. (1874)

31 Theodore N. Vail *Views on Public Questions* (New York 1913) 165

32 Richard McCormick 'The Discovery that "Business Corrupts Politics": A Reappraisal of the Origins of Progressivism' *American Historical Review* LXXXVI (1981) 247 74

33 The records of the McDougall inquiry can be found in CTA, City Clerk's Miscellaneous Papers. For a brief account see Armstrong and Nelles *Revenge* 121–8.

34 *Mail* 6 December 1894; *Grip* 14 November 1891

35 *Saturday Night* 14 December 1889

36 Hugh Heclo introduces this concept in *Modern Social Politics in Britain and Sweden* (New Haven 1974) 304–8.

37 CTA, Minutes, Appendix A, Report of the City Clerk on Elections, various years. The average number of years served by aldermen, controllers, and mayors for councils from 1900 to 1914 was: 1900, 4.6; 1901, 4.2; 1902, 5.5; 1903, 4.9; 1904, 5.4; 1905, 5.3; 1906, 6.0; 1907, 4.6; 1908, 5.4; 1909, 5.8; 1910, 5.3; 1911, 5.1; 1912, 5.3; 1913, 5.1; and 1914, 4.7. Each year in this period the councils checked averaged 5.1 years of previous service. Some war-horses served much longer: F.S. Spence for 12 years, Tommy Church 17 years, and Horatio Hocken for 7. Even longer-serving members included Robert Graham, 19 years, and George McMurrich, 18 years.

38 There are risks associated with giving an already vague category new meaning but

populism seems to us to be a more accurate description of the movement than progressivism as that term is currently understood. See McCormick ' "Business Corrupts Politics," ' and Ghita Ionescu and Ernest Gellner ed *Populism: Its Meaning and National Characteristics* (New York 1969), which licenses the use of the term 'populism' in an urban context. See especially the essays by Peter Worsley, 'The Concept of Populism,' and Peter Wiles, 'A Syndrome, Not a Doctrine.'

39 CTA, Minutes, Appendix C, Report of the City Clerk, 9 January 1901, and Mayor's Inaugural, 14 January 1901.

40 CGA, Minutes, 16, 21 December 1901; CTA, Minutes, 1902, Appendix A, Proposed Agreement between City and Consumers' Gas, 11 January 1902; CGA, Minutes, 16 March 1903

41 CTA, Minutes, 1904, Appendix C, Mayor's Message, 25 April 1904

42 CGA, Minutes, 6 December 1909, 7 February 1910

43 CTA, Minutes, 1900, Appendix A, Report of a Special Committee on Municipal Telephones, 19 October 1904; Canada, House of Commons *Report of the Select Committee to Investigate the Telephone* I (Ottawa 1905) 703

44 CTA, Minutes, 1900, Appendix A, Mayor's Inaugural, 22 January 1900; see Canada, House of Commons *Debates*, 6 March 1902, cols 786–8.

45 *Select Committee to Investigate the Telephone* I 703–13; Canada *Statutes*, 1906, 6 Edward VII cap 42 sec 17, 20, 30, 31, 35

46 Public Archives of Canada (hereafter PAC), Board of Railway Commissioners' Records, RG46, vols 18, 19; CTA, Minutes, 1914, Appendix A, Report of Board of Control, 13 November 1914; CTA, Board of Control Minutes, item 1400, 27 November ibid, 1919, Appendix C, Mayor's Message, 27 January 1919

47 On the public power movement see H.V. Nelles *The Politics of Development, Forests, Mines and Hydroelectric Power in Ontario, 1849–1941* (Toronto 1974) 223–88.

48 CTA, Board of Control Minutes, 1898, item 413, 20 June; Board of Control Papers, Box 2, J.K. Leslie and C.H. Rust to Controllers, 11 November 1898; the Conmee clause was *Statutes of Ontario*, 1899, 62 Victoria sec 35 subsec 4; on its repeal see CTA, Minutes, 1904, item 851, 15 December.

49 CTA, Board of Control Papers, Box 8, Urquhart to Ross, 31 January 1903; Nelles *Politics of Development* 241–6

50 Quoted in Nelles *Politics of Development* 257–8

51 CTA, Minutes, 1906, Appendix C, Report of City Clerk, 3 January 1907; CTA, Minutes, 1907, item 213, 15 March; Appendix A, Report of Board of Control, 22 November 1907; Ontario Hydro Archives, Toronto Electric Light Company Minutebook, 2 May 1907.

52 CTA, Board of Control Papers, Box 20, H.M. Pellatt to Emerson Coatsworth,

16 November 1907; CTA, Minutes, 1907, Appendix C, Report of City Clerk, 3
January 1908; CTA, Minutes, 1908, Appendix C, Mayor's Message, 16 March
1908; Nelles *Politics of Development* 292

53 Ontario Hydro Archives, Toronto Electric Light Company Minutebook, 17
March, 7 April 1911; CTA, Toronto Electric Commissioners *Annual Report[s]
of the Toronto Hydro-Electric System* 1911–23

54 See Nord 'Experts versus Experts' 221

55 Doucet 'Mass Transit: The Case of Toronto' 11–12; CTA, Minutes, 1909,
Appendix C, Report of the City Clerk, 4 January 1910; CTA, Board of Control
Minutes, 1910, item 429, March 10

56 CTA, Minutes, 1910, Appendix A, Board of Control Reports, 22 September, 21
October; CTA, Board of Control Minutes, 1910, item 2356, 29 October

57 CTA, Minutes, 1910, Appendix C, Report of City Clerk, 3 January 1912; CTA,
Minutes, 1913, Appendix C, Mayor's Message re Street Railways, 13 October
1913; CTA, Minutes, 1914, Appendix A, Mayor's Message, 9 February 1914;
Appendix C, Mayor's Message, 21 September 1914

58 Morton Keller *The Art and Politics of Thomas Nast* (New York 1968) 177–82

59 The eight cartoons, all by Samuel Hunter, appeared in the Toronto *World* on
the dates given; in this article they have been reproduced from original drawings in PAC, Picture Division, Samuel Hunter Collection.

60 'The Cartoonist's Armoury' in *Meditations on a Hobby Horse and Other
Essays on the Theory of Art* (London 1871) 130

61 See Nord 'Experts versus Experts' 221.

62 Board of Railway Commissioners *Seventh Annual Report* (Ottawa 1912) 289–93

63 Frisch *Town into City* 249

64 PAC, Charles Porteous Papers, vol 20, Porteous to James Ross, 2 August 1898

FRANCES FRISKEN

A triumph for public ownership

The Toronto Transportation Commission 1921–53

T HE OPENING IN 1954 of four and
one-half miles of subway along Yonge Street, Toronto's busiest north-south
artery, followed closely on the creation of Metropolitan Toronto and the
transformation of the city-owned Toronto Transportation Commission (TTC)
into a metropolitan transit authority. The event was a fitting conclusion to
Toronto's three decades of mass transit under city ownership, for it
highlighted the two characteristics on which the TTC had built a reputation for
success – financial self-sufficiency and high-quality service – long after many
North American companies had concluded that one required the sacrifice of
the other. Not only was the TTC able to finance the bulk of subway costs out of
its accumulated reserves, but it did so while it was making many other
improvements to a system suffering the effects of wartime overload. It was
also able to proceed in the knowledge of widespread public backing, for in
1946 city voters had approved the subway plan by a ratio of nine to one.
Transit patrons would soon register their approval in a different way – by
using the subway in numbers that surpassed the commission's most optimistic
forecasts.

Existing efforts to explain the TTC's successes are few in number and
sometimes inconsistent. Taken together, however, they point to the interplay
of several factors. The commission emphasized two of these – municipal
ownership and independence from politics – in a retrospective review of its
own accomplishments.[1] Municipal ownership, it said, freed the system's
operators from the need to realize a profit, thus allowing them to concentrate
on providing 'a maximum of modern and efficient service at the lowest
possible cost.' Separate and independent status, it added, enabled it to avoid

the 'inefficiency and financial failures of utilities administered under the interference of political expediency.' For Harold Kaplan, in contrast, the TTC's achievements were the result not of political isolation but of political skill – as manifested by the commission's ability to win support from the media and interest groups while maintaining staff loyalty and cohesion.[2] Michael Doucet suggests that it was the timing rather than the fact of public takeover that was important.[3] The change in ownership, he says, prompted large-scale improvements and additions to the streetcar system at a time when large capital outlays were rare in the industry. These investments, when added to the cost of purchase, gave Toronto too high a stake in its transit system to abandon it.

Donald Davis disagrees. Municipal ownership, he says, was not a panacea for the difficulties besetting urban transit systems, for there were other cities where it failed to prevent the decline in ridership and operating revenues that beset the industry in the 1920s.[4] The TTC managed to avoid those difficulties only because it operated in an environment that was particularly favourable to mass transit – one he attributes to 'some of the least admirable characteristics of Canadian society and life' – its 'relative poverty, conservatism, and technological backwardness.' Conservatism and greed led the TTC's predecessor, the privately owned Toronto Railway Company, to refuse to extend its lines to accommodate the city's outward growth – a policy that contributed to a population density and a ridership habit that were higher than those found in most North American cities. It was relative poverty that prevented Toronto residents from switching to automobiles as early and in as large numbers as their counterparts in the urban United States. Finally, he argues, conservatism and technological backwardness led the TTC to cling to the streetcar long after other transit systems were deciding to switch to buses, even though buses were less expensive to operate and more adaptable to the transportation needs of the decentralizing city, besides being what the public preferred.

Davis's appraisal is a useful reminder that history and environment help to shape political options and establish some of the conditions for organizational effectiveness. It still leaves important questions unanswered, however. First, how did the TTC manage to sustain an environment that was favourable to its operations over a thirty-year period in North American history that brought severe hardship to most members of the transit industry and disaster to some? While less prosperous than some of the wealthiest American cities, Toronto was still better off than many cities in both the United States and Canada, and its residents were just as susceptible to the lure of the automobile. Statistics compiled by the TTC in 1929 showed, in fact, that motor vehicle registrations were higher in Toronto than in 10 of the 22 US cities and one Canadian city surveyed.[5] None the less the average number of riders per capita was higher on the Toronto system than on all but those serving the three largest cities in the United States. The smallest of those three (Brooklyn) was four times the size of Toronto. The TTC was also the only one of twelve North American systems serving populations of 500,000 or more that actually experienced an increase in ridership between 1925 and 1928. The pattern persisted, for by 1950 the TTC's per capita ridership, though declining, was still well above the US average and higher than that of all other large Canadian cities.[6] There was more to the TTC's achievements, it would seem, than an auspicious beginning.

A second set of questions relates to the apparent anomaly between the TTC's conservatism and 'technological backwardness' and its ability to command the support of the city's government and population. If, as Davis suggests, the TTC defied a widespread public preference for buses when it decided to invest heavily in new streetcars in the late 1930s, why did it compound that folly by renovating and further adding to its streetcar fleet after the Second World War? And why were Toronto's government and citizens apparently so satisfied with their 'backward' company that they were prepared to sanction another and still more costly commitment to a fixed-rail mode at the same time? Finally, how was the commission able to put those investment decisions into effect, using its own funds, at times when other public transit companies were trying to reduce costs in order to remain solvent?

These questions are of more than historical interest. They bear directly on a problem that plagues public transit companies everywhere – that of reconciling demands for operating 'efficiency' with demands for more and better service. It is a problem that has been with the transit industry since its beginning, perturbing relationships between city governments and their transit suppliers in ways that often hurt the interest of both parties. As we consider the history of the TTC decade by decade from the 1920s through the 1940s, we should look for reasons why the TTC managed to surmount this problem. But first let us consider the reasons why its predecessor failed to do so, and the probable influence of this failure on the arrangements the city made for operating its transportation system once it had acquired it.

Toronto's decision to take over its public transit system in 1921 terminated a long history of disagreements, both political and legal, between the city and the privately owned Toronto Railway Company (TRC) to which it had granted a thirty-year franchise in 1891.[7] Underlying much of the discord was the company's refusal to extend its lines beyond the city's 1891 boundaries, a position that the city found increasingly unacceptable as it pushed its boundaries outwards by a succession of annexations that almost doubled its size between 1893 and 1920. As time went on the list of grievances grew, with each party contributing to it. City politicians reacted to company intransigence with frequent attacks on the quality of service but refused to allow the TRC to build the additional downtown lines that would relieve the overcrowding and congestion of which they complained. The company responded to talk of public takeover by cutting back on capital improvements and allowing its excess revenues to accumulate in a reserve account earmarked for repairs and replacements, thereby enraging its critics still more.

Those familiar with the early history of public transit in North America are inclined to see an element of irrationality in the TRC's behaviour. The orthodox view of the period depicts street railway companies as only too eager to expand their operations in advance of city growth, either to promote the development of their own real estate holdings or to assure monopoly access to the riders and thus the profits that would follow development.[8] This view fails to take account of the many and varied circumstances that influenced the calculations of individual suppliers. Not all street railway companies speculated in real estate (there is no evidence that the TRC did so) and not all could base their investment decisions on equivalent expectations of profitable returns, even in times of rapid population growth and outward expansion. Much depended on the nature of their agreements with municipal councils about fare structures, conditions of operation, and disposition of receipts. The 1891 agreement between Toronto and the TRC was a particularly restrictive example of its genre.[9] It gave the city engineer extensive powers to approve the location and supervise the construction of new lines and to oversee virtually all details of operation, thereby limiting the company's right to decide even the most technical matters. While it granted the company the right to charge the standard five-cent fare (considered generous or excessive at the time), it also required it to offer special, reduced-price tickets (at eight for 25 cents) for use during the hours when most people were travelling to and from work. Finally, it imposed taxes that exceeded those in effect in any other Canadian city and probably in any city in North America. They included the normal taxes levied on all city property owners, a graduated tax on revenue that rose to a maximum of 20 per cent on gross receipts of $3,000,000 or more, and an annual charge of $800 per mile of single track – this last to compensate the city for the costs of paving streets on which the railway operated.

Not only were the conditions imposed on the TRC onerous by the standards of the day but they were also undoubtedly a strong deterrent to expansion, for they failed to make allowance for the rise in operating costs and fall in passenger volumes that accompanied the extension of public transit into outer and less heavily populated districts. The city made no move to relax them during its efforts to persuade the company to make such extensions, however. In fact, it apparently insisted that the TRC agree to similar terms if it wanted council to approve its plans to solve the suburban transportation problem in another way – by bringing into the city electric radial lines that the TRC operated between towns outside Toronto or by connecting those lines to the city system at its outer terminals.[10] This was the way that Montreal and Vancouver suburbs achieved direct service into the city at about this time, but it did not occur in Toronto. Instead city council decided in 1910 to build its own lines in those parts of the city not served by the TRC – the first of the several formal actions that propelled it toward acquisition of all transit lines within its boundaries.

The intensity of Toronto's struggles with the TRC help to explain why public takeover gained widespread approval in the city. It does little to account for the venture's success, however. Many other cities had a similar history of controversy surrounding street railway issues but the subsequent development of their transit systems was very different.[11] In a few cases, discord culminated in moves to public ownership that were much less successful than Toronto's. Typically, however, city governments left their transit systems in private hands and continued to treat them as privileged monopolies that could afford to pay high taxes while operating on fares kept low by regulation. At the same time they allowed and sometimes encouraged the outward spread of populations into low-density suburbs that transit companies found difficult to serve. When challenged to provide transportation to those areas, they often devoted local tax monies to the construction or improvement of local streets and adopted other measures that facilitated automobile use but did little to aid mass transit. The result was a steady decline in the financial fortunes of most transit operators and in the quality of service they provided, with a corresponding decline in public support. This leads one to ask whether there were circumstances attending the Toronto takeover that led the city to adopt an administrative approach that gave the TTC advantages not enjoyed by most of its peers.

The city no sooner acquired its street railway system in 1921 than it placed it in the hands of a commission composed of three appointed members, none of whom could be sitting members of city council. It then empowered that commission to act on its behalf in all transportation matters that lay within the city's jurisdiction, retaining only the right to appoint commissioners, approve capital borrowing for new construction, and review the commission's financial records on a regular basis. This speedy devolution of authority seemed to violate the principle of public control that local politicians had been asserting for more than a decade; in agreeing to management by commission, council was endorsing an administrative model promoted by those political reformers who tempered their desire to strengthen local government with a distrust of elected legislatures. The move is understandable, therefore, only if one assumes that the challenges confronting the operators of the city's transportation system entailed greater risks than its government wanted to take. The most obvious of these was the immediate need to consolidate, rehabilitate, and expand transportation services for a land area almost twice the size of that served by the old TRC. Such a program implied a large capital investment in new plant and equipment just at a time when many transit companies were in serious financial difficulties and the industry's future was uncertain.[12]

The TRC had not escaped the problems that beset the street railway industry after the First World War, despite its conservative stand on expansion and the widespread belief that it was still making large profits. Although its passengers and gross revenues increased every year except 1915, its costs began to outstrip those increases during its last ten years of operation and the size of its profits fell.[13] In 1918 it asked for permission to raise its fares. The city opposed the request, citing the company's failure to respond to repeated demands for better service, and the Ontario Railway and Municipal Board refused to approve it.[14] By 1920 the TRC had not only stopped paying dividends but was also dipping into its surplus revenue to cover operating costs.

There was little reason for the city to be concerned about the TRC's financial difficulties as long as the lines remained in private hands. The policy of taxing gross receipts meant that its returns from company operations were increasing as company profits fell. These continuing financial benefits, together with the size of the company's accumulated surplus (which exceeded $5 million after 1915), might have induced council to disregard signs of impending difficulty if it had not had direct experience with the problems of making a transit operation pay its own way. The civic lines lost money from the beginning – a situation that civic officials attributed to council's initial insistence on setting a low rate of fare (at two cents a ride) and its subsequent refusals to raise it.[15] These same officials attacked the policy of providing service below cost not only because it entailed ratepayer support for a service that benefitted only one section of the community but also because 'it provides one of the most potent and damaging arguments urged against public ownership.' Council finally approved a one-cent increase in 1919, but the move merely slowed the rate of loss. By 1920 the lines had an accumulated deficit of more than $1 million.

These ominous portents for transit operations were appearing at a time of generalized fiscal retrenchment in civic administration. The city's financial situation changed radically in the years following council's 1910 decision to build street railways in the outer parts of the city. The pre-war period had been one of rising prosperity – a time when rapid assessment growth allowed council to maintain a constant mill rate while expanding local services and assuming sizeable capital debts. Wartime depression and inflation took their toll, however, slowing down the rate of assessment growth and increasing the costs of government. The mill rate increased rapidly, from 19½ cents in 1913 to 30¼ cents in 1918.[16] Members of city government began to emphasize the need to economize, including the need to put city-owned enterprises on a financially self-supporting basis.[17]

The city's preoccupation with protecting its financial interests is apparent in the wording of the by-law in which it outlined the powers and responsibilities of its new transportation commission.[18] That document said little about the standard of service the city expected. It merely empowered the TTC 'to locate, construct and operate ... such street railway lines and extensions to existing lines ... as will with the existing civic street railway lines *provide an adequate system of street railway transportation* [italics added].'

It was no more specific about the commission's operating responsibilities, except in one respect. The commission was

To take charge of, manage, control and operate all transportation facilities owned or controlled by the City as may from time to time be committed to it by by-law of the Council – to regulate and control all matters relating thereto, including the fixing of all tolls and fares *sufficient to make the system self-sustaining*, including the maintenance of the property in good condition and due provision for renewals, depreciation and debt charges, to make rules and regulations and enforce the same concerning all matters within its powers and *generally to do and perform all things necessary to fully and effectually accomplish the purposes of the Commission within its powers.* [italics added]

One message was clear: the TTC must ensure that its activities made no demands on city coffers. What remained to be worked out in the years ahead was what in fact constituted 'an adequate system of street railway transportation' and exactly what the commission could or must do 'to fully and effectually accomplish [its] purposes.'

There was one important feature of the arrangement that did not appear in the city by-law or in the provincial legislation that succeeded it. This was the city's decision to relieve the TTC of any taxation based on its earnings and to exempt it from all forms of property and business taxation except that levied for school purposes. The change occurred over the objections of the city's finance commissioner, who saw the exemptions as a form of taxpayer subsidy to the streetcar system.[19] That same official, however, strongly supported another council action with just as important implications for the TTC's future performance: a decision taken in 1918 not to annex any more territory outside the existing city limits unless the owners were prepared to pay the full cost of making service improvements up to city standards.[20] Both these decisions were significant departures from the city's treatment of the TRC, and the first gave the TTC a financial advantage denied to most of its contemporaries.

The TTC's mandate also freed it from direct council supervision and regulation to a degree not enjoyed by the TRC or by many other companies, public or private, operating at the time. This was a tenuous advantage, however, for what one council had given another could try to remove. This possibility guaranteed that the TTC's partial isolation from the city's elected government did not mean it could be indifferent to its views – an operational constraint that became increasingly apparent as the TTC moved through its first decade of operation.

The three-man commission appointed in August 1920 to run the city's transit system conformed well to the administrative model promoted by municipal reformers, for its members were all local businessmen who had never held elective office. They were not all newcomers to civic affairs, however, for two of them – P. W. Ellis and George Wright – were already members of the city's Hydro Electric Commission. Ellis had been chairman of that body since 1911 and had earlier helped to found the provincially owned Ontario Hydro-Electric Power Commission. The TTC gained further access to the experience of an existing public corporation by engaging as general manager H.H. Couzens, a British engineer who had come to Toronto in 1913 to manage the city's newly created hydro commission. It also ensured continuity in transit operations by absorbing those members of the city's works department who had worked on the civic lines and all but the most senior members of the TRC staff.

The commission faced the immediate problem of setting fares for its services, bearing in mind the need to keep the system self-sustaining. It sought advice from two sources: works department employees who had been operating the civic lines and a street railway official brought in from London, England, to study the system. Both agreed that a fare increase was necessary. City staff compiled statistics to show that the TRC had been operating at a lower average fare and had realized lower profits than virtually all other street railway companies on the continent.[21] The commission could operate on an average fare of no less than 5.46 cents without incurring a deficit, they said, and then only if it could minimize its financial obligations to the city, keep its expenses down, maintain existing ridership and wage levels, and not try to make improvements in mileage, speed, or methods of operation.[22]

The British consultant took a bolder approach.[23] He recommended an extensive plan of improvements that would help the TTC increase the speed, convenience, and accessibility of its services. These could be financed in one of two ways, he said: by zone fares or by an increase in the flat fare charged throughout the system. The zone fare might be fairer to the individual passenger, but it did not encourage the spread of population into the outer and healthier parts of the city. For that reason he recommended a flat rate of five cents, a rehabilitation surcharge of two cents, and no discounts or concessions.

The commission faced a difficult choice: either to risk the public outrage that a substantial increase would bring, or to follow the politically expedient course of adopting a smaller increase that would leave it less able to satisfy those clamouring for more and better service. It decided to take the risk, and announced in August 1921 that fares on the consolidated system would be 7 cents, with four tickets selling for 25 cents. There would be free transfers on all lines, but there would be no limited-hour (or 'workingmen's') tickets. General Manager Couzens told the board of control that the increase would enable the TTC to begin to rehabilitate the system, using a higher standard of maintenance and construction than had hitherto prevailed.[24] Even with the higher fare, rehabilitation would have to occur gradually because of the many challenges facing the commission and the extent of its financial responsibilities. Couzens explained that the commission was abandoning limited-hour tickets because they were contrary to the act under which it operated. Not only would they have been in effect at times when operating costs were higher than average, he pointed out, but they also helped to increase congestion and discomfort at those times.

The report drew swift reaction from council. Some aldermen tried to get the TTC to lower the size of its increase; others insisted that it should be council and not the TTC that determined fares. The mayor said that he would not sign the by-law transferring the railway to the commission on 1 September, but would instead turn it over to the works commissioner to operate at the old rate.[25] Council eventually approved the report, but by only one vote.

Having passed this hurdle, the commission moved quickly ahead with a program of rehabilitation, extension, and improvement. Within three years it had rehabilitated a total of 64 miles of track, partially rehabilitated 11½ miles more, added 26 miles in extensions, and rerouted the entire system. It had built new car houses and repair shops and had laid 18½ miles of track in its own yards. It had also purchased 575 new streetcars (scrapping more than half the 830 cars acquired from the TRC) as well as eight double-deck, seven single-deck, and four trolley buses.[26] It used these buses to provide feeder service to street railway lines in the city's outer districts. In addition, it introduced a non-stop service at a premium fare between a low-density upper-income neighbour-hood in north Toronto and downtown and began to operate sight-seeing and charter services to points outside the city.[27]

All these activities took place during an economic recession that was having its effects on TTC operations. The number of passengers on the city system fell from a 1921 high of 197.8 million to 181 million in 1925, and revenues behaved accordingly. The TTC responded to these trends by tempering its initiatives with concessions to fiscal prudence. It abandoned trolley coaches in 1925 because it found them more costly to operate than motor buses. It insisted that the higher cost of operating buses in general made them unsuitable for all but special purposes. It also made a distinction between 'coaches' and 'buses' – specifying that 'buses' were those vehicles used on the single-fare city system to supplement streetcars; 'coaches' were the better-appointed, more comfortable vehicles used for special services, sightseeing, and trips to outside points. The distinction was financially important, for the commission wanted to emphasize that 'coach passengers were not eligible for the free transfer privileges accorded to users of the city system.'[28] It proclaimed as a matter of policy 'that extensions or additions to the system should not be made unless they will earn sufficient additional revenue within a reasonable time to meet all the expenses of operation and fixed charges.'[29]

Fiscal prudence had both political and practical significance. The TTC had to reassure city council that its investment was in capable hands. Arbitrators had set the final price of the TRC property at $11.5 million – $4.5 million more than the city had expected to pay. The TTC's improvement program had increased that figure to more than $40 million, or one-quarter of the city's total indebtedness.[30] While the commission was responsible for paying interest on that debt and retiring it at the end of thirty years, the city government would have to step in if the TTC defaulted. Any sign that the transportation system might be in financial difficulty was likely to prompt city officials to take an immediate interest in TTC affairs to the point of challenging the commission's right to operate the system. The TTC gave the city no cause for such action. Instead it was able to assure an American critic of public ownership in 1925 that it had met all its financial obligations at no cost to the city.[31] The period ended on a harmonious note, with both city council and the city finance commissioner expressing appreciation for the TTC's good performance during a depression.[32]

These expressions of satisfaction did not mean that the TTC had managed to avoid political controversy altogether, for it had to defend itself from recurring protests about its services, its fares, the disruptions caused by its rehabilitation program, and its decision to convert many of its lines from two-man to one-man operation.[33] The most significant political skirmishes in which it engaged, however, were those that had to do with the scope of its operations and the extent of its jurisdiction. The earliest of these concerned an ambitious scheme promoted by Adam Beck, chairman of the Ontario Hydro-Electric Commission, for a massive network of interurban or 'radial' electric railway lines covering most of southern Ontario, a plan that the city supported.[34] The TTC saw the plan as a direct threat to its monopoly rights because some of the proposed lines would traverse the city to bring suburban passengers into downtown Toronto, and it even went so far as to hire an outside consultant to argue its case. It was not TTC opposition that finally persuaded the city to withdraw its support, but rather the fact that the province and other municipalities had already done so.

City council was more supportive of TTC motor bus initiatives, telling private operators in 1925 that there was nothing it could do to stop the commission from using its buses for sightseeing and charter purposes. It did so, however, only after hearing from the city solicitor that the TTC had a legal right to operate buses under powers granted the city in 1912. It took a different position in a situation where that legal right did not exist, assuring a delegation of taxicab owners a short time later that it opposed the idea (then only a rumour) of the TTC getting into the taxicab business.[35]

It was clear before many years had passed, then, that the TTC could not rely on the city to support initiatives and positions that the law did not allow or anticipate, especially if city council was under pressure to act in a different way. This became a more serious problem as the decade wore on and the TTC's disagreements with the city began to involve issues similar to those that had contributed so much to the city's disaffection with the TRC: suburban service, and the way the commmission managed its surplus revenues. These disputes became so serious, in fact, that they ended in a judicial inquiry that challenged the city to reconsider the way it wanted its transit system to be managed and operated.

The disputes that marred the TTC's relationship with the city of Toronto after 1925 centred on three specific matters: the disposition and mode of operation of electric radial lines that the city acquired from TRC subsidiaries after 1921; the TTC's decision to set up its own subsidiary to acquire and operate commuter and long-distance bus services outside the city; and a proposed purchase of new streetcars to supplement those already in use on city lines. In their different ways, all three disputes involved a clash between two conflicting views on the same issue – the nature of the TTC's obligation to the city. One view emphasized the agency's obligation to remain financially self-sufficient; the other stressed its responsibility to serve those interests that managed to find champions in the local political arena. Among the more active of those interests were persons living outside the city or having a stake in suburban development.

The radial dispute had its genesis during the period of transition from private to public ownership, when the city found it necessary to purchase all suburban radial lines owned by TRC subsidiaries because it had to own one of those lines before the TTC could extend the city system into North Toronto. The TTC became responsible for all portions of the lines that lay within city boundaries, but city council turned the outer portions over to Ontario Hydro to operate, under an agreement that required the city to pay any operating deficits. At the time it expected the lines to become part of the Hydro radial system. The Hydro radial scheme fell through, however; the suburban lines consistently lost money; and the city was soon looking for a way to rid itself of a bad investment. Some members of council favoured turning the lines over to the TTC to operate and adding their deficits to the TTC's capital debt. The TTC agreed to take over the lines but refused to be responsible for past deficits, saying that these would make it impossible to make the lines self-supporting.[36] It advised the city that it would be better to abandon the lines altogether than to risk the discredit to public ownership that accumulating deficits would bring. The city eventually paid off the debt to Hydro and turned the lines over to the TTC to operate on the same terms that governed city operations, with the added provision that the city would continue to pay operating deficits. The commission soon began to abandon the less profitable lines – a policy that provoked cries of outrage from affected communities and objections from their sympathizers on city council.[37] These objections soon faded, however, when it became clear that most suburban governments were unwilling to pay any part of the operating deficits.

The principal reason for the radials' difficulties – in Ontario as elsewhere – was growing competition from private bus companies. The city addressed this problem by appealing to the provincial legislature (which regulated inter-urban services) to prevent the companies from competing with the radial lines. This the province was not prepared to do. The TTC took a different approach, which led to the second controversy. In 1925 it set up its own motor coach department and began to buy up the private companies and operate inter-urban services of its own. Then in 1927 it used $1,000,000 of its reserve funds to establish an independent subsidiary – Gray Coach Lines Ltd – to take over its inter-urban operations.[38]

The city government showed little initial concern with these activities, and some of its members may have been encouraging them. Opposition soon developed outside, however. The city of Hamilton protested that TTC buses would induce Hamilton shoppers to spend their money in Toronto, a complaint that led the provincial legislature to approve Gray Coach routes only on condition that buses would bypass Hamilton. The Central Council of Ratepayers' Associations protested the commission's decisions to spend money on buses without ratepayer approval. Towns that received Gray Coach as a replacement for radial service joined the chorus of protest because fares on the buses were higher than the radial fares (which had been held down by franchise restrictions).[39]

It was not long before members of council and the board of control, civic officials, and the local press were choosing sides in the controversy. Debate focused on three related issues: whether the TTC had the right to make capital expenditures or other decisions affecting the nature of its operations without first consulting council and the local ratepayers; whether it had the right to use its reserves to set up Gray Coach Lines and provide it with working capital; and whether it had legal authority to operate buses outside the city at all.

TTC officials assured their critics that the establishment of Gray Coach Lines conformed to accepted business practice and yielded no personal advantage to commission members or their staff. The venture served the city's interests, they said, because it increased TTC efficiency by employing equipment, staff, and shop facilities at times when these would otherwise be underused; it prevented outside competition with city-owned transportation properties; and it would help the city recover its losses on the radials. They assured the board of control that money used to set up Gray Coach and buy out bus companies was drawn from funds that were kept quite separate from those set aside to take care of debt repayment and depreciation. The commission would not only pay off its debts, they insisted, but would also maintain the property in good condition.[40]

The dispute climaxed in a dramatic meeting of city council in April 1929 at which General Manager David Harvey (who had succeeded Couzens in 1924) urged council to go against the recommendation of its powerful board of control and approve the purchase of four additional bus lines (the board having approved only one).[41] He managed to carry the day, but only after a hard fight. 'One member of the council observed that from the grilling Mr. Harvey had been subjected to it is evident that the path of public ownership is a hard one, adding that if the TTC was a private company, the lines would have been acquired without delay and Mr. Harvey's salary raised.'[42]

Council not only approved the lines, however, but also agreed to seek the legislative changes that would allow the commission to carry on its inter-urban business. The matter might have ended there if another dispute had not surfaced almost immediately, raising new questions about the commission's conduct of its affairs.

Somewhat ironically, the third dispute arose because of the TTC's success in combating automotive competition to its city lines. After the disappointing results of its first few years, the TTC's fortunes began to improve in 1926 and by 1928 ridership on the system was higher than it had been in any year since 1921. The improvement turned out to be a mixed blessing. Streetcars were becoming increasingly crowded, especially at rush hours, and the situation was beginning to attract the attention of local politicians and the local press. Critics proposed a variety of remedies. Some talked of the need for a subway; others insisted that the TTC should use buses instead of streetcars on the busier downtown streets. A third group insisted that the TTC needed more streetcars to handle the load.

TTC spokesmen told critics that Toronto's population was not yet large enough to support a subway and that buses would increase downtown congestion, not reduce it. The commission did add several new bus routes in outlying districts, however. It also considered buying 110 new streetcars to supplement existing equipment – but decided against the purchase on the advice of General Manager Harvey. Coming as it did in the early stages of the Gray Coach controversy, that decision suggested to some that the agency was neglecting its responsibility to city riders in order to expand its operations throughout the province and beyond. Criticism continued to mount, and by the end of 1928 the TTC's activities had become an election issue. Soon after the election the board of control asked the commission to report on the problems of overcrowding and delays on its lines.

Harvey answered the board with statistics documenting improvements in street railway service since 1921.[43] He insisted that most of the system's current difficulties stemmed from two conditions that were beyond TTC control: an increasing volume of rush-hour travel (a consequence of the standardization of the workday) and delays caused by other traffic. In response to his suggestions the board arranged a conference with the chief constable to consider a variety of traffic control measures.

At this point events gave rise to a situation unprecedented in TTC history – an open disagreement between the commission and members of its senior staff.[44] The disruption occurred early in 1929, after one of the two original commissioners died and the second became ill, leaving the agency in sole charge of Edward J. Lennox, a Toronto architect and builder who had joined the commission in 1923. Lennox used his new authority to instruct the general manager to call for tenders for the 110 streetcars that Harvey had advised against in 1927. Harvey complied, though without enthusiasm. After receiving bids from three companies he recommended that the contract should go to a firm that had supplied the commission in the past, maintaining that this firm was the one best able to produce cars to TTC specifications. Lennox disagreed, insisting that the contract should go to the firm that had submitted the lowest bid, and immediately asked the city to release unspent capital funds held in reserve for the TTC. The city decided instead to appoint as temporary commissioners the two outside persons who were likely to be most knowledgeable about the TTC's financial affairs – its current and former commissioners of finance, George Wilson and George Ross. The reconstituted commission met three times before voting down the streetcar purchase, Lennox being the only one to support it.

Wilson and Ross explained their position in letters written to Lennox before the final meeting.[45] They could find no evidence, they said, that Harvey had ever been strongly in favour of buying the new cars. Citing detailed statistics compiled by TTC staff, they went on to argue that ridership on the Toronto system was still lower than it had been in 1922, despite the recent increases, and that seating capacity on the system had increased faster than ridership. They warned that transit patronage could easily decline in the future if the number of motor cars in the city continued to increase and that a large capital outlay of this sort was likely to lead to an increase in fares. In short, they took the position that operating and financial considerations should outweigh all others in decisions as to how and whether the system should expand.

Lennox defended his position to the city's mayor and board of control in an angry letter outlining a different set of views on the prospects for mass transit and the responsibilities of those who operated it. He dismissed his opponents' detailed statistical arguments as irrelevant to the existing situation and went on to relate recent ridership increases to the rapid growth that had accompanied a period of prosperity. Citing his long experience in the building industry to support his belief that prosperity and growth would continue, he maintained that the TTC needed new streetcars both to accommodate that growth in the city and the suburbs and to lessen the 'indecent, inhuman and unhealthy conditions' that currently existed. He noted further that the question of additional cars had been an issue in the last election, when the commission had become the target for unpleasant accusations of every possible type, and when 'the citizens who offered themselves for Municipal Honors were interrogated and exacted promises from, that they would support a proposition to buy additional cars.' Finally he suggested that Harvey had turned against the streetcar purchase only after Lennox had overruled his choice of supplier – a thinly veiled suggestion that Harvey's choice had been influenced by considerations of personal advantage. Similar considerations, he hinted, had influenced commission purchases in the past.

This was too much for Wilson and Ross. Characterizing Lennox's letter 'a direct charge of negligence, inattention to duty and general supineness' against former and present members of the commission and a serious criticism of its former and present general managers, they called on the city to launch a full judicial inquiry into TTC affairs.[47] Council complied, asking Judge James Herbert Denton of York County Court to investigate not only the streetcar controversy but also the TTC investment in Gray Coach and virtually all other aspects of TTC operations.

The Denton inquiry lasted from November 1929 to March 1930 and featured testimony from city and TTC officials, their legal advisers, and outside consultants brought in to evaluate the quality of TTC service. The judge's report largely exonerated TTC officials from all charges of corruption or financial mismanagement, accepted the testimony of expert witnesses that TTC service excelled that provided by any other municipally owned company in North America, and criticized Mr Lennox for having assumed too much authority while in sole charge of the commission and for other actions of questionable propriety.[48] At the same time, his conclusions and recommendations indicated that Judge Denton felt that the TTC had strayed too far from the 'ideal' model for an organization of its type – failing at times to exercise 'that restraint or check upon expenditures that the public would like to see' and embarking on a venture (Gray Coach) that lay outside its statutory authority and was perhaps inappropriate for a public company, the primary aim of which should be to give service, not make a profit. These criticisms did not stem from any finding that the TTC had jeopardized its financial position, however, for the judge also concluded that the agency had produced a greater surplus than its bookkeeping indicated and could afford to spend more on improvements to local service. What those improvements should be, and whether they necessitated the purchase of new streetcars, he left it to the commission to decide. He did not favour a decrease in fares, however, concluding that TTC fares were already among the lowest on the continent and that any decrease would mean a substantial loss of revenue.

While reaffirming the commission's right to decide what best served the interests of the city's transportation system, Judge Denton attributed many of the TTC's recent difficulties either to weaknesses within the commission itself or to faulty interactions among the TTC, the city government, and the public at large. Noting a recent and growing tendency for the commission to rely heavily on its staff, he observed that it was not enough for commission members to have business experience; they should also be in an active stage of life and able to withstand outside influence.[49] And they should be paid – something that council, in response to ratepayer pressures, had consistently refused to endorse. Further, the judge recommended that the city should conduct a more thorough annual audit of the TTC's affairs – not because he had uncovered evidence of wrongdoing but in the interest of opening them up to public scrutiny and allaying public suspicions. Finally he advised the commission to take the public into its confidence more than it had in the past: 'This does not mean that their meetings should be open to the public or the press, or that the public should be advised as to the details of what they have done or propose to do; but it does mean that in the larger matters of public concern the inclination should be to furnish, rather than withhold, information.'[50]

City council's first act in response to the Denton Report was to identify the commission as the agency responsible for studying and implementing most of its recommendations. There were a few matters that council could not delegate, however. One was the recommendation for a more comprehensive audit of TTC affairs. The city auditor assured council of the thoroughness of his annual review of TTC finances and pointed out that Judge Denton's recommendation implied an inquiry not only into accounts but also into the management and business practices of this and all other city commissions.[51] Council decided it would consult Judge Denton first before giving the auditor the authority and the money to do this and never discussed the matter again.

The second task was to reconstitute and strengthen the commission. Council wasted little time in deciding that henceforth commission members would be paid. It chose those members only after prolonged debate, however, during which it rejected all nominees who had already expressed opinions on how the commission should conduct its affairs.[52] Among those approved was William C. McBrien, a Toronto real estate specialist who had already served on both the harbour commission and the board of education. McBrien would remain with the commission until his death in 1954, acting as chairman for much of that period, and would gain a reputation as the person primarily responsible for the TTC's operating and political successes.[53]

The third matter demanding the city's attention was the future and scope of Gray Coach. Judge Denton had suggested that council might want to restrict the company's operations to the immediate environs of Toronto. The city auditor was advising the city to abandon the venture altogether, saying that it was too much of a gamble and an unfair burden on the streetcar system.[54] Council decided to compromise – asking the province to validate the commission's existing investments in inter-urban buses and bus routes while stipulating that the TTC could not put any more capital in Gray Coach or add any new services outside the city limits without council's consent.[55]

The new commission began its work in circumstances that posed a greater challenge to the city's transit operators than any encountered thus far. The number of revenue passengers on city lines fell from 206.8 million in 1929 to a low of 147.6 million in 1933 and rose only slightly until the end of the decade. The commission reacted to its difficulties by reducing service on uneconomic routes and cutting back on management salaries and operating personnel. These economies reduced operating costs from $9.1 million in 1929 to $6.3 million in 1933, for a decrease of 30.8 per cent. (The average decrease in the cost of city services from 1931 to 1935, by comparison, was 16.6 per cent).[56] By 1936 it was able to announce that it had weathered the difficult years and termed its record a 'triumph for public ownership.'[57] That triumph was more than a consequence of frugal management; it was also a vindication of Gray Coach. Passenger revenues on the inter-urban services exceeded expenses throughout the period, allowing the TTC to obscure its losses on the city system by issuing a consolidated annual report (and a separate report for Gray Coach). Noting that this technique had enabled the TTC to show a slight surplus for 1932 when in fact there had been a small loss, one city officer observed: 'It would undoubtedly be deemed reprehensible on the part of a private corporation to submit its revenue statement in such a way as to practically hide from its shareholders the fact of a loss being incurred for the year.'[58] The city made no move to end the practice, however.

The Great Depression severely restricted the commission's ability to make those improvements to the local system that Judge Denton had deemed both possible and desirable, but it did not prevent them altogether. While ruling out the purchase of new streetcars until business conditions improved, the commission hired American street railway consultant Albert S. Richey to review the system and its service and on his recommendation added at least two new bus routes in the outer parts of the city. The main value of Richey's report, however, was as a contribution to the principal technique that the TTC used to repair its damaged reputation – a campaign to improve its image and status in the community by publicizing its present merits and past accomplishments. Richey concluded that the TTC not only provided satisfactory service to practically all parts of the city, but was also superior to other North American systems in terms of the harmonious workings of its personnel, the completeness of its record and data collection, the physical condition of its equipment, the lower fares, the average speed, the frequency of service, and its safety record.[59] These judgments supplemented the TTC's own public relations activities, which took the form of newspaper advertisements documenting improvements in Toronto's urban and suburban transportation since 1921 and a tenth-anniversary report that claimed credit for such benefits to the city as less congested living environments, new business districts, increased property assessment, and fares below the continental average.[60]

These efforts, viewed in conjunction with the agency's responses to aldermanic requests for new services, did not mean that the change in the commission had yielded a significant change in operating philosophy. What they amounted to instead was a clarification of that philosophy and a refinement of the rules the commission had always used to evaluate requests for improvements in service. Those rules were little different from the ones observed by any private company. They required staff to weigh the benefits of any proposed service against its probable costs, taking into account such matters as stage of development or size of population of areas requesting service (indicators of potential ridership) or number of riders using services already available.[61] At Richey's instigation, the TTC added one other criterion – distance to nearest available service – that allowed it to discriminate among requests on the basis of relative need.

The combination of vigorous self-promotion and selective additions to service had the desired effects. The TTC was able to announce in 1936 that 99.5 per cent of the city's population was now within 2,000 feet of service.[62] It had also experienced a gradual decline in the number of complaints, criticisms, and demands that aldermen directed at its performance. This did not mean that all disagreements were at an end, for the TTC's strategies were of little help in dealing with some of the more fundamental issues underlying but not resolved by the Denton inquiry: ongoing suburban expansion and the growth in demand for suburban transportation and the degree to which the TTC controlled its surplus revenues and the use it made of them. The TTC's post-war activities were a direct outgrowth of the way these issues were handled after 1930.

The demand for suburban transportation service was never a matter of indifference to the TTC. Not only had the commission established Gray Coach Lines to provide short-distance as well as long-distance service outside the city, but it had also contracted during the 1920s to provide either streetcar or bus services to several outlying municipalities under agreements that required their governments to cover operating losses. When two of those municipalities sought annexation to the city in 1928 and again in 1931, the TTC joined forces with several city department heads who opposed the idea, claiming that it would almost certainly mean increased transit operating costs and an increase in fares over the entire system.[63] What it probably feared was that annexation would generate irresistible political pressure to incorporate the new territory into the uniform fare system.

Ironically, the TTC and other opponents of annexation convinced the city to hold firm to its non-expansionist policy just after council had decided to restrict the further development of Gray Coach Lines, thereby making it difficult for the TTC to serve the suburbs in its preferred way. As soon as Gray Coach had proven its financial worth, therefore, the TTC urged city council to remove restrictions on additions to Gray Coach services.[64] It pointed out that the Ontario Municipal Board had recently told the city that it could not adopt a 'dog in the manger' attitude – that it had to respond to the desire of people in the suburbs to get to the city at the lowest possible cost. The city made the requested change, and Gray Coach was soon adding bus routes once again.[65] Annexation pressures surfaced intermittently during the years that followed, but the TTC did not have to address the problems of serving an expanded area until after its absorption into the Metropolitan Toronto system in 1954.

Financial disagreements were more protracted. One of these concerned the TTC's right to maintain reserve funds and to decide how to allocate them. The city agreed to let the new commission retain these funds after General Manager Harvey and its own auditor pointed out in the early 1930s that they were helping to cover losses resulting from sharp declines in ridership.[66] While specifying at the time that the TTC could make no further capital investment in Gray Coach without its permission, it left unclear the purposes for which the reserves could be used. In 1934 the TTC faced a second judicial inquiry, after Controller Sam McBride challenged its right to purchase two pieces of property, one of which had belonged to TTC Chairman McBrien. This time the outcome was unequivocally favourable to the TTC. The presiding judge found that McBrien had sold his property to the commission for the price he had paid for it and had stayed out of all discussions pertaining to it. He also concluded that the TTC had not paid exorbitant prices for the properties (as McBride had charged) and that the purchases were justified.[67] McBride pressed on, none the less, insisting that the TTC was spending money it should be setting aside for retirement of the city's debt. He urged council to require the TTC to obtain its permission before making capital improvements of any kind.[68] The TTC responded that it was using its funds to maintain and improve the system 'where the interests of the community warranted' and insisted that council's approval was not required unless there were to be a radical change in the means of transportation.[69] The TTC now constituted a $55,000,000 investment with only a $28,000,000 debt, it said, and that achievement owed much to council's willingness to give it a free hand.

The issue divided the city bureaucracy. The city's auditor and commissioner of finance sided with McBride but the solicitor backed the commission, telling the board of control early in 1935 that the TTC's enabling legislation allowed it to set up reserves and use the money for any purpose within its competence.[70] If the city didn't want the TTC to do those things, he said, it should legislate to that effect. The board decided to take no further action.

The outcome was important because the TTC had almost $10,000,000 in a reserve fund for replacements and debt retirement by 1935, at a time when the city government was having to adjust its own spending to Depression conditions and the public mood was running against large public outlays. It enabled the commission to undertake an immediate program of renovation and rehabilitation of the Peter Witt cars it had bought in its first years of operation.[71] It also enabled it in 1938 to order 140 recently designed and newly built PCC (President's Conference Committee) cars and to add to their number thereafter, and so retire some of the last remaining cars it had acquired from the TRC.[72] And it meant that the TTC was able to accumulate the funds that would make possible its extensive post-war improvements. For that accumulation to proceed, however, the TTC first had to win other battles in the struggle to keep its financial interests and requirements separate from those of city government.

The struggle for fiscal autonomy frequently found the TTC resisting city efforts to make it assume costs the city would otherwise have to bear or to tap TTC revenues for city purposes. Its refusal to assume the debts of the failing radial lines in 1925 was an example of this type of resistance. So was an unsuccessful attempt in 1933 to get the city to assume all or part of the cost of providing free transportation for the blind and for war amputees – benefits that dated back to the system's beginnings or earlier.[73] It maintained on these and similar occasions that deficits incurred by unprofitable services or special fare concessions should be a charge on the whole community, not just on transit riders. The transit system should not be looked on as a source of relief for local taxpayers. It took the same position in its responses to the city's recurrent efforts to make it pay various costs associated with the paving and repair of streets used by streetcars. The city maintained from the beginning that the TTC should pay most or all of these costs, as street railways had always done, because it was the principal user of the streets. The TTC countered that it was the most efficient user because it carried 75–80 per cent of all passengers but accounted for only 8–15 per cent of all vehicles.[74] There was no reason why only some users should have to pay for an improvement that was available to all. This argument worked for a while, until the Depression years found the city government under increasing pressure to improve the local street system and its financial watchdogs increasingly zealous in their concern to relieve the burden on local taxpayers. They insisted that the TTC should pay not only a share of paving costs but also charges for other 'local improvements' – such as snow removal and the widening of streets – that had been accumulating since the beginning of its operations. The TTC resisted such claims and also asked the city to reimburse it for the costs of removing tracks and wires during street-widening operations. The parties finally took the matter to court in a 'friendly action' that yielded a split decision of both immediate and long-term financial benefit to the TTC.[75] The judge ruled that the commission had to pay the costs of local improvements but that it should not have to pay any costs arising from street widenings. Not only was the city fully responsible for looking after its highways, he said, but railway lines were public property and a public body was entitled to compensation for loss or damages. Otherwise streetcar riders would have to bear a considerable share of the costs of street improvements.

The Depression also strengthened the hand of those business groups, property owners' associations, and city financial officers who had always insisted that public utilities were no different from other businesses and should be taxed as such. By 1939 these interests had managed to persuade council to set up a special committee to consider the abolition of all or some of the property and business tax examptions it had granted municipally owned utilities in a more prosperous time. The TTC told that committee that the only way it could pay additional taxes was by increasing its fares, for it was nearing the limit of what it could do to economize on its operations.[76] Experience in the United States suggested, however, that a fare increase did not necessarily mean an increase in revenue; it could mean a decrease in riders instead. Besides, 'it would be most unjust to the car riders to increase the fare because of the immense community value of transportation to the City. It has built up district after district, increasing property values, assessment and City revenue. The car riders, at their own expense, have furnished these benefits to the taxpayers. Public transportation is vital to all the large financial and commercial institutions of the City and to all citizens, even motorists, who use it only as a standby service.' The committee recommended against the change, and council went along.

The TTC's victory over the tax-hunters was short-lived. A change in its circumstances soon forced it to reach accommodations with the city on the taxation issue. With the advent of the Second World War came that upsurge in transit patronage that was to make the 1940s the most successful decade – in passenger volume and revenue – in North America since the early years of the century. After increasing by less than 1 per cent a year between 1933 and 1939,

TTC ridership rose by 9 per cent between 1939 and 1940 alone and had almost doubled by the end of the war. This increase, coupled with government restraints on spending for new equipment, contributed to a rapid increase in both gross and net revenues and brought renewed demands that the TTC turn over a larger portion of its revenues to the city. Leading this campaign was Toronto's board of trade, which claimed that the tax exemptions granted to the TTC were unfair to other ratepayers. After an unsuccessful attempt to get the city to say it would use increased tax revenues to make street improvements that would benefit transit, the TTC agreed to pay a tax on its buildings (but not on plant and equipment) plus a business tax.[77] It also continued to pay a share of costs for snow clearing and street paving, as well as 60 per cent of the costs of transporting war amputees and the blind – all charges not levied on private businesses.

The steady improvement in the TTC's financial position also brought renewed demands for a fare decrease. The commission successfully resisted by referring to the exigencies of the wartime situation and by voicing the opinion that the majority of patrons preferred improvements in speed, comfort, and conveneince to a small saving on fares.[78] It offered instead to contribute $750,000 toward street improvements that the city was unwilling to make. Council accepted the offer.

These belated financial concessions to city demands may have simply been an admission that TTC reserves were becoming too large to defend with the old arguments. More likely, however, they were intended to prepare council and the public to look favourably on a much more extensive modification to the local transportation system than any the TTC had promoted so far. That change was an outgrowth of another long-standing irritant in relations between the commission and the city government – the increasing use of the private automobile and the city's responses to it.

From the 1920s onward the automobile created two serious problems for transit operators. First, it contributed to a sharp decline in transit use and thus posed a serious threat to the long-term viability of local transit systems. The problem having more direct and immediate impact on transit politics, however, was its effect on day-to-day operations. Toronto was no different in this respect than other cities. As early as 1921 H.E. Blair had identified traffic congestion and on-street parking as factors inhibiting street railway operations. Judge Denton and Albert Richey had made the same point in their later evaluations of the Toronto system. And the TTC itself undertook very early to educate the city's government and citizens to the adverse effects of traffic congestion on street railway movement and to recommend steps to alleviate it.

The task was never easy. There was strong resistance to parking restrictions, especially from local merchants, and the defenders and promoters of automotive interests multiplied quickly. In 1926 the TTC actually withdrew from the Toronto Traffic Board, a committee set up by council to study traffic problems, hinting at a 'conflict of opinion' between a body representative of the general public and one representative of 'special interests.'[79] Those 'special interests' already included the Ontario Motor Truck Owners Association, the Ontario Motor League, and the Toronto Automobile and Trades Association, as well as representatives of business and commercial associations. The TTC renewed its campaign for traffic regulation in 1929 and 1930, however, in the face of criticisms of congestion and delays on its own lines. The city responded with several measures to restrict parking and control the flow of downtown traffic, although not as wholeheartedly as the TTC would have liked.[80] Council had decided by this time that the problem of congestion called for more draconian solutions, for in 1929 it appointed an Advisory City Planning Commission to consider large-scale improvements to the downtown street system.

The report prepared by the commission dealt principally with improvements of much more obvious benefit to automobiles than to public transit – to the point of calling for the removal of streetcar tracks from some streets altogether. The first two versions of the report did not ignore transit entirely, however, for they suggested that the best way to remove congestion on Yonge Street would be to replace surface streetcars with an underground subway.[81] The first draft contained the additional suggestion that subways built to relieve surface congestion and assist automobile movement should not be a charge on transit users, but should be considered part of the costs of maintaining city streets. The city's department heads quickly dismissed this suggestion as financially impracticable and scarcely relevant to the report – in marked contrast to their enthusiastic reception of the report's proposals for arterial road improvements.[82] These, they said, would be a proper charge on taxpayers because of the great benefits they would bring to the city. The version of the report that finally reached council in 1931 carried no reference to subways at all.[83] None the less the board of control asked the TTC to comment on the idea. Its chairman told the board that subways could not be built without the city's financial help, but pointed out that a double-track subway would transport the same number of people as could be carried on as many as ten streets used entirely for free-wheel traffic.[84] The city should make the financial comparison, therefore, before deciding where to invest its money.

The times were not conducive to large commitments of any kind, however, and council retreated to a position of supporting only those street and traffic improvements that involved no capital outlays. Congestion continued to increase. At the end of the decade the TTC acted on its own, hiring two consultants to study subway alternatives. One of these was Norman D. Wilson, a Toronto-based consulting engineer who had been director of the short-lived Advisory City Planning Commission (1929–30) and was undoubtedly the author of the controversial subway idea. Wilson was well acquainted with both the city's transportation system and the problems of the transit industry in general, for he had advised the city on transportation matters in the years preceding public takeover, had served the TTC as engineer of traffic study in the years immediately following, and had been a transportation consultant to several cities in South America.[85] He would become not only one of the principal architects of Toronto's first subway but also one of the most vigorous advocates of public transit to participate in Toronto planning circles in the two decades that followed.

The beginning of the TTC's subway study coincided with the upsurge of transit patronage that followed the advent of the Second World War. It was not long, therefore, before the TTC staff and consultants were able to convince the commission that traffic on the Yonge line had increased to the point where it was advisable to separate it from other traffic, preferably by putting it underground. The commission agreed. It hired DeLeuw Cather, a Chicago-based engineering firm, to advise and direct the project and set up a rapid transit department to work with him.[86]

Planners began with the assumption that post-war traffic would quickly fall back to pre-war levels and looked first at a system that conformed to the Boston model, with streetcars running in depressed or buried rights-of-way. Wilson soon convinced his colleagues of the inadequacy of this approach by pointing out that such a system could not accommodate any increase in demand that might accompany the city's growth. The group then produced a rapid transit plan that included a full subway along Yonge Street (with a capacity of 40,000 persons per hour), convinced the city's newly constituted planning board to incorporate it into the city's first master plan (1943), and set out to win the support of the commission, the public, and the city government.

It was a challenging task. Despite transit's wartime revival, most transportation experts clung to the opinion that the day for large-scale investments in this mode had passed. The job now was to serve the automobile. Even transit supporters insisted that a city needed a population of 1 million to support a subway, and Toronto had fewer than 700,000 people at the time. (The population of the metropolitan area was approaching 1 million, however.) Commission members had already said publicly that Toronto did not need a full subway, that a streetcar subway would do. Staff persuaded them to change their minds by pointing out that the cost of building a full subway ($35.5 million) was not substantially higher than the cost of an underground streetcar line (about $30 million), that operating costs on the subway would be lower, and that a subway would yield extra advantages in the form of increased speed, savings in loading time, increased convenience, and fewer accidents.

Once the commission had accepted these arguments it threw its energies into a vigorous campaign to win community support. It prepared an illustrated brochure and arranged meetings with local businessmen, bankers, and representatives of local trust companies, service clubs, and church groups, where it stressed the financial and other benefits that a subway would bring to the city. When it finally turned its attention to council, it found that its aggressive tactics might backfire. Council members were irritated at having been bypassed for so long, and the mayor was telling the board of control that not one five-cent piece would be spent on this folly.

The moment of truth came on 30 November 1945, when council met to decide whether the matter should go to the city's voters. As time for a decision approached the outcome began to look increasingly doubtful. Then the meeting took a dramatic turn. In the words of a participant:

Things weren't going well. The Mayor, the Board of Control, the Council were opposed. Then one of the aldermen said, 'I understand, Mr. McBrien, that you have a consultant here from Chicago. I would like to hear from him'. DeLeuw talked about the dilemma of transportation in the United States. 'It all started with automobiles,' he said. 'We developed a system of federal intercity highways to accommodate automobiles. The cities had very poor roads. Aggressive legislators managed to get state funds to help pave city streets. Then there were so many cars in cities that it led to unacceptable congestion. Some cities have gone after state and federal government funds to support public transit. (He gave Chicago's State Street subway as an example.) It's the way cities are going to have to go. We can't solve our problems with highways and automobiles. We need public transit.'

Then the alderman said, 'Are we going to let this happen to Toronto? Or are we going to be progressive legislators?' He won over the whole council.[87]

Thus it was that council decided by unanimous vote to take the matter to the city's electors, who gave their overwhelming assent to the following question: 'Are you in favour of the Toronto Transit Commission proceeding with the proposed Rapid Transit System provided the Dominion Government assumes one-fifth of the cost, and provided that the cost to the ratepayers is limited to such amounts as the City Council may agree are necessary for the replacement and improvement of city services?'[88] The wording is significant, for it implies that all of Mr DeLeuw's persuasive powers would have done little to further the TTC's plans had it not been for two important factors. One was the $25 million that the TTC had managed to accumulate in its reserve accounts by the end of the war. The second was an indication that the dominion government was prepared to include 20 per cent of the costs of subway construction in a projected program of financial aid to alleviate the effects of an expected post-war depression. The prospect of that assistance had allowed the TTC to strengthen its appeal to the city government before the crucial council vote by withdrawing a request that the city 'contribute to the cost of the Rapid Transit project by acquiring and paying the cost of and incidental to the properties required for the rights-of-way.'[89]

The expected depression failed to materialize and so did the dominion government's contribution. Before many years had passed the TTC had to ask the city to borrow once again to secure what its commission had determined was 'an adequate system of street railway transportation,' even as it paid off the last of the debt incurred for that purpose in 1921. By the time it made that request the subway was already under construction and the city could not easily refuse. It would be more than a decade, however, before the system's new owners (the Metropolitan Toronto Council) would reluctantly act in accordance with the principle introduced into and later dropped from the Advisory City Planning Commission's Report of 1930 and later rejected by the city during its consideration of the TTC's subway proposal in 1945: that the subway was an underground street that benefited all kinds of traffic and so should be a charge on the whole community, not just on transit users.[90] This is hardly surprising, for local politicians and city officials first had to give up an idea that had persisted in the city since the days of private street railway operation: that a public transit system should be a source of financial support for the city government, and not the other way around.

There was nothing remarkable about the way the Toronto Transportation Commission conducted its affairs during the thirty years that followed its creation in 1920. It pursued practices that were generally considered necessary to the financial health of any enterprise of its type – gearing level of service to level of demand, replacing old equipment when it was no longer serviceable but repairing equipment that could still be used, and trying to avoid commitments that threatened to bring a low or negative rate of financial return. If it had followed these practices alone it would have seemed 'conservative' in the extreme. It did more, however. It expanded its operations in directions that seemed speculative or unorthodox at the time, but that later attested to an astute assessment of urban development trends and their long-term implications for the city's transportation system. The investment in Gray Coach Lines was one such venture, the Yonge Street subway another. Thus the agency took risks, but prudent ones, in the interest of protecting or enhancing the value of the properties entrusted to its care.

Even the most ardent devotee of private enterprise would have to concede, then, that the TTC's approach to its responsibilities was sound. What was truly remarkable about the TTC's record was its ability to take that approach during a period when most transit agencies, both public and private, had neither the financial security nor the operating flexibility to behave in a similar way. Four factors help to account for that achievement. One was a legal mandate so generous and imprecise in its wording that it left the commission with a good deal of freedom to decide where its duty lay. A second was a large measure of freedom from city taxation, which allowed the commission during prosperous times to deposit surplus earnings into reserve accounts. It later used these to offset losses during periods of depression and to make improvements to its plant and equipment. A third was the consensus reached between the commission and its staff about the principles that should guide the decisions of such an agency. That consensus broke down only once, with damaging consequences for the TTC and its relations with the community. At other times it allowed the commission to devote its energies to persuading, cajoling, or educating the city government and the public to recognize the merits of its activities. The fourth factor made it easier than it might have been to tailor those activities to the agency's financial requirements. This was a 1918 city council decision not to annex additional territory unless its owners were prepared to pay the full cost of servicing it. The immutability of the city's boundaries allowed the TTC to serve suburban districts on a 'cost of service' basis while maintaining a uniform fare within the city – to operate a zone fare system in the lower-density parts of the urban area, in other words, by making use of the operating latitude provided in its original mandate.

The TTC had no guarantee that any of these factors would persist. There were always elements within the community who wanted to divert a larger share of TTC revenue to city or other purposes or to impose a service philosophy that elevated demand-responsiveness over revenue stabilization. Two additional factors prevented these elements from effecting fundamental changes in the TTC's operating mandate or in the ideological bias of its governing board. One was the large debt that the city had incurred to launch the operation and its government's determination that the transportation system should not become either a charge on city taxpayers or a liability to the city's credit or the city's reputation. The second was the political importance attached to transit fares and the reluctance of local politicians to provoke the TTC into making a fare increase for which they might be held accountable.

Toronto's high stake in its public transportation system did play a role in that system's development, then, but less as an incentive to city support for new and better services than as a deterrent to political interference and financial exploitation. This does not mean that the commission was able to ignore the political implications of its own behaviour, for it remained a convenient target for politically motivated attacks by those who sensed any stirrings of public dissatisfaction with its performance. The TTC usually managed to neutralize such attacks by conducting its affairs in a manner that withstood careful scrutiny and by adhering to a set of performance criteria that gave it a comparative advantage over other operators of its type. While these criteria never allowed the commission to depart very far from its financial objectives, they did include a standard of equity that required it to assess requests for new service in terms of the level of service already available to the residents of other areas. The application of that standard helped to make transit accessible to virtually everyone in the city in a relatively short period of time and may have helped build a base of support within the community.

Public support never amounted to an unequivocal political expression of preference for mass transit, however. Toronto residents switched to automobiles even in periods of economic depression, and Toronto's public officials seemed as ready as officials elsewhere to respond to that trend with measures that discriminated against public transit in favour of the newer mode. It was only because the TTC succeeded so well in persuading them to fear the financial consequences of ignoring its requirements that it was able to accumulate the funds necessary to improve the system in ways that helped it to meet the automotive challenge. If it had not managed to do this it is doubtful if Toronto would have replenished its streetcars or built a subway when it did, and the subsequent development of its transportation system might have been very different.

NOTES

1 Toronto Transportation Commission *Wheels of Progress* 5th ed (Toronto 1953) 23, 25
2 Harold Kaplan *Urban Political Systems* (New York and London 1967) 131–2
3 Michael J. Doucet 'Mass Transit and the Failure of Private Ownership: The

Case of Toronto in the Early Twentieth Century' *Urban History Review* No. 3–77 (1978) 3–33

4 Donald F. Davis 'Mass Transit and Private Ownership: An Alternative Perspective on the Case of Toronto' *Urban History Review* No. 3–78 (1979) 60–98

5 City of Toronto Archives (hereafter CTA), Toronto City Council Minutes (hereafter Minutes), 1919, Apendix A, 1762–3

6 Metropolitan Toronto Transportation Plan Review *Strengths and Weaknesses* Part I *Public Transportation* (Toronto 1973) 28

7 The following works provide alternative perspectives on the nature of the difficulties and their underlying causes: Christopher Armstrong and H.V. Nelles *The Revenge of the Methodist Bicycle Company* (Toronto 1977); Christopher Armstrong and H.V. Nelles 'Suburban Street Railroad Strategies in Three Canadian Cities: Montreal, Toronto, and Vancouver, 1890–1920' paper prepared for the Conference on Canadian-American Urban Development, Guelph, Ontario, 27 August 1982; Davis 'Mass Transit'; Doucet 'Mass Transit'; F.S. Spence 'Some Suggestions as to Toronto Street Railway Problems' in Paul Rutherford ed *Saving the Canadian City: The First Phase 1880–1920* (Toronto 1974) 59–63

8 The orthodox view owes much to Sam Bass Warner, Jr *Streetcar Suburbs: The Process of Growth in Boston, 1870–90* (Cambridge, Mass, 1978). For a more general treatment of the same idea, see Charles N. Glaab and A. Theodore Brown *A History of Urban America* 2nd ed (New York 1976) 148–9.

9 See *The Charter of the Toronto Railway Company Together with Subsequent Statutes, Agreements and Judgements Relating to the Said Company and the Corporation of the City of Toronto: From April 14, 1882 to December 8, 1905* (Toronto 1906).

10 I have inferred the city's position on the matter of radial entrances from the advice given council at the time, together with the fact that no agreement was reached. See W.T. Jennings 'Report on Electric and Steam Railways, also the Marsh Area,' Minutes, 1903, Appendix C, 11, and 'Letter from R.C. Harris, Property Commissioner, to E. Coatsworth, Mayor,' Minutes, 1906, Appendix A, 1306–7. For a discussion of differences in the approaches taken to suburban service in Montreal, Vancouver, and Toronto, see Armstrong and Nelles 'Suburban Street Railway Strategies.'

11 Donald N. Dewees 'The Decline of the American Street Railways' *Traffic Quarterly* XXIV (1970) 574–8; Mark Foster 'City Planners and Urban Transportation, The American Response, 1900–1940' *Journal of Urban History* V (May 1979) 365–96; Stanley Mallach 'The Origins of the Decline of Urban Mass Transportation in the United States, 1890–1930' *Urbanism Past and Present* VIII (summer 1979) 8–14; Wilfred Owen *The Metropolitan Transportation Problem* (Washington, DC, 1956) 67–89

12 In the United States the problems had become so acute by the end of the First World War that President Wilson appointed a special commission to investigate them. Its *Proceedings* constitute a thorough examination of the way different interests viewed the state of the industry and the remedies they prescribed for it. See *Proceedings of the Federal Electric Railways Commission* 3 vols (Washington, DC, 1920).

13 'Toronto Railway Company Profit and Loss Account' 28 September 1922; CTA, R.V. Harrison Papers, 'Memorandum of Toronto Railway Company Revenue (Exclusive of Taxes)' 22 January 1936

14 See Minutes, 1918, Address of Mayor T.L. Church, Appendix C, 5. The Ontario Railway and Municipal Board was a provincially appointed commission established in 1905. Its principal function was to regulate municipal street railways and arbitrate disputes between those railways and municipal governments, but it also had more general responsibilities for municipal affairs. These latter powers were expanded in 1932 when the board's name was changed to the Ontario Municipal Board.

15 Ibid, Appendix A, 141–3

16 Ibid 871

17 See, for example, Address of Mayor T.L. Church.

18 Minutes, 1919, Appendix A, 1251

19 CTA, Harrison Papers, Letter to T.L. Church (Mayor) and Members of the Board of Control, 17 May 1921

20 Minutes, 1917, Appendix A, 874–5; Minutes, 1918, Appendix A, 879; Minutes, 1920, Appendix A, 755–8

21 'Report on Operating Costs and Revenues of Major Transit Companies' Toronto Civic Railway, 1921, a collection of papers, letters, memoranda, and statistics prepared for the Toronto Transportation Commission, Metropolitan Toronto Library

22 Ibid 'Report on Fares'

23 Toronto Transportation Commission *Blair Report on the Transportation problem in Toronto* (1921)

24 *Canadian Railway and Marine World* XXIV (1921) 486–7

25 Ibid

26 Ibid XXVI (1923) 404; XXVII (1924) 82–3

27 Ibid XXVI (1923) 234; XXVIII (1925) 192

28 Ibid XXVIII (1925) 626; CTA, Harrison Papers, Letter from D.W. Harvey, General Manager, Toronto Transportation Commission, to George H. Ross, Commissioner of Finance, City of Toronto, 20 April 1925; *Canadian Railway and Marine World* XXVIII (1925) 301

29 Toronto Transportation Commission *Fifth Annual Statement* December 1926

30 Minutes, 1926, Appendix C, 1–2

31 See the exchange of letters between H.C. Mitchell, Old Colony Trust Company, Boston, Mass, and D.W. Harvey, General Manager, Toronto Transportation Commission, 5 January and 10 January 1925 in CTA, Harrison Papers.
32 *Canadian Railway and Marine World* XXVIII (1925) 420, 464
33 Ibid XXV (1922) 580; XXVI (1923) 348; XXVII (1924) 38, 191
34 W.R. Plewman *Adam Beck and the Ontario Hydro* (Toronto 1947) 317–24
35 *Canadian Railway and Marine World* XXVIII (1925) 192, 301–3, 520
36 Ibid XXIX (1926) 197–8, 257, 548, 600–1
37 Ibid XXXII (1929) 515
38 Ibid XXVIII (1925) 365–6; XXX (1927) 227, 555
39 Ibid XXX (1927) 227; XXXII (1929) 245; Minutes, 1927, 7 March, Item 237
40 *Canadian Railway and Marine World* XXX (1927) 487–8, 612; XXXI (1928) 681, 746–7; XXXII (1929) 40, 455
41 Ibid XXXII (1929) 321–2; Minutes, 1929, Appendix A, 778–9
42 *Canadian Railway and Marine World* XXXII (1929) 321
43 Ibid XXXII (1929) 157
44 The account of the streetcar controversy and its outcome derives principally from Toronto Transportation Commission Judicial Investigation *Report of His Honour Judge Denton* (November 1929–March 1930), and Minutes, 1929, Appendix A, 1749–91.
45 Minutes, 1929, Appendix A, 1749–53
46 Ibid 1768–77
47 Ibid 1778–87
48 TTC Judicial Investigation *Report* 61, 9, 61, 27
49 Ibid 62
50 Ibid 63
51 Minutes, 1930, Appendix A, 1237–43
52 *Canadian Railway and Marine World* XXXIII (1930) 313; Minutes, 1930, 6 May, item 612; 20 May, item 673; 30 May, items 684, 685; 6 June, items 745–8; 16 June, item 777
53 Timothy Colton *Big Daddy* (Toronto 1980) 165; Kaplan *Urban Political Systems* 131
54 TTC Judicial Investigation *Report* 62; *Globe* 3 June 1931
55 CTA, Toronto City Council Papers, Toronto Transportation Commission, 'Notes regarding amended legislation of 1930 which requires City Council authority before the Toronto Transportation Commission or Gray Coach Lines Limited may establish or acquire a motor vehicle transportation service outside the limits of the City of Toronto,' 8 November 1935
56 *Canadian Railway and Marine World* XXXIX (1936); Minutes, 1936, Appendix A, 371–2
57 *Canadian Railway and Marine World* XXXIX (1936) 328, 173

58 CTA, Harrison papers, Private Memorandum to George Wilson from R.V. Harrison, 9 May 1933
59 Albert S. Richey *The Local Transportation Service of the Toronto Transportation Commission* (Worcester, Masachusetts, 1934)
60 *Canadian Railway and Marine World* XXXIII (1930) 38; Toronto Transportation Commission and Gray Coach Line *Ten Years of Progressive Public Transit Service* (Toronto 1931)
61 Minutes, 1925, Appendix A, 185–7; Minutes, 1927, Appendix A, 184–5; Minutes, 1928, Appendix A, 511–13; Minutes, 1929, Appendix A, 620–1; Minutes, 1930, Appendix A, 952–7; Minutes, 1931, Appendix A, 696–703; Minutes, 1933, Appendix A, 276–8
62 *Canadian Railway and Marine World* XXXIX (1936) 118
63 CTA, Toronto City Council Papers, 'Reports Submitted by Heads of Departments re Proposed Annexation of the Townships of York and East York,' March 1931
64 TTC 'Notes regarding amended legislation of 1930'
65 *Canadian Railway and Marine World* XL (1937) 360
66 CTA, Harrison Papers, Letter from D.W. Harvey, General Manager, Toronto Transportation Commission, to George Wilson, Commissioner of Finance, 24 October 1930, and Letter from City Auditor to William J. Stewart (Mayor) and Members of the Board of Control, 22 May 1931
67 *Canadian Railway and Marine World* XXXVII (1934) 357
68 Ibid XXXVIII (1935) 118
69 CTA, Harrison Papers, Letter from City Auditor, Commissioner of Finance, and City Solicitor to James Simpson (Mayor) and Members of the Board of Control, 17 December 1935; *Canadian Railway and Marine World* XXXVII (1934) 357
70 CTA, Harrison Papers, Letter from City Solicitor to the Mayor and Members of the Board of Control, 5 February 1936
71 *Canadian Transportation* XL (1937) 295
72 S.I. Westland 'The TTC PCC Story' *Upper Canada Railway Society Newsletter* No. 214 (November 1963) 161–74
73 *Canadian Railway and Marine World* XXXVI (1931) 522; XXXVII (1934) 73
74 CTA, Harrison Papers, Letter from P.W. Ellis, Chairman, Toronto Transportation Commission, to Thomas Foster (Mayor) and Members of the Board of Control, 'Division of Costs of Paving Maintenance,' 11 February 1925
75 CTA, Harrison Papers, Corporation of the City of Toronto versus the Toronto Transportation Commission, 'Copy of Reasons for Judgement of Kingstone, J., delivered October 29, 1936'
76 Minutes, 1939, Appendix A, 1812–14
77 *Canadian Transportation* XLIV (1941) 939; XLV (1942) 474

78 Ibid XLVI (1943) 375, 430, 431, 656

79 *Canadian Railway and Marine World* XXIX (1926) 495

80 Ibid XXXI (1928) 733; XXXIII (1930) 369; XXXIV (1931) 157

81 City of Toronto, Advisory City Planning Commission *Report with Recommen-dations for the Improvement of the Central Business Section* (Toronto 1929) 4. The manuscript of an earlier draft of this report, dated 11 February 1929, is contained in CTA RG265.

82 CTA, Toronto City Council Papers, 'Report of Civic Department Heads Re the Advisory City Planning Commission Report for the Improvement of the City of Toronto,' 1929

83 City of Toronto Advisory City Planning Committee *Report on Street Extensions, Widenings and Improvements* (Toronto 1930)

84 Minutes, 1931, Appendix A, 703–7

85 'Mr. Norman D. Wilson's Appointment' *Town Planning Institute of Canada Journal* VI (December 1928) 159

86 This account of events leading up to the decision to build the subway comes from three sources: W.E.P. Duncan 'Rapid Transit in Toronto' *Canadian Transportation* LII (1949) 673; Toronto Transportation Commission and DeLeuw Cather and Company *Report on Subways for the City of Toronto* (Toronto 1944); and interview with Walter Howard Paterson, retired general manager of Subway Construction, Toronto Transit Commission, 14 October 1976.

87 Interview with W.H. Paterson

88 Minutes, 1945, Appendix A, 269–70

89 Minutes, 1946, Appendix A, 481

90 W.E.P. Duncan 'Rapid Transit in Toronto'

GUNTER GAD and DERYCK HOLDSWORTH

Building for city, region, and nation

Office development in Toronto 1834–1984

Toronto's modern downtown silhouette in 1984, dominated by the CN Tower and the adjacent mass of tall bank towers, suggests a newfound status as Canada's financial and corporate capital. While some of the downtown structures do indeed symbolize Toronto's recent dominance over its earlier rival Montreal, most are merely the latest phase in a long process of creating more and more office space within which the economy of Toronto, Ontario, and much of Canada could be controlled.

Each phase of Toronto's economic growth produced landmark office buildings, and it is only familiarity with the silhouette of the most recent phase that makes earlier office structures seem inconsequential. The sleek towers of the last two decades were simply added to an already dense concentration of office buildings, including the thirty-four-storey Canadian Bank of Commerce building, in 1931 the tallest structure in the British Empire. While the Bank of Commerce tower marked Toronto's important role in the Canadian economy in the early twentieth century, the nine-storey Temple Building of 1895 announced the beginning of change in both building technology and the structure of Toronto's economy. Even in the middle of the nineteenth century, when the city's skyline was still dominated by its numerous church spires, office buildings were beginning to change land use patterns and the townscape.

This paper focuses on office buildings and the establishments that occupy them.[1] It examines their collective location within Toronto (particularly as that reflects the formation and expansion of office districts), size, appearance, and patterns of occupancy. Attempts to document the evolution of Toronto's office buildings and office districts have encountered a number of problems, particularly the availability of sources[2] and the ordering of an uneven stream of data, but the major challenge arises in interpreting or even periodizing 150 years of change. An understanding of office development in Toronto necessitates some knowledge of the city's changing role in the Canadian economy as well as the recognition that office development in Toronto is also an outcome of global economic transformations.

We would suggest that there are four stages in Toronto's economic history:[3] first, as colonial capital and the early centre for trade, transportation, and finance for an agricultural hinterland (1793 to the 1840s); second, as the centre for regional trade, transportation, and finance, with its own emerging industrial base (1840s–1880s); third, as a manufacturing centre with a parallel role as financial and head-office city for an increasingly larger area (1880s–1920s); and, fourth, as a national business centre (since the 1920s).

Much office growth, both in terms of employment and buildings, is simply the result of an ever-increasing division of labour or lengthening of production chains, throwing up an ever-increasing number of economic branches housed in both factories and offices. Increases in the size of firms, greater planning and control of production, and standardization of products or services have all profound implications for office development: the emergence of large-scale standardized production leads first to capital intensification in manufacturing, the relative if not absolute decline of blue-collar or production jobs, and the increase of white-collar jobs. In the second stage, white-collar work itself is affected by this dynamic: services produced by office workers (for instance life insurance policies) become standardized, and many aspects of office work become first mechanized and then automated. This second stage is quite well conceptualized in the context of the transition from entrepreneurial to corporate capitalism, which took place in the late nineteenth and early twentieth centuries.[4]

Since there is no general history or theory of the emergence of the white-collar labour force, we can present only tentative statements toward a meaningful framework of economic change relevant to the interpretation of office development in Toronto. However, the particular knowledge of offices in Toronto also becomes an interpretive link: ultimately, the Toronto examples are just as important in what they reveal of wider structural changes as they are in telling us about the fascinating place that was and is nineteenth- and twentieth-century Toronto.

Although offices constituted only a small part of the economy and landscape of Toronto in 1834, the study of the early town is more than appropriate, since most of the spatial dynamics concerning the emergence and enlargement of the nineteenth-century office concentrations were clearly visible. In 1833 there were only five structures that could be described as office buildings and only about 120 persons who could be called 'office workers.'[5] Most of these were government officials or government clerks and messengers, reflecting Toronto's role as colonial administrative centre in a thinly settled frontier agricultural region. Only large metropolitan centres (such as London, Paris, New York, or Boston) could boast of any sizeable set of banks, insurance companies, or other commercial office functions. The city directory for 1833–4 could list almost everybody working in offices, from the highest government official to the messenger. The government of Upper Canada was the largest employer of persons in offices. About fifty people worked for the executive council, the legislative council, the house of assembly, and various government departments or agencies. Most of these government offices were located in the Parliament buildings at Front and Simcoe streets, and a few of them in three other buildings in the vicinity (see Figure 1). Local affairs were directed by the lower courts and by the administration of the Home District. Most of these functions were housed in the court house, located at the northwest corner of King Street East and Church Street. About ten full-time officials and clerks had their offices there. Three other important government offices were the post office, the customs house, and the county registry office. Only one official is listed for each of these, and no clerks are documented.

The largest business office was the Bank of Upper Canada, with one cashier and ten clerks, tellers, and mesengers; a branch of the Commercial Bank of the Midland District had a cashier and two clerks. An exchange dealer completed York's financial phalanx! Apart from the Bank of Upper Canada, the only sizeable business office was that of the Canada Company,[6] employing two commissioners and eight other officers and clerks. There were also the offices of three land agents and about six newspapers. Although three British insurance companies were represented in Toronto in 1833, their agents were primarily involved with other businesses.

Only five buildings were designed with specific administrative or financial functions in mind: the Parliament buildings (built 1829–32), the court house (1824), the county registry office (1829), Osgoode Hall (1829–32),[7] and the Bank of Upper Canada (ca 1830). Although the Parliament buildings housed the largest number of 'office workers,' they, along with the court house and Osgoode Hall, were essentially meeting places rather than office buildings. The Bank of Upper Canada was in the style of a gentleman's house and contained the apartments of the cashier as well as the banking rooms. This leaves only the registry office as a 'pure' office building. All other office

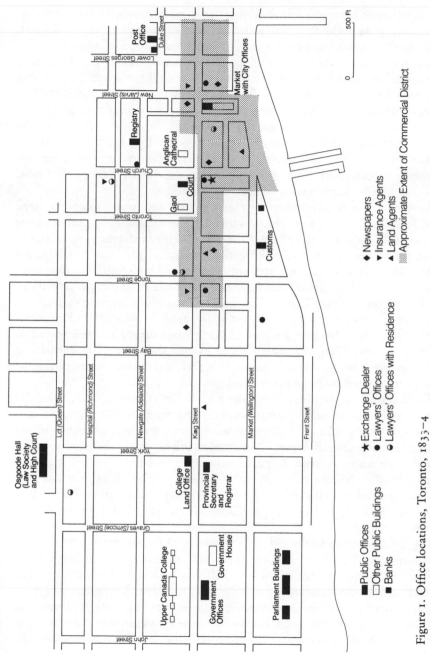

Figure 1. Office locations, Toronto, 1833–4

SOURCES: York Commercial Directory 1833–4; H.W.J. Bonnycastle and S.O. Tazewell *City of Toronto: The Capital of Upper Canada 1834* (lithographed map)

functions were conducted in buildings that were primarily residences or general-purpose buildings, in which retail, storage, manufacture, residential, and office functions were combined in various forms of admixture.

Although there was only one 'genuine' office building, an astonishing number of administrators, professionals, and clerks worked in premises separated from their residences. At least six of the thirteen barristers had offices separate from their residences, even if only three or four properties apart. The Parliament buildings, the court house, and some of the smaller government offices did not seem to contain any dwelling space, but both the post office and customs house also served as habitation for postmaster and customs collector, respectively. In the case of the other dozen or so offices, residence and business were generally combined.

Government and business offices were distributed over a relatively large area. This distribution, however, was by no means random. Most offices were found within a block of King Street (the principal business artery) and Church Street (as secondary artery, linking the wharf and the principal business street). There is also a clear spatial differentiation between offices that were primarily related to the commercial and daily life of the town and those conducting the affairs of Upper Canada. The local administration in the court house, the post office, and the customs house, as well as most of the barristers' and newspapers' offices were either on King Street east of Yonge Street or in its vicinity, occupying the most central part of the town. The Parliament buildings and other provincial offices, however, were at the western fringe of town, surrounded by large homes and gardens of the élite.

The juxtaposition of these two poles resulted in a dynamic that guided the direction of office development throughout the nineteenth century. Most of the new offices would be in the western part of the town rather than in the section east of Church Street. Also, those offices established before 1833 would later move westward. Parliament itself had been moved from the eastern to the western extremity of the town in the 1820s, the customs collector moved from the east to the centre in 1829, and the post office would follow in 1839, the Bank of Upper Canada in the 1860s, and eventually city hall in the 1890s.

The incorporation of the city of Toronto in 1834 was also marked by the establishment of the first city offices located in the market building at King and Jarvis streets. In 1844 a new city hall was built just to the south of the market, and for more than fifty years the neoclassical brick structure, together with the market, formed a distinct civic nucleus. However, fundamental economic changes in the second part of the nineteenth century made both the market and the modest city hall obsolete. The site, too, became obsolete: the expansion of wholesaling, retailing, and offices took place more and more to the west and northwest of the market and city hall, transforming the old civic and business nucleus into a marginal location.

Between 1834 and 1891 the population of the city of Toronto grew from about 9,000 to over 180,000. This dramatic increase was associated with the expansion of trading functions and financial services, and they in turn led to the formation of a central business district in the older, already developed part of the city. Throughout this period, offices played an increasingly important role in the articulation of the business district. In the early 1860s two spatially and (to a large degree) functionally distinct office concentrations were visible. By the early 1880s no fundamental changes had occurred, but many new office buildings were added to the two office concentrations. The 1880s, however, witnessed a departure from the patterns prevailing before.

After the government of the United Province of Canada was removed from Toronto in the 1840s, the city's economy did not collapse. Toronto had already established its role as regional trade centre, and this was to be consolidated in the 1850s through the construction of many railway lines. The most important economic activity of the regional trade centre, namely wholesaling, will be discussed briefly, before the office landscape is described as it presented itself in 1860, 1880, and around 1890.

Between the 1840s and 1880s wholesaling and related activities were the 'engine' for Toronto's economic growth.[8] Not only was the wholesale function important in terms of money earned for Toronto's economy, but it also spawned other businesses such as banks, insurance companies, building and loan societies, and settlement societies. It also played a considerable role in the expansion of Toronto's railway network.

The importance of the city's wholesale trade for the development of banking is particularly clear. In 1834 there was only one bank head office in Toronto and one branch of a Kingston bank. By 1862 there were two Toronto banks in existence, supplemented by seven branches of non-Toronto banks, and by 1880 the number of Toronto banks had increased to seven. In the case of at least four Toronto banks in existence in 1880, wholesalers either played the most important part or at least a vigorous role in establishing them.[9] The link in ownership was complemented by day-to-day functional links involved in financing imports and exports.[10] Toronto's wholesale merchants were also involved in the establishment of insurance companies, and, as in the case of banking, strong functional linkages seem to have existed between wholesalers and companies offering insurance related to transportation and storage.

The importance of wholesaling was partially reflected in the way offices fitted into the emerging central business district. By the early 1860s the principal wholesale quarters were found south of King Street, while King Street East between Jarvis and Yonge was the focus of most of the city's high-order retail establishments.[11] The wholesale district included several small office buildings and offices in buildings primarily constructed for wholesale businesses. The offices here were predominantly banks, insurance companies, and a variety of commercial agents. With one exception, all Canadian chartered banks represented in Toronto in 1861 could be found south of King Street, between Church and Bay, in the emerging wholesale district.

To the north of King Street a second concentration of offices overlapped with the King Street retail axis and the cluster of public buildings around Adelaide and Toronto streets. Only one of the chartered banks could be found here,[12] but most of the barristers, building societies, savings banks, and architects had their offices in this area. There were also many insurance companies and insurance agents, which were probably used by a wider spectrum of the population than the chartered banks.

While there were hardly any office buildings other than those of government in 1834, the 1840s and 1850s witnessed the appearance of the first purpose-built office structures for commercial users.[13] Bank and insurance company buildings were prominent among these new office buildings, along with the first multi-tenant, speculative office structures. One of the latter was the Masonic Hall, or Nordheimer Building, erected in 1857–8 on Toronto Street. With its bulkiness and Gothic styling, it inserted a more brash, energetic appearance into a street that had been solidly neoclassical to that point. Other multi-tenant office buildings were the Toronto Exchange on Wellington Street, the York Chambers on Toronto Street, and the Jordan Chambers at Jordan and Melinda.[14]

There seem to have been at least six purpose-built bank and insurance company premises in existence in 1861.[15] Most of these, like the Bank of Montreal building of 1845, were three storeys high and generally set back from the sidewalk. These small elegant bank and insurance company buildings resembled the gentlemen's clubs of London[16] and, at the time of construction in the 1840s, fitted into an élite residential area rather than an emerging wholesale district.

In 1861 at least five easily identifiable public office buildings were located in the business district: the city hall at the eastern edge; the customs house at Yonge and Front, wedged between wharfs to the south and the emerging wholesale district to the north; and the post office, registry office, and court house, all near the juncture of Toronto and Adelaide streets.

Royal Insurance Building, ca 1868. Built 1861, at the southeast corner of Yonge and Wellington streets, altered or demolished ca 1927. An early office building in the wholesale district (O. Thompson *Toronto in the Camera* [Toronto 1868])

TABLE 1

Separation of residences and offices, selected businesses or occupations, 1861

Business or occupation	Office and residence separate	Office and residence together	Uncertain	Total
Bank manager	4	4	1	9
Savings bank secretaries/treasurers	9	1	–	10
Assurance company managers, secretaries, etc	12	1	–	13
Barristers, solicitors	105	26	1	132
Accountants	8	10	–	18
Architects and civil engineers	7	3	–	10

SOURCE: City Directory 1861–2

Offices were also housed in general commercial buildings, especially those along the principal shopping streets such as King, Yonge, and Church. Here offices, together with small workshops and dwellings, occupied the second and third floors above shops. In addition, many houses on Toronto, Adelaide, and other streets near the core of the commercial area were exclusively used by one or several office establishments or had offices coexisting with dwellings or other uses.

Associated with the emergence of a number of specialized buildings is a remarkable development of home–work separation (see Table 1). Although most of the early bank buildings contained an apartment for the principal operating officer of the company – usually the cashier – by 1861 half of the bank managers no longer lived at their place of work.

Most of the lawyers lived separately from their places of work, and the key persons of some other businesses commuted to their offices. Particularly along Toronto and Wellington streets, small areas emerged without a residential population. Wholesalers had also begun to move away from their places of business, a process that was virtually completed by 1876.[17] This early process of home–work separation most probably preceded the development of public transportation. The first horse omnibus was introduced in the early 1850s, offering only a rudimentary one-line service. Tracked horse-streetcars were introduced in 1861, at a time when the home–work split was already well developed.

After 1861 office development slowed. Only two bank buildings were erected in the early 1860s (the Ontario Bank in 1862 and the Bank of Toronto in 1863), and then a pause set in until the end of the decade. This hiatus was followed by a boom, which seems to have lasted, in terms of the Toronto office scene, until 1890. Between 1869 and 1880 at least eighteen office buildings were constructed, most of them in the highly ornamented Second Empire and Gothic Revival fashions.[18] Almost all these buildings were three or four storeys high, although some of them could be recognized as five-storey buildings, if one included both semi-basement and attic floors (e.g. the Dominion Bank building of 1879). Generally, these buildings were still very small, typically 5,000 to 15,000 square feet (gross),[19] with only a few reaching 20,000 square feet.

By the 1880s the basic outlines of the business district already visible in the early 1860s were consolidated into a densely developed commercial area with distinct subareas (see Figure 2). Many of the row buildings erected between the 1830s and early 1850s were redeveloped for new structures; commercial buildings were erected on vacant lots and in garden spaces; and, in still other cases, houses were converted to business premises. Offices were an essential part of this remarkable intensification of land use, but the basic pattern of office location observable in the early 1860s was not altered.

The great majority of office buildings constructed between 1861 and 1880 were located in the wholesale district and the office concentration centred on Toronto Street. Several insurance company buildings were erected within the wholesale district, which by 1880 had reached its maturity. The whole area south of the King Street retail artery down to the north side of Front Street and stretching from the market at Jarvis Street in the east to Bay Street in the west was extremely densely developed, with wholesale warehouses, banks, insurance company buildings, and a few general-purpose office buildings. A similar density of buildings emerged on Toronto Street, which by 1880 had a single land use. Both sides of the street were exclusively lined with the façades of office buildings. At the northern end of this short street stood the splendid federal post office, built in the Second Empire style, flanked by more office buildings along Adelaide Street. On King Street West between Yonge and the west side of Bay some tentative incursions by office buildings were made, representing a deviation from the well-established spatial pattern. In the early 1870s the then Hamilton-based Canada Life Assurance Company erected a three-storey building, and in the late 1870s the Dominion Bank as well as two newspapers (the *Mail* and the *Evening Telegram*) moved into their new office buildings.

If office establishments are considered, irrespective of the kind of building they are accommodated in, a similar picture emerges (see Table 2): in 1880

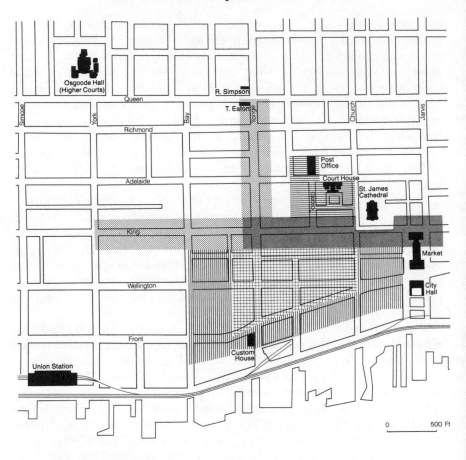

Functional Districts
▓ Principal Retail Street
░ Secondary Retail Street
‖‖ Wholesale District
▦ Wholesale and Offices
≡ Offices

Figure 2. Toronto's central business district, 1880

TABLE 2
Distribution in 1880 and 1914 of selected activities in downtown Toronto
(vertical line Yonge Street, horizontal, King)

	1880		1914	
Chartered banks	1	0	5	2
	5	6	10	2
Building and loan companies (1880), trust companies (1914)	1	15	5	7
	0	0	1	1
Insurance company offices	1	26	20	36
	0	17	7	42
Stockbrokers (members of the Toronto Stock Exchange)	1	11	8	7
	2	1	15	8
Law firms ('barristers')	7	120	106	140
	4	21	21	33
Chartered accountants	1	4	24	23
	2	8	14	20
Architects	3	19	13	28
	0	1	6	15

SOURCES: City Directories 1881 and 1915; Report of the Superintendent of Insurance 1880 and 1914; *Annual Financial Review* 1915

there were two principal concentrations east of Yonge Street (stretching only as far east as Church and contained by Front in the south and Lombard in the north), and a less dense concentration west of Yonge (stretching nearly to Bay, with King West as the northern boundary and Front as the southern edge). The northern part of the wholesale district, particularly Wellington and Yonge streets between Front and Colborne, was still the principal locale for the chartered banks (see Figure 3). Only two of them had King Street West addresses: the Montreal-based Molson Bank occupied part of the Canada Life Building, and the Dominion Bank, as mentioned above, had a new

Adelaide Street East between Victoria and Church ca 1880. Imperial Building (second from left), built ca 1876, demolished ca 1956; General Post Office (third from left), built 1869–73, demolished ca 1958. Both buildings are part of the late-nineteenth-century office district north of King Street East. (Michael Filey Collection)

head office building at the southwest corner of King and Yonge streets in 1879. King Street between York and Jarvis, especially the south side, was still the city's principal shopping street.

During the 1880s some important changes occurred: a new office concentration emerged on King Street West between Yonge and Bay, and the size of office buildings began to change dramatically. These new trends are the beginnings of the dramatic transformation of the business district, which occurred primarily after the recession of the 1890s and up to the beginning of the First World War.

The trend toward larger buildings was already visible around 1880. The *Mail* newspaper building had floor space of 37,000 square feet (gross), and its turret reached a height of 100 feet, dominating the silhouette around Bay and King. The North of Scotland Chambers and the Manning Arcade were built with broad frontages and façades organized in a modern grid fashion. Two other buildings of the mid-1880s are of interest, because they replaced older office premises: both the Bank of Montreal and the Bank of British North America buildings of 1845 were replaced by larger bank buildings in 1885. These were most probably the first instances of the redevelopment of office buildings for new office buildings; up to this date office buildings replaced dwellings and general commercial structures, or were even built on 'green' sites provided by ample garden space or undeveloped lots.

At the end of the 1880s, a short-lived boom set in, which produced the first set of 'modern' office buildings, six to seven storeys high, with between 50,000 and 75,000 square feet of (gross) floor space each.[20] The Toronto Board of Trade Building was the first one with a steel skeleton,[21] although this was masked by the customary stone façade. Confederation Life, in contrast, built a chateau-roofed building at the northeast corner of Richmond and Yonge that had immensely thick sandstone walls. The new structures, like most of the preceding general-purpose office buildings, were multiple-occupancy speculative buildings. The only novelty in this respect seemed to be the banks, which before 1880 generally had been sole occupants of their buildings. However, the Bank of Toronto of 1863, the Royal Canadian Bank of ca 1871, and the Dominion Bank of 1879 already had space for lease; the new Canadian Bank of Commerce building of 1889 continued this trend, with at least five of its seven floors for rent.

The new large buildings of the 1880s were predominantly found on King Street west of Yonge, signalling a major shift in the location of offices. By 1890 three of the banks, including the new head office of the Canadian Bank of Commerce, were located on King Street West, and in subsequent decades most of the banks would desert the nineteenth-century wholesale district and

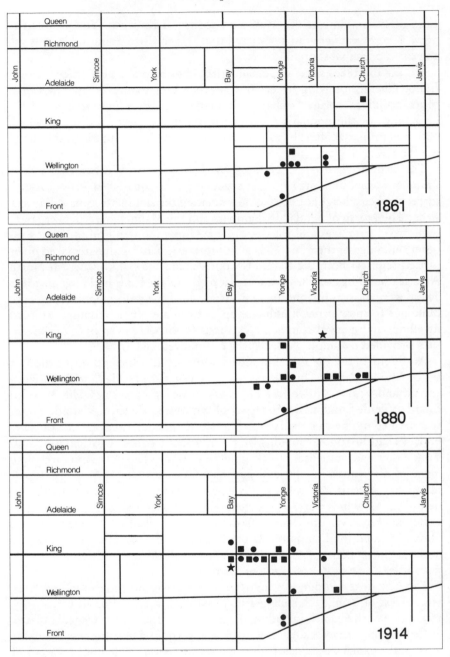

Figure 3. Bank and stock exchange locations, 1861–1984

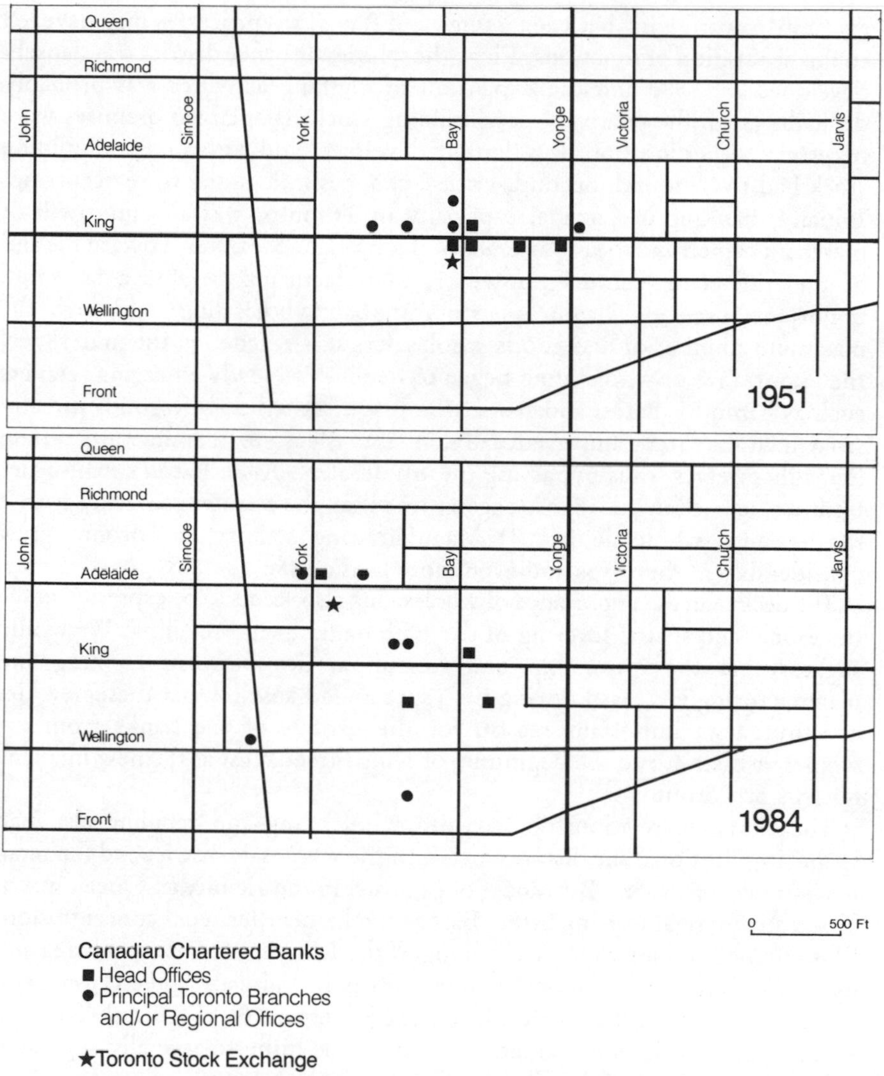

Queen
Richmond
John
Simcoe
Adelaide
York
Bay
Yonge
Victoria
Church
Jarvis
King
Wellington
Front
1951

Queen
Richmond
John
Simcoe
Adelaide
York
Bay
Yonge
Victoria
Church
Jarvis
King
Wellington
Front
1984

0   500 Ft

Canadian Chartered Banks
■ Head Offices
● Principal Toronto Branches
  and/or Regional Offices

★ Toronto Stock Exchange

gravitate toward King between Yonge and Bay. Two processes may have led to this separation of functions. First, the wholesale office district was densely developed by 1880 and the expansion of banking activities was probably difficult, given the relatively new building stock. If enlarged premises were necessary, other locations less densely developed and with an older building stock had to be found. Second, critical changes in banking were occurring. Initially, banking in Canada, especially in Toronto, was an outgrowth of merchant capital and the requirements of long-distance trade. Toward the end of the nineteenth century, however, manufacturing became a far more important force in Toronto's economy than wholesaling. Although the maximum number of dry-goods wholesalers was reached in the mid-1870s, the importance of wholesaling began to decline.[22] Newly emerging retailers such as Timothy Eaton and Robert Simpson started to buy goods directly from manufacturers and eventually, in the 1890s, to manufacture certain items themselves, thus bypassing the wholesalers. Also, Eaton's mail-order business, started in the 1880s, began to weaken the country store and with it the Toronto wholesale firm.[23] Manufacturing activity in Toronto grew considerably in the 1870s and even more in the 1880s.

The decline in the importance of wholesaling also seems to be expressed in the functional and spatial severing of ties with banking and retailing. We would suggest that the ownership and functional ties between banking and manufacturing increased during the 1870s and 1880s and that these new ties constituted an important reason for the exodus of the banks from the wholesale district and the beginning of King Street West as the new financial nucleus of Toronto.

The changing relationship between wholesaling and retailing also had spatial implications: the distance between the wholesale district and the retail nucleus became larger. By 1890 Yonge Street in the vicinity of Queen was at least a strong rival to King Street East as the high-order retail concentration. This competition led to the weakening of the King Street East retail area and its encroachment by offices. By 1890 offices had already spilled over from Toronto Street onto the north side of King Street East (see Figure 4). This was the first step in the amalgamation of the three hitherto spatially separated office nuclei into one fairly large office district by 1914.

Until the late 1880s offices, shops, and wholesale warehouses existed in architectural harmony. Almost all the office buildings, retail emporia, and the palaces of the wholesale merchant princes were built of stone or had stone façades at least. They were all a fairly uniform height of three or four storeys and had richly textured street façades. The office structures of the late 1880s started to rise above dwellings, shops, warehouses, and older office buildings.

King Street West between Bay and Yonge, ca 1926. Left to right: Cawthra House, built 1851–2 as residence, after 1885 used as office building, demolished ca 1946; Canada Life Assurance Building, constructed 1889, demolished ca 1946; and the John Kay store, built 1898. Commercial street with influx of first generation of large-scale office buildings in the 1880s (City of Toronto Archives, James Collection 7098)

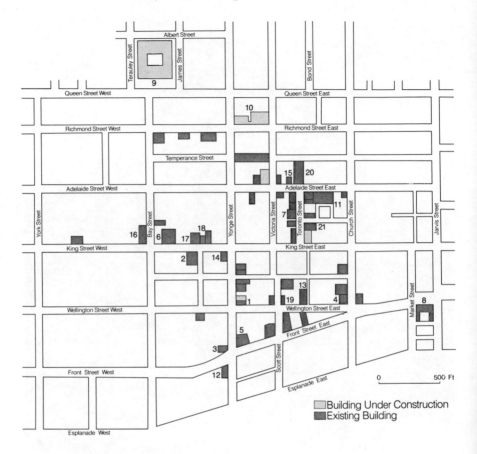

**Office Buildings Mentioned in Text
(with approximate construction dates)**

1 Bank of British North America (c. 1885)
2 Bank of Commerce Building (1889-90)
3 Bank of Montreal (1885-6)
4 Bank of Toronto (1863)
5 Board of Trade Buildings (1888-90)
6 Canada Life Building (1889-90)
7 Canada Permanent Buildings,
   originally Masonic Hall (1857-8)
8 City Hall (1844-5)
9 City Hall and Court House (1889-99)
10 Confederation Life Building (1890-2)
11 Court House (1852-3)

12 Custom House (1876)
13 Dominion Bank Chambers (1879)
14 Imperial Bank,
   originally Toronto Exchange (1855)
15 Imperial Loan Buildings (c. 1876)
16 Mail Building (c. 1880)
17 Manning Arcade (1884)
18 North of Scotland Chambers (1878)
19 Ontario Bank (1862)
20 Post Office Building (1869-73)
21 York Chambers,
   originally Gaol (converted c. 1850)

Figure 4. Distribution, 1890, of principal office buildings (10,000 or more square feet [gross] of office floor space)

They were, however, still of stone, still carrying on an old tradition. Many spots on the geological map of Canada, the northeastern United States, and Italy were represented in the building fabric of Toronto's office district. A wide variety of limestones, sandstones, granites, marbles, and more exotic stones, together with exotic woods, decorated the palaces of business.[24] They were also decorated with scrolls, swags, garlands, virile heads, and bare-breasted women, providing a sharp contrast to the stern looking, darkly clothed men standing at office desks. These small groups of men represented the 'old office.' In the subsequent period, much of the work inside the offices would start to change quite dramatically.

During the second half of the nineteenth century distinct concentrations of offices had become discernible; in the early years of the twentieth century these merged into a fairly large, cohesive office district. Most of the new office buildings appeared to the west of the old concentrations. Included with these additions was the first generation of skyscrapers, which marked a fundamental change in Toronto's silhouette: from now on the temples of commerce rose higher than the temples of God. These enormous changes in downtown Toronto are imbedded in the vigorous economic growth experienced by Canada at the turn of the century and also part of the transition from entrepreneurial to corporate capitalism.

The pace of development was not even between 1890 and the outbreak of the First World War. Although there was a noticeable slump in building activity during the 1890s, because of depressed economic conditions, these years saw an important transition in office development. The 9-storey Temple Building, at Richmond and Bay, was completed in 1895 as the head office of the Independent Order of Foresters, an insurance company. Together with the new city hall, begun in 1889 and ready for occupancy in 1899, it must have seemed like a beacon to the northwesterly expansion of the emerging office district. Between 1900 and 1914, Toronto was gripped by an unprecedented building boom. In 1906 the 15-storey Traders' Bank Building set a new record in height for non-religious buildings in Toronto. In 1913 the 15-storey Canadian Pacific Railway (CPR) Building was opened, followed in 1914 by the Dominion Bank Building with 10 floors. Finally, late in 1914 or early in 1915 the 20-storey Royal Bank Building was completed. Until the 1920s this was the largest of Toronto's office buildings.

Apart from these tall structures, many other office buildings of a more moderate scale were part of the changes that affected the streetscapes of the business district. About a dozen office buildings of between six and ten storeys, such as the Standard Bank Buildings on King Street West or the

Imperial Life Building on Victoria, added to the stock of office accommodation. Not all new important office buildings were necessarily tall. One of the most impressive with fewer than six floors was the Bank of Toronto head office building, erected in 1912–13. Its monumental *beaux arts* façade, stretching over 120 feet along King Street and 134 feet along Bay, made it one of the most notable features of the office district.

The area most profoundly affected by change was King Street between Church and Bay (see Figure 5). Here, not only were small older office buildings replaced by larger new ones, but also the sites of many shops and general commercial buildings were redeveloped for offices. On the north side of King Street East and on King Street West between Yonge and Bay, the fashionable retail shops that had been the pride of the 1880s were almost completely ousted. On the south side of King Street East the large King Edward Hotel complex began to break up the row of shops, and the CPR office building replaced stores at the southeast corner of King and Yonge. Henceforth, Toronto's principal retail district expanded around the intersection of Queen and Yonge, separate from the office district.[25] The new King Street office artery forged the concentrations on Toronto Street, Wellington Street East, Wellington Street West, and King Street West into one office district. New office construction also occurred on Bay Street between Melinda and Queen, and at Victoria and Adelaide, as well as at various other points. Church Street remained a stable eastern boundary,[26] although in the area just west of Church and south of King the first signs of decline of office activity and wholesaling had set in by 1914. Together with the offices already existing in 1890, the new stock formed a district reaching from Front to Queen and from Church to the west side of Bay.

Associated with the formation of the office district was a new distribution pattern of the various kinds of office activities (see Table 2). The most conspicuous was the new banking cluster on King Street (see Figure 3). By 1914, twelve of Canada's chartered banks had either their head office or principal Toronto office there. In the short stretch of King Street West between Yonge and Bay were seven bank head offices and three principal Toronto offices. The south side was completely dominated by banks: starting at Yonge and walking toward Bay one could pass the office buildings of the Dominon Bank, the Standard Bank, the Canadian Bank of Commerce, the Quebec Bank, the Bank of Nova Scotia, the Union Bank, and, finally, the Bank of Toronto. Six of the seven buildings occupied by these banks were constructed between 1902 and 1914. It would be wrong to describe this artery only in terms of financial activities. Most of the bank buildings were fairly large and housed a multitude of tenants.

Figure 5. Construction in the central business district 1890–1914: distribution of principal office buildings (six or more floors or with 20,000 or more square feet [gross] of office floor space)

Office Buildings Mentioned in Text
(with approximate construction dates)

1 Bank of Nova Scotia (1902-4)
2 Bank of Toronto (1911-3)
3 Canadian Northern Building (1890)
4 C P R Building (1911-3)
5 City Hall and Court House (1888-99)
6 Dominion Bank Building (1913-4)
7 Imperial Life Building (1911-2)

8 Royal Bank Building (1913-4)
9 Standard Bank Building (1910-1)
10 Temple Building (1895)
11 Toronto General Trusts Building (1910-1)
12 Toronto Stock Exchange (1912-3)
13 Traders' Bank Building (1905-6)
14 Union Bank Chambers (1910-1)

The King Street banking cluster was partially the result of the arrival of newcomers, such as the Royal Bank and the Bank of Nova Scotia, and partially the result of relocations within Toronto's business district. The most spectacular of these moves took the Bank of Toronto half a mile from the eastern edge of the office and wholesale cluster at Church and Wellington to the western 'frontier' of office development at Bay and King in 1913. The northwest shift of banks was accompanied by the move of two key institutions in the downtown activity system. In 1913 the Toronto Stock Exchange moved from King Street East (near Toronto Street) to Bay just south of King Street West, where it stayed for seventy-one years until it moved one block northwest in 1983. City hall had already moved at the end of the 1890s; parallel to the move of municipal government from Jarvis and Front to Queen and Bay was the move by the county courts from Toronto and Adelaide to the new city hall. The move of these key institutions undoubtedly helped to shift associated activities, such as stockbrokers and lawyers, from the area east of Yonge Street to the area west of it. Indeed, by 1914 the distribution pattern for most kinds of office activities was fairly evenly balanced on either side of Yonge Street (see Table 2).

Beyond documenting the changes in building stock and office location patterns, it is important to relate these to the rapidly rising demand for office space and, above all, to the increasing diversity of the 'content' of the office district. In order to do this, we must pay some attention to Canada's 'great transformation,'[27] involving western settlement, new resource exploitation, and vigorous industrial growth, and to the transition from entrepreneurial to corporate capitalism.

Western settlement had a great impact on banking. Both the Montreal- and Toronto-based banks developed large branch systems west of Ontario between 1890 and 1914.[28] The Toronto-based Canadian Bank of Commerce, for instance, opened its first branch west of the Ontario border in 1893 (in Winnipeg) and by 1914 had opened almost 200 branches in the Canadian west.[29] Each branch manager was required to submit weekly reports on crop conditions, employment prospects, and other aspects of economic activity,[30] and it is not difficult to imagine the avalanche of paper work descending on the Toronto head office. Settlement, land, trust, and insurance companies located in Toronto's office district also took part in western expansion, and their involvement probably meant increases in office staff in Toronto. The prairie boom encouraged a Toronto syndicate to build a third Canadian transcontinental line, the Canadian Northern Railway;[31] its head office, also involved in railway and electric light companies in South America, employed a large office staff in several buildings at King and Toronto streets.

Union Bank Building, ca 1915. Built ca 1910–11 at southwest corner of King West and Bay; later steel frame incorporated in Imperial Bank head office building. Toronto General Trusts Building, right, constructed ca 1910–11, later demolished. Both from consolidation phase (1900–15) of King West office district. (Royal Bank of Canada Archives)

The connection between the development of mining on the Canadian Shield and the development of offices in Toronto is equally striking. In 1881 no mining companies were listed in the classified section of Toronto's city directory; in 1891 there were 4; and in 1915, 73 were listed. Similarly, the number of mining engineers expanded from 2 in 1891 to 16 in 1915. Apart from these offices, the development of mining also meant the appearance of all kinds of companies specializing in machinery, general supplies, or the construction of mines.[32] A further impact of mining on demand for office space was felt through the increased activity in stock trading. Trading on the Toronto Stock Exchange expanded so much that by 1913 new quarters had to be found. Also, two new exchanges were formed as a result of the discovery of gold in northern Ontario: the Toronto Stock and Mining Exchange (1896) and the Standard Stock and Mining Exchange (1897),[33] and the number of firms listed in the city directory as stockbrokers increased from 31 in 1891 to 87 in 1915.[34] The links between the office district and the north are also suggested in the publications of and for the business community. The *Year Books* of the Toronto Board of Trade between 1910 and 1915 contain many drawings and photographs of new office buildings, while at the same time providing news and commentaries regarding Ontario's mineral wealth.[35] The *Toronto Annual* similarly juxtaposes the new high-rise office buildings at King and Yonge with a photograph of mining prospectors moving their canoes through the northern wilderness.[36]

Another aspect of rapid economic expansion at the turn of the century involved the enormous growth of manufacturing. In Toronto manufacturing accounted for about 26,000 jobs in 1891, about 42,000 in 1901, and 65,000 by 1911.[37] The growth of manufacturing in southern Ontario in general, as well as in Toronto, resulted in yet another facet of Toronto's office complex. The maturing of industrial activity was associated with the introduction of electricity and a wide range of electrical machinery, the appearance of the internal combustion engine and related products such as tires and gasoline, and the adoption of new materials such as chemicals or aluminum. The content of downtown Toronto offices reflected these changes. There one could find in 1914, for instance, the Hydro-Electric Power Commission of Ontario, Canadian Westinghouse, General Electric of Sweden, Siemens of Canada, Rolls Royce, Imperial Oil, Canadian Aniline and Chemicals, or Northern Aluminum next to firms involved in more traditional products such as Sun Brick, Canada Malting, or Rolland Paper.[38]

The demand for increasing amounts of office space originated from the addition of new firms within existing kinds of businesses (e.g. more law firms, architects, or stock brokers),[39] the addition of new industries (e.g. offices of manufacturers, mining companies, or consulting engineers),[40] and the growth of already existing firms (e.g. banks, insurance companies, or law firms). The rapid growth of a small number of companies to unprecedented size was an international phenomenon at the turn of the century, and the rise of large corporations had profound implications for office development in large cities of most western countries. In a competitive environment, companies attempted to secure their profitability and survival through attempts to control an increasing market share or to enlarge their market by branching out into new territory. An expression of the attempt to secure safe markets were the two waves of mergers that took place in various branches of the Canadian economy, between 1899 and 1914 and again through most of the 1920s.[41] Banking was especially affected by mergers, with the number of Canadian chartered banks decreasing from 37 in 1899 to 22 at the end of 1914.[42] Together with their expansion in the Canadian west and into other countries, mergers transformed a number of Canadian banks from regional businesses into national and even international organizations. The Canadian Bank of Commerce, for instance, absorbed four Canadian chartered banks between 1900 and 1912 and had six branches in the United States, Mexico, and the United Kingdom by 1911.[43] Life insurance companies grew only slightly through mergers, but expanded aggressively outside Canada between the mid-1890s and 1914.[44]

The merger wave gripped manufacturing between 1909 and 1913 and many nineteenth-century family enterprises or small partnerships were reorganized into a few dominant corporations. Among the results were new offices in the business districts of Toronto and Montreal. An example in Toronto was the office of the Provincial Paper Company, formed in 1913 out of three different firms. Other examples of newly formed large corporations with offices near King and Yonge were the Lake Superior Corporation (steel), the Maple Leaf Milling Company (flour), and the Canadian General Electric Company.[45]

The struggle for larger markets was also expressed in the attempts to broaden the range of customers. Although the first 'city branch' of a bank was opened in 1871 in Toronto, these kinds of branches were still infrequent in 1890.[46] By 1914, however, bank branches could be found at almost every major street corner and life insurance companies had also begun to develop branch systems within Toronto.[47] Henceforth, bank and insurance company branches took part in every wave of urban expansion and office decentralization.

Finally, the quest for larger markets led to the establishment of new types of business services. The most prominent example is the spread of advertising agencies. In 1890 there were only five of these in Toronto; by 1914 their number had increased to 38,[48] among them J. Walter Thompson and several other American firms. These US firms in Toronto by 1914 are a reminder that not only did manufacturing, mining, banking, and insurance become part of an international network, but also business service firms.

The transformation of business from relatively small companies, mostly owned and operated by families, to large corporations is frequently described with reference to the terms entrepreneurial (or high) capitalism versus corporate (or late) capitalism. It was this transition that was at the base of the growing demand for office space and the articulation of the whole collectivity of office establishments into an increasingly complex array of activities. In what specific ways was this transition linked to the emergence, by 1914, of the large new office buildings?[49]

The growth of large corporations did not translate immediately into large office establishments. In 1914, few offices in Toronto had more than 50 employees and only very few had more than 100.[50] There were only about a half-dozen head offices with 100 to 200 employees. The combined head office and main branch of the Canadian Bank of Commerce, probably Toronto's largest non-government office establishment, employed about 150 people. The head offices of Canada Life and Manufacturers' Life insurance companies may have employed about 100 persons each,[51] the CPR had about 100 employees in its skyscraper at Yonge and King, and both the Canadian Northern Railway group of companies and Consumers Gas may have had office staffs of over 100 in the King Street East and Toronto Street precincts. The other large bank establishments had between 50 and 100 employees, and two other bank head offices employed only about 25 and 15 persons each.

The largest buildings in this new generation of structures, often known by a corporate name, were in effect oversized with respect to that company. Almost all the large office buildings were occupied by dozens of different establishments (Table 3). Only the large banks and insurance companies occupied more than two floors. Few establishments occupied an entire floor; most were shared by several tenants, and it was not uncommon to have up to ten on a fully rented floor. There was not only a plethora of small law offices, advertising agencies, stockbrokers, and agents of various kinds, but also many small insurance companies.

Offices of manufacturing companies were also very small. Although Toronto was increasingly an industrial city, very few Toronto firms had a significant white-collar work-force by 1914. Office functions seemingly remained on or near the actual production site. If head offices were downtown, they did not seem to involve more than ten persons in most cases. Many of them were even smaller, and quite often one can find several head

TABLE 3

Selected office buildings: Completion date, size, and occupancy in 1914

Name of building	Date of completion	Approximate number of floors	Approximate floor space (gross, in square feet)	Tenants (1914)
Manning Arcade	1884	5	27,000*	24
Board of Trade	1890	7	50,000	44
Canadian Bank of Commerce	1890	7	50,000	2
Canada Life	1890	7	75,000	23
Temple	1895	9†	100,000	44
Traders Bank	1906	15	130,000	100
CPR	1913	15	100,000	49‡
Bank of Toronto	1913	5	75,000	5
Dominion Bank	1914	10	160,000	39‡
Royal Bank	1914	20	200,000	138§

*Without annex
†In 1901 a tenth floor was added
‡Many vacancies, including one full floor
§In 1921
SOURCES: 1915 City Directory; City of Toronto assessment rolls: 1890 for 1891 and 1914 for 1915; Goad's (fire insurance) atlases; E. Arthur *Toronto: No Mean City* (Toronto 1964); W. Dendy *Lost Toronto* (Toronto 1978); I. Franco *Tall Buildings in Toronto, 1889–1930* (Toronto 1979)

offices of manufacturing companies on the same floor of one of the large new office buildings together with several other kinds of office establishments.[52] In the case of the newly emerging giant corporations, of which both street directories and assessment rolls give abundant evidence, the downtown offices were even smaller: boiler manufacturer Babcock and Wilcox was represented by one person, Siemens of Canada by three, and Canadian Westinghouse by seven (including five travellers!). The downtown Toronto offices of these companies were obviously not much more than sales offices.[53]

This mismatch between building size and staff size of individual organizations was often only temporary. For example, when the Canadian Bank of Commerce moved into its 1890 building at King and Jordan it had about thirty-five employees in the head office and main branch and shared the building with seventeen other firms. By 1912 the bank's head office had grown to the extent that it took up almost the whole building. Only one tenant, the law firm that acted as chief legal adviser to the bank, remained. Some head office departments could not be accommodated: the archives were moved to what was then a suburban manufacturing district, the stationery department was temporarily moved to the King and Spadina area (an emerging industrial district close to downtown), and, according to the bank's chronicler, 'numerous' departments were forced to rent quarters elsewhere. At that time properties adjacent to the head office building were acquired, and plans formulated to erect a 'new and commodious' head office bulding. The advent of war prevented the execution of these plans, and the adjacent buildings were adapted instead; the stationery department and other parts of the bank were reunited with the head office in 1916.[54] These painful adjustments of buildings and staff must have been a lesson heeded in the 1920s, when the new head office building was constructed some thirty-four floors high. The size of this new building was calibrated for the bank's use; tenants were regarded as being in the building only temporarily.[55]

Making provision for expansion was not incompatible with other objectives, however. Little is known about real estate and building economics in Canadian cities around 1914. There are interesting indications in company histories and annual reports that large corporations watched their real estate dollars carefully. The Bank of Commerce felt that a building with room for tenants was necessary to carry the costs of 'one of the most valuable sites in the Dominion of Canada.' [56] A rather narrow economic calculus led the Canada Life Assurance Company (which moved to Toronto in 1899) to dispose of its former Hamilton head office building in 1914; the building was too large for the branch office, and the interest earned on investment 'did not give a satisfactory showing.'[57] Although the 'advertising value' of the building was acknowledged, it was not deemed sufficient to warrant continued ownership.

A further rationale for large buildings undoubtedly involved their prestige and symbolic values. Most of the owners of large office buildings seem to have been financial institutions such as banks, insurance companies, and trust companies. A large impressive building was less likely an item of conspicuous consumption than it was an important element in the struggle of banks and insurance companies to persuade potential depositors or policy holders that they were stable, solid, and legitimate. Almost routine bank failures,[58] and problems in the American life insurance industry at the turn of the century, had spread considerable anxiety; by 1906 a government inquiry was needed to reassure policy holders of the soundness of life insurance in Canada.[59] The confident scale of construction, together with the rich architectural imagery and the luxurious banking halls inside, had a subtle economic value.

Although the various symbolic meanings conveyed by impressive buildings were an important element in the genesis of these structures, it is also quite evident that they were considered as revenue-producing properties or appreciating investments. Above all, there are strong indications that they were calibrated against the expectations of rapid staff growth and anticipated problems of providing a rapidly expanding corps of office workers with a place for their desks. A contemporary climate of turbulent economic growth and faith in 'Canada's Century' must have reinforced the courage to think big.

The changes in the Canadian economy, including the rise of the large corporation, not only left their imprint on the morphology and business system of downtown Toronto, but also redefined the city's position in the Canadian urban system. By 1914 Toronto's 'progress' had resulted in the existence of two undisputed business capitals in Canada: Montreal and Toronto. Events such as the move of the Royal Bank from Halifax to Montreal, the Bank of Nova Scotia from Halifax to Toronto, or Canada Life from Hamilton to Toronto,[60] and the wave of mergers in banking and manufacturing, led to an increasing concentration of mangement functions in Canada's two largest cities and virtually eliminated the chances of other cities to challenge Toronto.

Of the two business capitals, Toronto was still occupying the second rank. In 1914 Montreal was still Canada's undisputed management centre: its banks and insurance companies controlled more assets than their Toronto equivalents; the value of transactions on the Montreal Stock Exchange was larger than that on the Toronto Stock Exchange; and more of the large Canadian 'industrial' corporations had their head office in Montreal than in Toronto. However, the gap between Montreal and Toronto had become small and Toronto was poised for gaining control.

Between 1914 and 1984 Toronto wrested the role of national management centre from Montreal. This was a slow process, however, and occurred in several important steps: by 1911 Toronto already had more people employed in 'finance' than Montreal; by 1924 a larger value of bank cheques was cleared in Toronto than in Montreal;[61] in 1932 the volume of transactions on the Toronto stock market exceeded that on the Montreal market;[62] during the 1950s Toronto took the leading role in insurance;[63] and by 1974 the number of head office employees in manufacturing companies was larger in Toronto than in Montreal.[64] As far as bank head offices are concerned, each city was home to 4 of the 11 Canadian chartered banks in 1984, with Montreal banks controlling 50 per cent of assets and Toronto banks 48 per cent. Significantly, Toronto houses several of the head office executives and departments of Montreal banks,[65] whereas Toronto banks do not seem to have moved any head office functions east. Also, of 58 new foreign banks in Canada in 1983, 46 are based in Toronto and only 6 in Montreal.[66]

Toronto's rise to hegemony was accompanied by many waves of new office buildings. Office construction slowed down but did not cease during the First World War. There were major booms in office development at both the beginning and the end of the 1920s. During the difficult 1930s the Imperial Bank head office building at the southeast corner of King and Bay, the Toronto Hydro building on Carlton (just east of Yonge), and the Toronto Stock Exchange redevelopment were prominent representatives of a whole set of office buildings that suggest the relative health of Toronto within the Canadian economy. Not all the projects of the 1920s and 1930s were brought to fruition: for example, the Bank of Montreal and the Bank of Nova Scotia buildings at the northwest and northeast corners of King and Bay were not finished until 1948 and 1951 respectively.

New office construction between 1914 and 1951 generally occurred west of Yonge Street, partially redeveloping the pre-1914 office district and also extending it from Bay to York streets, especially along King, Adelaide, and Richmond (see Figure 6). Among the most important changes within the existing office district were the moves of the Imperial Bank from Wellington Street East (1934) and of the Bank of Montreal from Yonge and Front (1948) to King and Bay, thus concentrating all principal banking offices in Toronto on King Street between the east side of Yonge and the west side of Bay (see Figure 3). Apart from these changes within and contiguous to the old office district, a fundamentally new phenomenon occurred: large office buildings sprang up detached from the traditional office district south of Queen Street. Office buildings arose on University Avenue between Queen Street and the Ontario legislature at Queen's Park, Dundas Square (near Yonge and Dundas), Carlton near Yonge, and Bloor Street East near Jarvis (see Figure 6). The new buildings outside the traditional office district were associated with some important head office relocations: the Hydro-Electric Power Commission of Ontario moved from Bay and Adelaide to University Avenue and College in 1915; Manufacturer's Life from King and Yonge to Bloor Street East in 1924; and Canada Life from King and Bay to University Avenue and Queen in 1931. Many organizational changes in the conduct of life insurance business rendered the tight cluster of offices obsolete.[67]

The construction of large office buildings, sometimes with more than twenty storeys and with 300–400,000 square feet (gross) of floor space,[68] was accompanied by the appearance of large head offices, the largest of which counted their staffs in hundreds rather than in tens as they had in 1914. For instance, Manufacturer's Life had 200 head office employees in 1921 and 445 in 1931; Canada Life about 650 in 1931 and close to 1,000 in 1951.[69]

The office of the 1920s was the 'new' (or modern) office.[70] The numerous

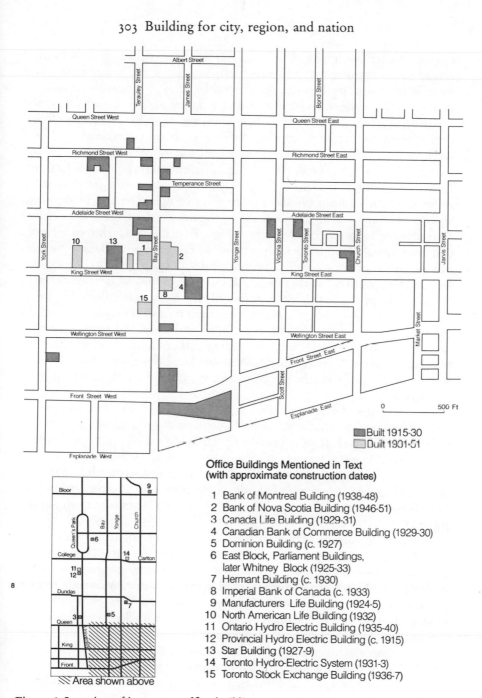

Office Buildings Mentioned in Text
(with approximate construction dates)

1 Bank of Montreal Building (1938-48)
2 Bank of Nova Scotia Building (1946-51)
3 Canada Life Building (1929-31)
4 Canadian Bank of Commerce Building (1929-30)
5 Dominion Building (c. 1927)
6 East Block, Parliament Buildings,
  later Whitney Block (1925-33)
7 Hermant Building (c. 1930)
8 Imperial Bank of Canada (c. 1933)
9 Manufacturers Life Building (1924-5)
10 North American Life Building (1932)
11 Ontario Hydro Electric Building (1935-40)
12 Provincial Hydro Electric Building (c. 1915)
13 Star Building (1927-9)
14 Toronto Hydro-Electric System (1931-3)
15 Toronto Stock Exchange Building (1936-7)

Figure 6. Location of important office buildings constructed between 1915 and 1951

employees, including many university-trained specialists, were organized according to departments and subjected, at least at the lower ranks, to a formalized work process. A considerable array of machines, such as typewriters, telephones, addressographs, printing presses, punch cards, and Hollerith machines, was used as 'labour-saving' equipment. Female clerical employment rose rapidly: in 1891 only 14.3 per cent of Canada's clerical workers were women, by 1911 32.6 per cent and by 1931 45.1 per cent were women.[71] In 1931, 49 per cent of all head office employees of Manufacturers Life were women.[72] Staff in the office began to be polarized: there was a sharp difference in the responsibility and earnings of managers and professional specialists on the one hand and clerks on the other. Managers and specialists were delegated more and more power by boards of directors who retired more and more from running the daily activities of a company. Clerical workers experienced a considerable decline in economic power. Until 1941, in Canada as a whole, clerical workers earned more than production workers in manufacturing; after 1941 the new role of the 'clerk' was reflected in lower salaries.[73] This 'new' office stood in sharp contrast to the 'old' office of the nineteenth century: that had been small, all male, and had relied on a wide range of skills of the clerks, who were often part not only of an 'office family' but also a real one. The conduct of business had been closely supervised by weekly meetings of the board of directors rather than delegated to hired management.

The expansion of white-collar work, including a wide range of occupations and occupational levels, between the 1890s and the Second World War was only a modest overture to the extremely rapid growth of this segment of the labour force from the 1940s to the 1970s. In 1941 white-collar workers accounted for 25.3 per cent of the Canadian labour force: by 1971 they accounted for 42.4 per cent.[74] In 1982, 43 per cent of all jobs in Metropolitan Toronto were jobs in office establishments as defined for the purposes of this paper.[75]

The 440,000 jobs in offices in Metropolitan Toronto are part of a very complex office landscape, which has emerged since the early 1950s. The 'old' office district south of Queen Street expanded further westward, while many buildings east of Yonge were demolished in the 1960s and 1970s and served as parking lots until very recently. Between Yonge and York, and Front and Queen, the majority of the pre-1951 offices were redeveloped, including the demolition of quite recent buildings such as the twenty-three storey Star building (completed in 1929) or the Bank of Montreal building (built in 1948). The texture of the 'old' office district, still maintained by the skyscrapers of the 1910s and 1920s, with moderately sized lots, buildings

King Street between York and Yonge, 1936. North American Life Building (left), built 1932, demolished 1975; Star Building (left of centre), built 1927–9, demolished 1972; and Canadian Bank of Commerce Building (right of centre), built 1929–30. All part of the westward expansion of the office district during the 1920s and 1930s (City of Toronto Archives, Salmon Collection 81)

aligned right up to the lot line, and richly ornamented stone façades, gave way (in the 1960s and up to the mid-1970s) to 'centres,' 'places,' and 'plazas' with large set-backs and glass-sheeted towers without ornament. Since then the morphology of the downtown and mid-town office district has become shaped by the design guidelines of the Central Area Plan.[76]

One further stage in office expansion emerged in the post-war period. Offices spilled out from the 'container' south of Queen Street and expanded around many nodes of the Yonge Street subway from Queen all the way north to Eglinton, four miles to the north. By 1971 this so-called central corridor, including the southern section below Queen, contained about 140,000 workers in office buildings.[77] Even this vast area, unlike the 'old' office district, could not contain the offices of the metropolis: since the mid-1960s, an increasingly large proportion of office space could be found outside the central corridor. In 1966 only 7 per cent of Metropolitan Toronto's office floor space was located outside central Toronto: in 1983 the 'suburbs' accounted for 31 per cent of this floor space.[78]

Behind the walls of the 650 office buildings of substantial size (over 20,000 net square feet),[79] in themselves a complex set of buildings of various age, size, architectural features, and location, lies an increasingly complex occupancy system and pattern of spatial distribution. With offices bursting out of the small area south of Queen Street and especially with their dispersion throughout the entire metropolitan area, a completely different geographical scale permeates location decisions. The vast area over which offices are now distributed is associated with the development of highly differentiated location patterns. Certain kinds of offices, such as those of architects and consulting engineers, have almost completely moved out of the old office district; others, such as the head offices of insurance and manufacturing companies or the offices of advertising agencies, have at least partially vacated the area south of Queen. Offices of film, radio, and television companies never had much of a presence in the old office district.

The 1960s and 1970s have seen the emergence of very large head offices. The largest head offices of banks, insurance companies, utilities, oil companies, and publishers now have several thousand employees; some have even as many as five to seven thousand.[80] Although there are only two or three dozen head offices in the metropolitan area with more than a thousand persons, there are a large number of firms, including 'service' firms, such as stockbrokers, accountants, and law and engineering firms, with hundreds of employees.

The largest head offices are seldom housed in one office building, introducing yet another complexity to the current office scene. Beginning in the late 1960s, several large data processing facilities were separated from the downtown head offices and 'decentralized' to the suburbs. Other head office functions such as sales, billing, mortgage, consumer loan, and credit card departments are also being dispatched to suburban office parks.[81] These departments are engaged in standardized, large-volume work, requiring a clerical work-force, most probably with a high percentage of women and almost no face-to-face contact with the public. The head office components remaining downtown have a relatively high percentage of male professional and executive personnel. The social distance between the clerk and manager, which developed between the two world wars, is becoming aggravated by spatial separation.[82]

Offices have been an important element of Toronto's townscape since the mid-nineteenth century. They have become more numerous and more conspicuous, and they have also become subject to changing public opinion. Most nineteenth-century observers of Toronto offices seem to have interpreted them as symbols of success and progress.[83] With the advent of tall buildings after the turn of the century, especially at the time of construction of the Traders Bank building in 1905–6 and the CPR, Dominion Bank, and Royal Bank buildings around 1911–14, a more differentiated opinion came to the surface. In the heated debate about the 'skyscraper issue' many city politicians, civic administrators, members of the press, the Guild of Civic Art, architects, and even real estate promoters voiced their opposition to the tall buildings. They warned about danger in case of fire, inadequate air and sunlight in and around the tall buildings, traffic congestion due to increased employment densities and sky rocketing real estate values in a very small area.[84]

From 1907 onwards, city council, under its authority to regulate the safety of buildings, attempted to restrict heights, thus taking the first major step in shaping the character and appearance of office buildings.[85] These early height controls, however, were difficult to implement. Facing the threat of projects being cancelled, the city government granted frequent exemptions from the 1907 by-law.[86] The debate carried on into the 1920s, when the then emerging city planning authorities put the issue of building heights in the downtown district on the agenda of town planning problems in Toronto and suggested regulating these buildings with the aid of the newly emerging instruments of planning, the zoning by-laws.[87]

Although Toronto grew dramatically in the 1950s, much of this growth occurred outside the political boundaries of the city. In order to counteract these trends, the city government, assisted by the private Downtown

Redevelopment and Advisory Council, encouraged large-scale office construction in the central area of the city. It is difficult to determine whether the liberal provisions of the first comprehensive zoning by-law (1954), giving property owners the right to build offices at twelve times coverage, was part of this attempt. It is on the record, however, that the new city hall, completed in 1965, was an attempt to encourage private investment in downtown projects.[88] City planners also seem to have encouraged the Toronto Dominion Bank to seek a partnership with a real estate development company in order to not just build another bank head office, but the vast Toronto Dominion Centre complex.[89] Along Wellington Street East between Yonge and Church, the city acquired land and buildings under the umbrella of an urban renewal scheme and successfully cleared away what was considered a blight: the dense tangle of bank, insurance, and telegraph offices, together with some of the wholesale warehouses from the 1860–90 period.

The city, however, soon found it impossible to tame the forces it had unleashed. The massive office boom of the 1960s and early 1970s decimated the city's heritage with alarming rapidity, created an awkward single-land-use district with an intolerable micro-climate, and began to put a renewed strain on the transportation system. The revision of the official plan, passed by city council in 1976 and approved by the province of Ontario in 1979, attempted to reverse some of these trends by instituting a complex set of policies and controls with regard to office development in central Toronto. At the same time the metropolitan government and the suburban municipalities tried to encourage and control offices in the suburbs.[90] The implications of these planning adventures of the 1970s are still unfolding. Among the results in the central office district are mixed-use buildings, incorporating offices and residential units. Some of these bring back a land use constellation of housing and offices that existed there in the 1860s and fell prey to a century of office development.

The changing office landscape of Toronto is not only a vehicle for the conduct of business, but also a mirror of Toronto's history in general. The moderate scale of office buildings up to the 1880s and their blending with commercial structures of various kinds and even residences are a reflection not only of limited technological abilities, but also of shared values and narrow social differences among the classes possessing wealth and power. The large towers of the decades after the turn of the century and the different opinions they engendered reveal the much more complex economic and social structure that had developed by then. The fierce debates caused by the huge towers of the 1970s revealed conflicts in existence since the turn of the century: between large and small business, between industrial and finance capital, between central-area and suburban property owners, between renters of business premises and providers of office accommodation, and between architects and planners as independent thinkers and architects and planners in the employ of large organizations. Many, if not most, of the 440,000 persons working in Metropolitan Toronto's office buildings, however, are clerical workers who have no way to articulate their collective attitudes toward offices as buildings or work places. They have stood, and still stand, on the sidelines. As such, the most visible elements of Toronto's silhouette reveal not only Toronto's role as national management centre, but also some of the basic divisions in contemporary society.

NOTES

We would like to thank Sue Friedman, Leila Gad, Cecil Houston, James Lemon, and Shoukry Roweis for a critical reading of an earlier draft and Shelley Laskin and Susan Laskin for their cartography.

1 In considering offices, we have included all buildings that for some time in their lifespan served to accommodate office work. This includes not only purpose-built office structures, but also dwelling houses, warehouses, and factories that had been converted to offices. We exclude, however, office structures or office rooms that are or were part of a factory, warehouse, or shop (for instance, the Massey Harris complex on King Street at Strachan contained not only the manufacturing plant and warehouse space but also significant clerical and management office functions at the same time). Once a firm moves part of its office function away from the plant, then it falls under our definition.

Individual organizational units occupying office buildings are considered to be establishments (e.g. a law firm, the head office of a bank, the sales office of a manufacturing company.) We include all sectors of the economy insofar as they appear in the office buildings defined above. Thus we do not restrict ourselves to the 'service sector' or so-called quaternary activities. The offices of mining companies (primary sector) or manufacturing companies (secondary sector), as long as they are not part of the plant, are included.

2 This paper can be only a survey, suggestive rather than definitive. Our knowledge of the context is fragmentary, and we have only begun to explore the very rich data sources available in Toronto. City directories, assessment rolls, fire insurance atlases, and several photo collections in the City of Toronto Archives and the Metropolitan Toronto Library served as the principal primary data sources. A great deal of this primary material was gathered and analysed in the

context of the *Historical Atlas of Canada* project, funded by the Social Sciences and Humanities Research Council of Canada. We acknowledge the assistance of Susan Friedman and Murdo MacPherson in constructing a series of detailed land use maps, and also University of Toronto research papers by students in our Advanced Urban Workshop (GGR 349, 1980–1) and Professor J. T. Lemon's Historical Toronto (GGR 336, 1984) courses.

An important secondary literature concerned with architectural history was useful in dating office buildings, especially: E. Arthur *Toronto: No Mean City* (Toronto 1964; 2nd edn, 1972); A.D. Burek 'The Evolution of Early Modern Office Buildings in Toronto' BA thesis, Erindale College, University of Toronto, 1978; W. Dendy *Lost Toronto* (Toronto 1978); I. Franco *Tall Buildings in Toronto, 1889–1930* (paper for FAH 488F, University of Toronto, 1979); Toronto Historical Board *City of Toronto: Inventory of Buildings of Architectural and Historical Importance* 2nd edn (Toronto 1981).

Another important secondary literature we drew upon deals with the formation of nineteenth-century business districts. Two papers are of particular importance: D. Ward 'The Industrial Revolution and the Emergence of Boston's Central Business District' *Economic Geography* 42 (1966) 152–71, and M.J. Bowden 'Growth of Central Districts of Large Cities' in L.F. Schnore ed *The New Urban History* (Princeton 1975) 75–109.

3 For the periodization of Toronto's economic history, we rely on the following: D. Cosgrove 'Dry and Fancy Goods Wholesaling in Nineteenth Century Toronto' MA thesis, University of Toronto, 1971; D.C. Masters *The Rise of Toronto 1850–1890* (Toronto 1947); G.S. Kealey *Toronto Workers Respond to Industrial Capitalism 1867–1892* (Toronto 1980); and J. Spelt *Toronto* (Toronto 1973).

4 The earliest exposition of these ideas can be found in W. Sombart *Der Moderne Kapitalismus* 2nd edn 3 vol (Munchen, Leipzig, 1916–27). Mainly based on the U.S. American experience are C. Wright Mills *White Collar: The American Middle Classes* (New York 1951) and H. Braverman *Labour and Monopoly Capital: The Degradation of Work in the Twentieth Century* (New York 1974). Many of these ideas are substantiated in the Canadian context by D. Coombs 'The Emergence of a White Collar Work Force in Toronto, 1895–1911' PhD thesis, York University, 1978; and G.S. Lowe 'The Administrative Revolution: The Growth of Clerical Occupations and the Development of the Modern Office in Canada, 1911–1931' PhD thesis, University of Toronto, 1979; see also G.S. Lowe 'The Administrative Revolution in the Canadian Office: An Overview' in Katherine L.P. Lundy et al ed *Work in the Canadian Context: Continuity Despite Change* (Toronto 1981) 153–73, and G. S. Lowe 'Class, Job and Gender in the Canadian Office' *Labour/Le Travailleur* x (1982) 11–37.

5 *The York Commercial Directory Street Guide and Register 1833–4* (Toronto, n.d.) allows us to form a reasonably detailed picture of the variety of offices and their location in early Toronto. Although the directory has no classified section, an untitled part lists government departments and selected businesses (such as banks, insurance companies, land agents, barristers) together with the names of government officials, business representatives, and clerks in both government and business employ. A search in the street section reveals a few additional businesses such as newspapers that could be classified as offices.

6 The Canada Company was a private land development company that purchased large areas of Upper Canada from the British government with the object of selling land to settlers. The Huron Tract, some 1 million acres of land, and the town of Guelph were their main concerns. See J.M. Cameron 'The Canada Company and Land Settlement as Resource Development in the Guelph Block' in J.D. Wood ed *Perspectives on Landscapes and Settlement in Nineteenth Century Ontario* (Toronto 1975) 141–58.

7 Osgoode Hall was the home of the treasurer and benchers of the Law Society of Upper Canada, founded in 1797 but modelled in the tradition of the Honourable Societies of the Inns of the Court in England. Although the hall contained space and offices for the Court of King's Bench, the Court of Chancery, and other higher courts of Upper Canada or Ontario at various times, its primary function was for the benchers 'to uphold the legal standards which they had imbibed, to impart their knowledge to others, to examine candidates and to call the qualified to the Bar of Upper Canada'; M. MacRae and A. Adamson *Cornerstones of Order: Courthouses and Town Halls of Ontario, 1784–1914* (Toronto 1983) 45.

8 This point is forcefully made by Cosgrove 'Dry and Fancy Goods' 1–3 and 67–80. However, Kealey *Toronto Workers* 3–34 draws attention to the importance of manufacturing in Toronto. Both sectors of the economy existed side by side, and it is difficult to measure exactly the economic importance of each of them. Judging by the prominence of wholesale merchants in civic and financial affairs, one could conclude that wholesaling was more important than manufacturing until about the 1880s. Around this time the number of wholesale firms started to decline, department stores began to buy directly from manufacturers, and manufacturing employment increased steeply.

9 The clearest example of this is the Canadian Bank of Commerce, founded in 1867 by dry goods wholesaler William McMaster. The Bank of Toronto, commencing business in 1856, was established by millers and grain dealers. See J. Schull *100 Years of Banking. A History of the Toronto-Dominion Bank* (Toronto 1958) 1–5. The Gooderham and Worts interests, which soon controlled the Bank of Toronto, consisted not only of distilling and milling

but also of export trade in agricultural commodities (ibid 3–5, 25). Other
banks, such as the Imperial or the Dominion, had wholesalers on their boards
of directors.

10 Although no direct evidence for these day-to-day functional links is available,
their existence can be deduced from the importance of credit facilities for wholesaling (see Cosgrove 'Dry and Fancy Goods' 60–1) and statements that until the
early twentieth century the primary customers of banks were wholesale and
other merchants. See, for example, Dominion Bank *The Dominion Bank 1871–
1921. Fifty Years of Banking Service* (Toronto 1922) 24.

11 As high-order retail establishments in 1860 we consider the following head-
ings from the classified section of the 1861–2 city directory: 'Dry and Fancy
Goods Retailers,' 'Dry and Fancy Goods Retailers and Wholesalers,' and
'Jewellers.'

12 This was the Bank of Toronto, located at 78 Church Street (between King and
Adelaide). In 1863 it moved into its own (and new) building at the northwest
corner of Church and Wellington, in the heart of the wholesale district.

13 Nikolaus Pevsner, an important authority on architectural history, states that the
first buildings erected specifically for office functions date from 1823 in London
and 1858 in New York. See N. Pevsner *A History of Building Types* (Princeton
1976) 214–15.

14 Like the courthouse and city hall, these buildings were still partly meeting places.

15 These were, with construction dates in brackets, the premises of: the Bank of
Upper Canada (1825–7), the Bank of Montreal (1845), the Bank of British
North America (1845), the Commercial Bank (ca 1845), the Edinburgh
Life Assurance Company (1858), and the Royal Insurance Company (1861).
Shortly after, in 1862 and 1863, the buildings of the Ontario Bank and the
Bank of Toronto were added.

16 A point made by Arthur *Toronto: No Mean City* 79

17 See Cosgrove 'Dry and Fancy Goods' 34.

18 These office buildings are (with approximate construction dates):
General Post Office, 36–42 Adelaide East (1869–73)
Trust and Loan Bldgs, 25–27 Toronto (1871)
Royal Canadian Bank, 36–38 Front East (ca 1871)
Toronto Union Block, 32–40 Toronto (1872–3)
Temple Chambers, 21–23 Toronto (1873)
Canada Life Assurance Co Bldg, 46 King West (ca 1873–4)
Consumers Gas Building, 19 Toronto (1876)
Customs House, 1 Front West (1876)
Imperial Buildings, 30–34 Adelaide East (ca 1876)
Union Loan and Savings Co Bldgs, 26–30 Toronto (1876–8)
British America Assurance Co Bldgs, 20–24 Front East (1877)

Queen City Fire Insurance Bldg, 22–26 Church (1877)
Equity Chambers, 22–24 Adelaide East (1878)
North of Scotland Chambers, 18–20 King West (1878)
Building and Loan Chambers, 13–15 Toronto (1879)
Dominion Bank, 1–3 King West (1879)
Western Assurance Co Bldg, 22 Wellington East (ca 1879–80)
Mail Newspaper Bldg, 50–54 King West (ca 1880–1)

19 Gross floorspace was determined from building outlines provided in fire insurance atlases. Minor irregularities in outline were ignored. In cases of attics or mansard roofs, usually declared as half-floors in fire insurance atlases, only one-half of the space within the building outline was added to the floorspace quantity, that is the sum of all the full floors.

20 From the late 1880s onward, it becomes increasingly difficult to quote floor numbers without ambiguity. Major buildings often had semi-basement floors, 'mezzanines' (partial floors in the upper part of two-storey banking halls), and turret floors.

21 See Arthur *Toronto: No Mean City* 215.

22 See Cosgrove 'Dry and Fancy Goods' 76–7.

23 Ibid 40

24 For examples of buiding material descriptions, see Dendy *Lost Toronto* 54, 61, 83, 94.

25 Important retail establishments already existed at Yonge and Queen in the early 1860s; Eaton's and Simpson's established their first stores in this area in 1869 and 1872 respectively; D. Kerr and J. Spelt *The Changing Face of Toronto – A Study in Urban Geography* (Ottawa 1965) 148. After 1880, however, retail expanded enormously at Yonge and Queen, while it began to stagnate on King. The separation of retail and office districts was not dramatic in terms of distance; to modern eyes they seem close. However, in the finely grained late-nineteenth-century city, there was a very clear difference between these two districts.

26 There was one notable exception: around 1890, a seven-storey office building was erected at the southeast corner of King and Jarvis.

27 For an excellent summary see R.C. Brown and R. Cook *Canada 1896–1921: A Nation Transformed* (Toronto 1974) 1–6.

28 For a discussion see A.B. Jamieson *Chartered Banking in Canada* (Toronto 1962) 35–40. The increase in branches, by provinces and territories, is documented in R.M. Breckenridge *The History of Banking in Canada* (Washington, DC, 1910) 162.

29 See the tabulation of branches of the Canadian Bank of Commerce in V. Ross *A History of the Canadian Bank of Commerce Volume* II (Toronto 1922) 556–72.

30 Ibid 112 and 255

31 For a brief history of the Canadian Northern Railway, see Brown and Cook *Canada 1896–1921* 150–3.

32 These mining-related companies are visible in the street section of the 1915 city directory. For instance, the tenants' lists of the Traders' Bank Building (61 Yonge Street) or the Temple Building (Bay and Richmond) give evidence of a number of these.

33 For the dates of establishment of these exchanges, see E.P. Neufeld *The Financial System of Canada: Its Growth and Development* (Toronto 1972) 478–9.

34 This listings in the classified sections of the 1891 and 1915 city directories include both Toronto Stock Exchange members and non-members. The relevant headings are for 1891 'Brokers (Stock)' and by 1915 'Brokers (Stock)' and 'Stock Brokers.' Many firms are listed twice in 1915; the figures in the text are based on counting each firm only once. Bond brokers and bond dealers are excluded.

35 For instance, Board of Trade of the City of Toronto, Canada *Year Book 1912* (Toronto 1913) 8 (photo of CPR Building) and 9–11 (section on development of northern Ontario in presidential address)

36 *The Toronto Annual (Heaton's) 1917* (Toronto 1917) 6, 18

37 Canada *Census* 1911, III 353. The table provides figures for 1891, 1901, and 1911.

38 The examples are taken from the 1915 city directory and the 1914–15 assessment rolls, principally by going through the tenant lists of the Trader's Bank, Dominon Bank, Canadian Pacific Railway, Confederation Life, Canada Life, Temple, and Board of Trade buildings.

39 Between 1890 and 1914 the number of law firms increased from 269 to 343, the number of architectural firms from 54 to 109, and the number of stockbrokers from 31 to 87. Our sources are the 1891 and 1915 city directories, using the following headings: 'Barristers' (1891), 'Barristers, Solicitors, Etc.' (1915), 'Architects' (both years), 'Brokers (Stock)' (both years), and 'Stock Brokers' (1915).

40 There were already a few manufacturers' offices in the downtown area by the 1880s. However, compared to the avalanche of new offices of manufacturing companies, the earlier ones pale to insignificance.

41 See Brown and Cook *Canada 1896–1921* 90–4 for a short summary. A more detailed analysis of mergers in the manufacturing and transportation sectors is provided by A.E. Epp 'Cooperation among Capitalists. The Canadian Merger Movement' PHD thesis, Johns Hopkins University, 1973.

42 See Neufeld *The Financial System* 79 and 97–101. A small proportion of the reductions in the number of banks was due, however, to the fact that there

were slightly more bank closures than openings of new banks between 1899 and 1914.

43 Ross *Bank of Commerce* 133, 199, 210–11, 226, 252–3, and 501 on merger dates and 556–64 for the dates of foreign branch openings up to 1911. In 1911 the bank had four offices in the United States, one in England, and one in Mexico.

44 On the expansion of Canadian life insurance companies abroad, see Neufeld *The Financial System* 255–7, and various company histories such as J. Schull *The Century of the Sun: The First Hundred Years of Sun Life Assurance Company of Canada* (Toronto 1971) 32–8, or Canada Life Assurance Company *Since 1847: The Canada Life Story* (Toronto, n.d. [ca 1967]) 25.

45 The examples in this paragraph are taken from Epp 'Cooperation' 224–7, 259–61, 336–43, and 687–9.

46 The Dominion Bank was leading in the establishment of 'city branches.' It opened its first one immediately after the establishment of the bank in 1871. The first branch, mainly a 'savings branch,' was located at Queen and Peter streets and moved to Queen and Augusta in 1872. (See Dominion Bank *The Dominion Bank* 45 and 65.) According to the city directory of 1891, there existed about fifteen 'city branches' in 1890.

47 According to the 1915 city directory there were about 170 'city branches' of banks in existence in 1914. Life insurance companies had about 7 branches in Toronto in 1914, not counting each of the first or principal branches of non-Toronto-based companies.

48 According to the 1891 and 1915 city directories, under the headings 'Agents (Advertising)' and 'Advertising Agents.' Double-counting has been eliminated.

49 The largest of the new buildings was the Royal Bank Building at the northeast corner of King and Yonge with twenty floors and approximately 200,000 square feet (gross). It was of exceptional size. Structures with 50,000–150,000 square feet (gross) could be considered as large-scale buildings at the turn of the century.

50 Unless otherwise stated, employment figures are based on assessment rolls. As Coombs points out, assessment rolls may have underestimated employment. See Coombs 'White Collar Work Force' 30.

51 According to Lowe 'The Administrative Revolution' 202, Manufacturers Life employed 93 persons in its head office in 1911 and 105 in 1915. No figures are available for Canada Life. Since the latter was somewhat larger in terms of assets, it is estimated that it had at least 100 head office employees in 1914.

52 It is a problem to account for these small head offices in the downtown area. Proximity to financial and other services, overlapping directorships, and proximity to customers could all have played a role in splitting off a small number of

executives from the plant. Alternatively there is the argument that they might have attempted to get away from a 'messy' physical and social environment.

53 This is confirmed by their staff compositions. Usually a manager, a stenographer or typist, a salesman or sales engineer, and/or 'travellers' are listed as occupations. However, these small offices may have been the vanguard of US manufacturing firms establishing themselves in a step-wise fashion in Canada at this time (S. Roweis, personal communication).

54 This picture of the accommodation problem of the Canadian Bank of Commerce is based on Ross *Bank of Commerce* II 220, 256, 351, 496, 505, and 507–8.

55 This was rather forcefully put forward by the bank's 'supervisor of bank premises': 'If you are to have tenants (and in our case they were necessary to carry the space provided for our future expansion) you must give them an attractive entrance,' and 'the Bank's requirements come first and ... the offices (for rental) are only incidental.' See D. Donald 'The Why and Wherefore of the New H.O. Building' *The Caduceus: Staff Magazine of the Canadian Bank of Commerce* XI 1 (1930) 22, 21. See also J. Nicoll 'Buildings of the Canadian Bank of Commerce' *Canadian Banker* XLV (1937–8) 205: 'The new building ... was planned so as to provide for all the requirements of the main Toronto office and to accommodate in one general scheme the various departments of Head Office. Until future expansion requires appropriations by the Bank, the surplus space is occupied by tenants.'

56 Stated in the Canadian Bank of Commerce *Annual Report* (29 November 1930) 42

57 A History of the Canada Life (unpublished manuscript, ca 1928, in the archives of the Canada Life Assurance Company) part 3, 27

58 See Neufeld *The Financial System* 81

59 Ibid 238–9. The *Report* of the Royal Commission on Life Insurance was published in 1907. The Canadian inquiry followed similar ones in the United States and the United Kingdom.

60 The dates of these transfers are Royal Bank of Canada, 1903, and the Bank of Nova Scotia, 1900. See W.R. Code 'The Spatial Dynamics of Financial Intermediaries in Canada' PhD thesis, University of California, Berkeley, 1974, 140, 207–11. The Canada Life Assurance transfer took place in 1899; see *Canada Life Since 1847* 20.

61 See Code 'Spatial Dynamics' 199.

62 See D. Kerr 'The Emergence of the Industrial Heartland' in L.D. McCann ed *Heartland and Hinterland: A Geography of Canada* (Toronto 1982) 94–5.

63 Our calculations are based on *Reports of the Superintendent of Insurance* for the years ending 31 December 1951 and 1961. Assets of all branches of insurance were considered with the exception of those of fraternal societies.

64 In 1972 in the Montreal Census Metropolitan Area (CMA) 26,412 persons were employed in 'separately located Head Offices, sales offices and auxiliary units,' and in the Toronto CMA there were 24,175. In 1974 the figures for the Montreal and Toronto CMAS were 24,758 and 27,004 respectively. No data were published for 1973. See Statistics Canada *Manufacturing Industries of Canada. Sub-Provincial Areas, 1972* Catalogue No. 31–209, 275, and Statistics Canada, ibid 1974, 265.

65 The Bank of Montreal has three 'executive office' locations: Montreal, Toronto, and Calgary. Of the five 'group headquarters,' four are in Toronto and ony one is in Montreal. See Bank of Montreal *165th Annual Report 1982* 80. Of the nine 'executive officers' of the Royal Bank of Canada, five are posted in Montreal, three in Toronto, and one in Calgary. See Royal Bank of Canada *Annual Report, 1982* 60. According to many press releases during the 1970s and early 1980s the Royal Bank has transferred substantial head office functions from Montreal to Toronto.

66 See Canadian Bankers' Association, Foreign Bank Secretariat *Schedule 'B' Foreign Bank Financial Positions* (Toronto 1984).

67 Some of the reasons for these moves are explored in G.H.K. Gad 'Die Dynamik der Burostandorte-Drei Phasen der Forschung' *Munchner Geographische Hefte* Nr 50 (1983) 29–59, based on the detailed histories of Montreal-based Sun Life, Toronto-based Canada Life and Manufacturers Life, and New York–based Metropolitan Life and New York Life, and arguments suggested by Braverman *Labour and Monopoly Capital* 293–358. The main reasons for these moves stem from organizational rather than purely technological changes.

68 The largest one was the thirty-four storey Canadian Bank of Commerce building at King and Jordan. Completed in 1931, it comprised approximately 450,000 gross square feet or 210,000 net square feet of office space (gross floor space according to City of Toronto Planning Land Use System, 30 November 1979; net floor space from A.E. LePage Ltd, office space listing, December 1975).

69 The employment figures for Manufacturers Life are from Lowe 'The Administrative Revolution' 202; those for Canada Life are from various unpublished documents in the archives of the company.

70 The distinction between the office of the nineteenth century, the 'old office,' and the office of the twentieth century, the 'new office,' was first made by C. Wright Mills *White Collar* 190–2 and 204–5 respectively. The terms *old office* and *new office* are Mills's. More recent accounts of technical, organizational, occupational, and social change in late-nineteenth- and early-twentieth-century offices can be found in Braverman *Labour and Monopoly Capital* 293–315, Coombs 'White Collar Work Force' passim, and Lowe 'The Administrative Revolution' passim.

71 Lowe 'The Administrative Revolution' 174

72 Ibid 202

73 Ibid 30. A similar reversal took place in the United States and the United Kingdom between the beginning and the middle of the twentieth century. See Braverman *Labour and Monopoly Capital* 296–8.

74 The 1941 figure is from S. Ostry *The Occupational Composition of the Canadian Labour Force* (Ottawa 1967) 50–1. The figure for 1971 is based on Statistics Canada *1971 Census of Canada* III part 5, Bulletin 3.5–11 (1975).

75 Based on Metropolitan Toronto Planning Department, Research Division *Metropolitan Toronto Employment Characteristics 1982* (Toronto 1983) 5

76 For a summary of recent planning measures concerning the 'Central Area' see G.H.K. Gad 'Face-to-Face Linkages and Office Decentralization Potentials: A Study of Toronto' in P.W. Daniels ed *Spatial Patterns of Office Growth and Location* (Chichester, UK, 1979) especially 285–90.

77 Ibid 291

78 Based on data from A.E. LePage *Toronto Office Leasing Directory* (Toronto, spring 1984) 6. The floorspace in Peel-Halton is excluded from these calculations.

79 Ibid 6

80 The largest office 'establishment' is probably that accommodating the major part of the Ontario Hydro head office. Approximately 7,000 employees work in a complex, consisting of three buildings, at University Avenue and College Street.

81 No systematic documentation of this phenomenon has been attempted. We rely on miscellaneous newspaper articles, company reports, job advertisements, telephone directory entries, and evidence in the field.

82 No systematic analysis of this process is available for Toronto. Some very interesting figures from American and British cities, however, show that in the central districts executive and professional jobs are growing faster than clerical jobs, whereas in the suburbs the opposite is the case. See J.D. Kasarda 'The Changing Occupational Structure of the American Metropolis: Apropos the Urban Problem' in B. Schwartz ed *The Changing Face of the Suburbs* (Chicago 1976) 113–36, and N. Spence et al *British Cities: An Analysis of Urban Change* (Oxford 1982) 38.

83 For example, see C.P. Mulvaney *Toronto Past and Present until 1882* (Toronto 1884) 227, regarding the 1877 building of the Queen City Fire Insura ice Company, or G.M. Adam *Toronto Old and New* (Toronto 1891) 194- 5 and 198, concerning the Canadian Bank of Commerce Building of 1889 and the (second) Canadian Life Assurance Company building, also of 1889.

84 For a brief discussion of the opposition to high-rise office buildings see J.C. Weaver *Shaping the Canadian City: Essays on Urban Politics and Polic*

1890–1920 (Toronto 1977) 32–7. A wealth of material on this issue has come to light recently in the research papers in Professor J.T. Lemon's course on Historical Toronto (GGR 366s, 1984) at the University of Toronto.

85 City of Toronto, By-Law 4861 (For Regulating the Erection and to Provide for the Safety of Buildings), 11 March 1907. The 100-foot limit was qualified by a further limit tied to the size of buildings at ground level. Buildings of skeleton construction could be built only to a height five times the building's least dimensions (length or width) at the ground. The by-law may have been amended by 1913 to allow for buildings of up to 124 feet in height.

86 By-law 4861 (see note 85) allowed exemptions in case of adquate fire-extinguishing equipment. Exemptions had to be approved by the inspector of buildings and by city council. The Dominion Bank Building (190 feet) and the Royal Bank Building (twenty storeys) are examples of these exemptions. See By-laws 6368 and 6369, both passed 24 February 1913.

87 See the paper by Toronto's city surveyor, T.D. Le May, 'Town Planning Problems in Toronto' *The Canadian Engineer* LVII 23 (1929) 779–81, and, by the same author, 'Skyscraper Problem in Town Planning' *The Canadian Engineer* LVIII 5 (1930) 189–91.

88 Nathan Phillips, mayor of Toronto, in 1955 called for decisions on the civic square, city hall, and court house projects, because they would provide a focal point for redevelopment. See N. Phillips *Mayor of all the People* (Toronto 1967) 110. Defending the city hall project at the Ontario Municipal Board, G.A. Burton, chairman of the Mayor's Advisory Committee on Redevelopment, claimed that 'developers must have confidence in the area' (ibid 147). See also City of Toronto Planning Board *Core Area Task Force. Technical Appendix* (Toronto 1974) 153.

89 According to R.W. Collier *Contemporary Cathedrals: Large-Scale Development in Canadian Cities* (Montreal 1974) 124–5.

90 For the office location policy of the metropolitan government see Metropolitan Toronto *Official Plan for the Urban Structure: The Metropolitan Toronto Planning Area* as approved to 23 September 1981.

PART THREE

The city that works

JAMES LEMON

Toronto among North American cities

A historical perspective on the present

'I HAVE SEEN civilization, and it works.' So concluded the prestigious journal *Science*, when promoting the 1981 meeting of the American Association for the Advancement of Science in Toronto. In the mid-1970s, commentators in other widely read American journals also heaped praise on Toronto. To *Fortune*, Toronto had become the 'new great city'; to *Harper's*, 'a city that works ... a model of the alternative future'; to *National Geographic*, 'worldly, wealthy, personable, and relatively problem free.' Los Angeles, it seems, had become passé.[1]

Even in the 1930s, when Toronto still invited American experts to evaluate its problems, the city was said to possess 'a marvellous organization and the finest [public] health service in the world ... a model among municipal health institutions.' Similarly, there was no comparable system to the Toronto Transportation Commission, 'where the entire personnel appears to be working so harmoniously to the one end of furnishing the best possible transportation service in the most economical manner.' To Ernest Hemingway, a young *Star Weekly* reporter in the early 1920s, however, Toronto's stability could not compensate for its dullness: 'Christ I hate to leave Paris for Toronto the City of Churches.' A touch of cosmopolitan excitement wedded with order has, it seems, changed perceptions. Alternatively, to latter-day Americans, cleanliness, safety, and civilized stability may command a higher premium than Parisian titillations. For Torontonians, however, the cost of 'civilization' may have been the loss of a measure of democracy.[2]

While Americans have praised Toronto, and more recently flocked to it for urban holidays and conventions, the city has not been without Canadian detractors. 'Toronto, one must understand, has no collective psyche,' westerner Alan Fotheringham asserts mischievously; the 'Big Lemon' has 'no real reason for being other than as a collection plate and siphoning pan for money created elsewhere.' Alberta's discovery of 'black gold' seems only to have accentuated the antagonism there to central Canada, meaning Toronto above all. Hogtown as a symbol is hardly new: that image was imprinted on children growing up in the 1930s and 1940s in southwestern Ontario. Toronto had everything, and not just meat packing. In 1946 Lister Sinclair could write a radio skit, 'We All Hate Toronto,' and the fact that the play was produced and broadcast in Toronto underlined Toronto's media power: this bit of self-deprecation cost Toronto nothing. The simple fact is that much of national (at least of anglophone) importance – finance and the media – has been increasingly concentrated in Toronto. All the big banks are run from King and Bay: what goes on 'This Country in the Morning' – now 'Morningside' – is decided in Toronto. But actually New York and Washington are fundamentally more influential in what happens in Canada.[3]

In considering the place of Toronto among North American cities, then, two issues should be addressed. First, and why is Toronto so different from US metropolises that it can conjure up the 'alternative' image? Second, what is Toronto's place among Canadian cities and regions? Only the first topic will be the major concern of this paper, though reference is made in passing to the other. I will survey the striking structural differences between Toronto and comparable US centres: a whole range of differences, such as Toronto's greater cleanliness, its relative freedom from crime, its efficient public transit, and the distinctive social character of its inner city and its suburbs. I will discuss also the special ethos and structure of municipal government in Toronto. After attempting to relate these differences to the distinctive historical circumstances of Toronto's growth, as against those of American metropolises, I will conclude with some thoughts on Toronto today: a metropolis of nearly 200 years of growth, facing an uncertain future.

In attempting to explain Toronto's distinctive character vis-à-vis comparable US cities, I should stress that Torontonians, and Canadians, have increasingly defined themselves largely in response to American ways. They filter out some impulses crossing the border while accepting others (if sometimes only gradually). Historically, Canadians have depended on British definitions of the workings of society. This influence persists, though muted by North American developments, while Americans still see themselves as un-European. Of course, Toronto shares with Vancouver, Philadelphia, and even Stockholm a history of liberal democracy and of entrepreneurial capital and, in this century, a degree of social democracy and corporate capital. What is most striking is how many American metropolises have declined, while big

Canadian cities seem to have become stronger and (at least superficially) more like western European cities.

Consider, first of all, cleanliness and health. Immediately apparent in Toronto are the tidy streets, a fact not lost on the commentator in *Science*. This is not new: in 1842 Charles Dickens noted that 'bustling' Toronto, then numbering only about 15,000 people, kept its sidewalks in 'very good and clean repair.' Today public works employees not only pick up garbage twice weekly but sweep the streets daily by hand and by machines.[4]

In Toronto, public health and crime have received a great deal of attention. A series of medical officers of health, the most noted being Dr Charles Hastings between 1910 and 1930, pushed Toronto to the forefront through pasteurization, control of communicable diseases, 'well-baby' clinics, and the like. Although much of the same sort was done in American cities during that period, today in many us inner cities public health has seriously deteriorated: witness rising infant mortality, worsening nutrition, and the hordes of 'bag ladies.' While Torontonians worry about signs of decline, and some try to war against them, the situation in many us central cities strikes many, not least Americans themselves, as being out of control. Toronto, like all Canadian cities, is seen to be safe, a perception supported by statistics on violent crime, if less so by statistics for crimes related to property. For many years Metropolitan Toronto, with over 2 million people, has witnessed only 40 to 50 homicides a year; compared to the worst us cities, such as Detroit, Miami, and Houston, the difference is staggering. Measures of violent crime generally show Canadian metropolitan areas at only one-quarter of us levels. The differences are even sharper between central cities: one-sixth. Most of central Toronto is as safe as the suburbs.[5]

Next, let us consider Toronto's spatial structure. Despite rapid and extensive post-war suburbanization on both sides of the border, Toronto's settlement pattern exhibits some striking contrasts to us cities with respect both to transportation patterns and to the inner city – suburban differentiations of housing and income.

In Canadian cities generally, public transit carries 2.5 times as many revenue miles of passengers per capita as it does in us metropolitan areas. A quarter of Canadian commuters rely on the public system, compared to only one-seventh in the United States. However, American metropolitan areas are criss-crossed by more freeways: 4.5 times the freeway lane mileage per capita. Canadians are also more inclined to share cars when commuting, to walk, and to ride bicycles. Overall, metropolitan Canadians commute somewhat shorter distances than Americans. In Toronto, the proportion dependent on public transport is also greater: a third or more, well over twice the us levels. In absolute ridership (400 million in 1983) the Toronto Transit Commission recently passed the much larger system in Chicago to take second place behind New York. By North American – if not European – standards Toronto stands out.[6]

Some of the difference may be attributable to the greater compactness of Toronto and other Canadian cities, but the data are hard to interpret because units of measurement are not easily comparable. However, the population density of metropolitan Chicago, for instance, would appear to be only 60 per cent of Metropolitan Toronto's. This trend is more certain when comparing central cities: the city of Toronto is clearly more densely populated than Boston and Cleveland, cities of similar area. Certainly Toronto appears more compact to the eye. Over the past three decades the number of multiple-unit structures has increased enormously. Visitors are struck by the number of high-rise apartments not only in the centre but also on the periphery. The sharp line between urban and rural at Steeles Avenue has dramatized the phenomenon, though that line has recently become more blurred as the towns of Vaughan and Markham become urbanized. The provision of commuter trains and bus service has undoubtedly widened the commutershed and so loosened Toronto to be more like the New York region.[7]

The relative success of Toronto's public transit may have been due in part to its greater compactness, but compactness was itself a result of policy. The Toronto Transit Commission (TTC), established in 1921, was merely emulating its predecessor, the privately run but publicly franchised Toronto Railway Company (TRC), when it refused to extend lines into lightly built-up areas beyond the city limits. The TRC had refused to extend its lines beyond the city boundaries of 1891, the year it was enfranchised, even though between 1903 and 1912 the city annexed nearly fourteen square miles of surrounding territory, almost doubling its area, and increasing its population to 410,000. Even though the city itself added a few civic lines, in 1911 an American consultant commented on the retardation of Toronto's peripheral growth and crowded streetcars, right in the middle of a major burst of population growth.[8]

In the 1920s, the TTC did extend lines beyond the city's boundaries, but, as elsewhere, with the advent of the automobile the system failed to grow as rapidly in ridership as expected. What helped to save the TTC, just when it was apparent that many other street railways and bus systems were weakening, was revenue from the Gray Coach Company's intercity operations in central Ontario. The TTC's decision in 1927 to buy out some private bus lines had paid off. It was a triumph for caution combined with astute public enterprise.[9]

As elsewhere, public transportation revived during the war. But unlike us cities, Toronto continued to forge ahead after 1945. In a 1946 referendum, 90 per cent of voters supported the building of rapid transit (touted since about 1908), showing considerably more enthusiasm for that than for the Don traffic artery (a predecessor of the Don Valley Parkway) and the Jarvis Street extension. It was clear by then, of course, that Toronto would have expressways. Just as New York in 1929, and Los Angeles in 1924 and 1939, had drawn up arterial road and expressway plans to accommodate the car, so had Toronto's planning board in 1943. The crucial difference between Toronto and these US cities was a commitment, if only dimly conceived at the time, to a 'balanced' system. When the Yonge Street subway was built, it simply replaced and speeded up the Yonge streetcar line. Undoubtedly, the devotion to public transit helped to maintain a better sense of proportion in the suburban growth of the 1950s, when enormous expansion occurred. Torontonians would buy nearly as many cars as Angelenos, but far more would leave them home while commuting, particularly into the central area. The successful resistance in the 1960s to the Spadina and the Scarborough expressways, and the quiet deletion of the Crosstown Expressway from Metro's plans, which together ruined the concept of an inner-city ring, obviously helped to maintain a balance. Political action on these issues reflected the community's underlying sense of a need for limits on the car.[10]

Toronto is distinguished most conspicuously from US cities by the spatial distribution of income groups in both the inner city and the suburbs. In the United States, inner-city residents have become poorer and the suburbs richer, while Toronto and other Canadian cities have halted and even reversed that pattern, though the pressures were never as strong as in the United States. In American inner cities, new office construction, persisting enclaves of high- and middle-income people, and (in some cities) the return of a miniscule number of 'gentrifiers' have all helped to support the property tax base. But the overwhelming reality has been decline in the twentieth century. Canadian cities have been maintained far better than any large inner US city. In Toronto one is hard put to find an abandoned dwelling; in New York officials and the Times have argued for 'planned shrinkage' and 'dedevelopment' – the withdrawal of public services from the large areas of the South Bronx and Brooklyn that now resemble bombed-out Dresden and Hiroshima. In 1975 New York experienced ten times as many fires (many set by paid arsonists) as it did in 1939, even though by then it was entirely built up. Most of Toronto's neighbours on the Great Lakes have experienced serious deterioration.[11]

What processes led to inner-city decay? Why has this not happened in Canadian metropolises? As a starting point, let us consider the notions of 'invasion and succession' and 'filtering down.'

In the 1920s a group of sociologists at the University of Chicago argued that

American cities could be described by positioning concentric zones focused on the central business district (CBD). These zones would move outward as the CBD expanded, as the city's population increased, and as the number of poor people in the inner zones increased. Gradually the affluent citizens on the outer edge would move farther out, being replaced by middle-income people, who would in turn be displaced by those less wealthy than they. Hence, housing 'filtered down' the income scale as the iron laws of 'invasion and succession' inexorably worked their dire effects. Certainly the model seemed to work then for Chicago, though the notions of income sectors and ethnic nuclei eventually modified the model to account for the persistence of the rich Gold Coast on the shoreline to the north and the poor Black Belt to the south. Zones themselves were eventually recognized in terms of age and size of families. No matter how the inner and outer suburbs might vary by income, however, the overwhelming pattern (with the exception of a few striking examples, such as the Gold Coast, New York's Central Park East, Boston's Beacon Hill, and several districts in San Francisco) was that the central residential areas had become poor and were universally considered as slums.[12]

In the late nineteenth and early twentieth centuries many of the poor in large American cities were eastern and southern European immigrants (instead of the earlier Irish and German Catholics). Italians and Jews flocked to New York's lower east side, to Boston's north end, to south Philadelphia. Some of these ethnic areas have remained stable, if often called slums. But little noticed until after 1900 was the flow of blacks from the south. This movement converted part of Harlem almost overnight into a ghetto, and during the First World War industrial jobs attracted even more. The largest influx of blacks to northern cities occurred during and after the Second World War. Together with Puerto Ricans, blacks now form large minorities, or even majorities, in northern and southern central cities. As a result, Chicago's southside Black Belt and the Harlem ghetto have increasingly become the norm. Central cities have witnessed block-busting, first refined in Harlem, and the flight of the whites: invasion and succession still remain realities.[13]

Coinciding with the migration of minorities in central cities was a weakening of the booster spirit expressed by businessmen and politicians from the mid-nineteenth century to 1914. Pushed by speculators, cities annexed surrounding communities and the urbanizing fringe. The suburbs, too, had been anxious to add water mains, sewers, and improved roads paid for from the central city's stronger revenue base. But generally by 1914 servicing costs and special arrangements for these services had obviated the need for still unattached areas to join. However, the poor minorities were now raising central-city social costs. Hence, increasingly, the new suburbs stayed out, creating a balkanized municipal environment. In the post-1945 United States only in the southern and southwestern Sun Belt have some central cities been able to appropriate surrounding areas. The older cities have been so immobilized that no annexations or other metropolitan arrangements have been possible.[14]

But that is only part of the story. The location of the new defence and space industries, with their highly skilled, white-collar work-force, in the Sun Belt also drew affluent whites away from the old cities; and post-war federal housing policy, with its tax concessions and guaranteed home-purchase loans helped to draw whites from the inner city out to the suburbs. Massive areas of central cities, increasingly black, were 'redlined' (deprived of mortgage, or even renovation money), while the large amounts of federal money spent on the urban poor created monolithic high-rise public housing ghettos. Federal aid went as well for interstate freeways, which tore up inner cities to connect the suburbs with the centre and one another. The inner city lost the middle-class taxpayers who would have sustained urban services, leaving only the poor (and, of course, undertaxed central office clusters). Henry Ford might have been pleased that public policy finally fulfilled his 1912 pledge that 'we shall solve the city problem by leaving the city'; Charles Dickens, however, would no doubt see the pathos of British cities during the 1840s being repeated in the New World.[15]

In Toronto the process of invasion and succession has operated to a lesser degree, despite intensive suburbanization since the Second World War. During the past two decades, in fact, it has even been reversed, in dramatic contrast to the trend in most American cities. In the late nineteenth century, wealthy Torontonians dwelt along the main north-south avenues, such as Sherbourne, Jarvis, University Queen's Park, and Beverley/St George, while more modest housing sprang up on the cross and interior streets. Directly south of the University of Toronto, for example, a remarkable variety of housing was built in close juxtaposition, as can still be seen today on Beverley, Cecil, and Huron streets. Along streetcar routes, the characteristic strips with stores at street level and apartments above them developed during these years and up to 1930. Thus, although there were a few homogeneous poor working-class neighbourhoods, such as Cabbagetown and The Ward, spatial differentiation based on income was on a very small scale.[16]

In the 1880s homogeneous upper- and upper-middle-class neighbourhoods started to appear in Toronto, as elsewhere. The central Annex was developed as a 'garden suburb,' albeit within the traditional grid pattern of streets, while the curving avenues of Rosedale (laid out in 1854) also began to be occupied. The larger scale of social differentiation heralded by these events would accelerate during the renewed period of rapid growth from 1905 to 1912, and again in the 1920s, though less markedly. North Rosedale, Lawrence Park, Forest Hill (immortalized in a 1950s study as *Crestwood Heights*), and the Kingsway were all developed at this time. These new suburbs so powerfully attracted the affluent from the more central districts that the Annex and even parts of South Rosedale remained prestigious only for a generation; 'deterioration' set in as the large houses were converted to rooming houses, undergraduate fraternities, and head offices of non-profit organizations serving anglophone Canada. Jarvis Street, an earlier scene of elegance punctuated by church spires, fell even further into the category of a red-light district. Downtown schools were closed.[17]

But during this period (1880–1930) Toronto did not experience growth to nearly the same extent as New York, Chicago, and Boston. The flood of immigrants to the land of opportunity was not matched in Canada. Moreover, most immigrants to Toronto were British. Despite the conspicuous Jews (who first occupied The Ward before expanding into a much wider area of the western inner city), the emergence of Little Italy at College and Grace, and modest clusters of several other non-anglophone communities, even in 1931 Toronto was still 80 per cent British. Of the foreign-born the British composed two-thirds. Reformers decried the blighted conditions in The Ward, ethnic groups segregated themselves (and were segregated), and racism directed against Jews was obvious. But Toronto only mildly reflected the American experience.[18]

The post-1945 influx of immigrants, first from Europe and later, after 1962, increasingly from southern and eastern Asia and the West Indies, paralleled in relative numbers the turn-of-the-century experience of New York and Chicago. Yet the results have been far less dramatic. Real incomes were higher in the post-war period than earlier. Even if Italians and Portuguese had to 'double up,' and more than one member of the household had to work to make ends meet, conditions hardly resembled those of the Bowery in 1900 or even The Ward in 1918. In fact, British working-class Torontonians and even some of the middle class had been doubling up before 1945.[19]

The urban form thus remained more stable in Toronto than in the United States. Invasion and succession continued but in a relatively benign way: the Jews moved north on the Bathurst corridor, the Italians north on the Dufferin corridor. Predominantly British high-income sectors persisted to the north and, less conspicuously, in central Etobicoke and the Beaches. Perhaps, too, vendor take-back mortgages helped many British and other working-class areas remain stable despite the construction of some high-rise developments and public superblock developments, which occurred on a much slighter scale than in the United States. Some central neighbourhoods did not change dramatically.[20]

Then, in the mid-1960s, just as the Watts, Detroit, and Newark riots erupted in the United States, middle- and upper-income families (and younger people with moderate incomes but wanting an inner-city life-style) began to move into formerly working-class districts of the city. The white-painting of Metcalfe Street, in the middle of Cabbagetown's skid row, was only the most dramatic indication of change. People's attitude toward old buildings shifted from negative to positive. Easy access to downtown services became more appealing now that factory and railway smoke diminished and the poor were less conspicuous. Like Americans, many post-1945 Torontonians had seen the suburban solution as the way to the good life: family-centred living, houses as self-contained entertainment centres on large lots. But not all did, and after 1965 a marked strengthening of the inner-city fabric occurred. Quite possibly more housing has filtered up the income scale over the past fifteen years than ever filtered down! Ironically, again in sharp contrast to the American experience, some of Metro's post-war suburbs have become poorly serviced reception areas for poorer immigrants.[21]

While American cities have continued to become more segregated by class (largely visible through race), Toronto has become more mixed. Recently this trend has been fostered by public policy, of which mixed public housing and the dispersion of group homes are two obvious signs. City housing projects built since 1972 have been designed to mix life-styles and income groups by mingling rental, co-operative, and private homeownership. In contrast to the superblock development of Regent Park North and its successors (if modest by American standards), the St Lawrence housing project on the old railway lands of the Esplanade brings varying income groups into a variety of housing styles. The St Lawrence project and others, such as Frankel-Lambert, are evidence that in Toronto the notion of social housing has come of age. Many years of argument had preceded the 1946 vote to build Regent Park, a project designed to separate the poor while improving their material condition. With less ideological struggle, the past decade has brought to the fore the idea of housing as a right for everyone, even if today it is conspicuously under-funded. In this respect, Toronto has become more European and less American. in the United States, the scale of segregated housing in the central city has continued in enormous high-rise blocks.[22]

Group homes for the retarded, the physically handicapped, ex-psychiatric patients, erstwhile addicts, and ex-criminals returning to society also signify the notion of mixed neighbourhoods. Some suburban communities, and even some neighbourhoods in the city of Toronto, have shown reluctance to accept them, but in the late 1970s, in response to unhealthy concentrations of such institutions in Parkdale and the Annex, the city of Toronto again led the way in opening neighbourhoods – every neighbourhood in theory, if not universally in practice – to this kind of mixing. When the topic was debated at city council, virtually every resident and ratepayer group ended up supporting the by-law. Beyond these two signs of social maturity, both city and suburban neighbourhoods increasingly – though not always without resistance, as shown in North York's past foot-dragging on allowing unrelated persons to live together – accept the mixing of incomes and life-styles. Perhaps most striking is the Sherbourne-Dundas area, where gentrification and skid row are conspicuously cheek by jowl! In the summer of 1982, a group of American urban historians touring the area were astonished at this spatial expression of social tolerance.[23]

Toronto's special combination of stability and social mixing was not achieved without a struggle and a reform of government. Until the 1960s neighbourhood stability was sought, often unsuccessfully, through social segregation, using the instrument of zoning by-laws. Soon after 1900 by-laws were increasingly used to exclude what were considered obnoxious land uses such as polluting industries. In 1912 apartments were prohibited generally, though the by-law varied frequently in many districts in the late 1920s and again in the late 1930s. In the 1920s many neighbourhoods specified only private dwellings, some only detached dwellings. By the mid-1930s a multitude of by-laws, and the inevitable plethora of amendments, had created a hodge-podge of regulations. Only then did the city act to create a zoning system, which followed American cities in imposing a sharp separation of used, for example keeping industry out of residential areas and vice versa. But even civic officials saw it more as an administrative device than as a stronger means to protect socially homogeneous districts. In Toronto's (and Ontario's) inimitably leisurely fashion, the system did not finally come into place until 1954.[24]

Before the 1940s, planning was used hardly at all to control and direct land use. Three substantial plans had been created: in 1909 the Guild of Civic Art's plan for the whole city; in 1912 the Toronto Harbour Commission's proposal for the waterfront; in 1929 the Advisory City Planning Commission's scheme for grand boulevards in the central area. Nothing of the first plan but some playgrounds and parks was ever put into place. The second was fulfilled in large measure: the reshaping of Ashbridge's Bay as a harbour and industrial site, the extension of the central waterfront southward, and the creation of Sunnyside amusement park were all carried out between 1912 and 1930, though the land allotted for manufacturing and grain elevators was never fully taken up and bridges were not built to the islands. Cautious Toronto rejected the 1929 plan, which was a scheme typical of that extravagantly speculative era. Only University Avenue was extended south of Queen to Front.[25]

The Great Depression was a great watershed in the Canadian experience, though Toronto felt the burden much less than other places. Apart from extensive home renovation support from the city and the federal governments from 1936 to 1939, and modest improvements of vehicular traffic flow, little was achieved in city planning. But the passivity of the 1930s was superseded in Toronto by rising expectations, and, particularly from 1941 on, much of the ideology of social change was expressed by the Co-operative Commonwealth Federation (CCF). This new, democratic socialist political party promoted economic, social, and land-use planning as well as civil and trade union rights. If centralized wartime economic planning was not carried on after 1945, universal social welfare programs eventually won public acceptance. In the United States the failure to follow up Franklin Roosevelt's social experiments redounded to the detriment of its cities. Canada, in contrast, moved haltingly to wider social protection of the individual. Although these social reforms hardly fulfilled all of the CCF's goals and did not lead the party to power in the province or even the city (let alone the country), the party's role in galvanizing governments to action can hardly be overestimated.[26]

It could be argued that a fixation on land-use planning diverted the public's interest from direct economic planning. Late in the war and afterward, land-use planning moved into the spotlight of the municipal stage. Rapid but orderly suburban development and the maintenance of environmental stability in built-up areas were central to public policy. Even though developers inevitably found ways to manipulate the rules, the system of development was more controlled than in the United States, where the inner city–suburban balance got out of hand. The organizational framework that was established in Toronto for the implementation of public policy showed how seriously the matter was taken. In 1942 the city had set up an advisory planning board, which delivered a general plan for the area late in 1943. The newly elected Progressive Conservative provincial government responded to pressure (from the CCF and others) by setting up a Ministry of Planning, which drew up a planning act with far more teeth than the acts of 1912, 1917, and 1918. Planning boards, with statutory powers, were required to produce official plans: Etobicoke, North York, and Toronto drew up theirs soon afterward. The Toronto and York (County) Planning Board was established in 1947 to control subdividing on the fringe of the expanding metropolis.[27]

The most significant organizational change in planning, however, was the creation of the Municipality of Metropolitan Toronto in 1953. After 1912, when the city stopped annexing large tracts as the solution to metropolitan growth, agitation for continuing the practice, or for the invention of an alternative municipal structure, was frequent, particularly on the part of the poorer townships of York and East York. Its failure exposed Toronto in the 1920s to the American experience of a proliferation of small suburbs, resulting in a fiscal crisis for all but the two richest (Forest Hill and Swansea) in the early 1930s. The province intervened through a restructured Ontario Municipal Board and tightened the reins on municipal borrowing. Then, in the late 1940s, the city reversed its long-standing opposition to annexation by proposing amalgamation of the whole urbanized area. But after considerable debate and protracted hearings by the Ontario Municipal Board, the province chose a metropolitan form of government, the most dramatic innovation in municipal administration since two-level structures were created for London and New York. Thirteen municipalities were brought under Metro's umbrella. Functions were divided, but with Metro providing the trunk water mains and sewers and the major transportation facilities. By establishing Metro as the prime agent in promoting orderly urban development, the province overrode parochial concerns, even though many local powers remained intact. The innovation was one that left the United States far behind. With the exception of some Sun Belt cities, twentieth-century attempts to create metropolitan structures in US cities have failed. American experts now came to Toronto, while Toronto's officials stopped relying on American advice.[28]

Metro's domineering first chairman, Frederick Gardiner, successfully transferred city tax revenues to provide services for suburban housing, industry, and shopping centres built by large corporations; he weakened local suburban political power; and, through building public housing on land banked by the provincial and federal government, he shifted some of the welfare burden from the inner city. The increased efficiency achieved in 1967, when the municipalities were reduced in number from thirteen to six and social services and welfare came under Metro's jurisdiction, smoothed out even more the social inequalities within the metropolis. But a good deal of local autonomy was lost in the process. The grant of virtually unlimited power to Gardiner, the 'maharajah of Metrostan,' substantially undercut the power of local politicians and brought the nineteenth-century municipal system in Toronto to an end. In effect, Metro, its chairman elected by an indirect system that entrenches him even more securely than any US 'machine' mayor, became and has continued to be a provincial commission as much as a local government.[29]

While Gardiner got the steam-shovels into farmlands of the outer townships in the heady days of the 1950s, the commitment to planning in the city of Toronto was gradually strengthening. Indeed, as if to compensate for the loss of power at the higher level, local politics eventually became more democratized. Backing off from the 1943 plan's extravagant provision of expressways, the city's planning board and council aided the car only modestly. Very important, too, was the planning board's 1944 report on the city's seventy-eight neighbourhoods. All but the 'sound' newer ones (in North Toronto especially) and those east and west of downtown that were described as 'blighted' were referred to as 'vulnerable' or 'declining' – a sure sign of accepting the notions of invasion and succession. In the wake of this report, and with more money, neighbourhood associations responded by campaigns to fix, clean, and paint; one group billed itself the 'First Tidy Toronto Block' committee. In the 1950s every May saw public 'clean up' campaigns. The 'vulnerable' Annex, much of it transformed between 1920 and mid-century to rooming houses and institutional uses, took up the challenge: through its 'Renaissance of the Annex' campaign, the district became known as a 'smart' place to live. In the mid-1950s the area east of Sherbourne and north of Wellesley Street, with the support of Alderman (later Mayor) William Dennison, resisted, successfully at first, the attempt to build what eventually became the high-rise cluster of St James Town.[30]

The remarkable flowering of residents' associations in the late 1960s and early 1970s was, therefore, not without antecedents. Traditional neighbourhood ratepayer groups, committed to protecting social homogeneity and property values, were already shifting, if often reluctantly, toward a wider conception of environmental protection and an acceptance of mixed populations. The drive toward public housing projects, residential high-rises, and downtown office redevelopment, which flourished from the mid-1950s to the late 1960s, pulled politicians including Dennison into the 'growth is good' syndrome, and the determination of Metro to proceed with the Spadina and Scarborough expressways seemed for a while unstoppable. But drawing on a traditional concern for stability, and helped by a burgeoning environmental movement and probably too by opposition to the war in Viet Nam, neighbourhoods mounted heroic resistance to the pressure for uncontrolled growth that they perceived in the 1964 Metro and the 1969 city plans. On the outskirts of Metro, groups opposed the proposal for a second major airport.[31]

The election of a reform city council in 1972 resulted in the rewriting of some of the rules: neighbourhood plans and municipal planners promoted a conception of stability based less on homogeneity than on diversity; redevelopers at every scale were encouraged to negotiate with both planners and residents' associations; the central area was replanned to reduce apartment densities (though less so office densities) and to provide for mixed-use structures. The push to develop the outlying city centres of North York and Scarborough, conceived in large measure by central-city activists in order to limit downtown development, helped to focus Metro planning even more on the improvement of public rather than private transit.[32]

Meanwhile, the province began to take a more active role in municipal affairs, to maintain stability, and to mediate disputes between Toronto and the suburbs. Financing became more complex with the creation of Metro, but the province gradually picked up more of the bills, at least until the mid-1970s. Education, social services, welfare, transit (first capital and later also operating costs), and highways all benefited from provincial largesse (which included transfer payments from Ottawa), thereby easing the pressure on property taxes. Metro's financial health has helped it maintain the highest possible credit rating for debenture borrowing from Moody's Investors Service of New York. By way of contrast, several large American cities, dependent on the caprice of their federal and often-unconcerned state governments, have slid down the rating scale. The control exercised by the province over the municipality has undoubtedly paid off, at least until recently.[33]

The province has also exercised control over development – indirectly through the Ontario Municipal Board and directly when issues dividing the city and the suburbs could not be resolved internally. The 1971 intervention that stopped the Spadina Expressway, and that of 1982 in favour of retaining residences on Ward's and Algonquin islands, are two cases in point. Since both of these extraordinary decisions were in favour of city, they were undoubtedly signals that the power of the city in the Metro federation had weakened over the years because of its progressively smaller representation on Metro council. Yet the province ignored virtually all reform proposals by former premier John Robarts's 1977 royal commission on Metro and shows no interest in further reforms. A future reversal of the Spadina decision too cannot be ruled out, and the islanders still find their status shaky.[34]

Toronto's development, then, has differed from that of comparable US cities in two critical respects. In terms of social morphology, Toronto has experienced far less drastic spatial segregation according to wealth. This relatively balanced development has been fostered by a distinctive governmental system that has contrived to give Toronto a more stable political environment than American cities have enjoyed. But what are the underlying differences in social ethos and dynamics that have helped to make Toronto's experience so remarkably divergent from that of comparable American centres?

In the United States, the flight to and now beyond the suburbs, and the consequent decline of central cities into dumping grounds for the poor, reflect three centuries-old characteristics of American social thought: an anti-city sentiment, a religious fervour for embracing the new as good and rejecting the old as bad, and a belief in a classless society. First, Thomas Jefferson's well-known view that cities were 'sores' on the body politic has been echoed and re-echoed, the few celebrators of cities (such as Jane Jacobs) notwithstanding. Paired with this negative view of the city has been the overwhelming symbolic promotion of the rural society of the frontier, or the small town with its village green or main street where one experiences liberty and fraternity while escaping the *anomie*, the alienation, of the city. To be sure, the image of Manhattan evokes excitement, but also fear. Americans often ignore the dominance of those Wall Street giants, the Chase Manhattan and Citibank, in an effort to convince themselves that their local county bank still benignly concerns itself with the needs of the ordinary person.[35]

The separation of a presumed tranquil rural life from the maelstrom of large cities provided the context for the disengagement of rural-dominated state legislatures and the courts from urban issues in the mid-nineteenth century. The cities themselves sought 'home rule,' allowing them to finance their own operations and to annex adjacent areas. But a nineteenth-century solution gradually turned into a twentieth-century quagmire. The costs of running older central cities increased, and then soared after 1945. The freedom of cities to act became a millstone as new, largely white suburbs successfully resisted sharing the social and material costs of central cities. Consequently, the federal government was drawn in, often riding roughshod over local needs. Wars on poverty and the like could not compensate for quite contrary federal policies encouraging suburbanization and inner-city expressways promoted for national security.[36]

Religion in the United States often sought to regenerate the individual and hence the society as a whole but has less frequently sought to sustain the collective experience. The periodic outbursts of religious fervour reinforce a powerful individualistic, even narcissistic tendency that has been present since the founding of the country. Exclusive sects and cults are thrown up, pulling people away from common public responsibility. When a bumper sticker proclaims that 'God, guns and guts' made the United States great, one is hard put to recognize the softer, more collective purpose of religion. One subtle urban outcome of this preoccupation with individual salvation and national power is the abandonment of old structures, especially when they impede a focus on the future. Ugly cities with strange people are obvious candidates for such neglect. The new person, the saved person, must have a new environment, and so the United States wastes more than any other society. Of course, the best of the old is preserved, but not in cities so much as in Disneylands, where pre-1890 horse-trams convince middle Americans that even cities may have been nice once upon a time: cities that the saved have long abandoned to be dump sites for the discarded and forgotten.[37]

Preoccupation with sentimental fraternity on the one hand, and paradoxically with excessive freedom on the other, leaves the perception of social equality and inequality largely out of the equation. A belief in classlessness remains a strong tendency in American social thinking, modified only by the notion that there is equality of opportunity. This is a false notion because people do not enjoy an equal start, though this fact is obscured in many ways, as by the United States leading the world in the number of students receiving post-secondary education. Colour hides the class issue. Blacks provide a ready-made lower class: in turn, in recent times, token black celebrities have only further clouded the condition of most persons who are visibly different, especially blacks. Over the past half-decade or so, the blacks' per capita income has fallen dramatically from 62 per cent to only 56 per cent of white income, Reggie Jackson's presumably included. The April 1983 Chicago mayoral election was billed, of course, as a race issue. What remained hidden was the problem of two competing groups of working-class people. Both depend on ex-mayor Richard Daley's job-patronage system, which reaches into lower-income jobs not yet replaced by a less biased method of hiring – such as that found in Toronto.

Periodically, Americans do become more conscious of class: in the early 1930s many people thought trade unions would disappear, but within a few years the Congress of Industrial Organizations arose, helped by the Wagner Act in 1935. As the weakness of an American economy dependent on military spending and the illusions of supply-side policies become clearer, another era of class consciousness may well emerge. But that consciousness has always been exceedingly fragile: insecurity and instability remain powerful, and the nation's strength has relied overwhelmingly on the freedom of market relations, through which labour and land are largely reduced to commodities. Even through social democratic channels status and equality are hard to come by, especially when times are bad.[38]

In contrast to Americans with their dogmas of life, liberty, and the pursuit of happiness, Canadians are stuck with the much more mundane slogan of peace, order, and good government. From what we have seen of Toronto's structure, stability would seem to be considered as high a virtue as growth, at least when dealing with the urban environment. The hedging in of private property rights and the provision of public services have been conspicuous, especially since 1945 (though weakening again since 1975), quite in contrast to American urban life. While the developers and real estate industry exert pressure for growth and preach the virtues of free enterprise, they operate within the tightened rules of the post-war period. Citizen participation too is designed to ensure order. Residents' associations have become more democratic than the older ratepayer groups, accepting tenants as members and so as full citizens. Neighbourhood environments are thus recognized not simply as aggregates of properties but as unitary public realities in which everyone has a stake. In the 'heroic' era of citizen participation, between 1965 and 1972, activists in Toronto effectively appealed to this sentiment through graphic descriptions of the horrors of American inner cities. Toronto's stability can be thus contrasted to the obsessive protectiveness shown in some American suburbs, where quasi-mediaeval walls, and even security forces, exclude strangers. Paradoxically, Toronto's situation allows more flexibility than the ideologically more open American society, where excessive freedom often begets an obsession with order in everyday relations – witness American litigiousness, which sometimes serves as a back door to fraternity by bringing people together. In that society, where business is the highest calling, as evangelist Jerry Falwell testifies in word and action, Alexis de Tocqueville long ago saw the problem in terms of tyranny of the majority and of conformity.[39]

A model of social persistence can usefully be considered here. For Canada, Gad Horowitz has modified Louis Hartz's paradigm for European overseas settlements. Like Hartz, Horowitz sees American society as overwhelmingly 'liberal,' that is, as one in which individual freedom is valued above equality and community (though, as we have seen, there is a certain hankering after fraternity). In anglophone Canada, according to Horowitz, liberalism also dominates – witness the constant calls to free enterprise – yet has been modified by conservative and social democratic impulses toward order and equality. The thinking of all three of Canada's, and Ontario's, major parties contains all of these ideological strands, though in varying degrees and differing weights. State-run enterprises are much more, albeit often grudgingly, accepted in Canada, and so is the universal welfare state, though consensus on this item has been strained in recent years. At the municipal level, Toronto balances liberal, conservative, and social democratic concerns. However, a conservative preoccupation with public stability, revealed in a willingness to check the unfettered exercise of private property rights, has loomed larger than the active promotion of equality and democracy.

Complacency, even fatalism, is obvious in this bureaucratized society and is exacerbated by nuclear doomsday threats.[40] While residents of other parts of Canada tend to define themselves culturally in juxtaposition to the dominant metropolis of Toronto, Torontonians spend little time on defining themselves against other parts of Canada. Consequently, they are more readily inclined than other Canadians to address the question of 'the Canadian identity.' Perhaps the very question is peculiarly a Toronto obsession – one evinced, for example, in Torontonian Pierre Berton's books on the war of 1812 and the winning of the west, in Torontonian Margaret Atwood's novel *Surfacing*, or in the definitions of morality propounded by the United Church's headquarters (also in Toronto). The massive immigration of non-anglophones and the even more recent emergence of substantial visible minorities has led to a new definition – multiculturalism. Yet Torontonians have always been more inclined to define themselves by reference to the United States and Britain them to their own country.

In recent times the American influence has been conspicuously greater than the British. As an American town on British soil (to reverse the oft-cited epigram) ever since the town of York was founded in the early 1790s, the place has absorbed American ways. Officials in York may have worried about republican tendencies among the loyalists and opportunists from below the border seeking free land, but connections were strong in economy and culture. Toronto's merchants did not take long to establish trade links via Oswego and the Erie Canal, and later by rail, to New York. The protectionist tariff, significantly known as the 'National Policy,' strengthened those ties; American investment increased, and Toronto and area increasingly became the locale of American branch plants. The southerly flow of dividends from American-owned companies is well known. Canada's twentieth-century resource development, much of it organized from Toronto, supplies America's almost bottomless demands. Even while Toronto gradually took the central role in the Canadian private financial sector from Montreal, the financing of economic activity came to be dominated more and more by American decisions. In this 'cold war' era, the Pentagon as much as Wall Street has come to define Canada's economic role. Although Ottawa too became increasingly active in setting up federal financial intermediaries in social welfare and in resource development, its ability to manoeuvre within Washington's rules is very limited. Western Canadians who complain of Toronto's 'siphoning pan' must consider these facts. Concern over recent attempts by the United States to weaken Canadian resistance to US economic control is justified, but is hardly a radical departure from past complaints of a small number of serious Canadian nationalists. Canada absorbs, and only weakly resists, the flows of capital both in and out.[41]

The 'lag' theory is thus sometimes thrown up to describe Canada's relationship to American culture: given enough time, Canada absorbs everything from the south. This is plausible, but in many respects not true. We are overwhelmed by American music and movies, by baseball and football and fast food outlets. More particularly, Toronto has followed US cities in styles and forms of the built environment. Toronto lagged behind in the telegraph, railways, horse-trams, electricification of street railways, sky-scrapers, automobiles, streamlined streetcars, urban expressways, public housing superblocks, subways, and metropolitan government, but did eventually embrace all of these American inventions. It seems almost that Toronto cautiously let American cities try them first before deciding to adopt them itself, whether a few years, or a generation, or even two generations later. The timing was partly a function of size: Toronto was still very small in the 1880s when skyscrapers appeared in New York and Chicago. The ostentatious landscape of the gilded age in America reflected the opulence of the super rich and could not be replicated here. Fundamentally, Toronto's lag in adopting American solutions reflects the city's caution and its anxiety to 'make haste slowly': Toronto is thus a very American city, though so modified as to be a successful invention itself, despite continual pressure from developers. Even these developers have learned from the Toronto experience as they rebuild New York, Houston and Los Angeles.

Clearly, not everything American has been accepted. Toronto has rejected certain American ways or solutions or altered them significantly. Because Canada allowed few American blacks to enter the country after the 1860s, Canadian cities, including Toronto, have not had to face the same questions of race and hence of class. That the United States has failed to move beyond tokenism (perhaps a step toward equality and integration) can hardly be a basis for parading a superior moral stance by Canadians. Toronto's visible minorities, still small in numbers when compared to those in most larger US cities, know that racism is not absent. In the United States hand-guns are the chief instrument of homicides; they cannot easily be bought in Canada. Rifle associations have less power.

In Canada efficiency in public action is valued more than in the United States, where the right to waste is taken much more for granted. Living on the edge of the United States and on the margins of the vast agricultural resources of North America, Canadians have been forced into somewhat greater caution in treating the environment. The caution shown in keeping out blacks and hand-guns is reflected too in the proportionately far fewer Canadians than Americans who risk investment in stock markets. Defending the British interest in the nineteenth century entailed care and efficiency, even planning. Note, for instance, Sanford Fleming's inventing Standard Time in Toronto.

Perhaps one should hesitate to suggest another Toronto invention, pablum, is an appropriate symbol for the city.

Canadian cities have been beneficiaries of a slower and more cautious pace of living. They are a considerable triumph for Canadian ingenuity. A sense of limits has helped. Toronto's public service has been comparatively uncorrupt and competent. Although formal planning started only in the 1940s, the 'planning mentality' can be discerned decades earlier. The subway is a case in point. As early as 1907, an east-west subway was promoted by Horatio C. Hocken, Toronto's most vigorous reform mayor during the era of rapid growth before the First World War; he advocated that the proposed Bloor-Danforth viaduct across the Don Valley provide not only a roadway but also space for what he called a 'tube.' The east-west subway was not opened until 1966! That was foresight! At the time too a north-south subway was rejected because Toronto was too small. A 1915 report suggested a million people were needed: the Yonge line replacing the heavily used streetcar route was built when Toronto eventually reached that threshold. Public officials such as Roland C. Harris, commissioner of works for decades, kept these ideas in their heads, it seems. The same could be said for the Metro solution, first suggested in 1914. Only in the 1950s was the process speeded up: ideas lying dormant for years were at last implemented under Gardiner.[42]

One final contrast with the American experience can be derived from a comparison between Frederick Gardiner and Robert Moses, New York's famous public developer of parkways, parks, bridges, public housing, and the unsuccessful 1964 World's Fair. Superficially, they acted in much the same way, as though entrepreneurs pushing ahead, getting things done. Privately they could boast to each other of their five-year plans (not publicly, of course). But the salient difference lies in Gardiner's greater straightforwardness and visibility, reflecting the greater legitimacy of his enterprise in the Canadian civic culture. Moses, in contrast, was often devious and secretive, because he could never hope to achieve the same degree of acceptance. Gardiner was public in his actions. As super mayor and chief provincial commissioner for the Metro region, he organized the whole region. Moses operated in an almost clandestine manner for many years from his obscure office on the Triborough Bridge approach, virtually a power unto himself, separate from state and city governments and providing less stability. Gardiner would not have brought the bulldozers into High Park under the cloak of darkness to remake it in his own image: Moses did that in Central Park. Moses shifted public and quasi-public funds around in a shadowy way to pay for his developments: Gardiner's books were undoubtedly clean.[43]

The 1929 Regional Plan of New York was a document privately generated from corporate and foundation funds. It never became fully public because many powerful New Yorkers and Americans were, and still are, against planning. Most of New York's expressways, none the less, including the infamous Cross Bronx built by Moses, were drawn from that plan. In Toronto the 1943 city plan was a public (if still only advisory) document and a partial guide for Gardiner. In New York planning could not be public or truly comprehensive: the 'people' would object. The result, as Moses's biographer notes in his title, was 'the fall of New York.' No one would say Toronto 'fell' under Gardiner. Moses developed, but contributed to disorder; Gardiner built with order, with stability as the goal, even if too much was conceded to private developers, even if suburban densities were too low, even if suburban high-rise apartments sprouted up too frequently. At the same time, local parochial community democracy was also quite explicitly overridden for the broader public good – a priority widely accepted in the 1950s and subsequently. Living cheek by jowl with the American giant, Canadians, Ontarians, and especially Torontonians have been moved, it seems, to exercise restraint. In short, Toronto's success as an urban environment has been wrought by looking over its shoulders at American cities.[42]

Toronto still defines itself against the British experience, too – even if the fact is hardly apparent today. As in Britain, the differences between town and country are not perceived as sharply as in America. But gone are the empire and the Orange order, formerly celebrated in this one-time Belfast of North America. Their virtual disappearance from the civic consciousness is possibly as much due to a reaction to the slaughter in the trenches of Flanders as to a decline of anti-Catholic consciousness among Torontonians (though Bolsheviks and Jews in the 1920s and early 1930s became the new scapegoats). British immigrants sustained the emotional and institutional connection to 'over home' from 1790 to 1914, but those arriving in the 1920s may well have been prime agents in weakening the sense of empire and so, indirectly, the Orange order, if only by waving the flag with less enthusiasm than before 1914. The marked political changes of the 1940s too may have been engendered partly in the pubs of Britain, where Canadian servicemen learned social democracy and the need for labour power from British fighting men. Possibly the long resistance to open Sundays in Toronto can be seen to be as much a Presbyterian and Methodist focus of the British past as an expression of un-American and indigenous sentiment. If the British influence is today less obviously direct, a residue of British ways remains.[45]

Toronto and most other Canadian cities have varied from Britain in the twentieth century in one major respect, namely in lacking political action through parties. Possibly infected by some of the late-nineteenth-century

American reformers who, as suburban Republicans, wanted to weaken the patronage power of big-city bosses of the Democratic party, Torontonians failed to pick up on the transition in British municipal politics to electioneering on political platforms and local government as a school for democracy. The overwhelming control of the Conservatives in Toronto's twentieth-century politics has probably contributed, too. It is no coincidence that Gardiner was a Conservative and a prime force in the party's transition to 'Progressive' Conservatism. Further, unlike Britain, where class distinctions have been sharper, and more like the United States, Canadian labour leaders earlier in the century generally followed Sam Gompers's 'business unonism' and so sought little direct involvement in politics. The recent concerted attempt by the New Democratic Party to push the important notion of defining goals and means in civic politics may mean that parties will become more important at the municipal level, though this is hardly clear at the moment.

One sure way to fulfil the Robarts Commission's recommendation of a directly elected Metro chairman would be through the introduction of a 'parliamentary' system where the chairman, elected in his or her own ward, is the head of a majority party. To the present provincial régime the current system is undoubtedly preferable. Even the theoretical possibility of Metro falling into the hands of someone like London's Ken Livingstone, that thorn in the side of Margaret Thatcher, is unacceptable to it. Alternative views on what should happen in Toronto remain muted. The plethora of resident, tenant, and social welfare organizations do not add up to a comprehensive program.[46]

Creating a liveable urban environment is an unending and important task. But today the larger questions are more clearly economic and social. Unemployment and the increasing polarization of income and wealth have become more serious. As in the United States and other Western countries, the numbers of Torontonians engaged in property and business, especially the financial sectors, have expanded, but so too have low-paid personal services. The middle has been weakening as unionized industrial work evaporates and the growth of public social service jobs is held in check as it has since 1975. A warning signal has been the appearance of a vast number of attractive but expensive restaurants: Toronto is running the risk of becoming a two-class society, with the poor and relatively poor waiting on the affluent and rich. The appearance of so many lottery shops in Toronto suggests a drift toward a symbolically picaresque society. American-style home security systems, now widely advertised among the affluent, are another sign of a problem. Even the appearance of closed newspaper boxes on Toronto's streets a decade ago signalled a less open society. Today, in Toronto and around the world, the barons of the liquor and tobacco corporations conspicuously advertise their control over major sports and many other areas of the consumer world.[47]

It would seem that *National Geographic* was correct: Toronto *is* 'worldly, wealthy, personable and relatively problem free.' But there are costs to this achievement. Symbolically, in the heyday of nineteenth-century entrepreneurial capital, the church spires scorned by Hemingway dominated the urban landscape. Today, the CN Tower and the banks reach for a different heaven. The material progress of Toronto, and the 'civilization' that developed around it, have, in the end, perpetuated social inequalities and cashiered local collective democracy. Toronto, too, has played a major role in tying Canada into the American system. By becoming the private financial city of Canada it has unwittingly aggravated regional tensions in Canada. If Toronto is to remain the 'city that works ... a model of the alternative future,' then its citizens will need to keep their wits about them.

NOTES

I wish to thank Norah Johnson, Alan Baker, Lydia Burton, Frances Frisken, David Morley, Pat Peterson, Paul Romney, Victor Russell, and James Simmons for reading earlier drafts. Various versions were presented at the Organization of American Historicans Conference, Detroit, 1982; the Urban History Conference, Guelph, 1982; the Toronto High School Teachers Conference, 1983; and the Popular Culture conference, Toronto, 1984. I am grateful to graduate and undergraduate students for writing papers on Toronto's past, and to staff of various libraries and archives, especially the City of Toronto Archives.

1 Arthur Herschman 'Foreign Travel' *Science* 210 (14 November 1980) 763; Edmund Futtermayer 'Toronto the New Great City' *Fortune* 90 (September 1974) 126–37; Anthony Astrachan 'A City That Works' *Harpers* 249 (December 1974), 14–19; Ethel A. Starbird 'Canada's Dowager Learns to Swing' *National Geographic* 148 (1975) 190–215
2 Robert Wilson *A Retrospect: A Short Review of Steps Taken in Sanitation to Transform the Town of Muddy York into the Queen City of the West* (Toronto 1934), pamphlet, City of Toronto Archives (hereafter CTA); Albert S. Richey, Worcester, Massachusetts, Local Transportation Service of the TTC, 1934, Municipal Reference Library, City Hall; Ernest Hemingway *Selected Letters, 1917–1961*, ed Carlos Baker (New York 1981) 84, 88, 95

3 On conventions see *Star* 18 june 1982; Alan Fotheringham *Malice in Blunderland or How the Grits Stole Christmas* (Toronto 1982) 87–8; more thoughtfully, John Warkentin 'Southern Ontario: A View from the West' *Canadian Geographer* (1966) 157–71; *Globe and Mail* 24 January 1946

4 Charles Dickens *American Notes and Pictures from Italy* (London and New York 1908) 203

5 Paul Bator 'Public Health Reform in Canada and Urban History: A Critical Survey' *Urban History Review* IX (October 1980) 87–102; some crime comparisons in 'The Urban Ebb and Flow' *Toronto Life* (August 1980) 13–14; J. Wreford Watson *A Social Geography of the United States* (London 1979) chap 6; Charles H. McGaghy *Crime in America* (New York 1980) 96, 114–15; *Globe and Mail* 1 March 1984. On various measures see John Mercer and Michael A. Goldberg 'Value Differences and Their Meaning for Urban Development in Canada and the U.S.A.,' paper presented to Comparative Urban History Conference on Canadian-American Urban Development, University of Guelph, August 1982, Table 3. See also John Mercer 'On Continentalism, Distinctiveness and Comparative Urban Geography: Canadian and American Cities' *Canadian Geographer* XXIII (1979) 119–39. Michael A. Goldberg and John Mercer 'Canadian and U.S. Cities: Basic Differences, Possible Explanations, and Their Meaning for Public Policy' *Regional Science Association Papers* XLV (1980) 159–84. Among their sources of data are those in Alex C. Michalos *North American Social Report* 5 vols (Dordrecht, Holland, and Boston 1980–2). Mercer 'On Continentalism' points out that urban geography text books obscure differences. I am grateful to John Mercer for discussing the data and issues. Stephen J. Arnold and James G. Barnes 'Canadian and American National Character as a Basis for Market Segmentation' in Jogdish N. Sheth ed *Research in Marketing* (Greenwich, Conn., 1979) 1–35

6 Goldberg and Mercer 'Canadian and U.S. Cities' 169–73; Mercer and Goldberg 'Value Differences' 54–6. Verbal communications 6 March 1981, Metro Planning Department and Ontario Ministry of Transportation and Communication, state transit community at one-third, but TTC Public Relations gives 43 per cent. Toronto *Star* 10 March 1982; Chicago's ridership one half New York's

7 On density gradients, R.C. Harris, F.H. Gaby, and E.L. Cousins *Report of the Civic Transportation Committee on Radial Entrances and Rapid Transit for the City of Toronto* 2 vols (Toronto 1915); Metropolitan Toronto Transportation Plan Review *Choice for the Future: Summary Report* Report 64 (Toronto 1975); Canada *Census* 1981; US *Census* 1980

8 Annexation data are in Harris, Gaby, and Cousins *Report*, and map, CTA. Population is from City Assessment Commissioner reports. Michael J. Doucet 'Politics, Space and Trolleys: Mass Transit – Early Twentieth-Century Toronto' in *Shaping the Urban Landscape: Aspects of the Canadian City-Building Pro-*

cess Gilbert A. Stelter and Alan F.J. Artibise ed (Ottawa 1982) 356–81; Donald
F. Davis 'Mass Transit and Private Ownership: An Alternative Perspective on
the Case of Toronto' *Urban History Review* No. 3-78 (1978) 60–98

9 Frances Frisken's essay in this volume.

10 Referenda results in City of Toronto *Council Minutes, 1945* (Toronto 1946)
Appendix C; City Planning Board of Toronto *The Master Plan for the City of
Toronto and Environs* (Toronto 1943)

11 Katharine L. Bradbury, Anthony Downs, and Kenneth A. Small *Urban Decline
and the Future of American Cities* (Washington, DC 1982); William K. Tabb
The Long Default: New York City and the Urban Fiscal Crisis (New York 1982);
Roger E. Alcaly and David Mermelstein ed *The Fiscal Crisis of American
Cities: Essays on the Political Economy of Urban America with Special Reference
to New York* (New York 1977); Ida Susser *Norman Street: Poverty and Poli-
tics in an Urban Neighborhood* (New York 1982) 162, 101, 180; David R. Gold-
field and Blaine A. Brownell *Urban America from Downtown to No Town*
(Boston 1979) chap 13; Larry Sawers and William C. Tabb ed *Sunbelt/Snowbelt:
Urban Development and Regional Restructuring* (New York 1984)

12 On the Chicago school see Peter G. Goheen *Victorian Toronto, 1850–1900:
Patterns and Process of Growth* University of Chicago Geography Department, Research Paper 127 (Chicago 1970). Following the modified model,
Robert Murdie *Factorial Ecology of Metropolitan Toronto, 1951–1961: An Essay
on the Social Geography of the City* University of Chicago Geography Department Research Paper 116 (Chicago 1969)

13 Upton Sinclair *The Jungle* (New York 1906); Gilbert Osofsky *Harlem: The
Making of a Ghetto: Negro New York, 1890–1930* (New York 1966); Thomas L.
Philpott *The Slum and the Ghetto: Neighborhood Deterioration and Middle
Class Reform, 1880–1930* (New York 1978); Bradbury, Downs, and Small *Urban
Decline* 75–6; Thomas L. Blair *Retreat to the Ghetto* (New York 1977). A 1974
Detroit poll reported that far more whites would move if blacks moved into
their neighbourhoods than was the case in Canadian polls; Mercer and Goldberg
'Value Differences' Table 2.

14 Jon C. Teaford *City and Suburb: The Political Fragmentation of Metropolitan
America, 1850–1970* (Baltimore and London 1979)

15 Larry S. Bourne *The Geography of Housing* (London 1981) compares policies,
especially on 210. Sam Bass Warner, Jr, *The Urban Wilderness: A History of
the American City* (New York 1972) 234–7; on Ford, James J. Flink 'Three
Stages of American Automobile consciousness' *American Quarterly* XXIV (1972)
451–73

16 Bureau of Municipal Research *What Is 'The Ward' Going to Do with Toronto?*
... (Toronto 1918)

17 James T. Lemon and Stephen Speisman 'The Building of a Suburb' in Lydia

Burton and David Morley ed 'The Annex Book,' manuscript, CTA; Peter W.
Moore 'Zoning and Planning: The Toronto Experience, 1904–1970' in
Alan F.J. Artibise and Gilbert A. Stelter ed *The Usable Urban Past: Planning
and Politics in the Modern Canadian City* (Toronto 1979) 316–41; Peter
W. Moore 'Zoning and Neighbourhood Change: The Annex in Toronto,
1900–1970' *Canadian Geographer* XXVI (1982) 21–36; John Punter et al
The Annex Study Urban Studies Program, York University (Toronto 1973);
on Rosedale, Isabel K. Ganton and Joan Winearls *Mapping Toronto's First
Century, 1787–1884*, forthcoming, based on an exhibit of the same name,
Royal Ontario Museum, 1984; John R. Seeley et al *Crestwood Heights*
(Toronto 1956)

18 Robert E. Harney and Harold Troper *Immigrants: A Portrait of the Urban
Experience, 1890–1930* (Toronto 1975); special issue 'Immigrants and the City'
Urban History Review 2–78 (1978); Stephen Speisman *The Jews of Toronto: A
History to 1937* (Toronto 1979); Michiel Horn 'Keeping Canada "Canadian":
Anti-Communism and Canadianism in Toronto, 1928–29' *Canada* III (September 1975) 35–47; population from *Census 1931*; BMR *What Is the Ward?*

19 Robert T. Allen *When Toronto Was for Kids* (Toronto 1961) chap 7.

20 On sectors, Murdie *Factorial Ecology*

21 Marvyn Novick (Social Planning Council) *Metro Suburbs in Transition* 2 vol
(Toronto 1979–80)

22 Albert Rose *Regent Park: A Study of Slum Clearance* (Toronto 1959); City of
Toronto Housing Department *Confronting the Crisis: A Review of City
Housing Policy, 1976–1981* (Toronto 1982); Metropolitan Toronto Planning
Department *Metropolitan Toronto Annual Housing Report 1981* (Toronto
1982)

23 Map of group homes, *Globe and Mail* 5 March 1984

24 Moore 'Zoning and Planning'

25 Kenneth Greenberg 'Toronto: The Unknown Grand Tradition' *Trace: a Canadian Magazine about Architecture* I 2 (spring 1981) 37–52. On playgrounds
developed, see Horatio Hocken 'The New Spirit in Municipal Government'
Canadian Club of Ottawa Addresses 1914 (Ottawa 1914) 85–97.

26 On the misery of the unemployed and deprived children, see the perceptive
recollections of Bernice Thurman Hunter *That Scatterbrain Booky* (Richmond
Hill 1981). Despite its misleading cover and obscure title, it should be read
alongside Hugh Garner's *Cabbagetown* (Toronto 1950, reprinted 1968). Michiel
Horn *The League for Social Reconstruction: Intellectual Origins of the Democratic Left in Canada, 1930–1942* (Toronto 1980); Gerald L. Caplan *The
Dilemma of Canadian Socialism: The CCF in Ontario* (Toronto 1973)

27 John David Hulchanski 'The Origins of Urban Land Use Planning in Ontario,
1900–1946' PHD thesis, University of Toronto, 1981

28 J.C. Boylen *York Township, 1850–1954* (York Township 1954); Roger E.
Riendeau 'A Clash of Interests: Dependency and the Municipal Problem in
the Great Depression' *Journal of Canadian Studies* xiv (1979) 50–8; Ross
Parry 'Post Mortem: Public Resentment against Rising Prices and Housing
Shortages Aided ccf Cause' *Globe and Mail* 10 June 1948; Timothy J.
Colton *Big Daddy: Frederick G. Gardiner and the Building of Metropolitan
Toronto* (Toronto 1980); Albert Rose *Governing Metropolitan Toronto: A
Social and Political Analysis, 1953–1971* (Berkeley 1972); Harold Kaplan *Urban
Political Systems: A Functional Analysis of Metro Toronto* (New York 1967);
Warren Magnusson and Andrew Sancton ed *City Politics in Canada* (Toronto
1983), especially Magnusson's introduction and essay on Toronto and Sancton's
concluding paper

29 Jacob Spelt *Toronto* (Toronto 1974) chap 6; James Lorimer *The Developers*
(Toronto 1978); Frisken 'Factors Contributing to Public Service. Equalization in
A Restructured Metropolis: The Case of Toronto' paper presented to Canadian
Political Science Association, 1981; Duncan Macpherson cartoon *Star* 28 May
1959, reproduced in Colton *Big Daddy* 150

30 City Planning Board of Toronto *Third Annual Report 1944* (Toronto 1945);
Report No. 1, Committee Surveying the Declining Areas of the City, 2 December
1946, Planning Board Papers, Box 3, File 6, cta; West Annex Neighbourhood
Association *Renaissance of the Annex as a Sound Convenient Congenial Neighbourhood* (Toronto 1954) mimeo; *Telegram* 4 June 1956; (Arthur Lowe) 'What
Might Have Been' *The Apartment Owner and Builder* ii (February 1957)
cover, 21

31 James T. Lemon 'Toronto: Is It a Model for Urban Life and Citizen Participa-
tion?' in David Ley ed *Community Participation and the Spatial Order of the
City* B.C. Geographical Series 19 (Vancouver 1974) 41–58; Michael Goldrick
'The Anatomy of Urban Reform in Toronto' *City Magazine* 3 (May–June 1978)
29–39. Besides John Sewell, David Crombie, William Kilbourn, and Karl
Jaffary *Inside City Hall* (Toronto 1971), mostly written by reform aldermen,
several books appeared between 1970 and 1972 by David and Nadine Nowlan,
Stephen Clarkson, J.L. Granatstein, James Lorimer, Alan Power (ed), John
Sewell, David Stein, and (on the proposed second airport) Sandra Budden and
Joseph Ernst.

32 Metropolitan Toronto Planning Department *Metroplan: Concepts and Objectives* (Toronto 1976)

33 Donald R. Richmond *The Economic Transformation of Ontario 1945–1973*
(Toronto 1974) and Lionel D. Feldman *Ontario 1945–1973: The Municipal
Dynamic* (Toronto 1974) (both books in Ontario Economic Council series,
The Evolution of Policy in Contemporary Ontario); Richmond and P.S. Ross
and partners *The Financial Structure of Metropolitan Toronto* Background

Studies in the Metropolitan Plan Preparation Programme (Toronto 1975);
John Mercer and Michael A. Goldberg 'The Fiscal Condition of American
and Canadian Cities' unpublished paper 1982, cited with permission

34 Ontario *Report of the Royal Commission on Metropolitan Toronto* 2 vols
(Toronto 1977)

35 Morton and Lucia White *The Intellectual versus the City* (Cambridge, Massachusetts, 1962); Donald W. Meinig 'Symbolic Landscapes: Some Idealizations of
American Communities' in Donald W. Meinig ed *The Interpretation of Ordinary Landscapes* (New York 1979) 164–92. For a British view see Raymond
Williams *The Country and the City* (New York 1973).

36 Teaford *City and Suburb*

37 This is more or less distilled from teaching two courses on the United States
and from my work on early America. Alexis de Tocqueville *Democracy in
America* (New York 1945) originally published 1835–40, especially chapters 15–17

38 On black income, *New York Times* 19 December 1982; Christopher Jencks
'Thomas Sowell vs Special Treatment of Black' *New York Review of Books*
xxx (3 March 1983) 33–9; David Brody *Workers in Industrial America:
Essays on the 20th Century Struggle* (New York 1980); Mary R. and Robert
W. Jackman *Class Awareness in the United States* (Berkeley 1983)

39 De Tocqueville *Democracy in America* chap 15

40 Gad Horowitz *Canadian Labour in Politics* (Toronto 1968) chap 1; David
V.J. Bell and Lorne Tepperman *The Roots of Disunity: A Look at Canadian
Culture* (Toronto 1979); Goldrick 'Anatomy of Urban Reform'

41 D.C. Masters *The Rise of Toronto, 1850–1890* (Toronto 1947); W. Randy Smith
Aspects of Growth in a Regional Urban System: Southern Ontario 1851–1921
York University Geographical Monographs 12 (Toronto 1982); Donald Kerr
'Metropolitan Dominance in Canada' in John Warkentin ed *Canada: A Geographical Interpretation* (Toronto 1968) 531–55; R. Keith Semple and W.R.
Smith 'Metropolitan Dominance and Foreign Ownership in the Canadian Urban
System' *Canadian Geographer* xxv (1981) 23; J. Tait Davis 'Government-
Directed Money Flows and the Discordance between Production and Consumption in Provincial Economies' *Canadian Geographer* xxvi (1982) 1–20; James
W. Simmons 'The Impact of the Public Sector on the Canadian Urban System' in
Alan F.J. Artibise and Gilbert Stelter ed *The North American City* forthcoming; on branch plants, N.C. Field and D.P. Kerr *Geographical Aspects of
Industrial Growth in the Metropolitan Toronto Region* (Toronto 1968); Wallace
Clement *Continental Corporate Power: Economic Linkages between Canada
and the United States* (Toronto 1977); Mel Hurtig 'Canadians Finance Own
Sellout' *Globe and Mail* 21 April 1983; Stephen Clarkson *Canada and the*

Reagan Challenge (Ottawa and Toronto 1982); James Laxer 'Canada's Economy a Prisoner of the US' *Star* 29 April 1984

42 *Telegram* October 1908, 22 December 1909; *Daily News* 29 June 1909; Harris, Gaby, and Cousins *Report*; Morley Wickett *Memorandum re Metropolitan Area* (Toronto 1913), noted in John C. Weaver *Shaping the Canadian City: Essays on Urban Politics and Policy, 1890–1920* Institute of Public Administration of Canada, Monograph on Canadian Urban Government (Toronto 1977) 66

43 Colton *Big Daddy* ix, 80, and my review in *American Review of Canadian Studies* 11 (autumn 1981) 107–9; Robert Caro *The Power Broker: Robert Moses and the Fall of New York* (New York 1974), and my review essay 'Of Power and Contemptuousness' *Canadian Review of American Studies* VII (1976) 88–92

44 Robert Fitch 'Planning New York' in Alcaly and Mermelstein ed *Fiscal Crisis* 264–84; Caro *Power Broker*

45 Cecil J. Houston and William J. Smyth *The Sash Canada Wore: A Historical Geography of the Orange Order in Canada* (Toronto 1980) chapter 8; Robert M. Stamp *The Schools of Ontario* (Toronto 1982) 92–5, on patriotism and imperialism; Paul Addison *The Road to 1945: British Politics and the Second World War* (London 1977)

46 Andrew Sancton 'Conclusion: Canadian City Politics in Comparative Perspective' in Magnusson and Sancton ed *City Politics in Canada* 291–317

47 Loren Simerl and Howard Goldfinger *Job Growth by Industry in the Toronto Area, 1941 to 1980* Social Planning Council Papers for Full Employment 6, March 1982. The 1981 census confirms this trend. In November 1983 Brian J.L. Berry, in a Toronto lecture, described Pittsburgh in similar terms; Lester Thurow, in January 1984, did the same for the United States generally.

Index